INDONESIAN PRIVATE INTERNATIONAL LAW

This book is the leading reference on Indonesian private international law in English. The chapters systematically cover the whole of Indonesian private international law including commercial matters, family law, succession, cross-border insolvency, intellectual property, competition (antitrust) and environmental disputes.

The chapters do not merely cover the traditional conflict of law areas of jurisdiction, applicable law (choice of law) and enforcement. The chapters also look into conflict of law questions arising in arbitration and assess Indonesian involvement in the harmonisation of private international law globally and regionally within ASEAN. Similar to the other volumes in the *Studies in Private International Law – Asia* series, this book presents the Indonesian conflict of laws through a combination of common and civil law analytical techniques and perspectives, providing readers worldwide with a more profound and comprehensive understanding of the subject.

Volume 2 in the series Studies in Private International Law – Asia

Studies in Private International Law – Asia

Editor: Anselmo Reyes

Advisory Editor: Paul Beaumont

Much has been written about private international law in the EU and the US. Less is known about the conflict of laws in Asia. Thus, little attention has been paid so far to the modernisation of private international law codes and rules that has been taking place over the last decade all over Asia. That trend continues. Now is the time to take stock of those reforms that have already taken place and suggest further improvements for the future.

Published under the celebrated series *Studies in Private International Law*, this monograph sub-series provides a forum for discussion and analysis of private international law in Asia. The series is not solely a survey of jurisdictions for practitioners. Comprising in-depth thematic and country-specific studies, each volume considers the private international law of Asian countries from a variety of perspectives. An underlying assumption is that private international law in different jurisdictions follow broad discernible patterns. Each volume in this sub-series highlights those patterns and discusses how rules in different Asian jurisdictions are either converging with, or diverging from, the patterns identified. Such an analytical framework will assist academics, judges, lawyers and legislators to envisage ways in which laws affecting cross-border relationships can be harmonised across jurisdictions and be made more responsive to the needs of citizens in Asia and elsewhere.

Volume 1: Recognition and Enforcement of Judgments in Civil and Commercial Matters
Edited by Anselmo Reyes

Volume 2: Indonesian Private International Law
Afifah Kusumadara

Indonesian Private International Law

Afifah Kusumadara

Contributors
Anak Agung Ayu Nanda Saraswati
Airin Liemanto
Diah Pawestri Maharani
Ranitya Ganindha
Ratih Dheviana Puru Hitaningtyas
Reka Dewantara
Rumi Suwardiyati
Setiawan Wicaksono

all at Faculty of Law, Brawijaya University, Indonesia

•HART•
OXFORD • LONDON • NEW YORK • NEW DELHI • SYDNEY

HART PUBLISHING

Bloomsbury Publishing Plc

Kemp House, Chawley Park, Cumnor Hill, Oxford, OX2 9PH, UK

1385 Broadway, New York, NY 10018, USA

29 Earlsfort Terrace, Dublin 2, Ireland

HART PUBLISHING, the Hart/Stag logo, BLOOMSBURY and the Diana logo are trademarks of Bloomsbury Publishing Plc

First published in Great Britain 2021

A catalogue record for this book is available from the British Library.

Library of Congress Cataloging-in-Publication data

Names: Kusumadara, Afifah, author.

Title: Indonesian private international law / Afifah Kusumadara ; contributors, Anak Agung Ayu Nanda Saraswati, Airin Liemanto, Diah Pawestri Maharani, Ranitya Ganindha, Ratih Dheviana Puru Hitaningtyas, Reka Dewantara, Rumi Suwardiyati, Setiawan Wicaksono, all at Faculty of Law, Brawijaya University, Indonesia.

Description: Oxford, UK ; New York, NY : Hart Publishing, an imprint of Bloomsbury Publishing, 2021. | Series: Studies in private international law – Asia ; volume 2 | Includes bibliographical references and index.

Identifiers: LCCN 2021000170 (print) | LCCN 2021000171 (ebook) | ISBN 9781509924332 (hardback) | ISBN 9781509924349 (pdf) | ISBN 9781509924356 (Epub)

Subjects: LCSH: Conflict of laws—Indonesia.

Classification: LCC KNW480 .K87 2021 (print) | LCC KNW480 (ebook) | DDC 340.909598—dc23

LC record available at https://lccn.loc.gov/2021000170

LC ebook record available at https://lccn.loc.gov/2021000171

ISBN: HB: 978-1-50992-433-2
ePDF: 978-1-50992-434-9
ePub: 978-1-50992-435-6

Typeset by Compuscript Ltd, Shannon

To find out more about our authors and books visit www.hartpublishing.co.uk. Here you will find extracts, author information, details of forthcoming events and the option to sign up for our newsletters.

FOREWORD

This is the inaugural volume of a number of books to be published within the series *Studies in Private International Law: Asia* focusing on the conflict of laws as practised and as being developed in specific Asian countries. Dr Afifah Kusumadara and her team of scholars from the Faculty of Law at Brawijaya University in Malang, Indonesia are to be congratulated for providing this up-to-date account of *Indonesian Private International Law*.

This is a book in which all readers may dip in and out and find something of interest. For the legal practitioner, there is detail. The book's style in respect of a given topic has been to provide a thorough discussion of present law on the subject, concluding with a brief summary of salient points before moving on to the next section. For the legal academic, by way of counterpoint to the detail just mentioned, there is lacuna. The book does not shy away from identifying gaps and other shortcomings in the present law and venturing views on how those problems should be addressed. For the general reader seeking insights into Indonesian history and sociology, there are not only references to how private international law has developed from Dutch colonial times to today. There are also glimpses into the pluralism of modern Indonesian society to be gleaned from the book's accounts of the facts underlying court decisions and from the book's discussion of the ways in which Roman law institutions continue to apply to contemporary Indonesia. It is in these senses that the book may be characterised as looking not just to the past or present, but also to the future.

As this book was being written, COVID-19 was at its height. It is likely to be with us yet for some time. One might wonder then whether in such circumstances private international law is relevant. The discourse of COVID-19 has been one of closure, not just of national borders, but also of commercial trade. The world is fast-becoming accustomed to a new normal of self isolation, social-distancing, quarantine, restricted travel and alienation. As a corollary, because of the economic recession that has come in the pandemic's wake, there are growing murmurs of anti-globalism, protectionism and discontent. Despite all this, the hope is that this book and the other volumes like it to come will prompt readers to answer the question just posed resoundingly in the affirmative.

By reason of history, trade, technology. religion, culture and family, cross-border issues will always be with us and will continue to arise in unexpected and novel ways. COVID-19 or not, the conflict of laws will inevitably play a significant role in our daily lives, as it has done for centuries. Accordingly, if we are to ensure that our day-to-day activities are affected for the better, it will remain important to understand our own laws and those of others or, more precisely, how our laws interact with those of others. Insofar as cross-border questions are concerned, we should be seeking to harmonise and unify the principles of private international law for the convenience and well-being of all. That is ultimately the premise underpinning the volumes of which *Indonesian Private International Law* is the first. At its heart, this book aims to promote, through a study of private international law, a better understanding of Indonesian society. This is meant to be for the benefit not just of Indonesians, but of everyone else.

Anselmo Reyes
Kyoto
22 September 2020
Autumn Equinox

CONTENTS

TABLE OF ABBREVIATIONS

AALCC	Asian-African Legal Consultative Committee
AB	*Algemene Bepalingen van Wetgeving voor Nederlandsch Indie* (General Provisions of Legislation for the Dutch East Indies)
ACIA	ASEAN Comprehensive Investment Agreement
APP	Asia Pulp & Paper, Co.
Arrest Convention	International Convention Relating to the Arrest of Sea-Going Ships
ASEAN	Association of Southeast Asian Nations
Astro	Astro Nusantara International BV; et al.
Ayunda	PT. Ayunda Prima Mitra
BCBC	BCBC Singapore Pte Ltd
Bank America	Bank America National Trust Company; et al.
BANI	Indonesian National Arbitration Board (*Badan Arbitrase Nasional Indonesia*)
BAPMI	Indonesia Capital Market Arbitration Board for capital market disputes (*Badan Arbitrase Pasar Modal Indonesia*)
BASYARNAS	National Syariah Arbitration Board for Islamic banking matters (*Badan Arbitrase Syariah Nasional*)
Bayan	PT Bayan Resources TBK
Berne Convention	Berne Convention for the Protection of Literary and Artistic Works
BIT/BITs	Bilateral Investment Treaty/Bilateral Investment Treaties
BKPL	PT Bangun Karya Pratama Lestari
BKPM	Investment Coordinating Board (*Badan Koordinasi Penanaman Modal*)
BT	Bankers Trust Company and Bankers Trust International PLC
BULOG	Indonesian Bureau of Logistics (*Badan Urusan Logistik*)
BW	*Burgerlijk Wetboek voor Nederlandsch-Indie* (Dutch East Indies Civil Code and current Indonesian Civil Code)

Cape Town Protocol	Protocol to The Convention on International Interests in Mobile Equipment on Matters Specific to Aircraft Equipment
Cape Town Convention	Convention on International Interests in Mobile Equipment
CISG	Contracts for the International Sale of Goods
CIF	Cost, Insurance, and Freight
Dit.	Direktorat
DNA	Deoxyribonucleic Acid
EKCP	East Kutai Coal Project
EOR	Enhanced Oil Recovery
FAS	Free Alongside ship
FOB	Free on Board
Garuda	PT Garuda Indonesia (Persero)
HCCH	Hague Conference on Private International Law
HIR	*Het Herziene Indonesisch Reglement* (Renewed Indonesian Code)
HKIAC	Hong Kong International Arbitration Center
HM Sampoerna	PT Hanjaya Mandala Sampoerna Tbk
HR	*Hoge Raad* (Supreme Court of the Netherlands)
ICC	International Chamber of Commerce
ICAO	International Civil Aviation Organization
ICSID	International Centre for the Settlement of Investment Disputes
ICSID Convention	Convention on the Settlement of Investment Disputes Between States and Nationals of Other States
IDERA	Irrevocable De-Registration and Export Request Authorisation
IDR	Indonesian Rupiah
ILR	International Law Reports
INCOTERMS	International Commercial Terms
IP	Intellectual Property
IS	*Indische Staatsregeling* (Dutch Colonial Constitution)
ISDA	International Swaps and Derivatives Association

ISDS	Investor-State dispute settlement
KADIN	Indonesian Chamber of Commerce and Industry (*Kamar Dagang dan Industri Indonesia*)
KBC	Karaha Bodas Company, L.L.C.
Kedubes	Embassy (*Kedutaan Besar*)
Kemlu	Ministry of Foreign Affairs (*Kementerian Luar Negeri*)
KPPU	Commission for the Supervision of Business Competition (*Komisi Pengawas Persaingan Usaha*)
KRL	Kangaroo Resources Limited
LCIA	London Court of International Arbitration
MA	Supreme Court (*Mahkamah Agung*)
Mahsin	Mahsin, SH.
MAR 91	New Marine Policy Form
Mayora	PT Mayora Indah Tbk
Menkumham	Minister of Law and Human Rights (*Menteri Hukum dan Hak Asasi Manusia*)
Menlu	Minister of Foreign Affairs (*Menteri Luar Negeri*)
Montreal Convention	Convention for the Unification of Certain Rules for International Carriage by Air, the 1999 Montreal Convention
New York Convention	United Nations Convention on the Recognition and Enforcement of Foreign Arbitral Awards 1958
NJ	*Nederlandse Jurisprudentie*
OIC	Organization of Islamic Conferences
Pertamina	*Perusahaan Pertambangan Minyak dan Gas Bumi Negara*
PKS	Perjanjian Kerja Sama (Cooperative Agreements)
PLN	*Perusahaan Listrik Negara* (State electric company)
PT. AHAP	PT Asuransi Harta Aman Pratama
PT FI	PT Freeport Indonesia
PTTEP	PTT Exploration and Production Public Company Limited
PTTEPAA	PTTEP Australasia (Ashmore Cartier) Pty Ltd
Rbg	*Rechtsreglement Buitengewesten* (Civil Procedure Code for Indigenous Outside Java and Madura)

RI	Republik Indonesia (Republic of Indonesia)
Rv	*Reglement op de Burgerlijke Rechtsvordering* (Civil Procedure Code)
SIAC	Singapore International Arbitration Centre
SICC	Singapore International Commercial Court
SKK Migas	Special Task Force for Upstream Oil and Gas Business Activities (*Satuan Kerja Khusus Kegiatan Usaha Hulu Minyak dan Gas Bumi*)
SLR	Singapore Law Reports
Soeharto	H.M. Soeharto
SOEs	state-owned Enterprises
SPIB	issuance of Port Clearance (*Surat Persetujuan Izin Berlayar*)
SSA	Subscription and Shareholders Agreement
TDM	Transnational Dispute Management
Texas District Court	US District Court for the Southern District of Texas
Time	Time Inc Asia; et al.
TRIPS Agreement	Agreement on Trade-Related Aspects of Intellectual Property Rights
UCP	Uniform Customs and Practices for Documentary Credits
UN	United Nations
UNCITRAL	United Nations Commission on International Trade Law
UNCTAD	United Nations Conference on Trade and Development
UNIDROIT	International Institute for the Unification of Private Law
UPICC	UNIDROIT Principles on International Commercial Contract
US	United States of America
UU	Regulation (*Undang-Undang*)
WA	Supreme Court of Western Australia
Warsaw Convention	Convention for the Unification of Certain Rules Relating to International Carriage by Air, the 1929 Warsaw Convention
WIPO	World Intellectual Property Organization
WNI	citizen of Indonesia (*Warga Negara Indonesia*)

TABLE OF CASES

Indonesia (published cases)

Indonesia (unpublished cases)

Australia

France

Hong Kong

Philippines

Singapore

The Netherlands

United Kingdom

United States

Other Jurisdictions

TABLE OF LEGISLATION

TABLE OF TREATIES AND CONVENTIONS

1

Introduction

I. The Subject Matter of Private International Law

Private International Law is the term used in Indonesia that governs private legal relations with foreign elements. In the US or the UK, it is known as the conflict of laws. Private International Law in Indonesia primarily deals with choice of law or applicable law. Rules in Indonesian Private International Law are used to determine what law Indonesian courts or authorities must apply to cases of private relations with foreign elements, because the parties, properties, and transactions are located in different countries or involve different nationalities.

The scope of Private International Law in Indonesia is narrower than that of Private International Law in other countries, particularly in Europe, which also has rules on choice of court and enforcement of foreign judgment. With these rules, Private International Law in those countries may restrict the jurisdiction of their courts when judging private cases involving foreigners and require them to recognise and enforce foreign judgments.[1] The constricted scope of Indonesian Private International Law derives from the principal sources of that law, namely Articles 16, 17, and 18(1) of *Algemene Bepalingen van Wetgeving voor Nederlandsch Indie* ('AB') (General Provisions of Legislation for the Dutch East Indies): [2]

> Statutory provisions governing the status and capacity of persons remain binding for Indonesian citizens (original text: inhabitants of the Dutch East Indies) during their stay abroad. (Article 16 AB)
>
> Concerning immovable property, the law of the country or place where the property is located applies. (Article 17 AB)
>
> Formality of a legal action is determined by the court in accordance with the law of the country or place where the action is performed. (Article 18 paragraph (1) AB)

These rules determine the applicable law in matters related to the status of persons, family matters, real property, and formality. Applicable law in other matters, such as contracts, torts, and status of legal entities, is determined by jurisprudence and doctrine found in the judgments of courts during the Dutch colonial era and following independence.

When involving Indonesian arbitration law, the scope of Indonesian Private International Law could be broadened to include choice of court and enforcement of foreign judgment. Act No 30 of 1999 concerning arbitration and alternative dispute resolution (the Arbitration Act 1999) and Presidential Decree No 34 of 1981 concerning

[1] G van Caster, *European Private International Law* 2nd edn (Hart Publishing 2016) 1–2.
[2] Promulgated in the State Gazette (*Staatsblad*) 23 of 1847.

ratification of the 1958 New York Convention, recognises choice of arbitral forum and enforcement of foreign arbitral awards.

In summary, the scope of Indonesian Private International Law is restricted, as the rules only govern choice of law or applicable law for private international cases, such as status of persons, family matters, real property, formality, and so on. Theoretically, the scope may be broadened if arbitration law is included in Indonesian Private International Law, as Indonesian arbitration law deals with choice of forum and the enforcement of foreign arbitral awards.

II. Sources of Private International Law

Because Private International Law is part of national law, the sources of Indonesian Private International Law are the same as the sources of other fields of law in Indonesia, namely:[3]

(i) Legislations (written law made and issued by State authorities).
(ii) Customary law or usage.
(iii) Jurisprudence (court precedents that are recommended as binding by the Supreme Court and classified as *Yurisprudensi Tetap* (stable jurisprudence) by the Supreme Court).[4]
(iv) Treaties or international conventions that have been ratified by the Indonesian Government.
(v) Doctrine (legal theories that are regularly considered in court judgments and serve as common references for legal practitioners to support their arguments before the court[5]).

The sources of Indonesian Private International Law come from both the Dutch colonial and post-independence eras, although most come from the former. The legitimacy of colonial law in the Indonesian legal system is based on Article II of the Transitional Provisions of the Indonesian Constitution 1945 (before amendment) that provides, 'All existing state institutions and regulations remain effective, as long as the new ones have not yet been provided under this Constitution.' Although the Transnational Provision of Constitution only validates state institutions and regulations of the colonial era, in practice other sources of law, including Dutch jurisprudence and doctrine, remain effective unless they violate Indonesia's public policy or have been revoked by newer instruments or cases.

As a country that adopted a civil law tradition created by the Dutch, the Indonesian legal system uses codified and written law, or legislation, as the main source of law. Other sources of law have been implemented to support legislation or to fill the legal gap where legislation is silent about a particular subject matter.

[3] PM Marzuki, *An Introduction to Indonesian Law* (Setara Press, 2011) 35–67; MS Is, *Pengantar Ilmu Hukum* (Kencana, 2017) 111–122.

[4] M Yasin, '*Bahasa Hukum: Sumber Hukum Formal Bernama "Yurisprudensi"* (*hukumonline*, 7 February 2018) www.hukumonline.com/berita/baca/lt5a7ad95871d1a/bahasa-hukum--sumber-hukum-formal-bernama-yurisprudensi (accessed 28 May 2018); AD Laiman and others, 'The Indonesian Legal System and Legal Research' (*Globalex*, September 2009) www.nyulawglobal.org/globalex/Indonesia.html#sourcesoflaw (accessed 29 May 2018).

[5] Laiman, 'The Indonesian Legal System' (n 4).

Until now, there has not been any codified Private International Law in Indonesia. Subject matter related to Private International Law have been governed by provisions scattered in different acts and regulations. Thus, Articles 16, 17, and 18 paragraph (1) AB mentioned above have become the main sources of Indonesian Private International Law to date. These three articles of the Dutch colonial period stipulate the applicable law in private matters related to the status of persons, family matters, real property, and formality with foreign elements.

The other sources of Private International Law, namely jurisprudence is used to govern private international matters that are not regulated by Articles 16, 17, and 18 paragraph (1) AB. Meanwhile, the courts and authorities also use doctrine such as *renvoi*, acquired/vested rights, proper law, and public policy (*ordre public*) when dealing with Private International Law subject matter.

After independence, the Indonesian Government passed several acts that contain provisions related to Private International Law matters. Examples are:

(i) Act No 5 of 1960 (Basic Agrarian Act 1960) has provisions regarding rights of foreigners over land situate in Indonesia.
(ii) Act No 1 of 1974 (Marriage Act 1974) has rules regulating marriages between Indonesians and foreigners (Articles 56–62).
(iii) Act No 23 of 2006 (Population Administration Act 2006), as amended by Act No 24 of 2013, has provisions regarding the civil status registration of Indonesian citizens outside Indonesia.

Further, the government has issued regulations that have become important sources of Indonesian Private International Law. Example are:

(i) Government Regulation No 54 of 2007 concerning procedures of adoption has provisions that govern intercountry adoption involving Indonesian children or Indonesian parents.
(ii) Presidential Decree No 34 of 1981 concerning ratification of the 1958 New York Convention, as further implemented by Supreme Court Regulation No 1 of 1990, sets out procedures for the enforcement of foreign arbitral awards.

These post-independence acts and regulations complement Articles 16, 17, and 18 paragraph (1) AB as well as jurisprudence and doctrine that has existed since before independence.

To date, Indonesia has not joined international treaties or conventions in the fields of Private International Law, except for the 1958 Convention on the Recognition and Enforcement of Foreign Arbitral Awards (popularly known as the New York Convention) and the 2001 Convention on International Interests in Mobile Equipment and its Cape Town Protocol.

Regarding legislation as the main source of Indonesian Private International Law, a hierarchy of legislation must be respected when dealing with Private International Law subject matter. According to a principle called *Lex superior derogat legi inferiori*, lower hierarchy legislation cannot conflict with higher legislation. The lower hierarchy legislation can be used independently only when the higher sources of law are silent on particular subject matter.

Based on Article 7 and its elucidation of Act No 12 of 2011 concerning the formulation of legislation (Formulation of Legislations Act 2011), the hierarchy of legislation in Indonesia is as follows:

(i) The 1945 Constitution.
(ii) Decrees of People's Consultative Assembly.
(iii) Acts/Government Regulations in lieu of Acts.
(iv) Government regulations.
(v) Presidential regulations.
(vi) Provincial regional regulations, including the *Qanun* applicable in Aceh Province, special regional regulations, and provincial regional regulations applicable in Papua Province.
(vii) Regency/city regulations, including the *Qanun* applicable in regencies/cities in Aceh Province.

Aside from the above-listed legislation, Article 8 of the Formulation of Legislations Act 2011 also recognises regulations made by the state apparatus, such as Supreme Court regulations, Parliament regulations, minister regulations, and so on.

The position of treaties or international conventions that have been ratified by the government within the hierarchy of legislation is not mentioned in the Formulation of Legislations Act 2011. Therefore, the status of ratified treaties or conventions as part of Indonesia's legislations is not clear. Although Article 11 of Indonesian Constitution recognises treaties, it does not stipulate whether a treaty shall become a law in Indonesia after being approved by the Parliament. In 2000, the government passed Act No 24 concerning international agreements (the International Agreements Act 2000). Like the Constitution, this Act does not mention when a treaty or convention becomes part of Indonesian law after being ratified or approved. The Act basically only governs the process of entering international agreements and other formalities. In addition, no stable jurisprudence exists to determine the position of ratified treaties in Indonesian law.[6] This situation raises questions about the role of treaties as a source of law in Indonesia. Legal scholars of this issue conclude that, in practice, a treaty or convention that has been ratified by the government and Parliament may not form part of Indonesian law until it is transformed into domestic legislation, such as by an Act or another type of regulation.[7] As a consequence, Indonesian authorities and courts may not implement a ratified treaty until it has been transformed into an Act or regulation. An example of this practice is the 1958 New York Convention on Recognition and Enforcement of Foreign Arbitral Awards that was ratified by the Presidential Decree No 34 of 1981. After ratification of the Convention, the Supreme Court maintained its refusal to enforce foreign arbitral awards. In the case of *P.T. Nizwar v Navigation Maritime Bulgare*, the Supreme Court held that while acknowledging the ratification of the 1958 New York Convention, Indonesian courts could not enforce foreign arbitral awards due to the lack of implementing regulations

[6] DD Agusman, 'Status Hukum Perjanjian Internasional Dalam Hukum Nasional RI Tinjauan Dari Perspektif Praktek Indonesia' (2008) 5 *Indonesian Journal of International Law* 488 http://ijil.ui.ac.id/index.php/home/article/view/178 (accessed 29 May 2018); S Butt, 'The Position of International Law Within the Indonesian Legal System' (2014) 28(1) *Emory International Law Review* 1 http://law.emory.edu/eilr/content/volume-28/issue-1/recent-developments/international-law-indonesian-legal-system.html (accessed 29 May 2018).

[7] ibid.

setting out in what court a request to enforce the awards should be filed and whether the Supreme Court should determine if an award violates Indonesian public policy.[8] Only after the Supreme Court issued Regulation No 1 of 1990 concerning the procedure for enforcing foreign arbitral awards, nine years after ratification, was the Convention implemented, thereby becoming part of Indonesian law enabling courts to enforce foreign arbitral awards. As such, while treaties are a source of Indonesian Private International Law, a ratified treaty may not be part of Indonesian Private International Law until an Act or regulation has been passed to implement it. In practice, the implementation of a treaty into Indonesian law may take many years after ratification.

As demonstrated, the sources of Indonesian Private International Law are the same as those of other fields of law in Indonesia. However, most come from the Dutch colonial era. There is no codified Private International Law in Indonesia. Provisions governing private international matters are scattered in different legislation from the pre-independence and post-independence eras. A ratified treaty, as one source of Private International Law, may not become law in Indonesia unless the treaty has been transformed into an Act or regulation.

III. History of Private International Law in Indonesia

The development of Private International Law in Indonesia started in the Dutch colonial era and continues through to today. The following section presents a brief account of the development of Private International Law before and after independence.

A. Before Independence

The foundation of Private International Law in Indonesia was established during the colonial era, when the Dutch colonial government passed a law that governed interpersonal legal relations among different groups of inhabitants, including foreigners, in the Dutch East Indies. The AB, passed in 1847, grouped the inhabitants into the Dutch, indigenous/natives, and foreigners (neither Dutch nor indigenous) who were granted residency (Article 4 AB). The newer law, *Indische Staatsregeling* ('IS') (Dutch Colonial Constitution), passed in 1926, added the group 'foreign oriental' as inhabitants of the Dutch East Indies (Article 163 IS). According to this article those who were not Dutch, indigenous, or foreign oriental were categorised as foreigners.

In private (civil and commercial) matters, the Dutch colonial Government did not unify the law, but rather allowed each group of inhabitants to apply its own private laws reflecting their beliefs and traditions. Article 131 IS provided applicable private law for each group: Dutch law for Dutch or European inhabitants; customary law for Indigenous and Foreign Oriental inhabitants; selected Dutch law for Chinese Foreign Orientals. The colonial government also developed the interpersonal law that governed private relations among these three groups of inhabitants as well as between them and foreigners.

[8] Supreme Court Decision 2944K/PDT/1983 (20 August 1984).

See, for example, Articles 16, 17, and 18 paragraph (1) AB mentioned above. Those articles governed interpersonal matters that related to the status of persons, family matters, real property, and formality. For other interpersonal matters, the court developed jurisprudence and used doctrine. As a consequence of accommodating a pluralistic legal system, the colonial government established a plural court system for all groups of inhabitants. Each court system had its own civil procedure law. The 1941 *Het Herziene Indonesisch Reglement* (Renewed Indonesian Code) was the civil procedure law in the Court for Indigenous Indonesians in Java and Madura. The 1927 *Rechtsreglement Buitengewesten* (Civil Procedure Code for Indigenous Outside Java and Madura) was for the Court for Indigenous Indonesians outside Java and Madura. The 1847 *Reglement op de Burgerlijke Rechtsvordering* (civil procedure code) was for the Court for the Dutch, European, foreign oriental, and foreigner inhabitants. Facing this diverse and complex legal pluralism in the Dutch East Indies, the colonial government relied more on jurisprudence (court precedents) than legislation to support Articles 16, 17, and 18 paragraph (1) AB. Jurisprudence became increasingly important as the source of law in interpersonal or intergroup cases.[9] Doctrine (legal theories) in the field of interpersonal matters was also developed by Dutch legal scholars during this time.[10]

The Japanese occupation in Indonesia from 1942 to 1945 did not bring change to the Dutch colonial legal system, as it was brief before Indonesia declared its Independence in August 1945. Article 3 of *Osamu Seirei* (Military Act) No 1 of 1942 also declared that, 'all state institutions and their authorities, law, legislations of the previous government remain valid temporarily, provided that they are not in contrary to the law of the military government'.

At the end of colonial era, Dutch legislation in interpersonal relations, jurisprudence, and doctrine laid the foundation of Indonesian Private International Law, as explained in the following section.

B. After Independence

Unlike the Dutch colonial Government that maintained legal pluralism especially in private law, the Indonesian Government preferred legal uniformity for the unity of the newly independent country. As the new Indonesian Government had not yet developed its legal system, it established Transitional Provisions in the 1945 Constitution to avoid a legal vacuum. Article II of the Transitional Provisions of the Indonesian Constitution (prior to the Fourth Amendment) provided that, 'All existing state institutions and regulations remain effective, as long as the new ones have not yet been provided under this Constitution.' With this Transitional Provision, the new government assimilated all Dutch colonial legislation into the Indonesian legal system, unless contrary to the Constitution. As a former Dutch colony, Indonesia also assumed the civil law tradition that made Dutch codified and written law preferable to indigenous customary (*Adat*) law which was unwritten and uncodified. This preference virtually transformed the Dutch law into Indonesian national law.

[9] R Lukito, *Legal Pluralism in Indonesia: Bridging the Unbridgeable* (Routledge, 2013) 130.
[10] S Gautama and H Wiknjosastro, 'Some Aspects of Indonesian Private International Law' (1990) 32 *Malaya Law Review* 417 www.jstor.org/stable/24865645 (accessed 26 May 2018).

To unify the country, the 1945 Indonesian Constitution also abolished the inhabitant grouping system, so that Indonesian law now only recognises Indonesian citizens and non-Indonesian citizens (foreigners). Article 26 of the Constitution states:

(1) Citizens are those who are indigenous Indonesians and persons of foreign origin who are legalised as citizens in accordance with the law.
(2) Residents consist of Indonesian citizens and foreigners residing in Indonesia.[11]
(3) Matters of citizenship and residency are to be regulated by law.[12]

These constitutional provisions abolished Articles 131 and 163 IS which segregated inhabitants into different groups with different private law. Since Indonesian law only recognises Indonesian citizens and non-Indonesian citizens, interpersonal law in Articles 16, 17, and 18, paragraph (1) AB are only used to govern matters between Indonesian citizens and foreigners. They are no longer used to govern matters among different groups of inhabitants. Consequently, Indonesian jurists agreed to redefine the phrase 'inhabitants of the Dutch East Indies' in those interpersonal laws as 'Indonesian citizens' to reflect post-independence circumstances. The three articles thereby became the main source of Indonesian Private International Law together with the jurisprudence and doctrine concerning interpersonal law developed during the colonial era.

The Indonesian Government also abolished the plural colonial court system but kept all three civil procedure codes left by the Dutch colonial Government. Particular emphasis was given to the 1847 *Reglement op de Burgerlijke Rechtsvordering* ('Rv'). Although Rv was civil procedure code for the court of Dutch and foreigner inhabitants, after independence, Indonesian courts began to use it to govern procedures related to arbitration and foreign judgments. Thus, Rv also became the source of post-independence Indonesian Private international law.

These Dutch laws – accompanied by scattered provisions found in different Indonesian codes that govern private relations between Indonesians and foreigners are still implemented today. For example, the Basic Agrarian Act 1960, the Marriage Act 1974, Act No 12 of 2006 concerning citizenship (Citizenship Act 2006), and Act No 25 of 2007 concerning investment (Investment Act 2007) have provisions that govern relations between Indonesians and foreigners. In 1981, the government also ratified the 1958 Convention on the Recognition and Enforcement of Foreign Arbitral Awards

The Indonesian Government has made some effort to codify Private International Law. The first and second efforts were in 1983 and 1997, but for unknown reasons, these Bills never reached the Parliament. The last effort was in 2014, when the Ministry of Law and Human Rights commissioned a team to write an Academic Paper on the Indonesian Private International Law Bill. Though completed in 2015, the Bill still has not reached the Parliament. Consequently, Private International Law in Indonesia has not changed much from colonial times. To date, Dutch colonial legislation, jurisprudence, and doctrine in Private International law matters remain applicable and operate as the main sources of law. This structure will change only if the Indonesian Government enacts its own private international code, and Indonesian court can develop its own jurisprudence to reflect new changes in its Private International Law.

[11] The 1945 Constitution of the Republic of Indonesia (Second Amendment).
[12] ibid.

IV. Preliminary Matters

Except for *renvoi*, Indonesian Private International Law has no clear rules on the general doctrinal matters discussed here. No legislation or jurisprudence has been developed on these matters since the Dutch colonial era. Thus, legal analysis on these matters in Indonesia is based on the doctrine and scholarly writing of Indonesian scholars who often cite cases and theories from classics textbooks, such as Dicey and Morris *The Conflict of Laws*. It is also based on the jurisprudence of courts outside Indonesia. Some attempts have been made to formulate rules on these matters in statutory Bills on Indonesian Private International Law, However, the Bills have yet to be passed by Parliament, so the rules set out in them have so far not become part of Indonesian Private International Law. This section will therefore analyse the relevant matters based on the writings of Indonesian scholars.

A. Characterisation

The term used in Indonesian Private International Law for characterisation is 'qualification' (*Kualifikasi*). Qualification is the process whereby a judge deals with a private international case by 'qualifying' or 'characterising' its essential nature. According to Sudargo Gautama and Sunaryati Hartono, two leading scholars in Indonesian Private International Law, once a court is seised of a case and has authority to adjudicate upon it, the judge must perform qualification to categorise the case into a branch of private law, such as tort, contract, capacity, formality, marriage, divorce, property, marital property, dependence, succession, and so on.[13] In determining whether a particular case should be qualified as, for example, one concerning breach of contract instead of tort, or matrimonial property instead of inheritance, these scholars suggest that Indonesian judges should use Indonesian law (*lex fori*) to qualify the case. As such, the facts of the case are analysed in accordance with Indonesian law and characterised as contract instead of tort, matrimonial property instead of inheritance, and so on, accordingly. However, some private international matters are not legally known in Indonesian law, such as trust[14] and civil child abduction. These matters are difficult for Indonesian judges to qualify. Sudargo Gautama has labelled this issue as one of 'Adaptation' (*Penyesuaian*) and suggested that Indonesian judges adapt a matter unknown to Indonesian law to the closest similar category in Indonesian Private Law.[15]

After an Indonesian judge is able to qualify a case into a certain branch of Indonesian private law, the judge must find the applicable law for that case (*lex causae*). To do so, the judge employs connecting factors known in Indonesian Private International Law, such as national law, domicile law, *lex situs*, *lex fori*, *lex loci*, etc. If the connecting factor of the case, for instance, is the nationality of the party, the Indonesian judge must use the national law of the party as the *lex causae* to decide the outcome of the case. In this case, the Indonesian judge will not use Indonesian law but rather the national law of the party.

[13] S Hartono, *Pokok-Pokok Hukum Perdata Internasional Indonesia* (Binacipta, 1976) 81; S Gautama, *Hukum Perdata Internasional Indonesia Jilid Dua Bagian Dua Buku Ketiga* (Penerbit Alumni, 1973) 120–121.
[14] Hartono, *Pokok-Pokok* (n 13) 77; Gautama, *Perdata Internasional Jilid II Bag 2* (n 13) 88.
[15] Gautama, *Perdata Internasional Jilid II Bag 2* (n 13) 89.

By way of example of the qualification procedure in Indonesian Private International Law, suppose an Indonesian judge must determine whether a private international case is one of capacity for marriage or one of marriage formality. Based on *lex fori*, the judge qualifies the case as the former instead of the latter. After qualifying the case, one must work out the applicable law to decide the case. Based on the connecting factor, which is the national law of the spouse or the couple (the party), the *lex causae* is the national law of the party.[16] Therefore, the Indonesian judge must decide the case by using the national law of the party – not by using Indonesian law, unless the national law of the party is contrary to Indonesian public policy. If, based on Indonesian law, the case is instead qualified as one of marriage formality, the judge must determine the applicable law accordingly. Based on the connecting factor, which is the *lex loci*, the applicable law for the case would be the law of the country in which the marriage took place.[17] If the couple were married in Indonesia, the applicable law would be Indonesian law. The *lex causae* is the same as the *lex fori*. Therefore, the judge will decide this case in accordance with Indonesian law.

This scholarly opinion was accepted in the 1983, 1997, and 2015 Bills of Indonesian Private International Law. Article 5 of the 1983 Bill of Indonesian Private International Law stated that an Indonesian judge shall perform qualification based on Indonesian law. Article 2f of the 2015 Bill of Indonesian Private International Law also emphasised that qualification for private international cases brought before the Indonesian court must be based on Indonesian law. The 2015 Academic Paper of the Indonesian Private International Law Bill also mentions adaptation (*Penyesuaian*) as part of the qualification process, but the Paper does not elaborate the adaptation. Neither do the Bills of Indonesian Private International Law.

To date there has not been any Indonesian Jurisprudence established on the characterisation or qualification. Therefore, the rules regarding qualification or characterisation in Indonesian Private International Law can only be found in doctrine or scholarly writings and the three Bills of Indonesian Private International Bill as explained above.

B. Incidental Question

Indonesian Private International Law's term for incidental question is 'preliminary question' (*Vorfrage*) because it must be resolved or answered by an Indonesian judge before making a judgment on a case. Because Indonesia has no legislation or jurisprudence on preliminary questions, Sudargo Gautama has defined the term for Indonesian Private International Law. He explained that the issue of preliminary question arises when a judge has decided to apply foreign law to a case (*lex causae*), but must resolve a preliminary question before making one's judgment. To resolve the preliminary question, the judge may use the *lex causae*. But the foreign law may be different from the law of the forum (*lex fori*). Because of the conflict between the *lex causae* and the *lex fori* on the preliminary question,

[16] Indonesian Private International Law follows the nationality principle to determine the status or capacity of persons. It means that a judge must use the national law of the party to decide his status or his capacity. See Art 16 AB and Indonesian jurisprudence.

[17] See Art 18(1) AB, which stipulates that formality of a legal action is determined in accordance with the law of the country or place where the action is performed (*lex loci*).

the judge must decide which law to implement to resolve the preliminary.[18] By way of illustration, Sudargo Gautama was fond of citing a classic situation drawn from Dicey and Morris's *The Conflict of Laws* and popularly known in Indonesia as 'the Greek Widow Case'.[19] This hypothetical case is referred to by other scholars, but adapted to and situated in Indonesia. The main question in the case has to do with succession. The Greek widow claims inheritance rights to her late husband's properties in Indonesia. The Indonesian judge applies Greek law (*lex causae*) to the matter but finds that the Court has to resolve a preliminary question before deciding the Greek widow's inheritance right. The preliminary question concerns the validity of her marriage to her late husband as the wedding had been performed in Indonesia. If the Indonesian judge applies Greek law to resolve this preliminary question, her marriage would be void as it was not performed by a Greek priest as required by Greek law. Therefore, the Greek widow would not be entitled to her husband's properties in Indonesia. On the other hand, if the Indonesian judge applies Indonesian law (*lex fori*), her marriage would have been validly contracted, as Indonesian law does not require marriage before a Greek priest. On this basis, she would be entitled to inherit her husband's properties in Indonesia. Sudargo Gautama suggested that judges in such situation must decide whether to apply foreign law as the *lex causae* or Indonesian law as the *lex fori* to the preliminary question, based on their consideration of justice and Indonesia's interest in the case.[20] For example, he suggested that, for the Greek Widow Case, Indonesian judges should apply Greek law for the succession matter and Indonesian law for the preliminary question. He argued that the marriage was performed in Indonesia and was consequently valid according to Indonesia law. Therefore, the Indonesian interest in this issue pointed to Indonesian law as being applicable to the preliminary question.[21]

Sudargo Gautama's opinion on preliminary questions has been accepted as doctrine in Indonesian Private International Law, although the 1983, 1997, and 2015 Bills of Indonesian Private International Law do not provide rules for dealing with preliminary questions. Sudargo Gautama admitted that the issue of preliminary question rarely arises.[22] As a matter of fact, there has not been any jurisprudence on preliminary question in Indonesian Private International Law.

C. Dépeçage

Dépeçage is the technique of applying different applicable laws to different issues in a case. French for 'break into smaller pieces',[23] *dépeçage* is meant to determine the law with the most significant relationship to the parties and each of the issues in a case with a view to leading to a just solution of the case overall. For example, an Italian investor agrees to buy a penthouse apartment on Bali Island, Indonesia, from a Balinese developer. After the Italian

[18] S Gautama, *Pengantar Hukum Perdata Internasional Indonesia* (Binacipta, 1985) 221, 223.
[19] S Gautama, *Hukum Perdata Internasional Indonesia Jilid II Bagian 5 Buku Ke enam* (Penerbit Alumni, 1988) 7.
[20] Gautama, *Pengantar Hukum* (n 18) 240.
[21] ibid, 24.
[22] ibid, 230.
[23] UM Drobnig, P Hay, and M Rheinstein, 'Conflict of Laws – Choice of Law' (*Encyclopædia Britannica, inc.*, 12 April 2018) www.britannica.com/topic/conflict-of-laws (accessed 21 June 2018).

investor pays the Balinese developer, he finds out that the penthouse does not belong to the Balinese developer, as it has been previously bought by a Singaporean. The Italian investor sues the Balinese developer in the Indonesian court. In his lawsuit, the Italian investor claims breach of the sales agreement by the Balinese developer and asks the judge for legal remedy and an *ex aequo et bono* decision (a decision according to what is fair and good). If the judge in this hypothetical case applies *dépeçage*, the judge would break the case down into its component issues and apply a choice of law analysis on each issue. A first component issue could be breach of the sales agreement, and a second one might be tort. After splitting the case into these two component issues, the Indonesian judge must determine the applicable law for each according to the Indonesian Private International Law. The judge could apply Singaporean law on breach of the sales agreement on the basis (say) of the *lex loci contractus* and Indonesian law for the tort component as *lex locus delicti*.

To date, there has been no case applying *dépeçage* in Indonesia. Nevertheless, academic legal writing in Indonesia recognises *dépeçage* in international business contracts. Indonesian scholars in general accept *dépeçage* doctrine in international business contracts whereby the parties to a contract subject different parts of their contract to different systems of law.[24] For instance, in a loan agreement between an Indonesian and Singaporean, the parties may agree that the security clause is governed by Indonesian law as the security is located in Indonesia, while the rest of the agreement is governed by Singaporean law as the agreement was executed in Singapore. Therefore, the Indonesian court must apply the *dépeçage* that has been agreed by the parties to the loan agreement, should the parties bring their dispute before the court.

Dépeçage by parties to a contract is also recognised in scholarly analysis of the first sentence of Article 42, paragraph (1) of the ICSID Convention (Convention on the Settlement of Investment Disputes Between States and Nationals of Other States) to which Indonesia is a contracting party. The first sentence of Article 42, paragraph (1) states that: 'The Tribunal shall decide a dispute in accordance with such rules of law as may be agreed by the parties'. Some scholars maintain that this provision allows the parties to make choice of law clauses that subject different parts of their agreement to different systems of law, also known as *dépeçage*.[25] In some cases, Indonesian scholars believe that d*épeçage* agreed upon by parties to a contract is better known than *dépeçage* imposed by the court. The application of *dépeçage* by parties to a contract supports the principles of party autonomy and freedom of contract. On the other hand, the application of *dépeçage* by the court carries the risk that the judge ends up making an *ultra petita* decision, which means that the court decides more than it has been requested by the parties to the dispute. The principle of *non ultra petita* is prescribed in Indonesian Civil Procedure Codes. See Article 178, paragraph (3) of *Het Herziene Indonesisch Reglement* and Article 189, paragraph (3) of *Rechtsreglement Buitengewesten*, which stipulate that the 'Judge is not allowed to decide matters that are not requested or to decide more than requested.' In Indonesia, application of *dépeçage* by the court can also make the proceeding increasingly complex, which does not comply with the

[24] Gautama and Wiknjosastro 'Some Aspects' (n 10) 430.

[25] GS Tawil, 'Dispute Settlement International centre for settlement of Investment Disputes (2.6 Applicable Law)' (*United Nations Conference on Trade and Development*, 2003) 8 http://unctad.org/en/Docs/edmmisc232add5_en.pdf (accessed 22 June 2018).

principle of the simple, quick, and economical judiciary required by Article 2, paragraph (4) of Act No 48 of 2009 concerning judicial power (the Judicial Power Act 2009). Although the Indonesian court has never applied *dépeçage*, an ICSID Tribunal did apply it in *Amco Asia Corporation and others v Republic of Indonesia.*[26] In this case, the ICSID Tribunal applied *dépeçage*, although it did not expressly mention it. The tribunal applied Indonesian law to an investment dispute between the parties and applied the law of the State of Delaware on the issue of Amco Asia's status and capacity.[27]

In summary, to date Indonesia has had no jurisprudence on *dépeçage*. But it exists in scholarly writing on Indonesian Private International Law. Indonesian scholars in general accept the doctrine of *dépeçage* as applied and agreed by parties to international business contracts. On the other hand, Indonesian scholars have not discussed the application of *dépeçage* by the Indonesian court to a Private International Law case. A case that involved the application of *dépeçage* in which Indonesia was a party was not adjudicated by an Indonesian court, but by an ICSID arbitral tribunal.

D. Renvoi and Transmission

Renvoi is recognised in Indonesian Private International Law. Textbooks on Indonesian Private International Law explain that, when the Indonesian court applies the law of another state, it includes that state's Private International Law. The rules of that state's Law could point to Indonesian Law (remission) or to the law of a third country (transmission).[28] 'Remission' and 'transmission' are categorised as single *renvoi.*[29] *Renvoi* as a choice of law doctrine has existed in jurisprudence and regulation in Indonesia since the Dutch colonial era. The Indonesian court applies it in cases concerning the status of persons, capacity, family matters, inheritance, and immovable properties of foreigners who domicile in Indonesia.[30] Because Indonesia follows the Nationality Principle, when Indonesian judges apply the national law of foreigners, they will include the Private International Law of the relevant countries. If the Private International Law refers back to Indonesian law, the judge will use Indonesian substantive or domestic law to adjudicate the case (remission). In fact, there has never been any jurisprudence or regulation on transmission in Indonesia. Like transmission, there is no jurisprudence or regulation in Indonesia concerning double/total *renvoi* (also called 'Foreign Court Doctrine').

Remission has been implemented since the colonial era. For instance, in 1925, a Sinhalese originating from British India but domiciled in the Dutch East Indies required

[26] International Centre for the Settlement of Investment Disputes *Amco Asia Corporation and others v Republic of Indonesia* (1992) 89 ILR 580.

[27] Oxford Academic, *AMCO v Republic of Indonesia: Resubmitted Case Decision on Jurisdiction* (ICSID Review 1998) vol 3(1) 183–184; see also Tawil 'Dispute Settlement' (n 25).

[28] Gautama, *Pengantar Hukum* (n 18) 89–90; IBR Supancana, *Naskah Akademik Rancangan Undang-Undang tentang Hukum Perdata Internasional (lanjutan)* (Badan Pembinaan Hukum Nasional Kementerian Hukum dan Hak Asasi Manusia RI, 2015) 14–15 www.bphn.go.id/data/documents/na_ruu_ttg_hukum_perdata_internasional_(lanjutan).pdf (accessed 8 July 2018).

[29] Gautama, *Pengantar Hukum* (n 18) 109; Supancana, *Naskah Akademik* (n 28) 14.

[30] Gautama and Wiknjosastro 'Some Aspects' (n 10) 426; Gautama, *Perdata Internasional Jilid II Bag 2* (n 13) 40.

the *Raad van Justitie*[31] of Medan to declare him bankrupt, as he could no longer pay his debts. He was 16 years old but already married to a native Indonesian. In dealing with this case, the judge had to answer the preliminary question of whether the petitioner was legally incompetent because of his minor age, or legally competent to file for bankruptcy. The judge decided to apply Dutch law to resolve this preliminary question with the consideration that law of British India as the national law of the petitioner referred to the law of the country in which he was domiciled to determine his status and capacity. Therefore, the judge of the *Raad van Justitie* applied Dutch law for foreign Oriental inhabitants (*Staatsblad*/State Gazette 1924 no 556) to determine the petitioner's status and capacity, as ethnically he was categorised as a foreign Oriental. Based on the law, the petitioner was found legally competent in spite of his young age and, therefore, the judge granted the petitioner's request to declare bankruptcy.[32] In this case, the judge did not expressly mention *renvoi* in his judgment, but clearly acknowledged the *renvoi* principles when indicating that the law of British India as the national law of the petitioner referred to Dutch law to determine the petitioner's legal status and capacity.

After independence, the *renvoi* principle continued to be applied by the Indonesian court. In a divorce case in 1987 the parties were an English husband and his Indonesian wife who had acquired British nationality. The couple were domiciled in Indonesia and their divorce case was brought to the South Jakarta District Court. The latter applied Indonesian law to the case. The judge accepted the *renvoi* principle, as the English law that was the couple's national law referred to the law of the country in which the couple were domiciled. Therefore, the judge applied the Marriage Act 1974 to the divorce.[33] The Indonesian Supreme Court approved the *renvoi* principle. In Decision No 2640 K/Pdt/2009, it upheld the decisions of the Jakarta High Court[34] and the South Jakarta District Court[35] regarding the divorce of an American couple domiciled in Jakarta. They held that although the nationalities of the couple were American, their domicile was in Indonesia and, therefore, the Marriage Act 1974 should be applied to their divorce.[36] Interestingly, in this case, the courts did not mention the *renvoi* principle to justify the application of Indonesian law. Instead, the courts only used the couple's domicile in Jakarta to justify application of Indonesian law. Nevertheless, their decision can be interpreted as a model of *renvoi* application by an Indonesian court.

As discussed, in Indonesia, the application of *renvoi* after independence has mostly occurred in divorce cases in which the husband and wife are foreigners domiciled in Indonesia, but originally from countries that apply the principle of domicile, such as the UK,[37] the US,[38]

[31] Under the colonial government, the *Raad van Justitie* was a Court for the Dutch, European, foreign oriental and foreign inhabitants.

[32] Medan Decision of the *Raad van Justitie* dated 4 December 1925, as described in Gautama, *Pengantar Hukum* (n 18) 105–106.

[33] District Court of South Jakarta Decision 112/Pdt.G/1987 (not published); see Gautama and Wiknjosastro 'Some Aspects' (n 10) 428.

[34] High Court of Jakarta Decision 141/PDT/2009/PT.DKI (not published) as cited on page 9 of the District Court of Denpasar Decision 172/Pdt.G/2014/PN.Dps. (6 May 2014).

[35] District Court of South Jakarta Decision 47/Pdt.G/2008/PN.Jak.Sel (not published) as cited on page 9 of the District Court of Denpasar Decision 172/Pdt.G/2014/PN.Dps. (6 May 2014).

[36] Supreme Court Decision 2640 K/Pdt/2009 is not published, but the legal opinion in the decision is cited on page 9 of the District Court of Denpasar Decision 172/Pdt.G/2014/PN.Dps (6 May 2014) (published).

[37] District Court of South Jakarta Decision 112/Pdt.G/1987 (not published).

[38] District Court of South Jakarta Decision 47/Pdt.G/2008/PN.Jak.Sel (not published); High Court of Jakarta Decision 141/PDT/2009/PT.DKI (not published) as cited on page 9 of the District Court of Denpasar Decision 172/Pdt.G/2014/PN.Dps. (6 May 2014); Supreme Court Decision 2640 K/Pdt/2009 (not published).

and South Africa.[39] This type of *renvoi* in which the national law of the parties refers back to the law of their domicile is categorised as 'remission'. The Indonesian court has accepted this type of *renvoi* since the Dutch colonial era. Conversely, the *renvoi* that refers to the law of a third country (transmission) has never been applied by an Indonesian court even during the Dutch colonial era. This fact supports the argument that Indonesia's acceptance of *renvoi* is simply to enable an Indonesian court to apply Indonesian law as much as possible. In relation to the reason of acceptance of the *renvoi* principle in Indonesia, Sudargo Gautama wrote:

> We are of the opinion that the acceptance of the *renvoi* principle is beneficial to Indonesia. It will result in the application of Indonesian internal law, and consequently, when Indonesian laws are applied, there is greater assurance that the correct law will be applied than when foreign laws are applied. Although we uphold the equality of Indonesian and foreign laws, the Indonesian courts will be more at ease if they can apply their own internal law.[40]

Acceptance of the remission type of *renvoi* has not only been by the court and judiciary, but also by the Indonesian Government. In 1922, the attorney general of the Dutch East Indies issued a circular letter dated 9 March 1922 to the Civil Registry offices. The circular letter sought to deal with the question of the capacity of foreigners to marry in the Dutch East Indies and whether adult foreigners under 30 years old had to obtain parental consent to marry. In the circular letter, the attorney general distinguished countries that adhered to the nationality principle from countries that adhered to the domicile principle.[41] The attorney general instructed the marriage registrars of the Civil Registry to apply the national law of foreigners from countries applying the nationality principle, but to apply Articles 42 and 48 of the 1847 *Burgerlijk Wetboek voor Nederlandsch-Indie* (Dutch East Indies Civil Code) to foreigners from countries applying the domicile principle, to determine issues of capacity to marry and the need for parental consent. The circular letter cited cases of German and French citizens who married in the Dutch East Indies. The applicable laws to determine their capacity to marry were German and French laws respectively. In the case of British citizens, the circular letter suggested the application of the Articles 42 and 48 of the Dutch East Indies Civil Code to determine their capacity and requirements to marry. Although the circular letter did not expressly mention the *renvoi* principle, it was clear that the attorney general applied the remission type of *renvoi* in instructing marriage registrars to apply the Dutch East Indies Civil Code to marriages of foreigners from countries applying the domicile principle.

Based on Article II of the Transitional Provisions of the Indonesian Constitution 1945,[42] the circular letter of 9 March 1922 has remained valid after independence as no new regulation superseded it. Therefore, it can be concluded that the present Indonesian Government should follow the *renvoi* principle as provided in the 1922 circular letter for matters related to the marriages of foreigners who domicile in Indonesia. The acceptance of the *renvoi* principle in Indonesia is further supported by the 1983, 1997, and 2015 Bills of Indonesian Private International Law that provide rules on *renvoi*. The Bills of Indonesian Private International Law provide that the national law of a person shall apply to matters

[39] District Court of Denpasar Decision 172/Pdt.G/2014/PN.Dps. (6 May 2014).

[40] Gautama and Wiknjosastro 'Some Aspects' (n 10) 429.

[41] Gautama, *Pengantar Hukum* (n 18) 101–103; Gautama, *Perdata Internasional Jilid II Bag 2* (n 13) 102.

[42] It provides that 'All existing state institutions and regulations remain effective, as long as the new ones have not yet been provided under this Constitution.'

relating to the person's status. But, if the person's national law refers back to Indonesian law, then substantive Indonesian law becomes the applicable law for that individual. The provisions in the Bills show acceptance of the remission type of *renvoi*, but not the transmission type of *renvoi*.

Therefore, it will be interesting to see how the Indonesian court will judge a case in which the national law of a foreign claimant refers to the law of a third country. No jurisprudence or regulation in Indonesia to date has applied the law of a third country. The Indonesian court is free to decide that the applicable law for the foreign claimant should be Indonesian law or the national law of the claimant – without referring further to the law of a third country. This approach is recommended because the underlying reason for Indonesia's acceptance of the *renvoi* principle is to enable the Indonesian court to apply Indonesian law as much as possible. In other words, there is no purpose of implementing the *renvoi* principle if the result is that the Indonesian court must apply the law of a third country, which is neither the *lex fori* nor the national law of the claimant. The Explanation to Article 2 of the 1983 Bill of Indonesian Private International Law confirms the underlying reason for the application of *renvoi* in Indonesia, is to increase the application of Indonesian law by Indonesian courts and authorities. On the other hand, scholars in Indonesia agree that application of the *renvoi* principle is limited to the fields of family law and to personal status and capacity. They maintain that, to respect the parties' freedom of contract, the *renvoi* principle should not be applied in the field of contract. Consequently, the law applicable to a contract or the law chosen by parties to a contract shall not include its Private International Law.[43] Another limitation to the *renvoi* principle is that it will not be applied in the field of tort.[44]

It is worth noting that the ICSID Convention, to which Indonesia is a party, recognises the *renvoi* principle in the second sentence of Article 42, paragraph (1):

> The Tribunal shall decide a dispute in accordance with such rules of law as may be agreed by the parties. In the absence of such agreement, the Tribunal shall apply the law of the Contracting State party to the dispute (including its rules on the conflict of laws) and such rules of international law as may be applicable.

The phrase '(including its rules on the conflict of laws)' in Article 42, paragraph (1) allows the ICSID Tribunal to implement the *renvoi* principle, and thus to apply Indonesian Private International Law where Indonesia has a dispute with a foreign investor. As stipulated in the second sentence of Article 42, paragraph (1), the application of *renvoi* by the ICSID Tribunal only takes place if the host state and the foreign investor have not agreed on a different law to govern their agreement or dispute. Should the parties have agreed on another law, an ICSID Tribunal will respect it and only apply the chosen substantive law (that is, excluding the designated state's Private International Law).

It can be concluded that *renvoi* has been recognised and implemented in Indonesia since the Dutch colonial era. There have been several examples of jurisprudence and regulation on *renvoi*. However, Indonesian Private International Law only recognises the remission type of *renvoi*, which points back to Indonesian law as the applicable law. The underlying reason

[43] Hartono, *Pokok-Pokok* (n 13) 110; Gautama, *Perdata Internasional Jilid II Bag 2* (n 13) 39–40.
[44] AJ Mayss, *Principles of Conflict of Laws* 3rd edn (Cavendish Publishing Limited, 1999) 9.

for accepting the *renvoi* principle is to enable the Indonesian court to apply Indonesian law as much as possible to cases brought by foreigners domiciled in Indonesia.

V. Connecting Factors

A. Nationality

i. Natural Persons

Indonesian Private International Law follows the nationality principle to determine the status or capacity of natural persons. Therefore, nationality is a significant connecting factor in Indonesian Private International Law. Article 16 AB and Indonesian jurisprudence dictate that judges and authorities should apply the law of a person's nationality to matters related to their status, capacity, family, and inheritance.

For instance, according to Indonesian Private International Law, the capacity of an Indonesian citizen to marry outside Indonesia is determined by Indonesian law, which is the law of the person's nationality (Article 16 AB). Likewise, the capacity of a foreigner to marry in Indonesia is determined by the law of the latter's nationality.

In a 1925 jurisprudence, the *Raad van Justitie* of Medan held that the Japanese law that allowed a married woman to conduct a legal act independently was applicable to a Japanese wife in Medan who lived in Medan and applied for bankruptcy. Therefore, based on Japanese law, her application for bankruptcy to the court without her Japanese husband's assistance or permission was valid,[45] although Articles 110 of the Dutch East Indies Civil Code would not have permitted her to do so.[46]

ii. Corporations

Indonesian Private International Law is generally silent on issues of the nationality and domicile of corporations in Indonesia. Therefore, one must refer to specific Indonesian legislation to determine answers concerning this issue. Article 5, paragraph (2) of the Investment Act 2007 requires foreign investors to incorporate companies in accordance with Indonesian law and to have the seat of such companies in Indonesia. Articles 30, 36, and 42 of the Basic Agrarian Act 1960 stipulate that foreign corporations are allowed certain rights in Indonesian land, only if they are incorporated in accordance with Indonesian law and have their seat in Indonesia. Based on those provisions, the Investment Act 2007 and the Basic Agrarian Act 1960, in principle, require all corporations to have Indonesian nationality or be incorporated in accordance with Indonesian law in order to operate and to have rights to land in Indonesia. This means that nationality is a significant connecting factor in determining the status and capacity of corporations in Indonesia.

[45] S Gautama, *Hukum Perdata Internasional Indonesia Jilid Kedua (Bagian Pertama) Cetakan Ke-3* (Eresco Bandung, 1986) 31.

[46] Article 110 stipulates that a wife may not appear in court without the assistance of her husband, although she is married without sharing matrimonial property with her husband, and has an independent profession.

iii. Ships and Aircraft

The nationality of ships and aircraft is a connecting factor to determine the applicable law for the ships or aircraft in their private law matters. Nationalities of ships and aircrafts are based on their flags. For example, the law applicable to legal relations between a Polish captain who works on an Indonesian-flagged vessel and its Indonesian owner would be the law of the vessel's flag, namely Indonesian law.[47]

B. Domicile

i. Natural Persons

Article 16 AB formerly stipulated:

> Statutory provisions governing the status and capacity of persons remain binding for inhabitants of Dutch East Indies during their stay abroad. However, if they are domiciled in the Netherlands or in one of the Dutch colonies, provided that they have residence there, their status and capacity will be governed by the law of the Netherlands or the law of the Dutch colonies where they are domiciled.

This original version of Article 16 AB had the consequence that, whereas Article 16 AB used nationality as a connecting factor to determine the status and capacity of Dutch East Indies inhabitants, it also used domicile as a connecting factor to determine the law governing the status and capacity of those living in the Netherlands or one of the Dutch colonies (such as Suriname and Curaçao). To be regarded as having a domicile in one of the latter states so as to be governed by its law, a person had to have a permanent home and earn a living in the relevant state (the domicile principle).[48] After Indonesia's independence, the second sentence of Article 16 AB ceased to be relevant. Thus, the domicile principle in the second sentence of Article 16 AB was deleted. Accordingly, Article 16 AB continues to have effect in Indonesia following independence. But the text has been slightly changed to: 'Statutory provisions governing the status and capacity of persons remain binding for Indonesian citizens during their stay abroad.' As a consequence, nationality has become the only connecting factor for determining the status and capacity of natural persons. However, Sudargo Gautama observed that, in cases having international elements, Indonesian courts often apply the Indonesian Civil Code (BW) to a party in relation to matters of personal status, capacity and family, regardless of the party's nationality. In practice, the courts will only consider the applicability of the national law of a foreign party if that party raises the possible application of his or her national law in a matter.[49]

Thus, under Article 16 AB, nationality determines the status and capacity of natural persons. However, in a given case, Indonesian courts will often simply use domicile (effectively permanent or long-term residence) in Indonesia as a connecting factor or basis for applying the Indonesian Civil Code to foreign nationals, unless such parties raise the issue of their national law applying.

[47] Gautama, *Perdata Internasional Jilid II Bag 1*(n 45) 47.
[48] Gautama, *Pengantar Hukum* (n 18) 31–32.
[49] ibid, 85.

ii. Corporations

As mentioned earlier, Indonesian Private International Law is silent on the issue of domicile of corporations in Indonesia. However, based on the Investment Act 2007 and the Basic Agrarian Act 1960, all corporations are required to establish their seat in Indonesia in order to operate and have rights to land in Indonesia. This condition means that the domicile (in the sense of statutory seat) is also a significant connecting factor to determine the status and capacity of corporations in Indonesia.

C. Residence

i. Natural Persons

Indonesian Private International Law, in following the nationality principle, does not regard residence of natural persons as a connecting factor to determine the law applicable to them. The law of residence is not applicable to matters related to the person's status, capacities, family matters, and inheritance. Although a foreigner can obtain temporary or permanent residency in Indonesia by holding a Limited Stay or Permanent Stay Permit Card, the law applicable to personal status and capacity would always be the person's national law and not the law of Indonesia as the place of the person's residence. However, as a matter of civil procedure, residence of a party would be a connecting factor to determine the jurisdiction of the Indonesian court in a case. Thus, for instance, the court that has jurisdiction in a particular matter will typically be the court situated in the place of residence of the defendant in an action or the residence of the plaintiff if the defendant's residence is unknown.

Article 100 of 1847 *Reglement op de Burgerlijke Rechtsvordering* ('Rv') allows Indonesians to bring claims against foreigners to Indonesian courts for obligations undertaken by the latter in Indonesia or elsewhere. According to Article 99 Rv, the court that has jurisdiction would be the court where the foreigner's residence is situated or, if it is unknown, where the plaintiff's residence is situated. Further, Article 99 *Rv* governs that:

(1) A claim against a defendant in a case of movable goods is brought to the court where the defendant's residence is situated.
(2) If the defendant does not have a residence, the claim is brought to the court where the defendant actually lives.
(3) If the defendant does not have a known residence in Indonesia, the claim is brought to the court where the plaintiff's residence is situated.

In summary, residence of a natural person is not a connecting factor for determining the law applicable to one's personal status, capacity, family matters, and inheritance. However, the residence of natural persons can be a connecting factor for determining the jurisdiction of a specific Indonesian court to adjudicate a dispute between persons.

ii. Corporations

For corporations, residence is a connecting factor for determining the status and capacity of corporations in Indonesia. Article 17 of Act No 40 of 2007 concerning corporations (the Corporations Act 2007) stipulates that:

(1) Corporations shall be domiciled in the city or regency within the territory of the Republic of Indonesia as specified in their Articles of Association.
(2) The domicile as written in paragraph (1) shall constitute the *Corporation's headquarter.*[50]

Based on Article 17, paragraph (2) of the Corporations Act 2007, to operate and have rights to land in Indonesia, corporations must have their headquarters in Indonesia. This means that their residence (headquarters) is a significant connecting factor in determining their status and capacity in Indonesia.

Like natural persons, a corporation's residence is also a connecting factor in determining the jurisdiction of an Indonesian court to adjudicate a case against the corporation.

VI. Substance and Procedure

Indonesian Private International Law has no clear rules governing which matters are categorised as substance and which as procedure. One must look at doctrine or scholarly opinion to understand the distinction between matters of substance and those of procedure. This section will explain matters of substance and procedure according to current doctrine.

A. Procedure

The discussion of procedural matters in Indonesian Private International Law involves two issues:

(i) International civil procedure based on Indonesian Civil Procedure Codes.
(ii) Formalities based on Article 18, paragraph (1) AB.

International civil procedure concerns that part of national civil procedure law that deals with cases having foreign elements. The subject matter of international civil procedure encompasses, among others, jurisdiction, evidence, judicial service, and the recognition and enforcement of foreign judgments and arbitral awards.[51] Those matters are governed in civil procedure codes, namely, the 1941 *Het Herziene Indonesisch Reglement* (Renewed Indonesian Code (HIR)); the 1927 *Rechtsreglement Buitengewesten* (Civil Procedure Code

[50] Emphasis added.
[51] S Gautama, *Hukum Perdata Internasional Indonesia Jilid III Bagian 2 Buku Ke Delapan* (Penerbit Alumni, 1987) 208, 315.

for Indigenous Outside Java and Madura (Rbg)); and the 1847 *Reglement op de Burgerlijke Rechtsvordering* (Civil Procedure Code (Rv)). For example, the jurisdiction of Indonesian courts over cases, including private international law cases, is governed by Article 118 HIR and Article 99 Rv. Those articles provide that the court having jurisdiction over a case is the court where the residence of a foreign defendant in Indonesia is situated or, if unknown, where the plaintiff's residence in Indonesia is situated.

In addition to international civil procedure, there are formalities that are also part of procedural regulations. These formalities are governed by Article 18, paragraph (1) AB that stipulates, 'Formality of a legal action is determined by the court in accordance with the law of the country or place where the action is performed.' This principle is also called *locus regit actum*. The formalities relate, among others, to civil registration, witness evidence, testaments, the authentication of deeds, and incorporation.[52] Based on Article 18, paragraph (1) AB, those matters are governed by the law of the country where the relevant action has been performed. Therefore, if the formalities are conducted in a country outside Indonesia and have complied with the legal requirements of that country, those formalities will be regarded valid in Indonesia. In certain situations, formalities are governed not only by Article 18, paragraph (1) AB, but also by other regulations, for example, by Article 945 *Burgerlijk Wetboek voor Nederlandsch-Indie* (BW) (the Indonesian Civil Code). The first sentence of Article 945 BW provides that, 'An Indonesian citizen who is in a foreign country, is not allowed to make a testament in any manner other than by an authentic deed and by respecting formalities that are commonly practiced in that foreign country.' Regarding weddings, Indonesian scholars are agreed that a religious wedding ceremony is not a legal formality, although it has ceremonial character. Instead, scholars qualify a religious wedding ceremony as a matter of substance. Therefore, it would not be governed by Article 18, paragraph (1) AB.[53] Further analysis of marriage procedures and substance in Indonesian Private International Law will be found in Chapter 3, section IV.

Finally, it must be remembered that to be regarded as valid by Indonesian law, a legal action must be valid not only according to matter of form or formality, but in accordance with the substantive requirements of that action. For instance, marriage by an Indonesian couple in Australia must comply with the formalities of marriage in Australia, such as marriage registration and the presence of witnesses, as well as any substantive requirements, such as capacity to marry as dictated by the Marriage Act 1974.

B. Substance

Indonesian Private International Law does not define what matters are categorised as procedure and that of substance. Therefore, one must consult doctrine as reflected in scholarly writings to know what are matters of substance in Indonesian Private International Law.

[52] S Gautama, *Hukum Perdata Internasional Indonesia Buku Ketujuh Jilid Ke-Tiga (Bagian Pertama)* (Penerbit Alumni, 1981) 291–294.

[53] ibid, 120–121.

In principle, 'substance' concerns the substantive rights and duties of the parties.[54] Examples are the status and capacity of persons, the status of goods, and parties' obligations are categorised. The law applicable to substantive matters is prescribed in Articles 16 and 17 AB as well as by the parties' choice of law and specific statutes. For example, the law applicable to the status and capacity of persons to marry is to be found in Article 16 AB and Articles 2 (requiring that a marriage comply with the rules of the couple's religion) and 6 to 11 of the Marriage Act 1974.

To conclude, there is distinction between substance and procedure in Indonesian Private International Law, although there is no rule for such distinction. One must learn from the doctrine as discussed above to find out what matters are categorised as substance and as procedure in Indonesian Private International Law.

VII. Proof of Foreign Law and Other Evidentiary Matters

A. Proving Foreign Law

Unlike in common law jurisdictions that categorise foreign law as a question of fact which must be pleaded and proved by a party, Indonesian Private International Law characterises foreign law as a matter of law. This means that a party does not need to plead and prove the applicability of foreign law in a case. Doctrine asserts that the Indonesian judge has the power and duty to apply foreign law *ex officio*, even though a party does not prove or plead it. This doctrine is a facet of the maxim *iura novit curi* ('the court knows the law'). The source of this doctrine can be found in Article 50, paragraph (1) Rv which stipulates, 'Judges in their *ex officio* consideration shall include legal grounds that may not be presented by the parties.' In this provision, legal grounds may be interpreted as including foreign law.[55] As a consequence of being characterised as a matter of law, foreign law may be applied at all levels of court: in trial, appellate, cassation, and extraordinary appellate courts. At all levels of courts, judges are free to decide which foreign law will be applied to a case. The application of foreign law by a judge to the case cannot be challenged or appealed by the parties.[56] If a judge fails to find the content of foreign law because of a lack of information about the law or because the judge is not convinced by the materials placed before the court relating to foreign law, there are some possible outcomes. First, the judge will use domestic law (*lex fori*). Second, the judge assumes that the foreign law is the same as national law, unless proven otherwise, Third, the judge will apply the law closest to the foreign law, for instance, the law in effect during a country's former colonial period. Finally, the judge rejects the plaintiff's claim.[57]

[54] S Peari, 'Substance and Procedure in Private International Law by Richard Garnett – Book Review' (2013) 14(1) *Melbourne Journal of International Law* 1 https://law.unimelb.edu.au/__data/assets/pdf_file/0011/1687448/11Peari1.pdf (accessed 11 August 2018).

[55] Gautama, *Perdata Internasional Jilid II Bag 5* (n 19) 187.

[56] The decision of the *Hoge Raad* (the Supreme Court of the Netherlands) on 26 November 1954, as cited in Gautama, *Perdata Internasional Jilid II Bag 5* (n 19) 202.

[57] Gautama, *Perdata Internasional Jilid II Bag 5* (n 19) 195–200; Supancana, *Naskah Akademik* (n 28) 24–25.

In summary, foreign law in Indonesian Private International Law is accepted as a law that does not need to be proven and pleaded by parties. The judge applies foreign law *ex officio* and in accordance with the *iura novit curia* principle. This doctrine is supported by Article 50, paragraph (1) Rv and accepted in Article 8 of the 1983 Bill of Indonesian Private International Law and in the 2015 Academic Paper of the Indonesian Private International Law Bill.

B. Taking Evidence in Indonesia for Use in Foreign Proceedings

Indonesia is not a party to the 1970 Hague Evidence Convention and Indonesian civil procedure codes do not have provisions governing applications to the Indonesian court by a litigant in foreign legal proceeding for the taking of evidence for use by the foreign court. The 1978 Agreement on Judicial Co-operation between the Republic of Indonesia and the Kingdom of Thailand governs applications by a litigant before the Thai court obtaining evidence in Indonesia for use in Thailand. This is done through the submission of a letter of request (letter rogatory) to the Directorate- General for General Court of the Indonesian Supreme Court. For litigants in foreign courts elsewhere, the only recourse would be Act No 1 of 1982 concerning accession to the 1961 Vienna Convention on Diplomatic Relations and Optional Protocol to the Vienna Convention on Diplomatic Relations Concerning Acquisition of Nationality and the 1963 Vienna Convention on Consular Relations and the Optional Protocol thereto (the Accession to Vienna Conventions on Diplomatic and Consular Relations Act 1982). Article 5 (j) of the 1963 Vienna Convention states that one consular function consists in:

> t]ransmitting judicial and extrajudicial documents or executing letters rogatory or commissions to take evidence for the courts of the sending State in accordance with international agreements in force or, in the absence of such international agreements, in any other manner compatible with the laws and regulations of the receiving State.

Based on that provision, a party in a foreign proceeding may obtain evidence in Indonesia through transmission of a letter rogatory to the Indonesian consular office, which is part of the Ministry of Foreign Affairs. The Ministry also uses the provision as the basis of its authority to transmit and receive letters rogatory to obtain evidence for service of judicial documents in civil matters.[58]

However, the Accession to Vienna Conventions on Diplomatic Consular Relations Act 1982 does not have an implementing law that sets out the procedure of taking evidence for use in foreign proceedings. To make up for the absence of procedural law in taking evidence in Indonesia for use in foreign proceedings, outside the Thai courts,[59] the Ministry of Foreign Affairs and the Supreme Court have entered into a memorandum of understanding (*nota kesepahaman*) and several cooperative agreements (*perjanjian*

[58] A Nursobah, 'MA Dan Kemlu Sepakati Kerjasama Penanganan Permintaan Bantuan Teknis Hukum Dalam Masalah Perdata Lintas Yurisdiksi Negara' (*Kepaniteraan Mahkamah Agung RI*, 21 February 2018). https://kepaniteraan.mahkamahagung.go.id/index.php/kegiatan/1578-ma-dan-kemlu-sepakati-kerjasama-penanganan-permintaan-bantuan-teknis%E2%80%A6 (accessed 27 September 2018).

[59] Indonesia and Thailand have a Bilateral Agreement on Judicial Co-Operation signed in 1978. This Agreement also governs the procedures of taking evidence and serving judicial documents in civil and commercial matters in Indonesia and Thailand.

kerjasama) to govern the procedure of transmitting letters rogatory to obtain evidence and service of judicial documents in civil matters. Their latest memorandum of understanding and cooperative agreements were executed in 2018.[60] That the scope of their cooperative agreements on letters rogatory and service of judicial documents specifically relates to 'civil matters' does not mean that their agreements exclude letters rogatory and service of judicial documents in commercial matters. Legal doctrine treats commercial law as part of civil law[61] and therefore the letters rogatory and service of judicial documents dealt by the Indonesian Ministry of Foreign Affairs and Supreme Court are for civil and commercial matters.

Based on the 2018 Memorandum of Understanding Between the Ministry of Foreign Affairs and Supreme Court No PRJ/HI/102/02/2018/01 No 01/NK/MA/2/2018 concerning request of judicial assistance in civil matters, the Ministry of Foreign Affairs in its website provides a flow chart that explains the procedure of transmitting letters rogatory from a party and authorities in a foreign country to Indonesian authorities, as shown in Figure 1.[62]

In line with Act No 24 of 2009, concerning the Indonesian flag, language, the state emblem, and the national anthem (the Flag, Language, State Emblem, and National Anthem Act 2009) requiring the use of Bahasa Indonesia in official documents, the Ministry of Foreign Affairs requires letters rogatory from foreign authorities to be accompanied by a translation into Bahasa, unless agreed otherwise in an agreement between Indonesia and another state.[63] However, the Ministry does not require that the translation be certified by an interpreter in contrast to the translation requirement in the Agreement on Judicial Cooperation between Indonesia and Thailand.

Based on the guidelines provided by the Ministry of Foreign Affairs in the flow chart, the transmission of letters rogatory to Indonesian authorities must be done through the court of the requesting state.[64] As such, letters rogatory may be used to obtain evidence intended for use in court proceedings only. They cannot be used for any other purpose, such as pretrial discovery (which is not recognised by Indonesian Civil Procedure Law) or in arbitration and administrative proceedings. Types of evidence that may be obtained in Indonesia by letters rogatory include documents, testimonials, and property.[65] Such evidence must be obtained through the Indonesian court in accordance with the Codes of Civil Procedure.

[60] Nota Kesepahaman Kementerian Luar Negeri Republik Indonesia dan Mahkamah Agung Republik Indonesia tentang Penanganan Permintaan Bantuan Teknis Hukum dalam Masalah Perdata No PRJ/HI/102/02/2018/01 No 01/NK/MA/2/2018; Perjanjian Kerja Sama Antara Kementerian Luar Negeri dengan Mahkamah Agung tentang Mekanisme Pengiriman Surat Rogatori dan Penyampaian Dokumen Peradilan dalam Masalah Perdata No PRJ/HI/103/02/2018/01; No 03/PK/MA/2/2018; Perjanjian Kerja Sama antara Kementerian Luar Negeri dan Mahkamah Agung tentang Standardisasi Surat Rogatori dan Surat Penyampaian Dokumen Peradilan dalam Masalah Perdata No PRJ/HI/104/02/2018/01 No 04/PK/MA/2018.

[61] R Soekardono, *Hukum Dagang Indonesia* (Dian Rakyat, 1983) vol 1, 1st ch, 1; HMN Purwosutjipto, *Pengertian Pokok Hukum Dagang Indonesia 1: Pengetahuan Dasar Hukum Dagang* 14th edn (Djambatan, 2007) 5–6.

[62] Dit. Hukum dan Perjanjian Sosial Budaya, 'Alur Masuk' (*Rogatory Online Monitoring)* http://rogatori.kemlu.go.id/flow2 (accessed 17 December 2018).

[63] Dit. Hukum dan Perjanjian Sosial Budaya, 'Ketentuan Nasional' (*Rogatory Online Monitoring)* 'Rogatory Online Monitoring' http://rogatori.kemlu.go.id/nasional (accessed 17 December 2018).

[64] See n 60.

[65] Nota Kesepahaman Kementerian Luar Negeri Republik Indonesia dan Mahkamah Agung Republik Indonesia tentang Penanganan Permintaan Bantuan Teknis Hukum dalam Masalah Perdata No PRJ/HI/102/02/2018/01 No 01/NK/MA/2/2018, Art 1(2).

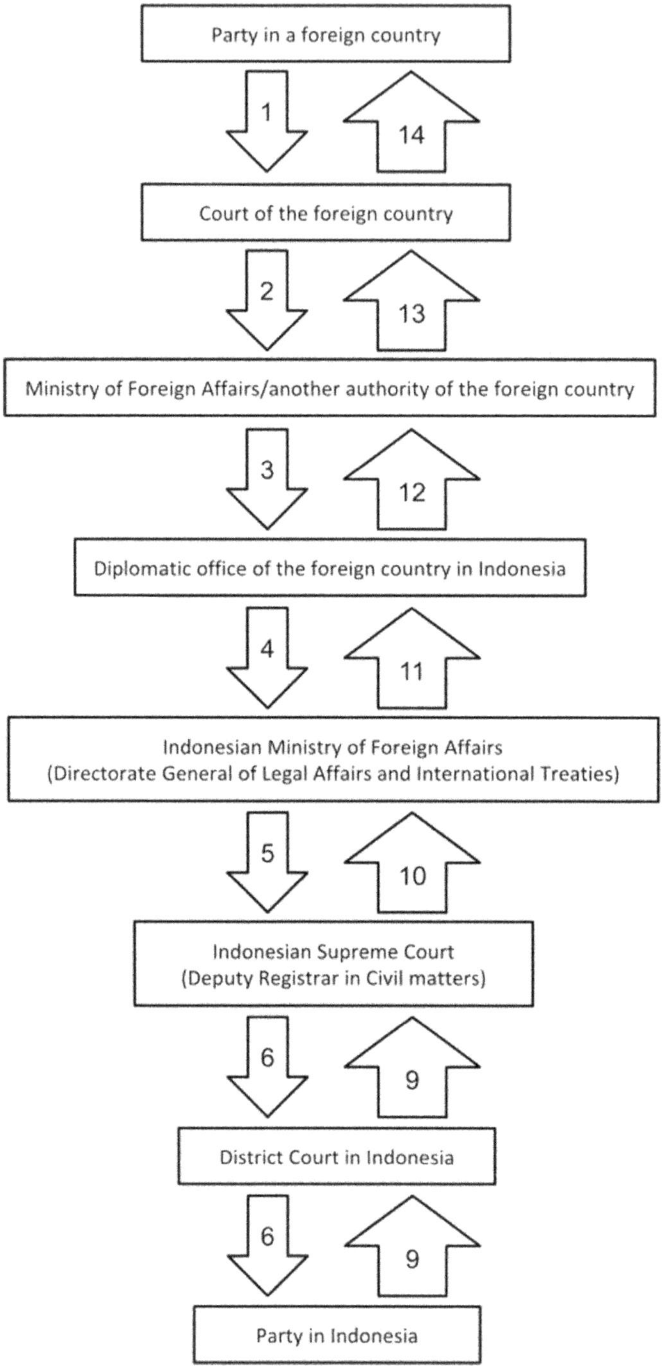

Figure 1 Procedure of transmitting letters rogatory from foreign countries to Indonesia

The foreign court in the requesting state is responsible for payment of all costs associated with the transmission of letters rogatory to and from Indonesia.[66]

Unlike in the 1970 Hague Evidence Convention and the Agreement on Judicial Cooperation between Indonesia and Thailand that govern the reasons of refusal by the requested state to execute letters rogatory on the grounds of sovereignty, security, impossibility, or impracticality,[67] the cooperative agreements between the Ministry of Foreign Affairs and the Supreme Court on the procedure of letters rogatory lack analogous provisions. This omission could allow the arbitrary refusal by Indonesian authorities to execute letters rogatory from other states and, as a consequence, may trigger reciprocal (retaliatory) treatment from other states that receive letters rogatory from Indonesia. Article 9 of the 1970 Hague Evidence Convention requires Member States to execute letters rogatory expeditiously while applying their own law as to the methods and procedures for so doing. In contrast, cooperative agreements between the Ministry of Foreign Affairs and Supreme Court on the procedure for letters rogatory do not dictate the period of time by which the letters rogatory must be executed by Indonesian authorities. This could mean that Indonesian authorities may take an unnecessarily extended period of time to comply with a letter of request. Once again, this omission could trigger reciprocal treatment from other states.

The Minister of Foreign Affairs, Retno Marsudi, noted that, between 2016 and 2017, there was a 91 per cent increase in the number of Indonesians who had civil disputes against foreigners or whose civil cases were pending outside Indonesia. According to the minister, in 2017 Indonesian diplomatic offices or consulates abroad, mostly in Singapore, Malaysia, the US, Hong Kong, and the UK, handled 1,767 requests for service in civil matters. She said that the 91 per cent increase was the consequence of increasing civil relationships between Indonesians, either individuals or legal entities, and foreigners.[68] In spite of the increase, the minister did not mention the need to accede to the 1970 Hague Evidence Convention. Instead, she said that the Ministry of Foreign Affairs planned to establish bilateral agreements for mutual legal assistance in civil matters with other countries, especially where the Indonesian diplomatic offices receive a high number of requests for service in civil matters. According to Ms Marsudi, the envisaged bilateral agreements will allow direct contact between Indonesian courts and other states regarding letters rogatory and the service of judicial documents.[69] Given

[66] ibid, Art 8.

[67] Article 12 of the 1970 Hague Evidence Convention allows the execution of a Letter of Request (Letters Rogatory) to be refused only to the extent that:

> *a)* in the State of execution, the execution of the Letter does not fall within the functions of the judiciary; or
> *b)* the State addressed considers that its sovereignty or security would be prejudiced thereby.
>
> Execution may not be refused solely on the ground that under its internal law the State of execution claims exclusive jurisdiction over the subject-matter of the action or that its internal law would not admit a right of action on it.

Article 15 of the Agreement on Judicial Cooperation between Indonesia and Thailand also has the similar provisions to Article 12 of the 1970 Hague Evidence Convention with addition of refusal because of the absence of the person or its inability to locate the person whose testimony is to be taken.

[68] RD Suastha, 'Kasus Perdata WNI Di Luar Negeri Meningkat 91 Persen' (*CNN Indonesia*, 20 February 2018) www.cnnindonesia.com/internasional/20180220174425-106-277523/kasus-perdata-wni-di-luar-negeri-meningkat-91-persen (accessed 3 October 2018).

[69] ibid.

that all countries (except Malaysia) mentioned by the Indonesian Minister of Foreign Affairs are parties to the 1970 Hague Evidence Convention, it is doubtful that those countries will agree to establish bilateral agreements with Indonesia as proposed by the minister. Those countries will prefer the 1970 Hague Evidence Convention to bilateral agreements, as the 1970 Hague Evidence Convention provides a more uniform mechanism for obtaining evidence than the bilateral agreements. With the current increase of requests for service abroad in civil matters and letters rogatory, it is time for Indonesia to acceded to the 1970 Hague Evidence Convention. This is because the majority of countries for which Indonesian diplomatic offices process requests for letters rogatory are parties to the 1970 Hague Evidence Convention.

C. Taking Evidence Abroad for Use in Indonesian Proceedings

As Indonesia is not a party to the 1970 Hague Evidence Convention, the only international agreement concerning taking evidence abroad entered by Indonesia is the 1978 bilateral Agreement on Judicial Co-operation between Indonesia and Thailand mentioned above. This bilateral agreement allows a litigant before the Indonesian court to obtain evidence from Thailand for use in the Indonesian proceedings, through the submission of a letter rogatory to the Office of Judicial Affairs of the Thai Ministry of Justice. Thailand apart, a party seeking to obtain evidence from abroad for use in an Indonesian court action must follow the procedure in Figure 2, stipulated by the Indonesian Ministry of Foreign Affairs, which is based on several cooperative agreements between the Ministry and the Indonesian Supreme Court:[70]

The litigant who is seeking evidence abroad must use the standard form of letter rogatory provided by the Indonesian Ministry of Foreign Affairs. The standard letter rogatory is written in Indonesian and English.[71] The litigant is responsible for the payment of all costs associated with the transmission of the letter rogatory. The remainder of the Ministry's rules regarding the taking of evidence abroad for use in Indonesian proceedings are similar to the rules of taking evidence in Indonesia for use in foreign proceedings. As there is no Central Authority similar to what is required by the 1970 Hague Evidence Convention, the proceedings for taking evidence abroad and in Indonesia must pass through the Ministry of Foreign Affairs, Supreme Court and Indonesian diplomatic offices abroad. The parties must follow the procedures laid down by the Ministry of Foreign Affairs, which are based on cooperative agreements between the Ministry and Supreme Court. Despite the possibility for simpler and more universal procedures offered by the 1970 Hague Evidence Convention, the Indonesian government has not shown interest in acceding to the Convention.

[70] Dit. Hukum dan Perjanjian Sosial Budaya, 'Alur Keluar' (*Rogatory Online Monitoring)* 'Rogatory Online Monitoring' http://rogatori.kemlu.go.id/flow1 (accessed 18 December 2018).

[71] Dit. Hukum dan Perjanjian Sosial Budaya, 'PKS Standardisasi Dokumen 2018' (*Rogatory Online Monitoring)* http://rogatori.kemlu.go.id/assets/pdf/PKS%20Standardisasi%20Dokumen%202018.pdf (accessed 18 December 2018).

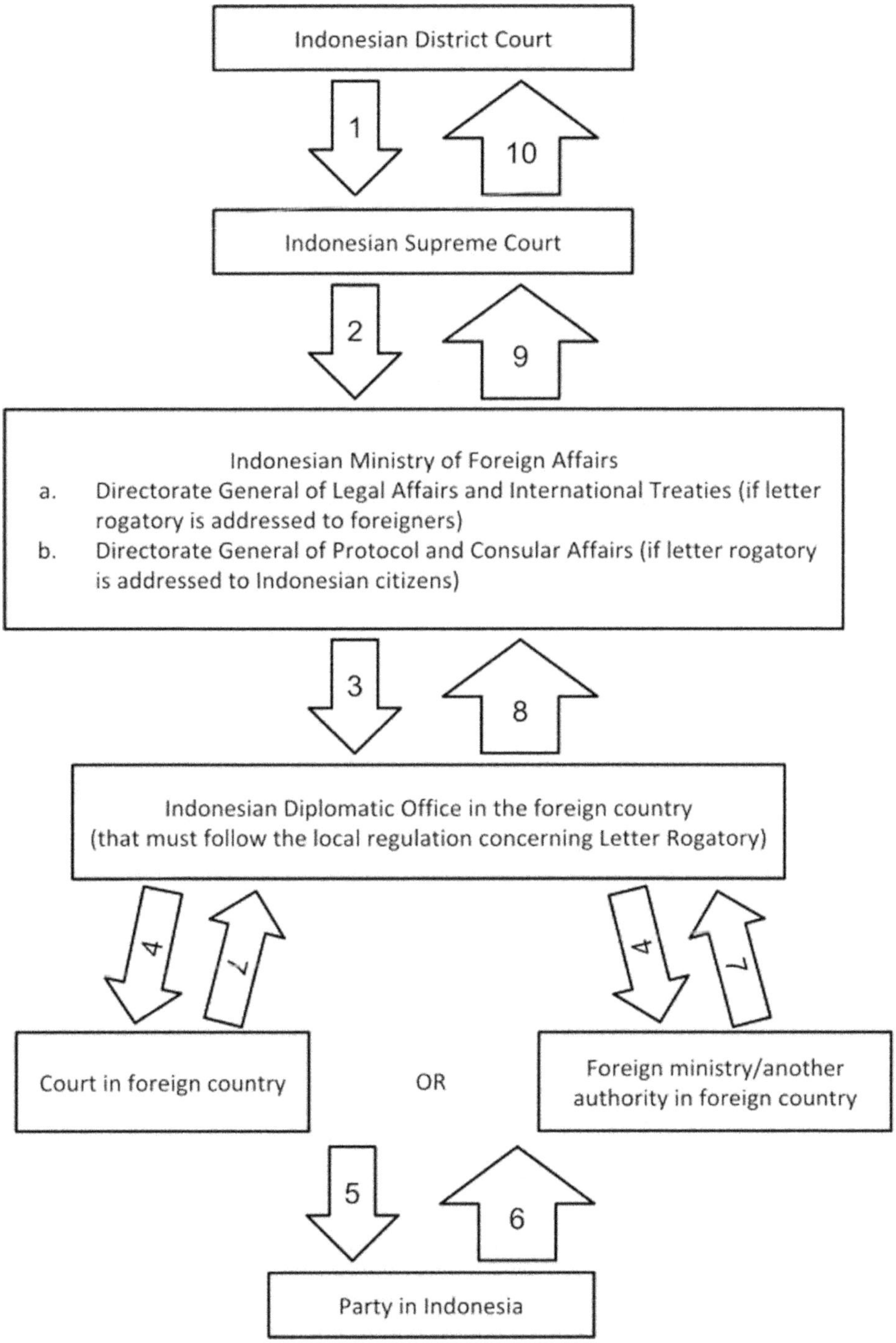

Figure 2 Procedure of taking evidence abroad for use in Indonesian proceedings

VIII. Mandatory Rules, *Ordre Public*, Public Law, and the Evasion of Law

A. Ordre Public and Public Law

The concept of *ordre public* is well accepted in Indonesian Private International Law. *Ordre public* is mentioned in Article 23 of the AB, which provides: 'The Laws that relate to *ordre public* and morality cannot be waived by any action or agreement.' This provision has been adopted in various acts and regulations since the Dutch colonial era. It continues to apply today. In Indonesia, *ordre public* is also referred to as 'public policy', *Openbare Orde*, or *Ketertiban Umum*. The concept of *ordre public* in Indonesian Private International Law has been developed since the Dutch colonial era particularly by the Dutch scholar Professor R D Kollewijn, who wrote a dissertation entitled *Het Beginsel Der Openbare Orde In Het Internationaal Privaatrecht* (The Principle of *Ordre Public* in Private International Law) in 1917. His discussion of *ordre public* has continued to be applied by Indonesian law scholars after Independence. Sunaryati Hartono, one of the leading scholars in Indonesian Private International Law, summarised some of Kollewijn's interpretations of *ordre public*: (1) *ordre public* limits freedom of contract; (2) *ordre public* is interpreted as order, peace, and security; (3) *ordre public* is synonymous with the legal order; and, (4) *ordre public* relates to justice.[72]

The 2015 Academic Paper of the Indonesian Private International Law Bill also addresses *ordre public*. It cites the opinion of Sudargo Gautama, another scholar in Indonesian Private International Law, who wrote that *ordre public* is the basic pillar of national law in the forum.[73] *Ordre public*, according to the paper, is a concept that is relative and dynamic, influenced by time and place. *Ordre Public* is also mentioned in the 2015, 1997, and 1983 Bills of Indonesian Private International Law. In the Bills, *ordre public* is connected to morality. Article 2c of the 2015 Bill of Indonesian Private International Law provides that 'a foreign law which is the *lex causae* of the case shall be disregarded if its application is contrary to *ordre public* and *morality* of the forum'.[74] These Bills, together with Article 23 AB, show that, in Indonesia, morality is another factor – besides *ordre public* – that can set aside the application of *lex causae* in private international cases. Despite the importance of *ordre public*, the 2015 Academic Paper and Article 3 of the 1983 Bill of Indonesian Private International Law caution against the frequent use of *ordre public*, as it will defeat the purpose of Private International Law by giving automatic preference to Indonesian domestic law. This caution is also expressed by Sudargo Gautama in his writings on *ordre public*.

Since Independence, Indonesian courts have invoked the doctrine *ordre public* several times. For instance, in 1953 the Jakarta District Court disregarded Chinese Marriage Law, which according to Article 16 AB was the *lex causae* of a divorce case brought by a Chinese wife against her husband. The couple were domiciled in Indonesia. The *lex causae*, Chinese marriage law, permitted divorce at the request of one of the parties, even

[72] Hartono, *Pokok-Pokok* (n 13) 119; See also S Gautama, *Hukum Perdata Internasional Indonesia Jilid Dua (Bagian Tiga) Buku Keempat* (Penerbit Alumni, 1973) 40.
[73] Supancana, *Naskah Akademik* (n 28) 17–19; See also Gautama, *Perdata Internasional Jilid II Bag 3*(n 72) 5.
[74] Emphasis added.

if that party did not have any justification for the divorce. The judge in the Jakarta District Court held that the application of Chinese marriage law would be contrary to *ordre public* in Indonesia, which required that divorce be based on a reason or justification as provided by Article 208 BW (Indonesian Civil Code).[75] The Indonesian court has also referred to the doctrine *ordre public* when it refuses enforcement of foreign arbitral awards or refuses to recognise an arbitration agreement. See, for instance, *P.T. Nizwar v Navigation Maritime Bulgare;*[76] *Yani Haryanto v E. D. & F. Man (Sugar) Ltd;*[77] *Bankers Trust Company and Bankers Trust International PLC v PT Mayora Indah Tbk;*[78] and *PT. Perusahaan Listrik Negara (PLN) v PT. Paiton Energy.*[79]

The 2015 Academic Paper of the Indonesian Private International Law Bill provides an example of the use of *ordre public* in relation to same-sex marriages. The paper explains that same-sex marriage is contrary to *ordre public* in Indonesia, although it is legal in some other countries. Therefore, it cannot be recognised in Indonesia.[80]

Regarding foreign public law, such as foreign fiscal law, administrative law, or penal law, Sudargo Gautama asserted that the same could not be applied in Indonesia, not because they violate *ordre public*, but because such laws are the public laws of foreign sovereign states. Therefore, those public laws are applicable only within territories of those countries.[81]

The doctrine *ordre public* is well accepted in Indonesian Private International Law and is regularly implemented by Indonesian courts. However, Indonesian scholars warn against the frequent use of *ordre public* as it could derogate from the function of Private International Law.

B. Mandatory Rules

The doctrine of mandatory rules has been developed by Indonesian law scholars, mostly in the field of contract. Sudargo Gautama wrote that some laws are considered mandatory rules and therefore must be applied to a contract irrespective of the parties' choice of law. He explained that Indonesian agrarian law, consumer protection law, employment law, and laws concerning export and import prohibitions, rental or lease, and exchange regulations are categorised as mandatory rules because they relate to Indonesian social and economic interests.[82] He referred in support to Kollewijn.[83] In addition, contracts in certain fields in Indonesia require the application of Indonesian law as mandatory law. For example, Article 38 of Government Regulation No 35 of 2004 concerning upstream oil and gas business activities, requires production sharing contracts for gas and oil

[75] Gautama, *Perdata Internasional Jilid II Bag 3* (n 72) 16–22.
[76] Supreme Court Decision 2944K/PDT/1983 (20 August 1984).
[77] District Court of Central Jakarta Decision 499/Pdt/G/VI/1988/PN.Jkt.Pst (29 June 1989); affd High Court of Jakarta Decision 486/Pdt/1989/PT.DKI (14 October 1989); affd Supreme Court Decision 1205K/Pdt/1990 (4 December 1991); see also G Soemartono, *Arbitrase dan Mediasi di Indonesia* (Gramedia Pustaka Utama, 2006) 41.
[78] District Court of Central Jakarta Decision 46/Pdt.G/1999 (9 December 1999).
[79] District Court of Central Jakarta Decision 517/Pdt.G/1999/PN/JKT/PST (13 December 1999).
[80] Supancana, *Naskah Akademik* (n 28) 18.
[81] Gautama, *Perdata Internasional Jilid II Bag 3* (n 72) 71.
[82] Gautama, *Pengantar Hukum* (n 18) 170, 205.
[83] S Gautama, *Hukum Perdata Internasional Indonesia Jilid II Bagian 4 Buku Ke 5* (Penerbit Alumni 1992) 238.

between foreign contractors and the Indonesian Special Task Force for Upstream Oil and Gas Business Activities (SKK Migas) to use Indonesian law as the applicable law. Article 4 of Government Regulation No 42 of 2007 concerning franchise requires that franchise agreements with foreign elements be in writing and use Indonesian law as the applicable law.

The doctrine of mandatory law has been used by the Indonesian court in several contract cases. The court has a wide discretion to decide what law to deem mandatory. In *Yani Haryanto v ED&F Man (Sugar) Ltd*, the Central Jakarta District Court held that the export-import agreement between ED&F Man (Sugar) Ltd (a British sugar exporter) and Yani Haryanto (an Indonesian sugar importer) was invalid as it violated Presidential Decree No 43 of 1971.[84] Presidential Decree No 43 ordained that, to stabilise the price and supply of sugar in Indonesia, the Indonesian Bureau of Logistics (BULOG) should be the sole importer and distributor of sugar in Indonesia. Therefore, no one else, including Yani Haryanto, was allowed to make an agreement to import sugar into Indonesia. In *PT Bangun Karya Pratama Lestari v Nine AM Ltd*, the West Jakarta District Court annulled a loan agreement between PT Bangun Karya Pratama Lestari (BKPL) (an Indonesian mining company/debtor) and Nine AM Ltd. (an American creditor) that had been executed in English only. It was held to violate Article 31 of the Flag, Language, State Emblem and National Anthem Act 2009, which requires all agreements involving Indonesian parties to be in Indonesian. As a consequence of the annulment, the judge ordered PT BKPL to make restitution of the loan monies to Nine AM Ltd. The judgment of the West Jakarta District Court was upheld by the Jakarta High Court and the Supreme Court.[85] The judges' interpretation of the mandatory status of Article 31 of the Flag, Language, State Emblem, and National Anthem Act 2009 was contrary to that of the government (as represented by the Ministry of Law and Human Rights), which argued, based on the principle of freedom of contract, that private contracts could be made in English only.[86] In his letter No M.HH.UM.01.01-35 dated 28 December 2009, the Minister of Law and Human Rights explained that private commercial agreements written in English only (without an Indonesian version) should be valid. He argued that the implementation of Article 31 of the Flag, Language, State Emblem, and National Anthem Act 2009 was still pending the issuance of a Presidential Regulation concerning use of Indonesian as stipulated by Article 40 of the Act.[87] Despite the minister's letter, the judgment of the Indonesian court on the mandatory status of Article 31 has prevailed, as the minister's letter is not legally binding. In both of the foregoing cases, it was the Indonesian defendants who, as the debtors, requested that the court annul their agreements with their foreign partners (creditors) for the reason that their agreements did

[84] District Court of Central Jakarta Decision 499/Pdt/G/VI/1988/PN.Jkt.Pst (29 June 1989); affd High Court of Jakarta Decision 486/Pdt/1989/PT.DKI (14 October 1989); affd Supreme Court Decision 1205K/Pdt/1990 (4 December 1991.

[85] District Court of West Jakarta Decision 451/Pdt.G/2012/PN.Jkt.Bar (17 June 2013); High Court of West Jakarta Decision 48/PDT/2014/PT.DKI (17 June 2013); Supreme Court Decision 601 K/Pdt/2015 (31 August 2015).

[86] Hukumonline, 'UU Bahasa Batalkan Kontrak Bisnis Internasional' (*hukumonline*, 12 October 2013) www.hukumonline.com/berita/baca/lt5258d22c06dfe/uu-bahasa-batalkan-kontrak-bisnis-internasional (accessed 17 January 2019).

[87] Hukumonline, 'Pernyataan Menkumham Bertolak Belakang dengan Suratnya' (*hukumonline*, 5 February 2010) www.hukumonline.com/berita/baca/lt4b6b97f03c20a/pernyataan-menkumham-bertolak-belakang-dengan-suratnya (accessed 17 January 2019).

not comply with Indonesian law. The court agreed that the laws had to be respected by the foreign parties with the consequence of the annulment of the relevant agreements for non-compliance.

The Indonesian court has handed down different interpretations of the mandatory status of Article 1266 of the Indonesian Civil Code. Article 1266 BW provides that:

(1) The resolutive condition is deemed to be always included in a mutual agreement in the case one of the parties fails to comply with its obligation. In such case, the agreement is not automatically dissolved by law, but *the dissolution shall be requested to the court.*[88]
(2) This request shall also be made, even though the resolutive condition due to the non-compliance of obligation is expressed in the agreement. If the resolutive condition is not expressed in the agreement, the judge shall be free, depending on the circumstances, to grant the defendant, at his request, a period to comply with his obligation, which period shall not exceed one month.

Although Article 1266 BW is mandatory, in practice parties in domestic and international agreements often waive it. The Indonesian court also allows the termination of an agreement by one party without a court order when the other party fails to comply with its obligation. In *Ir. Ermansyah Jamin v PT. Perusahaan Listrik Negara/PLN (Persero)*, the South Jakarta District Court approved the waiver of Article 1266 BW in respect of a Rental and Purchase Agreement and approved the dissolution of the agreement by the owner of the property, when the tenant of the property failed to pay the instalment to the owner of the property. The tenant did not accept the dissolution of the agreement by the owner and requested that the Court allow continuation of the agreement. But the Court approved the unilateral dissolution of the agreement and ordered the tenant to vacate and return the property to the owner. The Court also ordered the property's owner to give back 90 per cent of the instalment already paid by the tenant and keep the remaining 10 per cent after the tenant returned the property.[89] In *Tn Soegianto; Ny Ellies Soegianto v Tn Eka Gunawan; Ny Linda Soetanto*, the Court did not allow the parties to an Asset Purchase Agreement to waive Article 1266 BW, although the seller and buyer had agreed to waive the provision in case one of the parties wanted to dissolve the agreement because of non-compliance by the other party. In the case, the seller unilaterally dissolved the agreement because the buyer was ten months late completing the last instalment. The buyer sued the seller in the Bandung District Court and requested that the Court order the seller to continue with the agreement. The Court agreed with the buyer despite the parties' waiver of Article 1266 BW. The Court applied Article 1266 BW to prevent unjust enrichment by the seller, who would have benefitted from a clause in the agreement that allowed the seller to keep all the money already paid by the buyer in the case of termination of the contract. At the time that the seller dissolved the agreement, the seller had already received 75% of the total amount due. Therefore, the Court applied Article 1266 BW and ordered the seller to continue with the sale to the buyer.[90]

[88] Emphasis added.

[89] District Court of South Jakarta Decision 338/Pdt.G/2014/PN.Jkt.Sel (3 December 2014).

[90] District Court of Bandung Decision 168/Pdt.G/2008/PN.Bdg (7 January 2009); affd Supreme Court Decision 2821K/Pdt/2009 (18 March 2010); affd Supreme Court Extraordinary Appeal 738 PK/Pdt/2010 (2 May 2011); see also OM Rani, 'Pengesampingan Pasal 1266 dan Pasal 1267 Kitab Undang-undang Hukum Perdata Dalam Putusan Pengadilan' (Master thesis, Universitas Islam Indonesia 2015) 73–78; H Shietra, 'Aspek Hukum Uang Paksa (Dwangsom) dalam Praktik Litigasi Perdata' (Shietra and Partners, May 2016) www.hukum-hukum.com/2016/05/aspek-hukum-uang-paksa-dwangsom-dalam.html (accessed 4 January 2019).

Although in the above cases on Article 1266 BW, the contracts were domestic without foreign elements, the judgments of the courts in those cases can also be applied to international contracts involving Indonesian and foreign parties. With respect to industrial employment contracts in Indonesia, Article 1266 BW cannot be waived by the parties. It becomes mandatory, as Articles 151, 155, and 170 of Act No 13 of 2003 concerning manpower (the Manpower Act 2003) prohibit the termination of industrial employment contracts by the employers without the decision or permission from the institute for the settlement of industrial relation disputes. Failure to obtain the decision or permission will result in the termination of employment contract to become void.

The doctrine of mandatory rules has been developed by Indonesian law scholars and implemented by courts in Indonesia. In implementing the doctrine, judges have a wide discretion to determine what laws are deemed mandatory rules. Judges might invoke public policy and interest of the state to decide that a law is mandatory, as in *Yani Haryanto v ED&F Man (Sugar) Ltd*. They have also decided that a law is mandatory to protect the weaker party in a contract, as was done in *Tn Soegianto; Ny Ellies Soegianto v Tn Eka Gunawan; Ny Linda Soetanto*. In some circumstances, the mandatory nature of a law may be waived for economic and efficiency reasons. For example, Article 1266 BW is often waived in commercial contracts to speed up the process of terminating contracts by non-defaulting parties without having to pass through costly and lengthy court procedures.

C. Evasion of Law

Indonesian Private International Law has a doctrine of evasion of law. Evasion of law occurs when parties employ artificial or contrived arrangements to circumvent the application of mandatory provisions of the law to their situation. The 2015 Academic Paper of the Indonesian Private International Law Bill refers to evasion of law as a doctrine, although the Bill itself does not contain any provision concerning evasion of law. Most evasion of law in Indonesia arises in connection with the purchase of land in Indonesia of the purchase of shares in Indonesian companies by foreigners through nominee parties. Evasion of law also often happens in relation to the marriages of Indonesian couples and mixed couples[91] outside Indonesia.

Evasion of law in the purchase of land in Indonesia by foreigners occurs when the foreigners enter into a nominee relationship with Indonesians whereby the latter purchase land as the undisclosed agents of the former. Non-Indonesian parties enter into such nominee arrangements to circumvent the provisions of the Basic Agrarian Act 1960, which prohibits foreigners from holding certain rights in land and buildings in Indonesia, in particular, the right to own, the right to build, and the right to farm. The foreign party and the Indonesian nominee usually enter into several agreements to support their arrangement. The most common agreements are as follows:

(1) A loan agreement whereby the foreign beneficiary provides funds as a sham 'loan' to the Indonesian nominee to enable the latter purchase the land. The loan agreement

[91] Article 57 of the Marriage Act 1974 stipulates that, 'Mixed marriage under this Act is a marriage between two persons who in Indonesia are subjects to different laws, due to different citizenship, and one of them has Indonesian citizenship.'

is secured by a mortgage stipulating that the foreign beneficiary holds the land as collateral for the so-called loan.

(2) An ownership agreement whereby the nominee acknowledges that the land registered under his or her name actually belongs to the foreign beneficiary who provided the funds to purchase the land.

(3) An irrevocable power of attorney authorising the foreign beneficiary to conduct any activities on the land.

(4) A lease agreement whereby the nominee 'leases' the land to the foreign beneficiary for a specified period, with an option for an extension.

(5) A testamentary gift whereby the nominee grants the land and its building to the foreign beneficiary. By these means, a foreign party can conduct business or investment in land in a way that would otherwise be under the Basic Agrarian Act of 1960. A similar nominee arrangement is practiced when foreign investors become shareholders in Indonesian companies within business sectors classified by law as closed to foreign investment or as requiring more complex and costly procedures to be followed by foreign investors.

Indonesian authorities acknowledge the practice of nominee arrangement as anevasion of law, but agrarian law and investment law differ in how to govern the nominee practices. Article 33 of the Investment Act 2007 expressly prohibits and nullifies nominee arrangements in Indonesian investments. This means that all agreements derived from the nominee arrangement are deemed null and void by law. Article 33 stipulates that:

> (1) Domestic investors and foreign investors who make investments in the form of a limited liability company are prohibited from entering into an agreement and/or making a statement asserting that share ownership in a limited liability company is for and in the name of another person.
>
> (2) Where a domestic investor and a foreign investor enter into an agreement and/or make a statement as described in paragraph (1), such an agreement and/or statement is deemed void by law.

Article 33 of the Investment Act 2007 is supported by the Article 12, paragraph (6) of the Regulation of Investment Coordinating Board No 13 of 2017 concerning guidelines and procedures of investment permit and facilities that also prohibits the nominee agreement.

Unlike the Investment Act 2007, the Basic Agrarian Act 1960 is silent on nominee arrangements regarding land and building in Indonesia. There is no provision in the Basic Agrarian Act 1960 and other land regulations that expressly prohibit nominee arrangement for land and building. Therefore, the opinion has been expressed that nominee arrangements for land and buildings are valid, as manifestations of the principle of freedom of contract, until such arrangements are specifically declared invalid by the court.[92]

In *Susan Eileen Mather v I Nyoman Sutapa et al*, a nominee arrangement relating to land in Bali was made between Ms Mather, a foreign beneficiary, and Mr Sutapa, an Indonesian nominee. Their arrangement was supported by several agreements commonly found in nominee arrangements to protect Ms Maher's investment in the land. When

[92] M Sahabati, 'Perjanjian Nominee Dalam Kaitannya Dengan Kepasian Hukum bagi Pihak Pemberi Kuasa Ditinjau Dari Undang-Undang Pokok Agraria, Undang-Undang Tentang Penanaman Modal, Dan Undang-Undang Kewarganegaraan' (Master thesis, Universitas Indonesia 2011).

Ms Maher intended to sell the land, she found that Mr Sutapa had already sold it to Mr Said for a much lower price than the current market price. Ms Mather sued Mr Sutapa in the Denpasar District Court and before the National Land Agency in Bali, which had issued a new land certificate in favour of Mr Said. Judges in the Bali District Court in Decision No 82/PDT.G/2013/PN.DPS agreed that there was a nominee arrangement between Ms Mather and Mr Sutapa to evade Article 21 of the Basic Agrarian Act 1960. They held that the nominee arrangement was invalid, as were all agreements deriving from the nominee arrangement. The Court also held that the Land Purchase Agreement between Mr Sutapa and Mr Said was invalid because Mr Sutapa had been under undue influence to sell the disputed property to Mr Said because of his mounting debt owed to him. To compensate for the loss suffered by all parties involved, the Bali District Court ordered the auction of the disputed property to reimburse the loss of each party in the dispute.[93] The Bali High Court and the Supreme Court upheld the decision of the Bali District Court.[94] However, the Supreme Court, in an Extraordinary Appeal launched by Mr Said upheld the validity of the Land Purchase Agreement between Mr Sutapa and himself. The Supreme Court in Extraordinary Appeal Decision No 289 PK/Pdt/2018 found that Mr Said had acted in good faith and complied with all formalities when purchasing the land from Mr Sutapa and his rights consequently needed to be protected. Therefore, the Court ruled that the Land Purchase Agreement between Mr Sutapa and Mr Said was valid and overruled the decisions of the lower courts.[95]

The effect of evasion of law through nominee arrangement can differ, depending on the law sought to be circumvented. In cases involving the Investment Act 2007, nominee arrangements for share ownership by investors (foreign and domestic) are illegal by law. This means that all agreements derived and resulting from the relevant nominee arrangement are deemed invalid. With nominee arrangements for land ownership, some suggest that the same may be valid, until the court decides that a given arrangement constitutes an evasion of law and declares the same to be invalid. This is because the Basic Agrarian Act 1960 is silent on the issue of nominee arrangement and therefore requires the court to pronounce on the validity of a nominee arrangement. The effect of annulment on agreements derived from the nominee arrangement will vary, depending on the parties involved in each of the agreements. As demonstrated by *Susan Eileen Mather v I Nyoman Sutapa et al*, agreements between a beneficiary and a nominee are void once a nominee arrangement between them is held to be invalid by the court. In contrast, agreements resulting from the nominee arrangement but made with the third parties acting in good faith may continue to be valid.

Evasion of law often happens in the context of marriages between Indonesians or between an Indonesian and a non-Indonesian national celebrated outside Indonesia. Such couples may enter into non-religious marriages abroad with a view to avoiding Articles 2 and 8 of the Marriage Act 1974. Article 2 provides:

(1) A marriage is lawful if performed in accordance with the rules of religion and belief of each party.
(2) Each marriage is registered in accordance with the applicable law.

[93] District Court of Denpasar Decision 82/PDT.G/2013/PN.DPS (6 March 2014).
[94] High Court of Bali Decision 64/PDT/2014/PT.DPS. (22 July 2014); affd Supreme Court Extraordinary Appeal 3200 K/Pdt/2014 (9 June 2016).
[95] Supreme Court Extraordinary Appeal 289 PK/Pdt/2018 (25 April 2018).

Article 8.f rules that, 'Marriage is prohibited between two persons who according to their religions or other applicable law are not allowed to marry.' The requirement that a marriage must comply with religious rules has caused tremendous legal difficulties for couples who wish to have an interfaith marriage in Indonesia. Articles 2 and 8.f of the Marriage Act 1974 require a marriage to comply with religious rules, and some religious rules, such as in Islam, prohibit interfaith marriages. Although Articles 2 and 8.f of the Marriage Act 1974 only require a marriage to comply with religious rules and do not expressly prohibit interfaith marriage, most Indonesian registry officers interpret Articles 2 and 8.f as a prohibition of interfaith marriage. Therefore, those authorities regard interfaith marriage as unlawful and refuse to issue a marriage certificate to interfaith couples. This situation has forced interfaith couples, either Indonesian or mixed (Indonesian-foreigner) couples, to marry abroad. In countries that allow civil marriage without the need to abide by the religious rules on one faith, the Indonesian couple can have interfaith marriages recognised and registered by the authority in that country. They then obtain a marriage certificate from that country's registry office. The Indonesian Government, through its consulate in that country, will recognise and register the marriage certificate and issue an 'Excerpt of Marriage Certificate' to confirm the couple's marriage. Based on Article 56, paragraph (2) of the Marriage Act 1974 and Article 37 of the Population Administration Act 2006 as amended in 2013, the couple can register their marriage certificate and its excerpt at the Indonesian Civil Register Office within 30 days of returning to Indonesia. Their marriage should then be regarded as lawful. However, some family law scholars, such as Zulfa Basuki, regard this practice as an evasion of law.[96] Nonetheless, in practice, the Indonesian Government permits the practice and recognises the relevant marriage as lawful. By contrast, the government does not recognise same-sex marriage as lawful, even when a couple has lawfully celebrated their marriage in a country that allows same-sex marriage.

The government has thus adopted different approaches to evasion of law in interfaith marriage and same-sex marriage. The evasion of law in interfaith marriage by an Indonesian couple outside Indonesia is tolerated because the government and the court recognised and upheld interfaith marriages before the rise of Islamic political power in Indonesia in the 1990s.[97] The government became reluctant to recognise and register interfaith marriages after increasing demand by Islamists for stricter application of Islamic rules in Indonesia. Nonetheless, in the case of interfaith marriages performed outside Indonesia to the Marriage Act 1974, the government's approach has been lenient, as the marriage is performed outside Indonesia, far from the reach of Islamic politics. The government's lenient approach to interfaith couples evading Articles 2 and 8.f of the Marriage Act 1974 is further demonstrated by the enactment of the Population Administration Act 2006 as amended in 2013 that contains an implicit recognition of interfaith marriage. The Elucidation of Article 35.a of the Act explains: 'The meaning of a marriage ruled by the court is a marriage performed by an interfaith couple.' This provision, although only appearing in the Elucidation, indicates the government's acceptance of interfaith marriage. The practice of performing interfaith marriage outside Indonesia persists because of the complexity of obtaining a court ruling

[96] ZD Basuki and others, *Materi Pokok Hukum Perdata Internasional. Modul 5* (Universitas Terbuka, 2014) 28–29.

[97] Lukito, *Legal Pluralism* (n 9) 256–257.

on interfaith marriage in Indonesia. To deal with this, the Indonesian Government has issued several regulations for the recognition and registration of marriage certificates issued abroad in respect of marriages performed by Indonesians abroad, whether to same-faith or interfaith couples. The latest regulation is Presidential Regulation No 96 of 2018 concerning the requirements and procedure for population registration at the civil registry. Articles 38–40 of the Presidential Regulation provide the procedure of the registration of foreign marriages of Indonesians whether involving same-faith, interfaith, mixed nationality, or Indonesian couples.

On the other hand, the government does not tolerate circumvention of the domestic prohibition of same-sex marriages. Such unions are simply treated in Indonesia as contrary to public policy, which considers marriage as limited to unions between a man and a woman. This public policy is the foundation of marriage law in Indonesia, as found in Article 1 of the Marriage Act 1974, which provides that: 'A marriage is a physical and spiritual union between a man and a woman as husband and wife to establish a happy and lasting family founded in the belief of God Almighty.' This policy is also based on contemporary Indonesian socio-religious culture which does not accept same-sex marriage. The 2015 Academic Paper of the Indonesian Private International Law Bill also treats same-sex marriages by contracted by Indonesians abroad as contrary to public policy and consequently as evasions of law.[98]

In summary, Indonesian Private International Law has a doctrine of evasion of law. But its effect differs in different fields of law. The consequences of an evasion will depend on mandatory law, public policy, and socio-cultural factors bearing upon a particular field.

[98] Supancana, *Naskah Akademik* (n 28) 18, 34.

2

Jurisdiction

I. Jurisdiction *in Personam*

A. General Principles

i. Jurisdiction of the Indonesian Court

The jurisdiction of the Indonesian court over the personal liabilities or obligations of a person – whether the latter are created by agreements (contracts) or arise by operation of law – is primarily governed by Article 118 HIR and Article 99 Rv. In general, Indonesian civil procedure law applies the principle of *actor sequitur forum rei*. This principle, which requires the plaintiff to bring a legal suit in the defendant's forum, is found in Article 118, paragraph (1) HIR and Article 99, paragraph (2) Rv. These articles provide that the court with jurisdiction *in personam* is the court in the district in which the defendant's residence is situated or where the defendant actually lives. If there is more than one defendant, the court that has jurisdiction over the defendants is the court in the district that has been chosen by the plaintiff from among the districts where the defendants have their residence (Article 118, paragraph (2) HIR and Article 99, paragraph (6) Rv). In addition to the principle of *actor sequitur forum rei*, other principles in the HIR and Rv determine the court's jurisdiction *in personam*. Those principles will be explained in the following paragraphs.

In the case that the residence of the defendant is unknown or cannot be found, the court that has jurisdiction *in personam* is the court in the district where the plaintiff resides (Article 118, paragraph (3) HIR and Article 99, paragraph (3) Rv). These provisions can be applied in cases when Indonesians or foreigners are to be the defendants and do not have a known residence in Indonesia. In claims for debt against a holder of bearer shares or unregistered equity, the court that has jurisdiction *in personam* will be that where the plaintiff resides (Article 99, paragraph (4) Rv). Should there be more than one plaintiff, the court that has jurisdiction *in personam* is the court of the district where one of the plaintiffs resides, as elected by the plaintiffs (Article 99, paragraph (5) Rv).

A court will have *in personam* jurisdiction in mixed actions (that is, combinations of in *personam* and *in rem* actions), where the plaintiff brings a claim before the court of the district where the defendant resides (Article 99, paragraph (10) Rv). For example, a shipping claim can be characterised as a mixed action against the shipowner and the ship. The plaintiff would have a number of options as to where to bring such a claim. The plaintiff could bring the claim in the district where the ship is located (that is, the court having *in rem* jurisdiction) or in the district where the shipowner resides (that is, the court having *in personam* jurisdiction). In several cases,[1] the plaintiffs commenced their actions in the district courts of the shipowners' place of residence. The courts then exercised jurisdiction *in personam* over the shipowners, even though the underlying actions were a mixture of *in personam* and *in rem* claiMs When the parties have agreed on a choice of residence or domicile, the court that has jurisdiction *in personam* will be the court in the district of the chosen residence or domicile (Article 118, paragraph (4) HIR and Article 99, paragraph (16) Rv).

Indonesian courts also have jurisdiction *in personam* over the Indonesian Government and the agencies which represent the Indonesian state as plaintiff or defendant in a civil lawsuit. Although Article 99, paragraph (18) stipulates that the Jakarta Court has jurisdiction *in personam* over the Indonesian Government, judicial practice allows courts in other districts where the Indonesian Government has representatives to exercise jurisdiction *in personam*. M Yahya Harahap, a legal scholar and former Supreme Court Justice, has defended such judicial practice on the basis that it allows courts outside Jakarta to exercise jurisdiction in cases involving the government to implement in a simple, quick and economical manner as mandated by Article 2, paragraph (4) of the Judicial Power Act 2009.[2] Further discussion in relation to this matter will be found in Chapter 2, section III.A dealing with sovereign immunity.

Pursuant to Article 100 Rv, an Indonesian court has jurisdiction *in personam* over a foreigner, whether a natural or legal person, who is not present or does not have a residence in Indonesia, if the foreigner is under a legal obligation to an Indonesian plaintiff, regardless of whether such an obligation arises in Indonesia or elsewhere. Because the foreigner is not present or does not reside in Indonesia, the Indonesian court having jurisdiction will be the court in the district of the plaintiff's residence (Article 118, paragraph (3) HIR and Article 99, paragraph (3) Rv). For example, the Indonesian court will have personal jurisdiction over a non-resident foreigner, where the latter has incurred contractual or non-contractual obligations to an Indonesian national in respect of (say) intellectual property infringement, whether the alleged breach has occurred within or outside Indonesia. However, this jurisdiction will not exist if the Indonesian and the foreigner have entered into an agreement designating a particular court or forum other than Indonesian court for the resolution of their dispute.

The aforementioned principles and provisions of the court's personal jurisdiction also apply to legal entities or corporations. The court that has jurisdiction *in personam* over a legal entity is the court in the district of that entity's legal seat. For example, if a corporation's legal seat is in Bali, the Bali District Court will have jurisdiction over the corporation, depending on whether the corporation is the plaintiff or the defendant. This principle has been adopted by Article 56, paragraph (1) of Act No 16 of 2001 as amended by Act No 28 of 2004 dealing with foundations. That law states that the court's jurisdiction over a foundation is determined by the legal seat of the foundation. There are rules for determining the seat of a legal entity or corporation: First, there is the doctrine of incorporation, which means that the legal seat of a corporation is the place where it is incorporated. Second, there is the doctrine of statutory seat, which means that the legal seat of a corporation is that

[1] District Court of Jambi Decision 10/PDT.G/2013/PN.JBI. (31 July 2013); District Court of Central Jakarta Decision 23/PDT.G/2011/PN.JKT.PST (1 December 2011).

[2] MY Harahap, *Hukum Acara Perdata Tentang Gugatan, Persidangan, Penyitaan, Pembuktian, dan Putusan Pengadilan* 16th edn (Sinar Grafika, 2016) 136.

written in its memorandum of association. Third, there is the doctrine of central management, which means that the legal seat of a corporation is where the central management is situated. In Indonesia, the first and second doctrines are typically applied together, because in practice the place where a corporation has its statutory seat is also the place under whose law it was incorporated.[3] Consequently, Indonesia applies only two doctrines to determine the legal seat of a corporation: (1) an amalgamation of the doctrines of incorporation and statutory seat; and (2) the doctrine of central management. Articles 30, 36, and 42 of the Basic Agrarian Act 1960 apply the combination of the doctrines of incorporation and statutory seat to determine the rights to land of corporations in Indonesia. The Investment Act 2007 adopts the combination of doctrines of incorporation and statutory seat (Article 5) and the doctrine of central management (Article 17) in respect of corporations investing in Indonesia. Based on the foregoing doctrines, the courts that will have jurisdiction over the legal entities will be the courts in the districts where the statutory seats of the entities are located or the courts in the districts where their central management are situated.

Since Indonesia is a party to the Conventions for the Unification of Certain Rules Relating to International Carriage by Air (the 1929 Warsaw Convention and the 1999 Montreal Convention),[4] the Indonesian court has jurisdiction *in personam* over a foreign airliner that has a place of business or an establishment in Indonesia by which a contract of carriage was made. This principle applies even if the airliner does not have its legal seat or central management in Indonesia. This principle is stated in Article 28, paragraph (1) of the 1929 Warsaw Convention and Article 33, paragraph (1) of the 1999 Montreal Convention. Based on that principle, in *Sigit Suciptoyono v Singapore Airlines Limited*, the South Jakarta District Court exercised jurisdiction over Singapore Airlines because it had a representative office in South Jakarta that confirmed Mr Suciptoyono's flight reservation and accepted his ticket payment through his travel agent. The Jakarta High Court and the Supreme Court upheld the South Jakarta District Court's decision.[5] Where a foreign legal entity has neither a legal seat, central management, branch office nor representative agency in Indonesia, an Indonesian court may still have jurisdiction *in personam* over the foreign entity when it has incurred a legal obligation to an Indonesian plaintiff in Indonesia or somewhere else (Article 100 Rv). Because the foreign legal entity has no established legal seat, central management, or representative office in Indonesia, the court with jurisdiction will be the court in the district of the plaintiff's residence (Article 118, paragraph (3) HIR and Article 99, paragraph (3) Rv).

From what has been discussed, several principles determine the jurisdiction of the Indonesian court over the liabilities or obligations of natural and legal persons. The key principles are to be found in Article 118 HIR, Articles 99 and 100 Rv, the doctrines mentioned above, and the conventions relating to international air carriage that have been

[3] IBR Supancana, *Naskah Akademik Rancangan Undang-Undang tentang Hukum Perdata Internasional (lanjutan)* (Badan Pembinaan Hukum Nasional Kementerian Hukum dan Hak Asasi Manusia RI, 2015) 47.

[4] The Convention for the Unification of Certain Rules relating to International Carriage by Air, Warsaw 1929, is ratified by the Air Carrier Ordinance No 100 of 1939. The Convention for the Unification of Certain Rules for International Carriage by Air, Montreal 1999, was ratified by the Presidential Regulation No 95 of 2016.

[5] District Court of South Jakarta Decision 908/Pdt.G/2007/PN.Jak.Sel. (5 February 2008); affd High Court of Jakarta Decision 611/PDT/2008/PT.DKI (2 February 2009); affd Supreme Court Decision 1517 K/Pdt/2009 (18 April 2011).

ratified by Indonesia. The 1983, 1997, and 2015 Bills of Indonesian Private International Law do not have provisions concerning the jurisdiction of the Indonesian court in private international matters. If the Bill of Indonesian Private International Law is passed as an Act without provisions concerning the jurisdiction of the Indonesian court, the existing law and principles that have been discussed will continue govern relevant matters.

ii. Forum non Conveniens, Lis Alibi Pendens, Anti-suit Injunctions, Interim Measures, and Choice of Court Agreements

a. Forum non Conveniens

The doctrine of *forum non conveniens*, by which the Indonesian court may refuse to exercise jurisdiction because there is a more appropriate forum available to the parties, is well-known to Indonesian legal scholars and accepted in Indonesian judicial practice.[6] Nevertheless, this doctrine is not part of written Indonesian law.

In *Richard Bruce Ness v Jane Perlez and the New York Times Company*,[7] the Central Jakarta District Court applied the doctrine of *forum non conveniens* when dismissing the case. The Court took into account that all parties were not Indonesian nationals. Mr Ness was an American citizen domiciled in Jakarta and the president-director of an Indonesian mining company; Ms Perlez was an Australian journalist who had lived in Jakarta when writing articles about Mr Ness and his company. The New York Times Company was a US legal entity with its legal seat in New York. In this case, Mr Ness brought a tort lawsuit against Ms Perlez who had written three articles alleged to be defamatory of Mr Ness's reputation. He also sued the New York Times Company that had published Ms Perlez' articles. The articles had stated that Mr Ness as president-director of PT. Newmont Minahasa Raya, an Indonesian company, was responsible for serious mining pollution at Buyat Bay in North Sulawesi. The articles claimed that the cause of the pollution was mining activity by PT. Newmont under the leadership of Mr Ness. In accordance with Article 118, paragraph (2) HIR and Article 99, paragraph (6) Rv, Mr Ness brought his lawsuit against the defendants in the Central Jakarta District Court, because one of his defendants had a residence in the Central Jakarta. However, the defendants raised a motion of *forum non conveniens* against the jurisdiction of the Indonesian Court based on the fact that Ms Perlez no longer lived in Indonesia and had moved to Islamabad, Pakistan, sometime before Mr Ness brought his lawsuit. In addition, the New York Times Company did not have any representative in Indonesia. The defendants also argued that the judgment of the Central Jakarta District Court would not be enforceable against the defendants, as there were no treaties covering the recognition and enforcement of judgments between Indonesia and their countries of residence. The Central Jakarta District Court agreed with the defendant's motion of *forum non conveniens*.

In their judgment, the judges quoted M Yahya Harahap to the effect that the most appropriate forum was the one having the most real and substantial connection with a dispute. Mr Harahap had suggested a number of connecting factors that would assist in determining

[6] Harahap, *Hukum Acara* (n 2) 206.
[7] District Court of Central Jakarta Decision 181/PDT.G/2007/PN.JKT.PST. (8 October 2007).

the appropriate forum for a dispute: convenience and expense; availability of witnesses and documents; the place where the parties reside or conduct business; and the law governing the cause of action.[8] Based on Mr Harahap's list of connecting factors, the defendants' countries of residence, the nationalities of the parties, and the location where the articles were published, the Central Jakarta District Court determined that Indonesia was not an appropriate forum for the parties or for the subject matter. The Court also took into account the defendants' argument that any judgment may not be enforceable in the defendants' countries of residence. Accordingly, the District Court refused to exercise jurisdiction. Interestingly, Mr Ness then filed the same lawsuit again, but with an additional defendant who was an Indonesian residing in Central Jakarta. This time, the Central Jakarta District Court agreed to exercise jurisdiction over this case. In their interlocutory judgment concerning jurisdiction, the judges explained that, since the target of the *New York Times* article was located at Buyat Bay, the Court had jurisdiction to adjudicate the case. In the end, the Court delivered a judgment in the defendant's favour.[9]

It is worth noting that the Central Jakarta District Court referred to Mr Harahap's list of connecting factors in both of its judgments, given that Mr Harahap actually compiled the list on the basis of the House of Lords' judgment *Spiliada Maritime Corp v Cansulex Ltd*,[10] a leading common law decision on *forum non conveniens*.[11] That an Indonesian court should apply this doctrine demonstrates that, although Indonesia follows a civil law tradition that in general does not have such doctrine, judicial practice in Indonesia has accepted it.

b. Lis Alibi Pendens

The principle of *lis alibi pendens* provides that a court shall refuse to exercise jurisdiction when there is a parallel lawsuit pending in another forum or in another foreign court. To implement *lis alibi pendens*, the defendant in the later set of proceedings may ask the court seised to stay those proceedings. This principle is recognised in Indonesian civil procedure law. Article 134, paragraph (1) Rv stipulates that a court may be asked to stay a lawsuit that is pending in another court or in an arbitration, is between the same parties, and arises out of the same dispute. The request for a stay must be filed by the defendant before putting in a defence. However, in practice, the *lis alibi pendens* principle in Article 134 Rv applies to domestic proceedings only and does not extend to foreign proceedings. This means that the Indonesian court will refuse to exercise jurisdiction if there is a parallel lawsuit pending before another Indonesian court or in Indonesian arbitration proceedings. But if the parallel lawsuit is pending before a foreign court, the Indonesian court may continue to exercise jurisdiction, even if that might result in inconsistent judgments by the Indonesian and foreign courts.

For instance, in *PT. Indah Kiat Pulp & Paper Tbk. v Bank America National Trust Company; et al*, the Bengkalis District Court exercised jurisdiction over the dispute, although the same matter with the same parties was being litigated before a New York court.

[8] ibid. Harahap, *Hukum Acara* (n 2) 205.

[9] *Richard Bruce Ness v Jane Perlez*; et al, District Court of Central Jakarta Decision 408/Pdt.G/2007/PN.Jkt.Pst. (25 March 2009).

[10] [1986] UKHL 10, [1987] AC 460.

[11] AJ Mayss, *Principles of Conflict of Laws* 3rd edn (Cavendish Publishing Limited, 1999) 25.

The parties had entered into an indenture agreement, a loan agreement, and an underwriting agreement to fund PT. Indah Kiat Pulp's ('PT Indah Kiat') business expansion. The parties had stipulated New York law as the governing law of their agreements. The parties had further agreed to submit to the non-exclusive jurisdiction of any New York court or the US Federal court sitting in New York City. Despite the parties' choice of forum and choice of law, the Bengkalis District Court exercised jurisdiction over the case and applied Indonesian law. The defendants in this case, who were the holders of the bonds issued by PT. Indah Kiat's subsidiary, argued that the case was already pending in a New York court and that the plaintiff, PT. Indah Kiat, had appeared in the proceedings before the New York court. The defendants also argued that the case should be adjudicated based on New York, not Indonesian, law. However, the District Court decided in favour of PT. Indah Kiat and annulled all agreements between the parties. Accordingly, PT. Indah Kiat did not have to pay the bonds held by the defendants. The Riau High Court and Indonesian Supreme Court affirmed the District Court's judgment.[12] Subsequently, opponents of PT. Indah Kiat applied for an extraordinary appeal against those decisions to the Indonesian Supreme Court. The justices in the extraordinary appeal panel accepted the request and annulled the decisions by the previous courts, because those courts had not applied New York law, as the law chosen by the parties.[13] But the justices in the extraordinary appeal did not deny the jurisdiction of the Bengkalis District Court, because the parties' New York choice of court had not been exclusive. Therefore, the Bengkalis District Court could exercise jurisdiction, although the same case with the same parties was still pending in a New York court.[14]

In Case No 210/Pdt/G/1992/PN.JKT.Sel,[15] the South Jakarta District Court exercised jurisdiction in a custody dispute between an Indonesian husband and a German wife, although the German court had already proceeded with the same dispute and had issued a provisional ruling. The couple had two sons and used to live in Germany. In 1992, the wife filed for divorce in a German court and the German court granted her temporary custody of the children while the couple's divorce was being finalised. During the divorce process, the Indonesian father abducted the children to Jakarta.[16] He filed for divorce and sole custody for the children in the South Jakarta District Court. He also applied for his children to become Indonesian nationals. Responding to her husband's legal proceeding in the Jakarta Court, the German wife pointed out that there had been an interlocutory judgment by a German court granting temporary custody of the two children to her. The judges of the South Jakarta District Court refused to recognise the provisional ruling of the German court and exercised their own jurisdiction over the dispute. They granted a decree of divorce and, contrary to the German provisional ruling, awarded custody of the elder son to the father and custody of the younger son to the mother.[17]

These cases demonstrate that the *lis alibi pendens* principle in Article 134 Rv does not apply to foreign proceedings. The practice of not applying *lis alibi pendens* to foreign

[12] District Court of Bengkalis Decision 05/PDT.G./2003/PN-BKS (21 September 2004); affd High Court of Riau Decision 40/PDT/2004/PTR (16 June 2005); affd Supreme Court Decision 381 K/Pdt/2006 (24 May 2006).

[13] Supreme Court Extraordinary Appeal 445 PK/Pdt/2007 (19 August 2008).

[14] Supreme Court Extraordinary Appeal 445 PK/Pdt/2007 (19 August 2008) 193.

[15] Not published. See also Supancana, *Naskah Akademik* (n 3) 50.

[16] Indonesia is not a party to the 1980 Hague Convention on the Civil Aspects of International Child Abduction.

[17] Supancana, *Naskah Akademik* (n 3) 53.

proceedings may result in inconsistent judgments by the Indonesian and foreign courts. This practice is the consequence of Indonesia not recognising and enforcing foreign judgments due to Article 436, paragraph (1) Rv. The latter provides: 'All judgments delivered by foreign courts are unenforceable in Indonesian territory, except in the matters mentioned in Article 724 of Commercial Code and in other regulations.'[18] A stay of action in a dispute pending in a foreign court may be possible if the eventual judgment of the foreign court is one of the limited types of foreign judgments that the Indonesian court will recognise and enforce. But, if the judgment of the foreign court will not be recognised and enforced in Indonesia by virtue of the near blanket prohibition in Article 436 Rv, the Indonesian court will not decline jurisdiction on the basis of *lis alibi pendens*.

c. Anti-suit Injunctions

To prevent a party from forum shopping, the other party to a dispute can apply to the court for an injunction to restrain the other party from pursuing foreign proceedings. If the former party fails to comply with the injunction, the court can charge it with contempt. Based on the court's jurisdiction over the parties, an anti-suit injunction may be granted against a party pursuing foreign proceedings. It is never granted against a foreign court – to avoid interfering with a sovereign foreign court. Therefore, anti-suit injunctions in the UK and US are granted with caution, where certain criteria are met. For example, they are granted if the foreign proceedings are found to be oppressive or vexatious.[19] But they are not granted when the parties should have expected litigation in the foreign forum.[20]

In Indonesia, the law is silent on anti-suit injunctions. The rules concerning anti-suit injunctions can be gleaned from judicial practice. In *PT. Indah Kiat Pulp & Paper Tbk. v Bank America National Trust Company; et al* discussed above,[21] the parties agreed to submit to the non-exclusive jurisdiction of any New York court or the US Federal Court in New York City. When PT. Indah Kiat did not pay on its overdue bonds, the bondholders brought a lawsuit before a New York court in April 2003. PT. Indah Kiat took part in the New York proceedings. But on 14 November 2003 it also brought a lawsuit to the Bengkalis District Court for the annulment of all agreements between itself and the other parties relating to the bonds. On 25 November 2003, the New York court issued a temporary injunction against PT. Indah Kiat and its parent company, Asia Pulp & Paper, Co. ('APP'), to stop them from pursuing the Indonesian proceedings. But PT. Indah Kiat went ahead with the lawsuit in the Bengkalis District Court and applied for an injunction against its opponents. On 5 February 2004, APP argued in the New York court that the Indonesian court could not enforce any judgment from a US court obtained by creditors of APP and PT. Indah Kiat. The New York court accepted APP's argument and lifted the injunction order against APP and PT. Indah Kiat. In its ruling, the New York court observed that 'Litigation

[18] Further discussion on the recognition and enforcement of foreign judgments in Indonesia is presented in ch 1, section IV in this volume.

[19] Mayss, *Principles of Conflict* (n11) 40–43.

[20] L Aurora, 'New York Court Rules in Favor of Asia Pulp and Paper' (*Jawawa Indonesian Business & Finance News*, 16 February 2004) https://jawawa.id/newsitem/new-york-court-rules-in-favor-of-asia-pulp-and-paper-1447893297 (accessed 18 October 2019).

[21] See section ii.b.

was a pre-disclosed risk of investment that the plaintiffs had voluntarily accepted.'[22] On 4 May 2004, the Bengkalis District Court issued a provisional judgment restraining PT. Indah Kiat's opponents from taking any legal action (including a lawsuit, claim, insolvency proceeding, or enforcement of a judgment) inside or outside Indonesia, with a penalty of US$100,000 per day for non-compliance. On 19 May 2004, the Court issued a ruling stating that it had jurisdiction over the case. The lawsuit in the New York court therefore continued in parallel with the lawsuit in Indonesia. On 21 September 2004, the Bengkalis District Court delivered judgment, annulling all relevant agreements as the Court was of the view that the agreements had been entered into in bad faith and in violation of Indonesian law.

The Riau High Court and Indonesian Supreme Court affirmed the judgment.[23] However, at the extraordinary appeal level, a panel of Supreme Court justices quashed the decisions of the previous courts, on the basis that those courts had not applied New York law as the law chosen by the parties.[24] Justices in the extraordinary appeal panel also set aside the Bengkalis Court's provisional measure restraining PT. Indah Kiat's opponents from taking legal action inside and outside Indonesia. The provisional measure was quashed because it did not comply with Indonesian civil procedure law, namely Articles 191 Rbg, 54 Rv, and Supreme Court Circular Letter No 3 of 2000. In actuality, the Bengkalis District Court applied no clear standard or reason when granting the anti-suit injunction requested by PT. Indah Kiat, apart from the circumstance that it claimed to have jurisdiction over the case. This was in contrast to the anti-suit injunction issued by the New York Supreme Court, which was based on the fact that all the parties, including PT. Indah Kiat, had agreed to submit themselves to a New York court and had chosen New York law.[25]

Another case with a foreign anti-suit injunction issue is *Perusahaan Pertambangan Minyak dan Gas Bumi Negara* ('Pertamina') *v Karaha Bodas Company, L.L.C.* ('KBC'). In this case, Pertamina, an Indonesian state-owned company, entered into two contracts with KBC, a Cayman Islands company owned jointly by two US energy companies. The first contract was a Joint Operation Contract that granted KBC geothermal development rights in West Java, Indonesia. The second contract was an Energy Sales Contract, in which the state electric company (PLN) agreed to purchase from Pertamina the electrical energy produced at the KBC geothermal facility. The two contracts were executed in 1994. Because of the severe economic crisis that hit Indonesia in 1997 and to alleviate the state budgetary problems caused by Indonesia's growing debt, the Indonesian President issued a decree in September 1997 suspending the KBC geothermal project. However, KBC continued its geothermal project based on Pertamina's and PLN's assurances that the project suspension was only temporary.[26] The project was reinstated briefly by a presidential decree dated 1 November 1997. However, in January 1998, the Indonesian President issued another decree that terminated the project. As a result, Pertamina and PLN could not fulfil their contractual obligations to purchase the energy generated by KBC's facilities.

[22] n 20.
[23] District Court of Bengkalis Decision 05/PDT.G./2003/PN-BKS (21 September 2004); affd High Court of Riau Decision 40/PDT/2004/PTR.
[24] Supreme Court Extraordinary Appeal 445 PK/Pdt/2007 (19 August 2008) 193.
[25] T Mapes, 'New York Judge Orders APP to End Efforts to Nullify Bonds' (*Wall Street Journal*, 28 November 2003) www.wsj.com/articles/SB106995908981230100 (accessed 18 October 2019).
[26] See 190 F. Supp. 2d 936 (S.D. Tex. 2001) (4 December 2001).

In April 1998, KBC served Pertamina and PLN with its Notice of Arbitration. Pursuant to their contracts, the three parties arbitrated their disputes in Geneva, Switzerland, under the UNCITRAL Arbitration Rules. In December 2000, the arbitral tribunal held that Pertamina and PLN had breached their contracts with KBC. The tribunal found that, under the Joint Operation Contract and the Energy Sales Contract, Pertamina and PLN had accepted the risk of loss arising from a government-related event.[27] Accordingly, the tribunal awarded KBC US$111.1 million, the amount KBC had expended on the project, and US$150 million in lost profit. After obtaining the arbitral award, KBC sought to enforce it in the Southern District of Texas. Pertamina resisted enforcement of the award on the grounds of public policy and lack of due process in the arbitration. In December 2001, the Texas court ordered enforcement of the arbitral award. Pertamina subsequently appealed to the US Court of Appeals for the Fifth Circuit. In March 2002, Pertamina applied for the annulment of the Swiss arbitral award before the Central Jakarta District Court. In its petition for annulment, Pertamina sought an injunction against KBC to enjoin KBC from taking any legal action elsewhere in relation to the award, including enforcing the Swiss arbitral award. In response to Pertamina's action in the Jakarta court, KBC requested a temporary restraining order from the Texas court to prevent Pertamina's action proceeding in the Jakarta court. On 29 March 2002, the Texas court issued a temporary restraining order against Pertamina. The latter was limited to directing Pertamina to withdraw its application for an injunction against KBC in the Jakarta court. The Texas court did not enjoin Pertamina from defending itself against proceedings for the enforcement of the award commenced by KBC in Indonesia, because the Texas court did not intend to interfere with the jurisdiction of Indonesian courts.[28] Pertamina did not withdraw its injunction application and on 1 April 2002 the Jakarta court issued a provisional injunction against KBC. Consequently, KBC complained to the Texas court which found Pertamina in contempt. On 7 May 2002 Pertamina informed the Jakarta court of the Texas court's decision and requested that the Jakarta court suspend the proceedings indefinitely. However, the Jakarta court rejected Pertamina's request on several grounds. First, PLN, which was also a party to the proceedings in Indonesia, had filed an objection to suspension. Second, the Jakarta court held that it retained jurisdiction to hear the case.

Meanwhile, Pertamina appealed to the US Court of Appeals for the Fifth Circuit against the contempt order of the Texas court. In its judgment dated 18 June 2003 the US Court of Appeals decided in Pertamina's favour and vacated the injunction and contempt order of the Texas court. When lifting the injunction and contempt order, the US appeal court noted that, as an enforcing court under the 1958 New York Convention having only to decide whether or not to enforce the award, it was not for the Texas or appeal courts to protect KBC from hardship in a foreign country resulting from disputes over the arbitral award. The US appellate court was not convinced that the Indonesian injunction or annulment action would frustrate or delay the speedy and efficient determination of the cause. The award could be enforced in the US with or without the Texas court's injunction against Pertamina. Under the 1958 New York Convention, US courts have the discretion to enforce

[27] See *Karaha Bodas Co., L.L.C., v Perusahaan Pertambangan Minyak Dan Gas Bumi Negara; et al*, 364 F.3d 274, 9–10 (5th Cir. 2004).

[28] *Karaha Bodas Co., LLC v Perusahaan Pertambangan Minyak Dan Gas Bumi Negara*, 264 F. Supp. 2d 470 (S.D. Tex. 2002).

an award despite annulment in another country. The appellate court could not see how the court proceedings in Indonesia could add to any hardship experienced by KBC, as KBC had itself instituted court proceedings in other countries to enforce the Swiss arbitral award. Even if the Indonesian court were to enforce its injunction against KBC in Indonesia, its effect on KBC was unclear, as KBC did not have substantial assets in Indonesia. Given the absence of the injunction's practical effect, the US court should as a matter of comity avoid interfering with judicial proceedings in another country and stepping outside its role as an enforcing court under the 1958 Convention. Finally, the contempt order against Pertamina was not criminal, but civil in character, and accordingly should be vacated along with the injunction.[29] In August 2002 the Jakarta court set aside the Swiss arbitral award and confirmed its earlier provisional judgment by permanently enjoining KBC from seeking to enforce the arbitral award and imposing a penalty of US$500,000 per day against KBC for non-compliance.[30] KBC appealed the Jakarta court decision to the Indonesian Supreme Court. The Indonesian Supreme Court decided in favour of KBC and held that the Central Jakarta District Court did not have the jurisdiction to annul the Swiss award. The appellate court overruled the Jakarta court's annulment of the Swiss award and vacated the injunction against KBC.[31] The appellate decision was affirmed in an extraordinary appeal proceeding.[32]

Pertamina v KBC again demonstrates that the reasoning behind the Indonesian court's decision to grant an anti-suit injunction requested by an Indonesian party was simply that the court claimed to have jurisdiction over the case and to protect the assets of the Indonesian party from being seized by its foreign opponents. On the other hand, the anti-suit injunction issued by the Texas district court was based on transparent parameters and clear limitations on what was covered and not covered by its injunction.[33] Likewise, the US Court of Appeals provided a set of clear standards when terminating the injunction and contempt orders against Pertamina in its decision.

Given that the Indonesian civil procedure codes (HIR, Rbg, Rv) do not have provisions concerning anti-suit injunctions, the only legal source for the principles underlying the grant of an anti-suit injunction in Indonesia is court practice. However, judicial practice in Indonesia has not yet developed standard rules concerning anti-suit injunctions, apart possibly from a rule that an injunction can may be granted to protect the interests of Indonesian parties. Indonesian courts do not follow the standard tests or parameters commonly applied by the courts in the UK or the US when granting injunctions against foreign suits (such as vexatious or oppressive litigation in foreign courts, possible injustice to the parties, or breach of a choice of forum agreement by the parties). The available cases also indicate that there is no set of clear parameters when higher courts in Indonesia vacate anti-suit injunctions, apart from a finding that the injunctions do not comply with Indonesian civil procedure law.

[29] See *Karaha Bodas Co., L.L.C., v Perusahaan Pertambangan Minyak Dan Gas Bumi Negara; et al*, 335 F.3d 357 (5th Cir 2003) for a more complete explanation of the court's parameters in terminating the injunction and contempt orders against Pertamina.

[30] District Court of Central Jakarta Decision 86/PDT.G/2002/PN/JKT/PST (27 August 2002).

[31] Supreme Court Decision 01/BANDING/WASIT.INT/2002 (8 March 2004).

[32] Supreme Court Extraordinary Appeal 444 PK/Pdt/2007 (9 September 2008).

[33] See n 27 for a more complete explanation of the court's parameters in granting anti-suit injunction against Pertamina.

In *Astro Nusantara International BV; et al v PT. Ayunda Prima Mitra; et al*, the Indonesian courts viewed a foreign anti-suit injunction as interfering with Indonesian sovereignty and, consequently, refused to enforce an international arbitral award because it contained an injunction directing the Indonesian party to terminate ongoing Indonesian court proceedings.

In the case, the parties entered into a Subscription and Shareholders Agreement ('SSA') in 2005. Article 17.4 of the SSA provided that in the case of a dispute that the parties were unable to resolve amicably within 30 days, any party could commence arbitration proceeding at the Singapore International Arbitration Centre ('SIAC') under SIAC rules. Any arbitral award would then be final and binding on the parties. In addition, Article 17.6 of the SSA stated that the parties agreed that none of them were allowed to commence or maintain an action in any court with respect to the dispute, except for the enforcement of arbitral award.

In 2008 a dispute arose among the parties in the midst of negotiations to resolve their differences. On 2 September 2008 PT. Ayunda Prima Mitra ('Ayunda') brought a tort lawsuit against the other parties in the South Jakarta District Court. The lawsuit was registered under number 1100/Pdt.G/2008/PN.Jkt.Sel. Ayunda alleged that the other parties had misused the money invested in PT. Direct Vision, a joint venture company owned by Ayunda and the other parties.[34] A month later, Astro Nusantara International BV. ('Astro') brought the dispute to the SIAC in accordance with Article 17.4 of the SSA. The arbitration in the SIAC was registered under number 062 of 2008. Astro immediately sought an injunction from the SIAC against Ayunda's action in the South Jakarta District Court. The SIAC tribunal granted an anti-suit injunction against Ayunda in a preliminary award dated 7 May 2009. Despite the injunction, Ayunda did not suspend its lawsuit in the Jakarta court and on 13 May 2009, the South Jakarta District Court gave an interlocutory judgment holding that it had jurisdiction. Thus, the lawsuit in the Jakarta court continued in parallel with the Singapore arbitration. While the proceedings in the South Jakarta District Court were in progress, the SIAC tribunal issued four arbitral award. In its awards, the SIAC tribunal found in favour of Astro against Ayunda. Subsequently, Astro sought enforcement of the arbitral awards in Indonesia and various jurisdictions.

Pursuant to Articles 65 and 66(d) of the Arbitration Act 1999, Astro applied for exequaturs to the Central Jakarta District Court to enforce the SIAC awards. The court made five rulings concerning Astro's requests, all refusing to grant exequaturs.[35] The Central Jakarta District Court viewed, insofar as they related to the anti-suit injunction ordered by the SIAC tribunal, the SIAC awards constituted interference with the jurisdiction of the Indonesian courts. Furthermore, the anti-suit injunction was said to be outside the scope of commercial law, because injunction belonged to the field of civil procedure law. Therefore, the SIAC awards had violated Article 66(b) of the Arbitration Act 1999, which requires awards to be confined within the scope of commercial law. As a result, the Central Jakarta District Court ruled that the SIAC awards were not enforceable in Indonesia and were contrary to the Indonesian *ordre public*. In its appeal to the Indonesian Supreme Court, Astro argued

[34] Hukumonline, 'Gugatan PT Ayunda Terhadap Astro Tidak Dapat Diterima' (*hukumonline* 19 September 2009) www.hukumonline.com/berita/baca/hol23180/gugatan-pt-ayunda-terhadap-astro-tidak-dapat-diterima/ (accessed 25 October 2019).

[35] District Court of Central Jakarta Ruling 05/PDT.ARB.INT/2009/PN.JKT.PST (28 October 2009); District Court of Central Jakarta Rulings No 32 of 2009; No 6 of 2010; No 14 of 2010; No 41 of 2010 (11 September 2012).

that the anti-suit injunctions in the SIAC awards were not contrary to Indonesian *ordre public*, because the anti-suit injunctions were granted against Ayunda, over whom SIAC had *in personam* jurisdiction. The injunctions were not directed against the South Jakarta District Court. Astro also complained that the Central Jakarta District refused to enforce two other SIAC arbitral awards, despite the two awards having no connection with the anti-suit injunction. The Supreme Court rejected Astro's appeal and upheld the Central Jakarta District Court's decision.[36] An extraordinary appeal panel also upheld the Central Jakarta District Court's decision.[37]

Astro Nusantara International BV; et al v PT. Ayunda Prima Mitra; et al illustrates how, although the SIAC issued an anti-suit injunction in the exercise its jurisdiction *in personam* on Ayunda, the Indonesian courts interpreted the SIAC injunction as interference in Indonesia's sovereignty. This case also set a precedent that any judgment or award containing an injunction against a party pursuing a parallel action in Indonesia may be regarded by Indonesian courts as violating Indonesia's *ordre public*. However, unlike the anti-suit injunctions in *PT. Indah Kiat v Bank America National Trust Company;* and *Pertamina v KBC*, the anti-suit injunction in *Astro v Ayunda* was issued against a court proceeding in Indonesia that had commenced earlier than the foreign arbitration proceeding that issued the anti-suit injunction. The anti-suit injunctions in the two former cases were issued by foreign courts against court proceedings in Indonesia that commenced after the parties had participated in the foreign court proceedings. In other words, the anti-suit injunction in *Astro v Ayunda* was granted in relation to ongoing Indonesian court proceedings. Therefore, this kind of injunction was regarded as interfering with the jurisdiction of the Indonesian court and the sovereignty of the Indonesian state. The anti-suit injunctions in the other two cases were later revoked by the courts in New York and Texas before the Indonesian courts made their judgments. Therefore, in *PT. Indah Kiat v Bank America* and *Pertamina v KBC*, the Indonesian courts never dealt with the issue of foreign anti-suit injunctions.

Because Indonesian law is silent on anti-suit injunctions and clear rules of anti-suit injunctions have not been developed by Indonesian courts, it remains to be seen whether, in the future after *Astro v Ayunda*, foreign anti-suit injunctions will be regarded as interfering with the jurisdiction of Indonesian courts and with Indonesian sovereignty. It also remains to be seen whether international arbitral awards or foreign judgments that contain anti-suit injunctions will be regarded as contrary to Indonesian *ordre public*.

d. Interim Measures

The term 'interim measures' is not used in Indonesian civil procedure law. Instead, the civil procedure law uses the term 'provisional measures' and 'conservatory seizure' (*conservatoir beslag*) to characterise protective measures taken by a court pending its final decision in a dispute. Provisional measures are governed by Article 180 HIR (equivalent to Article 191 Rbg). Legal scholars agree that the definition of provisional measures is temporary orders against defendants to do or not to do certain actions, for example, an order against a tenant to vacate rented property or an order against a defendant not to plant anything on land.

[36] Supreme Court Decision 877 K/Pdt.Sus/2012 (26 March 2013).

[37] Supreme Court Extraordinary Appeal 26 PK/Pdt.Sus-Arbt/2016 (18 May 2016).

The application for provisional measures can be filed by disputing parties at all levels of court, in the trial court, appellate court, or cassation court. Although Article 180 HIR does not detail the procedure for obtaining provisional measures, in practice an application for provisional measures is filed by a claimant in a court as part of one's lawsuit. The application for provisional measures is not filed separately from the principal claim in a lawsuit.[38] To issue provisional measures, judges in lower courts must obtain approval from the chief justices of the higher courts (Supreme Court Circular Letter No 3 of 2000 concerning immediate (*uitvoerbaar bij voorraad*) and provisional judgments). Article 185 HIR provides that court decisions on provisional measures form part of the final judgment. Based on the aforementioned procedures, Indonesian courts will not grant provisional measures sought by parties whose disputes are being adjudicated by foreign courts. Pursuant to Articles 180, 185 HIR, 191 Rbg, and jurisprudence, courts have the power to decide on claims for provisional measures only if the claims are filed by claimants together with their principal claims in lawsuit.

The other interim measure, namely conservatory seizure (*conservatoir beslag*), has different procedures from provisional measures. Conservatory seizure is governed by Articles 226–227 HIR and 261 Rbg. Unlike the application for provisional measures, the claim for conservatory seizure can be filed in a court separately from the applicant's principal claim. The court will establish a separate proceeding in the presence of the claimant and defendant, to decide whether it will grant or deny the conservatory seizure claim. To grant conservatory seizure, the court does not need approval from a higher court. A judgment on conservatory seizure can be made by a court separately from its judgment on the principal claim. As a consequence, the conservatory seizure judgment can be separately appealed against by an affected party. Therefore, an Indonesian court theoretically may have jurisdiction to grant a conservatory seizure requested by a party whose dispute is being adjudicated outside Indonesia, insofar as the Indonesian court would have jurisdiction *in personam* or *in rem* over the merits of the case.[39] Nevertheless, although theoretically possible, the submission of such a conservatory seizure claim to an Indonesian court separately from a principal claim would be pointless, because pursuant to Article 436 Rv the foreign judgment on the parties' principal claim may not be enforced in Indonesia. As a consequence, it will be impractical for an Indonesian court to exercise jurisdiction on a conservatory seizure request, if the judgment of the relevant foreign courts on the principal claim cannot ultimately be enforced in Indonesia.

The above principle also applies to intellectual property cases. Although Indonesian copyright law, patent law, trademark law, and industrial design law give jurisdiction to the Indonesian commercial court to deal with claims for interim measures separately from the merits of the case, Article 15, paragraph (2) of Supreme Court Regulation No 5 of 2012 concerning interlocutory injunctions requires the claimant, within 30 days after the grant of an interlocutory injunction, to file the principal claim in an Indonesian commercial court. As such, it is impractical for the Indonesian commercial court to exercise jurisdiction on a bare claim for interim measures in an intellectual property dispute if the merits of the case will be adjudicated outside Indonesia.

[38] Harahap, *Hukum Acara* (n 2) 885.

[39] For the discussion on the jurisdiction of Indonesian courts, see section I.A.i above.

In *PT Bayan Resources TBK v BCBC Singapore Pte Ltd*, the dispute related to a joint venture agreement between BCBC Singapore Pte Ltd ('BCBC') and PT Bayan Resources TBK ('Bayan'). The two companies were incorporated in Singapore and Indonesia respectively. Their joint venture agreement was governed by Singapore law. In December 2011, BCBC sued Bayan in the Singapore court claiming damages for breach of the joint venture agreement. The case was transferred from the Singapore High Court to the Singapore International Commercial Court ('SICC').[40] Before the SICC entered judgment, in April 2012, BCBC applied to the Supreme Court of Western Australia ('WA') for freezing orders against Bayan's assets in Australia, to prevent the same from being removed from Australia, disposed of, or diminished in value.[41] While Bayan, as an Indonesian company, had assets in Indonesia, they also held shares in an Australian company named Kangaroo Resources Limited ('KRL'). On 5 April 2012 the Supreme Court of WA granted freezing orders against Bayan and KRL in respect of the shares held by Bayan.[42] Subsequently, on 17 May 2012 Bayan and KRL launched proceedings in the High Court of Australia in which they challenged the jurisdiction of the Supreme Court of WA to make the freezing orders. Bayan argued that the Supreme Court of WA did not have jurisdiction to make freezing orders in aid of proceedings being tried in a foreign court and KRL argued that the Court did not have power to restrain KRL, as a third party, from dealing with its shares and other assets. The Hight Court of Australia ordered the proceedings to be remitted to the Supreme Court of WA.

In response to Bayan's challenge, Justice Le Miere held that the Supreme Court of WA had inherent jurisdiction to make a freezing order against Bayan, because there was a sufficient prospect that the Singapore court would give judgment in favour of BCBC and the Singapore judgment would be registered in and enforced by the court pursuant to the Foreign Judgments Act 1991. In response to KRL's challenge, the judge held that the Court would not exercise its jurisdiction to make a freezing order against KRL, because KRL, as a third party, was not in a position of control or influence concerning Bayan's shares. The High Court of Australia upheld the decision of the Supreme Court of WA.[43] BCBC never applied for a freezing order or conservatory seizure against Bayan's assets to the Indonesian court, although Bayan had assets in Indonesia. This was understandable, because the Indonesian court would refuse to exercise jurisdiction on BCBC's claim for conservatory seizure as the Singapore judgment on the merits of the case could not be recognised and enforced in Indonesia pursuant to Article 436 Rv.

Regarding provisional measures and conservatory seizure in relation to a defendant's actions and property outside Indonesia, an Indonesian court theoretically has jurisdiction to order such interim measures, insofar as the court has jurisdiction over the merits of the case. However, it remains to be seen whether interim measures imposed by an Indonesian court will have extraterritorial effect, given that there is no civil contempt order in the Indonesian legal system against parties who are violating court orders outside Indonesia.

[40] D Lim, 'SICC Releases Its First Decision' (*Financier Worldwide*, August 2016) www.financierworldwide.com/sicc-releases-its-first-decision#.Xbs2ROgzaUk (accessed 17 November 2019).

[41] 'Supreme Court of Western Australia' (*AustLII*) www8.austlii.edu.au/cgi-bin/viewdoc/au/cases/wa/WASC/2013/239.html (accessed 17 November 2019).

[42] *BCBC Singapore Pte Ltd v PT Bayan Resources TBK* [2012] WASC 170.

[43] *PT Bayan Resources TBK v BCBC Singapore Pte Ltd* [2015] HCA 36.

In relation to interim measures in arbitration proceedings, there are no provisions in Indonesian civil procedure codes or the Arbitration Act 1999 that govern the jurisdiction of courts over the enforcement of interim measures ordered by arbitral tribunals. Article 32 of the Arbitration Act 1999 provides that an arbitration tribunal may order provisional measures and other interlocutory orders, including conservatory seizure, at the request of one of the parties. But Article 32 stops short of stipulating how courts are supposed to implement those arbitral interim measures. Hence, in the absence of procedural rules, Indonesian courts cannot exercise jurisdiction over claims for the enforcement of arbitral interim measures. In addition, pursuant to Article 11 of the Arbitration Act 1999, courts do not have jurisdiction over matters and disputes that the parties have agreed to settle by arbitration. Based on Article 11, only Indonesian legal scholars classify interim measures in arbitration proceedings as matters over which Indonesian courts do not have jurisdiction.[44] Pursuant to Chapter VI of the Arbitration Act 1999, Indonesian courts can enforce only final and binding arbitral awards, whether domestic or foreign (Articles 59–69). As such, Indonesian courts do not have jurisdiction over the enforcement of interim measures in arbitration proceedings, because interim measures are not final awards. This principle also applies to interim measures issued by foreign arbitration tribunals that are to be enforced in Indonesia. Indonesian courts will not exercise jurisdiction over claims for foreign arbitral interim measures, because interim measures are not final and binding arbitral awards under the 1958 New York Convention. To give jurisdiction to courts over claims for interim measures ordered in arbitration proceedings, there must be a regulation issued by the Indonesian Supreme Court similar to Supreme Court Regulation No 5 of 2012 concerning interlocutory injunction in intellectual property cases.

In summary, Indonesian courts have the power and jurisdiction to grant provisional measures and conservatory seizure in cases over which they have jurisdiction on the merits. However, Indonesian courts do not have jurisdiction over provisional measures issued by foreign courts, because Indonesian civil procedure law does not allow a claim for provisional measures to be filed separately from a principal claim. In the case of conservatory seizure, Indonesian courts theoretically have jurisdiction to grant a conservatory seizure in connection with foreign court proceedings, because a claim for conservatory seizure can be filed separately from a principal claim. But, since foreign court judgments on the principal claims are not enforceable in Indonesia pursuant to Article 436 Rv, it would be pointless to apply to the Indonesian courts for conservatory seizures in aid of foreign court proceedings. Indonesian courts also have jurisdiction to order interim measures against defendants outside Indonesia. But their jurisdiction would be ineffective, because judgments of Indonesian courts are not recognised beyond Indonesian territory and civil contempt orders do not exist in the Indonesian legal system to enforce interim measures outside Indonesia.

e. Choice of Court Agreements

Choice of court agreements are recognised by the Indonesian civil code (BW) and civil procedure codes (HIR/Rbg and Rv). Although choice of court agreements are a manifestation

[44] Sujayadi and Yuniarti, 'Pelaksanaan Sita Jaminan Dalam Hukum Acara Arbitrase' (2010) 25 *Yuridika* 227, 231–2 https://e-journal.unair.ac.id/YDK/article/view/255 (accessed 3 January 2020).

of the freedom of contract principle in Article 1338 BW, choice of court agreements in Indonesia are constrained by Article 118, paragraph (4) HIR, Article 99, paragraph (16) Rv, and Article 24 BW.

Article 24 BW provides that choice of court agreements shall be in writing. Article 118, paragraph (4) HIR and Article 99, paragraph (16) Rv provide that, while parties in a dispute may have entered into a choice of court agreement, it is up to the plaintiff to decide where to file a claim. Article 118, paragraph (4) HIR and Article 99, paragraph (16) Rv allow the plaintiff to file a claim in the court chosen by the parties, or to file the claim in the court in the district of the defendant's residence in accordance with the principle of *actor sequitur forum rei*. Therefore, M Yahya Harahap has suggested that the principle of *actor sequitur forum rei* stated in Article 118, paragraph (1) HIR may prevail over choice of court agreements, depending on the plaintiff's choice. According to Mr Harahap, in the case that the plaintiff chooses the court in the district of the defendant's residence notwithstanding the parties' choice of court agreement, the latter court will exercise jurisdiction and dismiss an objection by the defendant seeking to enforce the parties' choice of court agreement.[45] Indonesian civil procedure codes are silent on choice of court agreements that involve a foreign court. None of the abovementioned provisions expressly governs the situation in which the parties choose a foreign court. The 1983, 1997, and 2015 Bills of Indonesian Private International Law are also silent on this issue. The absence of rules concerning choice of foreign court in the codes is understandable because judgments made by foreign courts cannot be enforced in Indonesia pursuant to Article 436 Rv. Indonesian civil procedure codes are likewise silent on the issue of whether the parties can have choice of court agreements in all fields of civil law or only in the area of commercial law.

Although Article 118, paragraph (4) HIR, Article 99, paragraph (16) Rv, and Article 24 BW are silent on the choice of court agreements that involve foreign courts, there is no prohibition for parties in Indonesia to choose foreign courts. Indonesian scholars and judicial practice recognise the choice of foreign courts as part of the freedom of contract. Indonesian law allows parties to agree on a foreign court for the resolution of their disputes. Article 18, paragraph (4) of Act No 11 of 2008 as amended by Act No 19 of 2016 concerning electronic information and transactions (the Electronic Information and Transaction Act 2008 as amended in 2016) provides that parties have the power to designate a court, an arbitral tribunal, or some alternative dispute resolution body to settle disputes arising out of their international electronic transactions. Paragraph (5) of the latter Article states that in the case the parties do not choose a forum mentioned in paragraph (4), the principles of Private International Law shall apply to determine the forum that will settle the parties' dispute. Article 74 of Government Regulation No 80 of 2019 concerning electronic commerce stipulates that parties have the power to choose a court, arbitral tribunal, or other alternative dispute resolution body to settle disputes arising out of their international e-commerce transactions. In the case where the parties have not designated a forum, the principles of Private International Law are to apply to determine the forum that will settle the parties' disputes. However, because of the absence of procedural law concerning agreements designating a foreign court for the resolution of disputes, even where the parties have designated a foreign court by agreement, the Indonesian court

[45] Harahap, *Hukum Acara* (n 2) 200–202.

will still apply Article 118, paragraph (4) HIR, Article 99, paragraph (16) Rv, and Article 24 BW to determine whether an Indonesian court has or does not have jurisdiction to settle the parties' dispute.

As with the domestic choice of court, when parties designate a foreign court by agreement, it will be up to the plaintiff to choose in which court to file a lawsuit. One may file the suit in the foreign court chosen by the parties or file the suit in the court in the district of the defendant's residence. As such, an Indonesian court may have jurisdiction over parties who have chosen a foreign court, if the plaintiff prefers to file a suit in the Indonesian district court. In accordance with the *forum non conveniens* doctrine, the Indonesian district court may refuse to exercise jurisdiction over the suit only if there is a more appropriate forum to adjudicate the same.

The principles above were implemented in *Bali Energi Ltd v Mitomo Shoji K.K.* Bali Energi Ltd was a Bermuda registered company having its legal seat in Central Jakarta. Mitomo Shoji K.K. was a Japanese company having its legal seat in Japan. Bali Energi Ltd objected to the jurisdiction of the Central Jakarta District Court because in the investor financing agreement dated 27 October 2010 the parties had designated the Tokyo District Court as the forum to decide disputes and Japanese law as the applicable law. The parties in the investor financing agreement were Mitomo Shoji K.K. and two Japanese shareholders of Bali Energi Ltd. Mitomo Shoji K.K. brought its lawsuit against the two Bali Energi Ltd's shareholders as well as Bali Energi Ltd because of the breach of the investor financing agreement by the shareholders. Mitomo Shoji K.K. brought its action before the Central Jakarta District Court because Bali Energi Ltd had its residence in Central Jakarta. In their preliminary decision, the Central Jakarta District Court dismissed Bali Energi Ltd's objection and decided that it had jurisdiction over the dispute.[46] The decision was based on Article 118, paragraph (2) HIR, which stipulates that, if there is more than one defendant, the court in the district where a defendant has its residence may exercise jurisdiction. The Jakarta High Court affirmed the District Court's decision.[47] Bali Energi Ltd did not appeal to the Supreme Court. The case is an example of how Article 118 HIR can prevail over the parties' choice of court agreement.

In *PT. Pelayaran Manalagi v PT. Asuransi Harta Aman Pratama, Tbk*, an Indonesian shipping company (PT. Pelayaran Manalagi) sued PT. Asuransi Harta Aman Pratama ('PT. AHAP'), an Indonesian insurance company, in the Central Jakarta District Court, for breach of an insurance agreement. The plaintiff alleged that PT. AHAP had refused to pay on an insurance claim filed by the plaintiff which had lost a vessel in a fire during transit. According to the plaintiff, the loss suffered was covered by the Marine Hull and Machinery Policy dated 24 October 2005. In accordance with the *actor sequitur forum rei* principle in Article 118 HIR, PT. Pelayaran Manalagi had filed the lawsuit against PT. AHAP in the Central Jakarta District Court, because PT. AHAP's legal seat was in Central Jakarta. The District Court applied English law and practice as the applicable law of the parties' marine insurance agreement (Institute Time Clauses – Hulls). PT. AHAP objected to the jurisdiction of the Central Jakarta District Court and argued that the English court had jurisdiction because the applicable law of the parties' agreement was English law. On 29 July 2010,

[46] District Court of Central Jakarta Decision 359/Pdt.G/2011/PN. Jkt.Pst (31 July 2012).
[47] High Court of Jakarta Decision 186/PDT/2014/PT.DKI (23 July 2014).

the District Court issued a preliminary decision dismissing PT. AHAP's objection to the Court's jurisdiction and on 21 October 2010 the Court made its substantive decision in the plaintiff's favour. The Jakarta High Court affirmed the decisions.[48]

PT. AHAP appealed to the Supreme Court. There, PT. AHAP once again argued that the Central Jakarta District Court did not have jurisdiction over the case because the applicable law was English law. However, this time, PT. AHAP also presented evidence that the Institute Time Clauses – Hulls were an integral part of New Marine Policy Form (MAR 91) granting exclusive jurisdiction to English courts. MAR 91 stipulates that 'This insurance shall be subject to the exclusive jurisdiction of the English Courts, except as may be expressly provided herein to the contrary.' The Supreme Court held that the English court and not the Central Jakarta District Court had jurisdiction over the case. The reason was that the choice of law in the parties' agreement was English law, hence the court that had jurisdiction should be English.[49] Unfortunately, the Supreme Court did not refer to the choice of court provision contained in MAR 91 granting exclusive jurisdiction to the English court. This case is an example of choice of court and choice of law agreements designating a foreign court and foreign law being respected by the Indonesian court. Since there is no law, apart from Article 118, paragraph (4) HIR and Article 99, paragraph (16) Rv, governing agreements designating foreign courts, it is unclear whether the parties' choice of court is absolute or relative. The decisions of the lower courts indicate that the parties' choice of foreign court will not be regarded as absolute and can be ignored on the principle of *actor sequitur forum rei*. The Supreme Court, on the other hand, has shown that the choice of a foreign court by the parties, even if only implicit, may be treated as absolute and so prevail over the principle of *actor sequitur forum rei*.

In conclusion, based on existing civil procedure codes, an Indonesian district court may have jurisdiction *in personam* over parties who have chosen a foreign court, because Indonesian civil procedure codes allow a plaintiff to file a suit either in the foreign court chosen by the parties or in an Indonesian court in the district of the defendant's residence (following the principle of *actor sequitur forum rei*). But a choice of court agreement will most likely not be regarded as conferring exclusive jurisdiction to the chosen foreign court. Such an approach is a corollary to the principle that judgments of foreign courts will normally not be enforced in Indonesia pursuant to Article 436 Rv. Therefore, although choice of court agreements are permitted by the Indonesian legal system, in practice agreements that designate foreign courts are impractical for Indonesian parties because foreign judgments are generally not enforceable in Indonesia.

iii. Service of Process outside Indonesia

Once an Indonesian court has jurisdiction *in personam* over a party outside Indonesia,[50] it needs to effect proper service of process on the party. Service of process establishes the

[48] District Court of Central Jakarta Decision 52/Pdt.G/2010/PN.Jkt.Pst. (21 October 2010); affd High Court of Jakarta Decision 297/PDT/2011/PT.DKI (24 November 2011).

[49] Supreme Court Decision 1935 K/Pdt/2012 (14 January 2013).

[50] See section I.A.i above for the discussion on the jurisdiction *in personam* of Indonesian courts over persons outside Indonesia.

personal jurisdiction of the Indonesian court over the person served abroad. Indonesian civil procedure codes contain few provisions concerning service of process outside Indonesia.

Article 118, paragraph (3) HIR and Article 99, paragraph (3) Rv provide that a suit against a defendant whose presence and residence in Indonesia are unknown, shall be brought to the court in the district of the plaintiff's residence. A similar provision can be found in Government Regulation No 9 of 1975 on implementation of the Marriage Act 1974 (the Marriage Regulation 1975). Article 20, paragraph (3) of the regulation states that a divorce petition served on a defendant living abroad shall be filed in the court in the district of the petitioner's residence. The general principle is thus that the court that has jurisdiction over a defendant outside Indonesia is the court in the district of the plaintiff's residence.

In serving notice and related documents ('process') on defendants outside Indonesia, the courts in the plaintiff's district are to comply with Article 6, paragraph (8) Rv. The Article provides that the court shall serve process on the defendant through the court's public prosecutor. The public prosecutor is to deliver the process papers to the Indonesian Government. Service on the defendant abroad is to be effected by the Indonesian Government. Rv does not specify which office or ministry is to handle service of process outside Indonesia. In practice it is usually the Ministry of Foreign Affairs through its diplomatic or consular offices abroad that effects service. This is in accordance with the Accession of Vienna Convention on Consular Relations Act 1982 that implements the 1963 Vienna Convention on Consular Relations. Regarding a divorce petition to be served on a defendant living abroad, Article 20, paragraph (3) of the Marriage Regulation 1975 provides that the chief justice of the court in the plaintiff's district shall serve the petition on the defendant abroad via the Indonesian diplomatic office in the defendant's country. The foregoing provisions can be used in cases in which the defendant's location outside Indonesia is known. If the defendant's whereabouts are unknown, Article 390, paragraph (3) HIR and Article 6, paragraph (7) Rv will apply. The two Articles provide that process is to be effected by announcement (general convocation) attached to the court's main door in the plaintiff's district and by publication in a newspaper in the district or area closest to the district.

Service of process outside Indonesia only covers service of judicial documents that emanate from legal proceedings and which are directly connected with lawsuits, such as court summonses, court verdicts, notices and memorandums of appeal, notices and memorandums of cassation, authentic deeds, civil documents, etc. Service abroad of extrajudicial documents is unknown in the Indonesian legal system. This correlates to Indonesia not being a party to the 1965 Hague Convention on the Service Abroad of Judicial and Extrajudicial Documents in Civil or Commercial Matters.

Although the provisions in civil procedure codes concerning service of process outside Indonesia have never been revoked, in practice those provisions are no longer in use. For example, public prosecutors are no longer involved in the service of process outside Indonesia.[51] Several new regulations also have been issued by the Ministry of Foreign Affairs and the Supreme Court to regulate service abroad. In addition, in 1978 the Indonesian Government and the Kingdom of Thailand entered into an Agreement on

[51] Harahap, *Hukum Acara* (n 2) 224.

Judicial Co-operation. This agreement was ratified by Presidential Decree No 6 of 1978.[52] Article 1 of the Agreement states: 'The Government of the Republic of Indonesia and the Government of the Kingdom of Thailand agree to cooperate with each other in serving judicial documents and obtaining evidence in civil and commercial matters.' The service of process from Indonesian courts is to be made through the Office of Judicial Affairs of the Ministry of Justice, the Kingdom of Thailand (Article 3-4 of the Agreement). To serve process in other countries, besides adhering to Indonesian civil procedure codes, Indonesian courts follow the procedure stipulated by the Ministry of Foreign Affairs. This procedure was the result of agreements between the Ministry of Foreign Affairs and the Supreme Court in 2018.[53] The Ministry provides the following flowchart in Figure 3, setting out the procedure for service of judicial documents on a defendant with a known residence outside Indonesia.

The plaintiff in Indonesia is responsible for the payment of all costs associated with the service of process outside Indonesia.[54]

Since Indonesia is not a party to the 1965 Hague Service Convention, Indonesian courts must refer to Indonesian civil procedure codes in relation to serving process on defendants outside Indonesia. In addition, Indonesian courts comply with the procedure for service of process agreed between the Ministry of Foreign Affairs and the Supreme Court. For service on a party in Thailand, Indonesian courts adhere to the 1978 Agreement on Judicial Co-operation between Indonesia and Thailand.

iv. Service of Foreign Proceedings in Indonesia

In contrast to service of process outside Indonesia, Indonesian civil procedure codes do not have provisions on service of foreign proceedings within Indonesia. Despite the absence of regulations concerning the service of foreign proceedings, there is no prohibition for a plaintiff or a court outside Indonesia to serve process on a person within Indonesia. The 1978 Agreement on Judicial Co-operation between Indonesia and Thailand allows a plaintiff before the Thai court to serve judicial documents on a defendant in Indonesia through the Directorate- General for General Court of the Indonesian Supreme Court (Article 3). For plaintiffs in other countries, the Indonesian Ministry of Foreign Affairs and the Supreme Court issued the procedure outlined in the 2018 Memorandum of Understanding Between the Indonesian Ministry of Foreign Affairs and Supreme Court No PRJ/HI/102/02/2018/01 No 01/NK/MA/2/2018 concerning requests for judicial assistance in civil matters. A

[52] Presidential Decree No 6 of 1978 concerning ratification of Agreement on Judicial Co-operation Between the Republic of Indonesia and the Kingdom of Thailand.

[53] Nota Kesepahaman Kementerian Luar Negeri Republik Indonesia dan Mahkamah Agung Republik Indonesia tentang Penanganan Permintaan Bantuan Teknis Hukum dalam Masalah Perdata No PRJ/HI/102/02/2018/01 No 01/NK/MA/2/2018; Perjanjian Kerja Sama Antara Kementerian Luar Negeri dengan Mahkamah Agung tentang Mekanisme Pengiriman Surat Rogatori dan Penyampaian Dokumen Peradilan dalam Masalah Perdata No PRJ/HI/103/02/2018/01; No 03/PK/MA/2/2018; Perjanjian Kerja Sama antara Kementerian Luar Negeri dan Mahkamah Agung tentang Standardisasi Surat Rogatori dan Surat Penyampaian Dokumen Peradilan dalam Masalah Perdata No PRJ/HI/104/02/2018/01 No 04/PK/MA/2018.

[54] Supreme Court Registrar Office Circular Letter No 1747/PAN/HK.01/2018 concerning procedure to deliver rogatory letter and service of judicial documents in civil matter outside Indonesia.

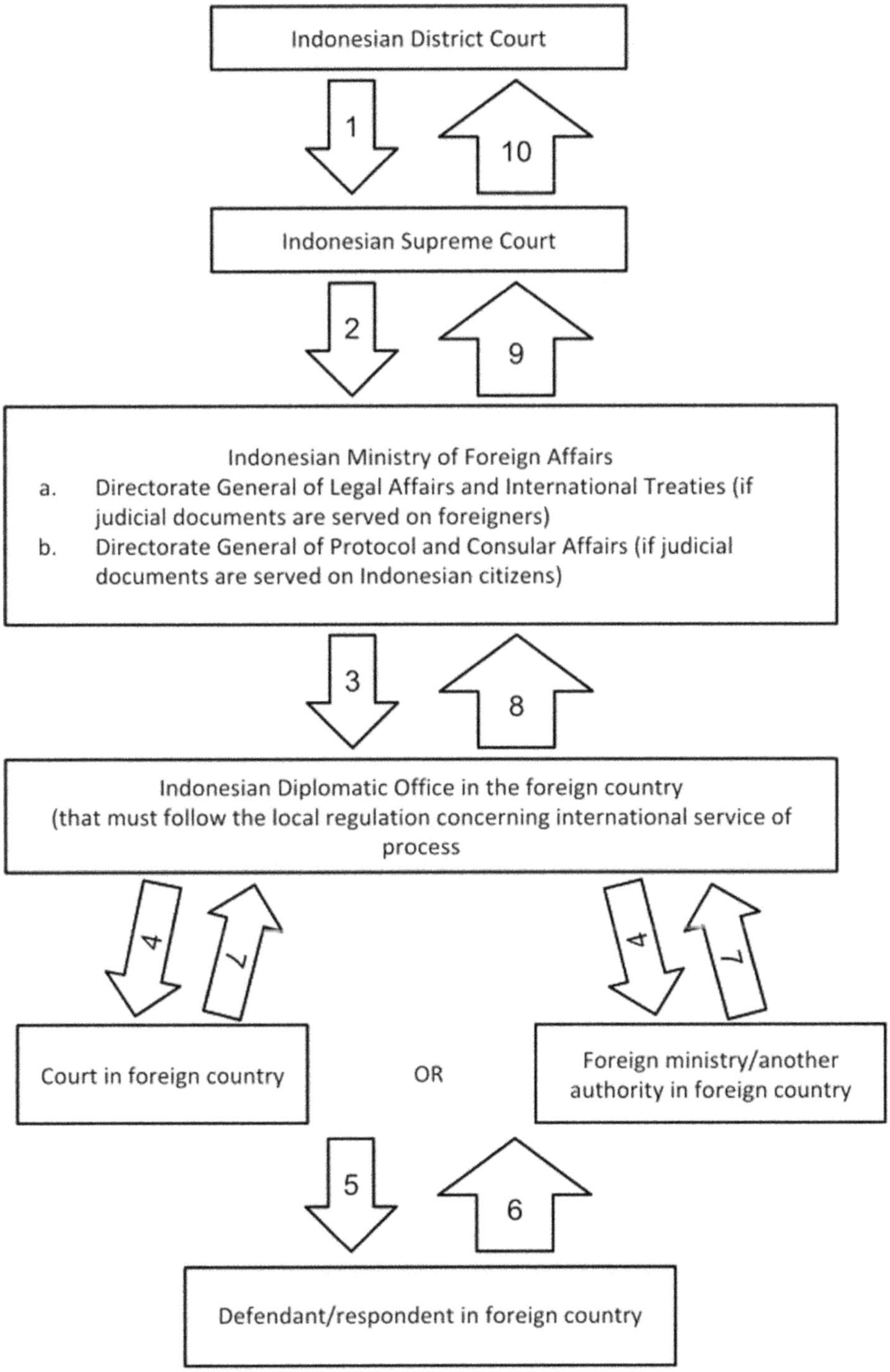

Figure 3 Procedure of service of process outside Indonesia

flowchart of that procedure was published in the website of the Ministry of Foreign Affairs. The following is an unofficial English version of the flowchart:

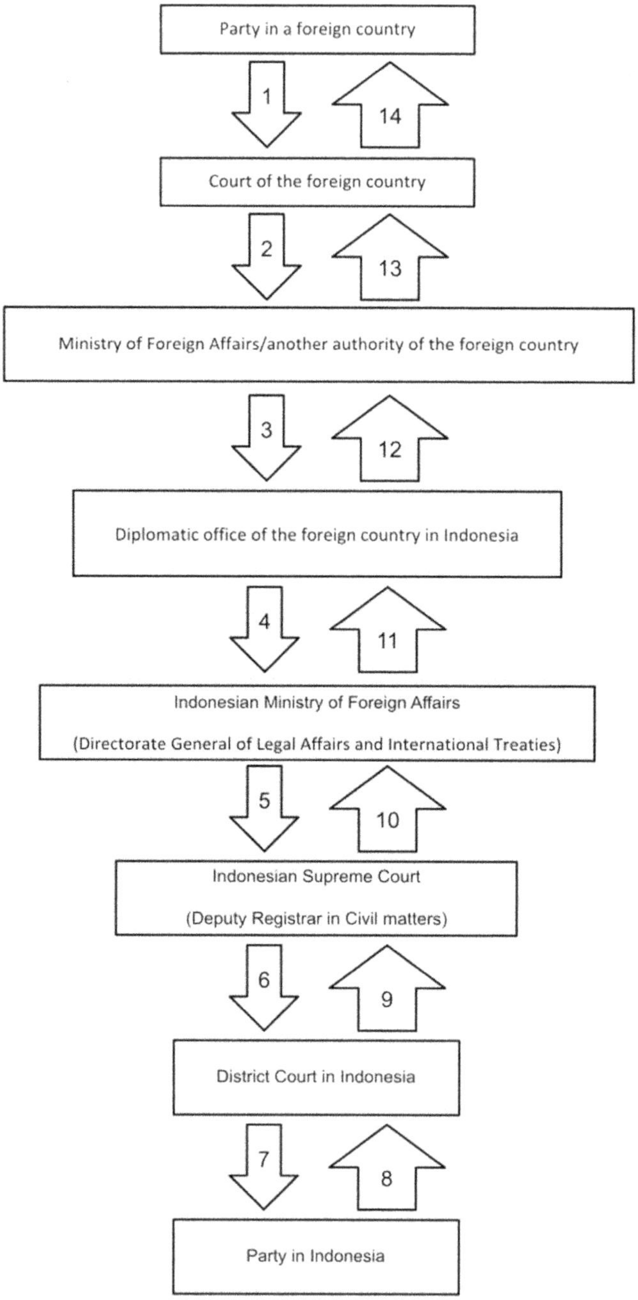

Figure 4 Procedure of service of foreign proceedings in Indonesia

In line with the Flag, Language, State Emblem, and National Anthem Act 2009, which requires the use of the Indonesian language in official documents, the Ministry of Foreign Affairs requires service of process from foreign authorities to be accompanied by an Indonesian translation, unless stipulated otherwise in an agreement between Indonesia and the relevant state.[55] However, the Ministry does not require that the translation be certified by a sworn translator in contrast to the requirement in the Agreement on Judicial Cooperation between Indonesia and Thailand. Based on the foregoing flowchart, service of foreign proceedings must involve the court of the requesting state. As such, service of foreign proceedings in Indonesia only covers the service of judicial documents that emanate from legal proceedings and which are directly connected with lawsuits in foreign courts, such as copies of the plaintiff's complaint, court summonses, witness summonses, court verdicts, notices of and memorandums of appeal, notices and memorandums of cassation, authentic deeds, civil documents, etc.[56] Plaintiffs in the foreign courts are responsible for the payment of all costs associated with serving process on respondents in Indonesia.[57]

Indonesian Foreign Minister Retno Marsudi has stated that in 2017 there was a 91 per cent increase from 2016 in the number of Indonesians in civil actions involving foreigners or pending outside Indonesia. According to the minister, in 2017 Indonesian diplomatic offices and consulates abroad (primarily in Singapore, Malaysia, the US, Hong Kong, and the UK) handled 1,767 requests for service in civil matters. She said that the 91 per cent increase was the consequence of the growing number of civil relationships between Indonesians (whether individuals or legal entities) and foreign nationals.[58] Despite the increase, the minister did not raise the need to accede to the 1965 Hague Service Convention. Instead, she said that the Ministry of Foreign Affairs was planning to establish bilateral agreements for mutual legal assistance in civil matters with other countries, especially where Indonesian diplomatic offices receive a high number of requests for service in civil matters. According to Ms Marsudi, the bilateral agreements will enable direct contact between courts in Indonesia and those of other states for the service of judicial documents.[59] However, given that the US, the UK, the PRC and many other countries are parties to the 1965 Hague Service Convention,[60] it is doubtful that those countries will agree to establish bilateral agreements with Indonesia as proposed by the minister. Those countries would instead prefer the mechanism of the 1965 Hague Service Convention to bilateral agreements, as the 1965 Hague Service Convention offers a more uniform mechanism for service of process than bilateral agreements. With the current increase of requests for service of process in civil matters, it is time for Indonesia to accede the 1965 Hague Service Convention.

[55] Nota Kesepahaman Kementerian Luar Negeri Republik Indonesia dan Mahkamah Agung Republik Indonesia tentang Penanganan Permintaan Bantuan Teknis Hukum dalam Masalah Perdata No PRJ/HI/102/02/2018/01 No 01/NK/MA/2/2018, Art 7.

[56] ibid, Art 1(3).

[57] ibid, Art 8.

[58] RD Suastha, 'Kasus Perdata WNI Di Luar Negeri Meningkat 91 Persen' (*CNN Indonesia*, 20 February 2018) www.cnnindonesia.com/internasional/20180220174425-106-277523/kasus-perdata-wni-di-luar-negeri-meningkat-91-persen (accessed 3 October 2018).

[59] Ibid.

[60] There are currently 78 contracting states to the 1965 Hague Service Convention.

B. Special Rules

i. Law of Obligations

Concerning obligations, both contractual and non-contractual, the provisions and principles in Indonesian civil procedure codes apply to determine which court has jurisdiction over the parties' obligations.[61] For obligations with foreign elements, beside the civil procedure codes, jurisprudence and doctrine apply to determine jurisdiction.

a. Specific Contracts

Specific contracts in the Indonesian legal system are typically contracts that have specific names given by legislation and which are specially regulated by such legislation. Most of the specific contracts are identified in Book III of the Indonesian Civil Code or BW. These include sale and purchase contracts, contracts for the hire of goods, partnership contracts, guaranty contracts, etc. Other specific contracts are governed by the Indonesian Commercial Code. Examples are contracts for the carriage of goods, negotiable instruments, and insurance contracts. Besides being governed by the Commercial Code, insurance contracts are also governed by the Insurance Act 2014. In addition, specific contracts are also regulated by other laws. For instance, consumer contracts are governed by Act No 8 of 1999 concerning consumer protection (the Consumer Protection Act 1999). Employment contracts are governed by various Indonesian labour regulations. Contracts for sale of land are governed by the Basic Agrarian Act 1960. Secured transactions are governed by Act No 42 of 1999 concerning Fiduciary (the Fiduciary Act 1999), Act No 4 of 1996 concerning Mortgage on Land and Its Related Objects (the Mortgage on Land and Its Related Objects Act 1996), and the BW. E-commerce is governed by Government Regulation No 80 of 2019.

There are also a growing number of specific contracts without a specific name and which are not governed by specific legislation. Instances of these are agency, leasing, franchise, and build–operate–transfer (BOT) contracts. These specific contracts are found in business practice and are governed entirely by the parties' agreement on the freedom of contract principle. Parties to such contracts are generally allowed to enter into choice of court agreements. The exception concerns specific contracts relating to land and employment in which the parties are not allowed to make choice of court agreements as a matter of public policy. Thus, in general, courts that have jurisdiction over such specific contracts are the courts expressly chosen by the parties in their written contracts. It shall be noted however, that as discussed in section I.A.ii.e above on choice of court agreements, case law suggests that Indonesian courts often exercise jurisdiction over contracts in which the parties have made choice of court agreements. The reason for Indonesian courts to exercise jurisdiction despite the parties' choice of court agreements is Article 118, paragraph (4) HIR and Article 99. paragraph (16) Rv.

In contracts in which the parties do not expressly make choice of court agreements, the courts that have jurisdiction over the contracts are determined by Indonesian civil procedure codes and by the specific laws that govern the specific contracts. In contracts relating

[61] See sections I.A.i and I.A.ii above for the discussion of rules and principles to determine court jurisdiction.

to movable goods (for example, contracts for the sale of goods, the hire of goods, and the carriage of goods), the principle of *actor sequitur forum rei* in Article 118 HIR and Article 99 Rv apply to determine the court that will have jurisdiction over a contract. The court in the district of a defendant's residence will have jurisdiction over such contracts. This principle also applies to contracts related to movable goods with foreign elements. In e-commerce in which the parties are Indonesian and foreign nationals, the principles of Private International Law (namely the basis of presence and effectiveness principles) are applied to determine the jurisdiction of a forum to settle the parties' dispute (Elucidation of Article 74, paragraph (2) of Government Regulation No 80 of 2019 concerning e-commerce). Since contracts relating to movable goods often involve end-users or consumers whose rights need to be protected, the Consumer Protection Act 1999 has special provisions dealing with jurisdiction in consumer contracts disputes, including e-contracts. To protect consumers, who are generally presumed to be the weaker party in a contractual relationship, jurisdiction provisions in the Consumer Protection Act 1999 supersede choice of court agreements between the parties found in consumer contracts. The latter contracts are often standard form contracts which many consumers sign without having read or understood. The jurisdiction provisions in the Consumer Protection Act 1999 also supersede jurisdiction provisions in Indonesian civil procedure codes.

Article 23 of the Consumer Protection Act 1999 stipulates that consumers can bring merchants who refuse to respond to consumers' claims or refuse compensation for damages suffered as a result of the breach of Article 19, to the Consumer Dispute Resolution Body or to the court in the district of the consumer's residence. Article 19 provides that a merchant shall compensate for damage, contamination or loss sustained by a consumer as a result of using the goods or services produced or traded by the merchant. Pursuant to Article 23, it is the situation of the consumer, not of the merchant, that determines the forum for a consumer contract dispute. The court or the consumer dispute resolution body that has jurisdiction over a consumer contract is the one in the district of the consumer's, not the merchant's, residence. By Supreme Court Regulation No 1 of 2006 concerning the procedure for objecting to the decision of the Consumer Dispute Resolution Body, consumers or merchants can file an objection to the court in the district of the consumer's residence (Article 3, paragraph (1)). A consumer who does not have a domicile in Indonesia shall file an objection to the court in the district in which the Consumer Dispute Resolution Body issued its decision (Article 3, paragraph (2)). To protect consumers, the jurisdiction provisions in the Consumer Protection Act 1999 override the *actor sequitur forum rei* principle and the parties' choice of court agreement.

The relevant principles were applied in *PT Garuda Indonesia (Persero) v Mahsin, SH.* There, Mahsin, a Garuda's passenger, sued PT Garuda Indonesia (Persero) ('Garuda'), an Indonesian airline, for the loss of checked-in baggage. Mahsin was domiciled in Medan and Garuda had its legal seat in Jakarta. On 7 October 2016, Mahsin flew with Garuda from Jakarta to Singapore. When arriving in Singapore, Mahsin could not find a suitcase that contained valuable items He reported the missing baggage to the Garuda staff at the Singapore Airport. Mahsin flew back to Medan. His baggage was eventually declared lost. Mahsin brought a lawsuit against Garuda for the loss of his baggage in the Consumer Dispute Resolution Body in Medan and the Resolution Body decided partly in favour of Mahsin. Garuda objected to the decision of the Resolution Body and brought their objection to the Medan District Court. Garuda objected to the jurisdiction of the Medan Consumer Dispute

Resolution Body over the dispute. The Medan District Court dismissed Garuda's objection. The Supreme Court affirmed the Medan District Court's judgment.[62] This case shows that, in consumer contract cases, the court or consumer dispute resolution body that has jurisdiction is always the one in the district of the consumer's residence. In a case between Mr Faisal Amri Nasution and PT Hanjaya Mandala Sampoerna Tbk ('HM Sampoerna'), an Indonesian cigarette company, the judges in the South Jakarta District Court dismissed Mr Nasution's tort lawsuit against HM Sampoerna because the South Jakarta District Court did not have jurisdiction over the case. Mr Nasution whose residence was in Bekasi, argued that he brought the tort lawsuit to the court in the South Jakarta district because the defendant had a management office in the South Jakarta district (the principle of *actor sequitur forum rei*). Mr Nasution claimed to suffer health problems after smoking a cigarette produced by HM Sampoerna and therefore sought compensation from HM Sampoerna. However, the judges in the South Jakarta District Court did not characterise the case as tortious in nature, but as one involving consumer protection. In accordance with the Consumer Protection Act 1999, the forum that has jurisdiction over consumer disputes is the Consumer Dispute Resolution Body or court in the district of consumer's residence. Consequently, on 15 May 2008, the South Jakarta District Court dismissed Mr Nasution's action and told him to bring his suit before the court in Bekasi.[63]

In relation to contracts related to immovable property, especially land and buildings on land,[64] the courts that have jurisdiction over the contracts are those prescribed by Article 118 HIR and Article 99 Rv. Pursuant to Article 118, paragraph (3) HIR and Article 99, paragraph (8) Rv, in the case that the main dispute in the contracts relates to the ownership or title of immovable property, the court that has jurisdiction is the court in the district in which the immovable property is located. But, if the dispute in the contract is a combination of action in *rem* and action *in personam*, the court that has jurisdiction is either that in the district where the immovable property is located or where the defendant resides, depending on the plaintiff's election (Article 99, paragraph (10) Rv). Those provisions also apply to contracts with foreign elements.

Regarding employment contracts, the Manpower Act 2003 recognises two types of contracts. First, an individual work agreement between an employee and an employer (Article 1, number 14). Second, a collective work agreement resulting from negotiations between a labour union and an entrepreneur or between a group of labour unions and a group of entrepreneurs (Article 1, number 21). The Manpower Act 2003 also recognises employment contracts between foreign workers and Indonesian companies (Chapter VIII of the Manpower Act 2003). The Act mentions four types of disputes that can arise out of those employment contracts, namely disputes over rights, interests, termination of employment, and disputes among several labour unions within the same company (Article 1, number 22).

[62] Consumer Dispute Resolution Body of Medan Decision 145/ARB/XII/2016/BPSK-Mdn. (9 February 2017); affd District Court of Medan Decision 125/Pdt.Sus-BPSK/2017/PN Mdn. (21 April 2017); affd Supreme Court Decision 1317 K/Pdt.Sus-BPSK/2017 (19 December 2017).

[63] Not published. See Hukumonline, 'Gugatan Konsumen Rokok Salah Alamat' (*hukumonline*, 15 May 2008) www.hukumonline.com/berita/baca/hol19246/gugatan-konsumen-rokok-salah-alamat/ (accessed 9 February 2020); Hukumonline, 'Gugatan Konsumen, Haruskah Sesuai Domisili?' (*hukumonline*, 29 May 2008) www.hukumonline.com/berita/baca/hol19346/gugatan-konsumen-haruskah-sesuai-domisili (accessed 9 February 2020).

[64] Indonesian law distinguishes between land and a building or other structure on land. Both are considered immovable property.

Pursuant to Article 56 of Act No 2 of 2004 concerning settlement of industrial relation disputes (the Industrial Dispute Settlement Act 2004), all four disputes are under the jurisdiction of the Industrial Relations Court, which is a special court established within the district court in capital cities of provinces. Indonesian civil procedure codes apply to proceedings in the Industrial Relations Court (Article 57 of the Industrial Dispute Settlement Act 2004). The general jurisdiction provisions and principles in the civil procedure codes, such as the *actor sequitur forum rei* principle, apply to determine the jurisdiction of the Industrial Relations Court over disputes in employment contracts. Since employees or workers are generally considered to be the weaker parties in employment situations, choice of court agreements are not allowed in employment contracts. To protect employees or workers, the Industrial Relations Court has jurisdiction over employment contracts. Article 29 of the Industrial Dispute Settlement Act 2004 allows parties to bring their dispute to an arbitration of industrial relations only if there is disagreement between the parties concerning the making or the amendment of working requirements in their employment contract. Other types of disputes arising out of employment contracts shall be brought to Industrial Relations Court.

In summary, jurisdiction over specific contracts is determined by the parties' choice of court agreements and principles of Private International Law. But, for specific contracts that involve the public interest in protecting weaker parties, such as consumer and employment contracts, the courts having jurisdiction are specific courts designated by laws regulating the specific contracts. For contracts relating to land, the courts having jurisdiction will always be an Indonesian court.

b. Specific Torts

In the Indonesian legal system, tort is categorised as an obligation arising by operation of law in respect of a wrongful act (Article 1353 BW). In the BW, the term used for tort is *onrechtmatige daad* (literally 'unlawful act'). Article 1365 BW stipulates that 'every unlawful act that causes damage onto another person obliges the perpetrator to compensate such damage'. The damage is the consequence of a wrongdoer's act, omission or recklessness (Article 1366 BW). There are other provisions in the BW that govern unlawful acts or tort. For example, Article 1367 concerns the responsibility of supervisors and guardians for the unlawful acts of persons, apprentices or minors under their supervision or guardianship. Article 1368 concerns the responsibility of owners of animals for their animals' unlawful acts; Article 1369 concerns the responsibility of owners of buildings for the collapse of their buildings. Articles 1372 to 1380 concern defamation. In 1919 in *Lindenbaum v Cohen*, the Dutch Supreme Court (*Hoge Raad*) broadened the meaning of 'unlawful acts' to include acts or omissions that are contrary to the social duty of care or are contrary to what are appropriate in society according to unwritten law.[65] This judgment was also applied to the Dutch East Indies (now Indonesia). Within that wider meaning of 'unlawful acts', conduct not listed in Articles 1367 to 1380 BW or other legislation can be categorised as torts.

[65] Lindenbaum/Cohen, HR 31 January 1919, NJ 1919, 161.

To determine which court has jurisdiction *in personam* over tortious or unlawful acts, one must apply the rules and principles in Indonesian civil procedure codes.[66] The same rules and principles apply to tort with foreign elements.

In the extraordinary appeal in *Time Inc Asia et al v H.M. Soeharto*, the Indonesian Supreme Court upheld the interlocutory judgment of the Central Jakarta District Court concerning its jurisdiction over the case. H.M. Soeharto ('Soeharto'), the Indonesian former president, filed a defamation lawsuit against Time Asia over an article in *Time* magazine in May 1999. The article reported that US$9 billion linked to Soeharto and his family had been shifted from a Swiss to an Austrian bank. The article accused Soeharto's businesses of paying less than 10 per cent of their tax obligation. The cover page of the magazine was entitled 'SUHARTO INC: How Indonesia's long-time boss built a family fortune'. Soeharto based his action on Article 1372 BW that specifically covered defamation. Time objected to the jurisdiction of the Central Jakarta District Court. It argued that Time Asia was a branch office of Time Inc., a company incorporated in Delaware with a management office in New York. Time Asia only had a branch office in Hong Kong, which was registered as an overseas company under Hong Kong law. Neither Time Inc nor Time Asia had a presence in Indonesia. *Time* also argued that based on the applicable Indonesian Basic Press Act, the individual who was responsible for the publication of the magazine was its editor-in-chief, not its Indonesian-based journalists or the Hong Kong editor who were also named as defendants in the case. *Time's* editor-in-chief did not reside in Indonesia. Therefore, according to *Time*, the Central Jakarta District Court could not have jurisdiction because all responsible parties did not have a presence in Indonesia. The Central Jakarta District Court dismissed *Time's* objection.[67] In its interlocutory judgment dated 9 September 1999, the Court did not refer to specific provisions in the Indonesian civil procedure codes to justify its jurisdiction over the parties. However, pursuant to Article 100 Rv, an Indonesian court has jurisdiction over a foreigner, either natural or legal person, who does not stay or reside in Indonesia, if the latter owes a legal obligation to an Indonesian plaintiff which has arisen in Indonesia or elsewhere. The Central Jakarta District Court could hear the case because it was the district court of the plaintiff's residence. The Court also stated that the Hong Kong branch of Time Inc. and the individual employees of Time Inc. could be personally liable for their acts. They were thus correctly joined as parties in the defamation action. The Jakarta High Court and the Supreme Court in extraordinary appeal upheld the judgment of the District Court.[68]

In the *Time* case, the Central Jakarta District Court exercised its jurisdiction based on the rules and principles in the Indonesian civil procedure codes. However, in *Richard Bruce Ness v Jane Perlez and the New York Times Company*,[69] the Central Jakarta District Court refused to exercise jurisdiction due to *forum non conveniens*. Mr Ness brought a tort lawsuit against Ms Perlez who had written three articles deemed harmful to Mr Ness's reputation. He also sued the *New York Times* for publishing Ms Perlez' articles. The articles accused Mr Ness as president-director of PT. Newmont Minahasa Raya, an Indonesian company,

[66] See sections I.A.i and I.A.ii above for the discussion of rules and principles to determine court jurisdiction.

[67] District Court of Central Jakarta Interlocutory Decision 338/PDT.G/1999/PN.JKT.PST (9 September 1999).

[68] High Court of Jakarta Decision 551/PDT/2000/PT.DKI (16 March 2001); affd Supreme Court Extraordinary Appeal 273 PK/Pdt/2008 (16 April 2009).

[69] District Court of Central Jakarta Decision 181/PDT.G/2007/PN.JKT.PST. (8 October 2007).

of serious mining pollution at Buyat Bay, North Sulawesi. The Central Jakarta District Court took into account that all the parties were not Indonesian nationals. Mr Ness was an American, although domiciled in Jakarta. Ms Perlez was an Australian journalist who had lived in Jakarta when writing the articles about Mr Ness and his company. The *New York Times* was incorporated and had its legal seat in New York. Although based on Indonesian civil procedure codes, the Central Jakarta District Court could have asserted jurisdiction over the case, but the judges considered that the Court was not an appropriate forum for the case. The Court lacked a connection with the defendants' countries of residence, their nationalities, and the place where the articles were published. The Court also took into account that its judgment may not be enforceable in the defendants' countries of residence. Accordingly, the Jakarta District Court declined jurisdiction.

As demonstrated above, the general rules and principles of the Indonesian civil procedure codes apply to determine the jurisdiction of an Indonesian court over torts with foreign elements, whether general or specific torts. The doctrine of *forum non conveniens* has also been used to refuse jurisdiction over tort with foreign elements.

c. Unjust Enrichment

In 1922, the New Netherlands Civil Code (*Nieuw Burgerlijk Wetboek*) introduced a provision on unjust enrichment in Article 6:212. But the Indonesian Civil Code only has provisions about performance rendered or payments made under the mistaken belief that there was an obligation so to act. The performance or payment in such circumstance give rise to a *condictio indebiti* (that is, an obligation to make restitution where a party has received a benefit not due to him or her). In Indonesia, the *condictio indebiti* is governed by Articles 1359 to 1364 BW concerning 'Obligations' (Book III). Article 1359, paragraph (1) BW provides that every payment implies a debt. What has been paid without being due may thus be reclaimed. A person who has inadvertently or knowingly accepted something that was not due, is obliged to return it to the person from whom one received it (Article 1360 BW). A person who mistakenly believes one's self to be a debtor and makes payment to the presumed creditor is entitled to reclaim the payment from the latter (Article 1361 BW). A person, who in bad faith has received money or goods that are not actually due, is to return the same, with (as relevant) interest or compensation for depreciation (Article 1362 BW). Anyone who in good faith has sold goods received as a payment for a debt that was not due, may remedy the situation by handing the purchase price over to the payer (Article 1363 BW).

Since Indonesian law only deals with *condictio indebiti* and not unjust enrichment generally, this chapter will only discuss the former. In the BW, the former is classified as an obligation arising by operation of law as a result of some act (Article 1353 BW). The obligation does not depend on the existence of a contract or tort. The *condictio indebiti* is therefore categorised as an action *in personam* rather than an action *in rem*. Jurisdiction *in personam* over obligations, including that under the *condictio indebiti*, is governed by Article 118 HIR and Article 99 Rv. In addition, Article 100 Rv governs the court's jurisdiction over *condicitio indebiti* involving foreign elements. Article 118, paragraph (1) HIR and Article 99, paragraph (2) Rv provide that the court that has jurisdiction *in personam* is the court in the district in which the defendant's residence is situated or where the defendant actually lives. In other words, the plaintiff shall bring the *condictio indebiti* lawsuit in the defendant's forum (*actor sequitur forum rei* principle). If there is more than one defendant, the court that has jurisdiction over the defendants is the court in the district where one of the defendants has a residence (at the plaintiff's election) (Article 118, paragraph (2) HIR and Article 99, paragraph (6) Rv). In the case that the residence of the defendant is unknown or a place of living cannot be found, the court that has jurisdiction *in personam* is the court in the district where the plaintiff resides (Article 118, paragraph (3) HIR and Article 99, paragraph (3) Rv). These provisions can be applied in cases when both Indonesians and foreigners as defendants do not have a known residence in Indonesia. Under Article 100 Rv, an Indonesian court has jurisdiction *in personam* over foreign nationals or legal persons without a residence or presence in Indonesia, if the foreigner has incurred a legal obligation to an Indonesian plaintiff in Indonesia or elsewhere. The Indonesian court that will have jurisdiction is the court in the district of the plaintiff's residence (Article 118, paragraph (3) HIR and Article 99, paragraph (3) Rv). For example, an Indonesian party to an export-import agreement with a Chinese party believes that their agreement requires it to pay the purchase price for certain items sold by the Chinese party. Later, however, their export-import agreement is found to be void because export of the items is prohibited by Chinese law. Therefore, the payment made by the Indonesian party is regarded as giving rise to a *condictio indebiti*. The Chinese party has an obligation to undo the performance of the Indonesian party by returning the received payment to the Indonesian party. Pursuant to Article 100 Rv, Article 118, paragraph (3) HIR and Article 99, paragraph (3) Rv, an Indonesian court in the district of the Indonesian party's residence will have jurisdiction *in personam* over the Chinese party. The same Indonesian court will have jurisdiction even though Indonesian plaintiff paid the money outside Indonesia.

Where (as in the export-import agreement example above) a person is enriched through an unlawful act at the plaintiff's expense, this enrichment does not give rise to a *condictio indebiti* under the BW. The latter action must be based on a lawful act by the plaintiff who makes payment or renders performance. The enrichment in the export-import agreement example cannot be qualified as a tort either, because the person who committed the unlawful act was not the defendant, but someone else. The BW does not have provisions to govern this type of enrichment. For instance, an Indonesian national receives an inheritance deposited in a bank in Singapore. Unbeknown to him, the money in the Singapore bank originated from a bribery payment paid to his deceased father. Obviously, this person has been enriched at the expense of his late father's employer in Indonesia. Nevertheless, the person's obligation to return the bribery payment to his late father's employer is not covered by the BW, because the BW only governs enrichment from a lawful act. Consequently, the right of the deceased's employer to demand restitution from the heir is not governed by the BW either. Accordingly, in this particular enrichment case, the Indonesian civil court cannot exercise jurisdiction *in personam* over the heir who has been unjustifiably enriched, because the enrichment does not create a personal obligation in accordance with the provisions of Book III of the BW. As a consequence, there is no recourse for the plaintiff to obtain restitution from the heir through the Indonesian civil court.

In conclusion, the jurisdiction of the Indonesian court over mistaken payments or performance is governed by Article 118 HIR, Articles 99 and 100 Rv. In the case of enrichment obtained by a person through an unlawful act of someone else, the Indonesian court will not have jurisdiction over the person enriched because the enrichment does not create an obligation in accordance with the Book IIII of the BW.

d. Trusts and Charitable Foundations

The concept of trust, which is based on English law, does not exist in the Indonesian legal system. Book III of the BW concerning obligations and Book II of the BW concerning property do not have provisions about trusts. In addition, Indonesia is not a party to the 1985 Hague Convention on the Law Applicable to Trusts and on their Recognition, so Indonesia does not have an obligation to recognise the existence and validity of trusts. The concept of ownership in a trust that gives a trustee only a legal ownership – because the beneficial ownership is vested in a third party (beneficiary) – is unknown to the Indonesian law. It contradicts Article 570 in Book II of the BW that defines ownership as the right to have full enjoyment of property and freely use the property to the exclusion of everyone else provided that the owner of the property respects the law and the rights of others. In a trust, a trustee has legal ownership of an entrusted property but is prohibited in equity from freely using the property and can only manage or use the same for the benefit of the beneficiaries. Therefore, under current Indonesian law, an agreement between a settlor and a trustee to transfer legal ownership of assets to a trustee for the benefit of a third party will not create any obligations on the trustee under Indonesian law. In other words, as far as Indonesian law is concerned, the trustee will have no personal liabilities to the beneficiaries. As a result, although the Indonesian court may have jurisdiction *in personam* over the parties to a trust agreement, the court will not exercise its jurisdiction. This principle also applies to trusts with foreign elements.

There are two types of 'trust-like' arrangement that are recognised by Indonesian law. First, the practice of bond trustees in the Indonesian security market is governed by Act No 8 of 1995 (the Capital Market Act 1995). The difference between a bond trustee (*wali amanat*) in the Indonesian security market and an ordinary trustee in English law is that the bond trustee is not the legal owner of any assets or collateral of the company that issues or sells bonds. The ownership of the assets or collateral remains with the company. The function of the bond trustee is merely to serve as the fiduciary of the bondholders and act in their best interest. Second, there is the trust practice governed by Financial Services Authority Regulation No 27/POJK.03/2015 as amended by Regulation No 25 /POJK.03/2016 concerning bank bailment and management services. By this trust regulation, a trustee is not entitled to own assets transferred by a settlor. An Indonesian bank or the Indonesian branch office of a foreign bank can become a trustee, but with the limited role of bailee or safekeeper and manager of a settlor's financial assets (cash, receivables, or commercial papers). In this context, the settlor retains ownership of the relevant assets.

In conclusion, the Indonesian legal system does not recognise trusts and, accordingly, trust agreements do not give rise to personal obligations or ownership rights under Indonesian law. Hence, the Indonesian court will not exercise jurisdiction over the parties to a trust agreement.

Unlike trusts, charitable foundations have been recognised since the Dutch colonial era. Based on the decision of the *Hoge Raad* (Supreme Court of the Netherlands) in 1882 which was adopted as jurisprudence in the Dutch East Indies, a foundation is recognised as a legal entity. After independence, the Indonesian Supreme Court held in decision No 124 K/Sip/1973 (27 June 1973) that a foundation would have legal personality if it satisfied three criteria: (1) it owns assets; (2) it has a specific purpose; and (3) it has a board of management. Legal personality is governed by Chapter IX of Book III of the BW on obligations.

Unlike partnerships, firms, or limited liability companies which are governed by specific provisions in the BW or Commercial Code, foundations are not governed in either code. Foundations (*Yayasan*) were only mentioned briefly in the BW. Foundations were, therefore, only regulated in accordance with custom, doctrine and jurisprudence. In 2001 the Indonesian Government enacted Act No 16 of 2001 as amended by Act No 28 of 2004 concerning foundations (the Foundation Act 2001 as amended in 2004).

Before the Foundation Act in 2001, a foundation was established when one or more natural or legal persons by a notarial deed transferred assets to it for a charitable purpose, such as the advancement of education, health, poverty reduction, religion, and so on. The notarial deed had to mention the specific purpose of the foundation. At that time, a foundation was not required to have Articles of Association or a Memorandum of Association. The notarial deed would suffice. Foundations were not required to be registered or to obtain government approval. The assets of a foundation could also come from public donations. As a legal person, the foundation was the owner of the transferred assets and could manage them by investing the same in business activities for the benefit of the foundation. The beneficiaries of the foundation could not be the founder or the persons managing the foundation but had to be the public at large or a class of specified persons. However, because charitable foundations were not well regulated and received certain kinds of tax exemption, it became common for charitable foundations to be established to hold assets for the benefit of the founders and the foundation's executives in addition to third parties.[70] An example may be seen in *Negara Republik Indonesia cq. Presiden Republik Indonesia v Yayasan Beasiswa Supersemar and H.M. Soeharto*,[71] in which the Supersemar scholarship foundation established by the Indonesian President Soeharto used its assets (that came in part from public donations) to invest in or give loans to companies belonging to Soeharto's children and cronies. The profit of the foundation's business activities went to the Supersemar foundation as well as to Soeharto's family and cronies. Foundations in Indonesia could also be established by foreigners provided that they complied with applicable jurisprudence, doctrine and custom. Prior to the enactment of the Foundation Act in 2001, the court jurisdiction over foundations and the parties involved were not specifically regulated. As such, the court's jurisdiction *in personam* over foundations and the parties involved was governed by the general rules and principles in Articles 118 HIR, 99 Rv, and 100 Rv.

The objective of the Foundation Act 2001 was to restore the function of foundations as charitable entities benefitting the public through social, religious and humanitarian activities. The Act was to eliminate the practice of establishing foundations to enrich the founders and executives of the foundation and of use foundations as the depository of illicit assets (General Elucidation of the Foundation Act 2001). The Foundation Act requires that a foundation be established by notarial deed. Further, before the foundation can come into being, its deed of establishment or memorandum of association (including its articles of association) must be legalised by the Minister of Law and Human Rights (Article 11).

[70] S Margono, *Kompendium Hukum Yayasan* (Badan Pembinaan Hukum Nasional Kementerian Hukum dan Hak Asasi Manusia RI, 2012) 10-11 www.bphn.go.id/data/documents/komp_2012_yayasan.pdf (accessed 15 March 2020).

[71] District Court of South Jakarta Decision 904/Pdt.G/2007/PN.Jak.Sel (27 March 2008); affd High Court of Jakarta Decision 465/PDT/2008/PT.DKI (19 February 2009); affd Supreme Court Decision 2896 K/Pdt/2009 (28 October 2010).

Thereafter, the deed of establishment is published in a Supplement to the Official Gazette by the Minister of Law and Human Rights (Article 24). All foundations established prior to the Foundation Act must revise and legalise their articles of association in accordance with the Foundation Act.

Foundations are established to achieve certain social, religion, and humanitarian purposes (Article 1, No 1 of the Foundation Act 2001) and are not allowed to share their profit with their founders or executives (Article 3, paragraph (2)). A foundation is allowed to invest a maximum of 25 per cent of its assets in its own or other parties' businesses (Article 7), but the profit gained from the businesses shall be returned to the foundation only. The Foundation Act implements principles of transparency and accountability by requiring foundations to have supervisors who are independent of its patrons and executives. Patrons include the founder and executives of the foundation. Supervisors constitute a separate organ of a foundations with different statutory obligations from the patrons (Chapter VI of the Act).

Foreigners alone or foreigners in cooperation with Indonesians, being natural or legal persons, are allowed to establish foundations in Indonesia by following the requirements in Government Regulation No 63 of 2008 as amended by Government Regulation No 2 of 2013 concerning implementation of the Foundation Act.

Besides providing new rules for the foundations and their organs, the Foundation Act 2001 also provides new rules as to the court's jurisdiction over foundations and the parties involved. Article 1, No 2 stipulates that the competent court is the court in the district in which the foundation has its legal seat. Basically, this court has jurisdiction over foundations and their organs. For instance, the court in the district of the foundation's seat, has jurisdiction to overturn the patron's appointment and oversee the termination or replacement of the foundation's executives and supervisors based on a request brought by interested parties or by a public prosecutor representing the public interest (Articles 34 and 46). The court also has jurisdiction to dissolve a foundation on grounds of public policy and morality, insolvency, or bankruptcy (Article 62). However, the court does not have jurisdiction over disputes between foundations and their executives (Article 36), because an executive cannot bring a lawsuit against the foundation that he or she legally represents. In dispute among patrons, executives and supervisors of a foundation, the court that has jurisdiction is the court in the district of the foundation's legal seat, because the dispute concerns internal matters within the foundation. In the case of a dispute between foreigners and their Indonesian partners concerning their foundation established in Indonesia, the court that has jurisdiction *in personam* is the court in the district of the foundation's legal seat. The same principle applies to a dispute between foreigners who establish a foundation in Indonesia without Indonesian partners. Different rules of jurisdiction apply when a dispute arises from a transaction between the foundation and third parties. An example would be where a foundation invests in another company or one of the foundation's businesses makes a loan to another party. In such cases, the rules and principles in the Articles 118 HIR, 99 Rv, and 100 Rv apply to determine which court has jurisdiction *in personam*. If the foundation is the defendant in the dispute, based on the principle of *actor sequitur forum rei*, the court that has jurisdiction is the court in the district of the foundation's legal seat. Otherwise, the court that has jurisdiction is the court in the district of the other party's legal seat or residence. Article 100 Rv applies if the defendant in a transactional dispute is a foreigner, whether a natural or legal person, that does have a residence or legal seat in

Indonesia. In such an instance, the court that has jurisdiction over the dispute is the court in the district of the plaintiff (the foundation).

In summary, under the Foundation Act 2001/2004, the court that has jurisdiction over a case relating to internal matters within a foundation, such as disputes among the foundation's organs and patrons, is the court in the district of the foundation's legal seat. For cases or disputes involving transactions with third parties, the court that has jurisdiction is the court specified in Articles 118 HIR, 99 Rv, or 100 Rv.

ii. Law of Property

a. Immovable Property

Based on Article 118, paragraph (3) HIR and Article 99, paragraph (8) Rv, the court having jurisdiction to determine the title or right to immovable property is the court in the district in which the immovable property is located. These provisions are the consequence of the *forum rei sitae* principle.[72] For cases that combine an action in *rem* and an action *in personam* in relation to immovable property, such as a lawsuit for the division of marital property that is immovable, the court that has jurisdiction is the court in the district where the immovable property is situated or where the defendant resides at the plaintiff's choice (Article 102 Rv). The same provisions apply to govern the jurisdiction of Indonesian courts in immovable property with foreign elements.

b. Intangible Property

Unlike movable and immovable property, Indonesian civil procedure codes do not have specific provisions concerning court jurisdiction over intangible property. Therefore, the rules to determine jurisdiction in intangible property cases follow the principles of jurisdiction over movable and immovable property. If the intangible property is related to immovable property (for instance, a land mortgage and hypothec),[73] Article 118, paragraph (3) HIR and Article 99, paragraph (8) Rv apply. The court with jurisdiction is the court in the district in which the related immovable property is located. This rule is recognised in the Mortgage on Land and Its Related Objects Act 1996. If the intangible property is not related to immovable property (for instance, security interests over movable property[74] and rights over shares or commercial instruments, Article 118, paragraph (1) HIR and Article 99, paragraph (1) and (2) Rv apply. They provide that the court that has jurisdiction is the court in the district in which the defendant's residence is situated or where the defendant actually lives. An Indonesian court will have jurisdiction over intangible property based on the principal of *actor sequitur forum rei*. A foreign claimant may start an action in respect of intangible property that is unrelated to immovables before the court in the district in which the defendant has a residence or actually lives. If there are multiple defendants, the claimant

[72] Harahap, *Hukum Acara* (n 2) 199.

[73] Land mortgage is governed under the Mortgage on Land Act and Its Related Objects 1996. Hypothec on all immovable properties, but land is governed under Articles 1162–1232 BW.

[74] Security interests on movable properties are governed in Articles 1150–1160 BW concerning lien and the Fiduciary Act 1999.

may choose the court of the district in which one of the defendants resides (Article 118, paragraph (2) and Article 99, paragraph (6)).

c. Succession to Property

Under Article 99, paragraph (12) Rv and Article 23 BW, the court that has jurisdiction over succession to property is the court in the district of the deceased's last residence. The court's jurisdiction covers succession to property, whether immovable or movable, tangible or intangible. After the enactment of Act No 3 of 2006 concerning amendment of the 1989 Religious Court Act (the Amendment of the 1989 Religious Court Act), the court that has jurisdiction over succession to property where the deceased was a Muslim, is the religious court in the district in which the deceased last resided. Otherwise, the court that has jurisdiction is the district court in the district where the deceased last resided.[75]

Indonesian Civil Procedure Codes are silent on the issue of court jurisdiction in succession to property when the deceased's last residence and deathplace are outside Indonesia. The last residence of the deceased stipulated in Article 99, paragraph (12) Rv and Article 23 BW refers to the deceased's residence in Indonesia, not overseas. Therefore, in the case of succession to the property of a deceased person who did not reside in Indonesia at death, the court that has jurisdiction is the court in the district where the deceased resided prior to leaving Indonesia. There are no published court judgments on this particular matter. The latter conclusion is instead based on the provisions in Article 7 Rv and Article 467 BW. Article 7 Rv stipulates that any notice and claims in respect of the deceased must be brought to the last residence of the deceased. Furthermore, Article 467 BW gives jurisdiction over succession to the property of a missing person to the court in the district of last residence before the person went missing and presumed to have died. The foregoing provisions in the Rv and BW indicate that jurisdiction over succession to property is to be exercised by the court in the district of Indonesia where the deceased last resided. This principle applies where a person has emigrated to or became a citizen of another country or is missing and presumed dead.

iii. Intellectual Property

Indonesian intellectual property law does not have specific provisions on jurisdiction in intellectual property matters whether or not it involves foreign elements. Therefore, intellectual property law adheres to the normal principles of civil procedure, in particular, the principle of *actor sequitur forum rei*. This principle is stipulated in Article 118, paragraph (1) HIR and Article 99, paragraphs (1) and (2) Rv, which provide that an Indonesian court that has *in personam* jurisdiction is the court in which the defendant's residence is situated or where the defendant actually lives. Thus, an Indonesian court will have jurisdiction over an intellectual property matter based on the defendant's residence (*forum rei*) and a foreign claimant may bring an intellectual property dispute to an Indonesian court in the district

[75] District Court is also called the State Court (*Pengadilan Negeri*) that exercises general subject matter jurisdiction in civil and criminal cases (Article 50 of Act No 2 of 1986 concerning Courts of General Jurisdiction (the Courts of General Jurisdiction Act 1986)).

in which the defendant resides or lives. In the case that there are multiple defendants, the claimant may choose the district court in the place where one of the defendants resides (Article 118, paragraph (2) HIR and Article 99, paragraph (6) Rv). As a consequence of their asserting jurisdiction based on the defendant's residence, Indonesian courts have jurisdiction over legal persons when they have places of business in Indonesia. In Indonesian doctrine, the entity's place of business is regarded as the entity's residence.[76]

Article 118, paragraph (1), (2) HIR and Article 99, paragraph (1), (2), (6) Rv do not require the claim to arise in Indonesia for Indonesian courts to assert jurisdiction. Therefore, Article 100 Rv allows an Indonesian court to exercise jurisdiction over a foreigner, either a natural or legal person, who does not stay or have a residence in Indonesia, if the latter has an obligation to an Indonesian claimant that has arisen in Indonesia or elsewhere. In the case of intellectual property, a foreign national who does not stay or have a residence in Indonesia can be sued before an Indonesian court for contractual or non-contractual obligations relating to intellectual property owed to an Indonesian citizen. To limit this wide-reaching jurisdiction over out-of-state defendants, it must be proven that the foreign defendants owe obligations to Indonesian claimants. In addition, the parties shall not have made a choice of forum agreement that designates a court or forum other than an Indonesian court. There is no distinction between registered and unregistered intellectual property for the implementation of Articles 118 HIR, 99 and 100 Rv. These articles apply to parties involved in all cases of intellectual property, whether requiring or not requiring registration, namely patents, trademarks, geographical indications, industrial designs, layout designs of integrated circuits, plant variety, copyright, and trade secrets. Although Indonesia adopts the civil law tradition and recognises *lis alibi pendens* as stipulated in Article 134 Rv, the principle only applies to domestic proceedings and does not extend to foreign proceedings. Indonesian courts maintain jurisdiction over parties in intellectual property disputes, even though the disputes are being litigated in foreign courts. In practice, Indonesian courts adjudicate on cases that are pending in other foreign courts.[77]

In summary, in intellectual property matters, the *in personam* jurisdiction of an Indonesian court is governed by Articles 118 HIR, 99 and 100 Rv. Articles 118 HIR and 99 Rv basically apply the *actor sequitur forum rei* principle. If the jurisdiction requirements of Articles 118 HIR, 99 and 100 Rv are met, the Indonesian court will always have jurisdiction even though the dispute is pending in a foreign court. The *lis alibi pendens* principle in Article 134 Rv only applies to domestic proceedings.

iv. Family Law

a. Marriage

The rules to determine jurisdiction over matters of marriage are found in the Marriage Act 1974, the Marriage Regulation 1975, and Act No 7 of 1989 as amended by Act No 3 of 2006 as amended by Act No 50 of 2009 concerning religious judicature (the Religious

[76] Supancana, *Naskah Akademik* (n 3) 47–49.

[77] For example, in the case of District Court of South Jakarta Decision 210/Pdt/G/1992/PN.JKT.Sel (not published), Indonesian judges in the Jakarta court kept processing a custody dispute between an Indonesian husband and a German wife, although a German court had already processed the same custody dispute and issued a provisional ruling earlier. See also Supancana, *Naskah Akademik* (n 3) 50.

Judicature Act 1989 as amended in 2006 and 2009). In general, the courts that have jurisdiction *in personam* over marriages are the district and religious courts and their respective appellate courts. District courts, High Courts, and the Supreme Court have jurisdiction over the parties who contract marriages based on religions other than Islam. Religious courts, Religious High Courts, and the Supreme Court have jurisdiction over parties who perform their marriages based on Islamic law. Besides having jurisdiction over matrimonial causes as will be discussed in the next chapter, the courts also have jurisdiction over pre-matrimonial causes, which essentially relate to permissions for or prohibitions against marriage. For instance, pursuant to Article 6 of the Marriage Act 1974, a written parental consent or (if not available) a written consent from a family member of direct parental lineage, a guardian, or a caregiver, is required for an adult under 21 years old to marry. If one fails to obtain the requisite consent, one can file an application for marriage to the court in one's district of residence. The court may issue a ruling of marriage permission after hearing the applicant and relevant parties (for example, the parents or surviving parent, a family member, or a guardian) (Article 6, paragraph (5) of the Marriage Act 1974). The district courts have jurisdiction over this matter, if the applicants are not Muslim. The religious courts have jurisdiction, if the applicants are Muslim (Article 49 of the Religious Judicature Act 1989 as amended in 2006 and 2009). A written parental or familial consent is also required by a foreign national under 21 years old who intends to marry an Indonesian national in Indonesia (Article 59 of the Marriage Act 1974). In case the foreigner fails to obtain a written parental or familial consent, the foreigner may file an application for marriage in the court of the district in which he or she resides in Indonesia to obtain a ruling of marriage permission.

In the case of an Islamic marriage, the law requires a Muslim bride to obtain the consent of her father or (if he is not available) her male relatives on the patrilineal side (*wali* or guardian) (Part 3 of Chapter IV Compilation of Islamic Law). If the bride cannot obtain such consent, she can request a religious court to issue a ruling appointing a *qadi* to give consent and to marry her to the groom in a wedding ceremony (Article 23, paragraph (2) of Compilation of Islamic Law). A *qadi* is an official appointed by the government to function as a *wali* (guardian) for a Muslim bride, in addition to other functions under the Compilation of Islamic Law. Although not expressly stated in Indonesian marriage law, a religious court in Indonesia will have jurisdiction over a foreign bride performing an Islamic marriage in Indonesia who cannot obtain the consent of her father or male relatives. The religious court can appoint a *qadi* to act as *wali* for her marriage. The competent religious court is the one in the district in which she stays in Indonesia.

The Indonesian courts also have jurisdiction over polygamous marriages, whether non-Islamic or Islamic. The General Elucidation of the Marriage Act 1974 writes that:

> The Act adheres to the principle of monogamy. Only if desired by the parties, because their law and religion permit, a husband can marry more than one wife. However, the marriage of a husband with more than one wife, although desired by the parties, shall be allowed only if it meets certain conditions and is decreed by the court.

Indonesian courts accordingly have jurisdiction to issue rulings to allow polygamous marriages provided that the requirements for such marriages are met. The district courts have jurisdiction over polygamous marriages, if the applicants are not Muslim. The religious courts have jurisdiction if the applicants are Muslim. The courts also have jurisdiction over polygamous marriages contracted by foreign nationals in Indonesia. Pursuant to the principle of *locus regit actum* of Article 18 AB, a foreigner, irrespective of nationality and domicile, who has capacity to enter into polygamous marriage in Indonesia must comply with all formal requirements of polygamous marriage in Indonesia, including obtaining a court ruling that allows him to marry more than one wife (Article 4 of the Marriage Act 1974 and Article 41 of the Marriage Regulation 1975). If the court denies the foreigner's application for polygamous marriage, the marriage cannot be performed. The court ruling is mandatory for polygamous marriages in Indonesia. A Certificate of No Impediment to Marriage issued by the foreigner's embassy in Indonesia is not a valid substitute for such a ruling. The court having jurisdiction over the matter is that in the district where the foreign national resides in Indonesia.

Finally, Indonesian district courts have jurisdiction over inter-faith marriages, either contracted by Indonesian or mixed Indonesian and non-Indonesian couples in Indonesia. Since some religions (for example, Islam) do not allow believers to marry those who do not embrace the same religion, adherents to such religions who wish to enter into inter-faith marriages must first obtain a court ruling permitting them to marry a person of a different faith. The court having jurisdiction over this matter is the district courts in the places of the intended marriage. The jurisdiction of district courts over inter-faith marriages is not governed by the Marriage Act 1974, the Marriage Regulation 1975, or the Religious Judicature Act 1989 as amended, but is governed by the Elucidation of Article 35.a. of the Population Administration Act 2006 as amended in 2013.

In conclusion, the jurisdiction of Indonesian courts over pre-matrimonial causes essentially concerns permissions for or prohibitions against marriages. In general, the courts that have jurisdiction over pre-matrimonial causes are the district and religious courts and their respective appellate courts. District courts have jurisdiction over the parties who will perform their marriages based on religions other than Islam. Religious courts have jurisdiction over the parties who will perform their marriages based on Islamic law. Applications for court rulings on permission to marry must be filed by applicants in the district or religious courts of their residence. Where the applicants are foreign nationals, the applications are to be filed in the relevant courts in the districts in which they reside.

b. Divorce, Nullity and Separation

The rules to determine jurisdiction over marital disputes are in the Marriage Act 1974, the Marriage Regulation 1975, and the Religious Judicature Act. The principles of court jurisdiction in those legislations and regulation are similar to those in the civil procedure codes (HIR, Rbg, and Rv). Marital disputes can result in divorce, nullity or separation. The parties in marital disputes may be mixed marriage couples, foreign couples having their domicile in Indonesia, or Indonesian couples having their domicile outside Indonesia.

Regarding divorce, Article 39, paragraph (1), Article 40, paragraph (1) of the Marriage Act 1974 and Article 65 of the Religious Judicature Act 1989 provide that divorce can only be obtained before a court following an unsuccessful attempt to conciliate the spouses. These provisions abolish the traditional *talaq* divorce which was commonly invoked by Indonesian Muslim husbands before the enactment of the Marriage Act 1974. In those cases, husbands would divorce their wives without need for court proceedings and without need to give reasons, simply by pronouncing *talaq* (repudiation) directly to their wives.[78]

Article 63 of the Marriage Act 1974 and Article 1 of the Marriage Regulation 1975 govern which courts have jurisdiction over marital disputes in Indonesia. Pursuant to those Articles, the courts that have jurisdiction over marital disputes, including divorce, are the district and religious courts. District courts have jurisdiction over parties who contract marriage based on non-Islamic religious rites. Religious courts have jurisdiction over the parties who contracted marriage pursuant to Islamic law. The Religious Judicature Act 1989 sets out the divorce procedure in religious courts. In addition, the Compilation of Islamic Law that was implemented based on Presidential Instruction No 1 of 1991, specifies divorce procedures similar to those in the Religious Judicature Act 1989.

Apart from Indonesian couples, mixed-marriage couples in Indonesia and foreign couples domiciled in Indonesia can file divorce petitions in district and religious courts The courts have jurisdiction not only over Indonesian nationals, but also over foreign nationals having a domicile in Indonesia. As discussed in section 4.4. on *Renvoi* and transmission, after independence, it was an established practice for Indonesian courts to exercise jurisdiction over divorces of foreign couples domiciled in Indonesia. In Case No 2640 K/Pdt/2009, the Supreme Court affirmed the jurisdiction of the South Jakarta District Court over the divorce of an American couple because both American spouses resided in the South Jakarta district. This principle was adopted by the Bali District Court in Case No 172/Pdt.G/2014/PN.Dps in which the Court exercised jurisdiction over the divorce of a South African couple because both South African spouses resided in Bali. In 1987 the South Jakarta District Court exercised jurisdiction over the divorce of an English husband and an Indonesian wife with British nationality, because the couple were domiciled in Indonesia.[79]

Parties, whether Indonesian or foreign nationals, are to submit their divorce petitions in accordance with certain rules. A Muslim husband who wishes to divorce his wife by *talaq* must file a request to that effect in the religious court in the respondent's residence. This is supposed to be done unless the respondent has moved out from the couple's shared residence without the petitioner's consent (Article 66, paragraphs (1) and (2) of the Religious Judicature Act 1989). However, the latter condition (namely, that the respondent (wife) has not left the couple's shared residence without her husband's consent) does not appear in the Compilation of Islamic Law. Article 129 of the Compilation of Islamic Law simply provides that the husband's request for a *talaq* divorce should be filed, either orally or in writing, in the religious court in the district of his wife's residence, along with the reason for the *talaq* divorce. Thus, it is submitted that the court having jurisdiction over the *talaq* divorce should now always be the court in the district of the respondent's residence, although the respondent wife has moved out from the couple's shared residence without the husband's consent. This would be in line with the general principle of *actor sequitur forum rei*. But it should be noted that the Compilation of Islamic Law is neither legislation nor regulation.

[78] C Subijakto, 'Tinjauan tentang Talak Setelah Berlakunya Undang-undang Nomor 1 Tahun 1974' (Undergraduate thesis, Universitas Airlangga, 1989) 27.

[79] District Court of South Jakarta Decision 112/Pdt.G/1987 (not published); see S Gautama and H Wiknjosastro, 'Some Aspects of Indonesian Private International Law' (1990) 32 *Malaya Law Review* 428 www.jstor.org/stable/24865645 (accessed 26 May 2018).

By the Preamble to Presidential Instruction No 1 of 1991, the objective of the Compilation of Islamic Law is to provide guidance in matters of Islamic marriage law, inheritance law, and *waqaf* (religious foundation). Therefore, it is up to the religious court that deals with the *talaq* divorce to decide whether to apply Article 66, paragraphs (1) and (2) of the Religious Judicature Act 1989 or Article 129 of the Compilation of Islamic Law to determine jurisdiction where the wife has moved out from the couple's shared residence without the husband's consent. A Muslim wife, whether Indonesian or foreign national, who wishes to divorce her husband is to file her petition in the religious court of the district of her residence, unless she has moved out from the couple's shared residence without her husband's consent (Article 73, paragraph (1) of the Religious Judicature Act 1989 and Article 132, paragraph (1) of the Compilation of Islamic Law). The consequence is that, when a wife has moved out from her shared residence with her husband without his consent, the principle of *actor sequitur forum rei* determines the court that has jurisdiction over her divorce. The petition should then be filed in the district court of the place where the husband resides.

Concerning jurisdiction over couples that were married under religions other than Islam, Article 20 of the Marriage Regulation 1975 and the Elucidation thereof stipulate that a petitioner, whether husband or wife, shall file the divorce petition in the district court of the respondent's residence. This provision applies to Indonesian couples and foreign couples having domiciled in Indonesia. Article 20 of the Marriage Regulation 1975 is in line with the principle of *actor sequitur forum rei*. In general, the rules in the Marriage Regulation 1975 concerning the jurisdiction of district courts over divorce are the same as the general rules of the Indonesian civil procedure codes (Articles 118 HIR and 99 Rv). So where the residence of the respondent is unknown, the respondent's place of living cannot be found, or the respondent's residence is outside Indonesia, the court that has jurisdiction over the divorce would be that in the district of the petitioner's residence (Article 20, paragraphs (2) and (3) of the Marriage Regulation 1975 and Article 66, paragraph (3) of the Religious Judicature Act 1989). These provisions can be applied to both Indonesian and foreign respondents. The Indonesian civil procedure codes, the Marriage Regulation 1975 and the Religious Judicature Act all apply the same principle, by which the court having jurisdiction over a defendant or a respondent outside Indonesia will always be the court in the district of the plaintiff's or petitioner's residence.

If Indonesian or mixed marriage couples domiciled outside Indonesia wish to divorce, there are different rules to determine the court having jurisdiction over their divorce. Article 41 of the Population Administration Act 2006 as amended in 2013 recognises divorce decrees obtained by Indonesian citizens from foreign courts and requires the divorce decrees from foreign courts to be registered in the civil registry offices in the cities of their residence in Indonesia within 30 days of their return to Indonesia. Based on this provision and as will be discussed later in Chapter 4, section I.B.iv.b on decrees of divorce, nullity and separation, where an Indonesian or mixed marriage couple is domiciled outside Indonesia, a petition may be filed in a foreign court, as long as both spouses agree with that court exercising jurisdiction over their divorce. A divorce petition can only be filed in an Indonesian court if one spouse refuses to submit to the jurisdiction of the foreign court.

Regarding an Indonesian Muslim or Muslim mixed marriage couple domiciled outside Indonesia who wish to divorce, they can file a divorce petition only in an Indonesian religious court, although both husband and wife agree to the jurisdiction of foreign courts. This different rule for Muslims is based on Article 66, paragraph (4) and Article 73, paragraph (3) of the Religious Judicature Act 1989. The Articles, which were written specifically for Muslim couples, provide that if the petitioner and respondent are domiciled outside Indonesia, the divorce petition should be filed in the court in the district in which the couple registered their marriage or in the Central Jakarta Religious Court. However, there are judges in the religious courts who have suggested that divorce decrees obtained by Muslim couples from foreign courts can be recognised and registered in Indonesia. There would then be no need for the couples to make a second petition to the Indonesia courts.[80] This would apply, however, only if both husband and wife agree on the jurisdiction of a foreign court over their divorce and the grounds for their divorce abroad are applicable under Indonesian law.

The practice of recognising foreign divorce judgment, despite the provisions of the Religious Judicature Act 1989 is premised on the doctrine of *lex posterior derogat legi priori* and the doctrine that categorises a divorce decree as a constitutive judgment. Those that adopt the doctrine of *lex posterior derogat legi priori* (a later law repeals an earlier law) assert that Article 41 of the Population Administration Act 2006 as amended in 2013 supersedes Article 66 paragraph (4) and Article 73 paragraph (3) of Religious Judicature Act 1989. Therefore the divorce of an Indonesian Muslim couple abroad should be recognised, although not decreed by a religious court in Indonesia.[81] The doctrine that categorises foreign divorce decrees as constitutive judgments posits that, because divorce decrees are not intended to condemn or punish parties, but only to create a new legal status, the decrees are constitutive in nature. Therefore, divorce decrees are outside the scope of Article 436 Rv that prohibits the enforcement of foreign condemnatory judgments in Indonesia.[82]

Pursuant to Article 39, paragraph (2) of the Marriage Act 1974, religious and district courts will exercise jurisdiction only if the divorce is based on sufficient grounds. Sufficient grounds for divorce are also required for *talaq* divorces and for petitions filed by foreigners in Indonesia as well by Indonesians in foreign courts. The valid grounds for divorce are listed in Article 19 of the Marriage Regulation 1975 as follows:

(1) one of the spouses commits adultery, is an alcoholic, drug addict, a gambler or exhibits other vices which are difficult to cure; or
(2) one of the spouses has left the other spouse for two consecutive years, without consent and without legitimate reasons or for the reasons beyond the couple's control; or
(3) one of the spouses has been sentenced to imprisonment for five consecutive years or a longer period of time; or
(4) one of the spouses has resorted to cruelty or severe ill treatment, endangering the life of the other spouse; or
(5) one of the spouses has developed a disability or disease, preventing him or her from fulfilling the duties of husband or wife; or
(6) the couple have irreconcilable differences.

[80] This opinion was given by Justice Tamah, a judge at the South Jakarta Religious Court during an interview with Astrid Pratiwi for her thesis. See A Pratiwi, 'Aspek-aspek Hukum Acara Perdata Internasional dalam Perceraian di Indonesia' (Undergraduate thesis, Universitas Indonesia, 2011) 118, 119; The same opinion was also presented by Justice Mohamad Thoha, a judge at the Ponorogo Religious Court in his writing titled: Hukum Perceraian di luar negeri, on http://pa-ponorogo.net. His writing was generated on 12 September 2008, but is no longer accessible online.

[81] M Yasmin, 'Akibat Perkawinan Campuran Terhadap Anak dan Harta Benda yang Diperoleh Sebelum dan Sesudah Perkawinan (Studi Banding Indonesia-Malaysia)' (Undergraduate thesis, Universitas Indonesia, 2011) 21, 23.

[82] Pratiwi 'Aspek-aspek Hukum' (n 80) 75–78.

For Muslim spouses, there are two other valid grounds for divorce, namely:

(1) the respondent renounces Islam; or
(2) the husband breaks his *taklik talak* (Islamic nuptial agreement).
(Article 116 of the Compilation of Islamic Law).

The general rules and principles of court jurisdiction over divorce that are regulated under the Marriage Act 1974, the Marriage Regulation Act 1975, the Religious Judicature Act, and Compilation of Islamic Law, are the same as the general rule in the Indonesian civil procedure codes. In fact, Article 54 of the Religious Judicature Act 1989 provides that the procedure law applicable to religious courts is the civil procedure codes applicable to district courts, save for procedures that are specifically governed by the Religious Judicature Act. The rules concerning court jurisdiction over the divorce of Indonesian couples having their domicile outside Indonesia may be different for non-Muslim and Muslim spouses, although later developments suggest that there may ultimately be no difference between the rules of jurisdiction over divorces of non-Muslim and Muslim spouses living abroad.

Regarding nullity of marriage, which is a declaration that a marriage is null or never existed, Article 37 of the Marriage Regulation 1975 stipulates that '[n]ullity of marriage can be declared solely by court of law'. No other institution has jurisdiction to annul a marriage (Elucidation of Article 37 of the Marriage Regulation 1975). In Indonesian law, there is no distinction between nullity and the annulment of marriages. Indonesian law uses the word *pembatalan perkawinan* that literally means 'cancellation of marriage', because the marriage was either void from the start or is voidable. The declaration of cancellation of a marriage by a court has no effect on children born as the result of the marriage and third parties acting in good faith who obtained rights before the declaration of cancellation of the marriage (Article 28, paragraph (2) of the Marriage Act 1974 and Article 75 of the Compilation of Islamic Law). Prior to the Compilation of Islamic Law by Presidential Instruction No 1 of 1991, all petitions for nullity had to be filed in the district court of the place of marriage or in the district court of the residence of the couple or either spouse (Article 25 of the Marriage Act 1974 and Article 38 of the Marriage Regulation 1975). But after the Compilation of Islamic Law, the latter two provisions are now only applied to annul non-Muslim marriages. For a marriage performed under Islamic law, the petition for nullity must be filed in the religious court of the place of the marriage or of residence of either spouse (Article 74 of the Compilation of Islamic Law). As such, the courts that have jurisdiction over nullity of marriage after the implementation of the Compilation of Islamic Law, become the district and religious courts.

The claimants in nullity of marriage are not only the husband and the wife, but also their families of direct parental lineage (their mother, father, grand-mother, grand-father, and so on), and other parties who have an interest in the nullity (Article 23 of the Marriage Act 1974 and Article 73 of the Compilation of Islamic Law). Applicants can be either Indonesian or foreign nationals. This is based on the general principle of Indonesian civil procedure law that allows foreign nationals to bring a claim in Indonesia. Theoretically, as in divorce, the Indonesian court should be able to exercise jurisdiction in respect of the nullity of a marriage in which both spouses are foreign nationals domiciled in Indonesia, provided the grounds for nullity are known in Indonesian law. However, to date, in Indonesia there have been no court judgments on the nullity of a marriage in which both spouses are foreigners.

But there are some court judgments on the nullity of mixed marriages between Indonesians and foreigners.

For example, in *Ludwig Franz Willibald Maria Josepf Leonhard Erbgraf von Waldburg-Wolfegg-Waldsee v Yesisca Iskandar*, Ludwig, Hereditary Prince of Waldburg-Wolfegg and Waldsee (mediatised),[83] filed a petition for nullity of his marriage to Ms Iskandar, an Indonesian actress, in the South Jakarta District Court in October 2014. Prince Ludwig resided in Germany when filing his petition for marriage nullity. Ms Iskandar lived in South Jakarta. Pursuant to Article 25 of the Marriage Act 1974, the South Jakarta District Court exercised jurisdiction over the petition for nullity because the wife's residence was in the South Jakarta district, their marriage had been solemnised in a church in South Jakarta, and the marriage was registered in a civil registry office in South Jakarta. The South Jakarta District Court decided in favour of Prince Ludwig and nullified his marriage to Ms Iskandar. Pursuant to Article 22 of the Marriage Act 1974 that provides that a marriage is voidable if the parties do not comply with marriage requirements, the court found that the marriage between Prince Ludwig and Ms Iskandar did not comply with the requirement of Article 2, paragraph (1) of the Marriage Act 1974. The Article stipulates: 'A marriage is lawful if performed in accordance with the rules of religion and belief of each party.' During the court proceedings, the Court found that their marriage had not been solemnised by an authorised Christian priest of the Church *Yesus Sejati* in South Jakarta. Therefore, their marriage had not been performed in accordance with their Christian religion. Accordingly, it was null under Article 2, paragraph (1) of the Marriage Act 1974. Besides that, the Court found that the Marriage Letter of Statement No 081/SKP/VII/2013 dated 11 December 2013 issued by the Church *Yesus Sejati* had been forged. Therefore, Marriage Certificate No 05/AI/2014 dated 8 January 2014 that was issued by the South Jakarta civil registry office was invalid, as it had been based on the forged church document. The nullification was regardless of a child having been born to the couple after marriage.

Another court judgment on the nullity of a mixed marriage was Case No 324/Pdt.G/2006/PA.Dpk dated 13 December 2006. This was between Elisa binti Udin Saragih (petitioner) and Darren Andrew Fourancre and Nia Erna Susanti (respondents). Ms Saragih, an Indonesian domiciled in East Jakarta district, filed a petition for nullity in the Depok Religious Court. She claimed that she was the wife of Mr Fourancre, an Australian citizen, and Mr Fourancre had married Ms Susanti without her consent and court approval. In this case, the Depok Religious Court had jurisdiction over the parties because Ms Susanti and Mr Fourancre, the respondents, had a shared residence in Depok and had registered their marriage in the Office of Religious Affairs in Depok. The petitioner argued that the respondents' marriage without court approval violated Article 4 of the Marriage Act 1974, Chapter VIII of the Marriage Regulation 1975 and Article 56, paragraph (1) of the Compilation of Islamic Law requiring a husband to obtain court approval to marry more than one wife. Therefore, the respondents' Marriage Certificate No 537/63/VII/05 dated 26 July 2005 issued by the Depok Office of Religious Affairs should be declared invalid because it had been issued based on a

[83] A De Gotha, 'Mediatized House of Waldburg' (*the Almanach de Saxe Gotha*) www.almanachdegotha.org/id108.html (accessed 28 March 2020); P Thereoff, 'Waldburg' (9 December 2019) www.angelfire.com/realm/gotha/gotha/waldburg.html (accessed 28 March 2020).

forged document stating that Mr Fourancre was not married. The Depok Religious Court decided in favour of the petitioner and nullified the respondents' marriage.[84]

Indonesian religious and district courts will exercise their jurisdiction over the nullity of marriage, only if the petitioners have sufficient grounds to nullify the marriages. For example, suppose there was a lack of consent to the marriage because of duress, mistake, or misrepresentation on the part of one of the spouses. If six months later, the couple remain together, the court will refuse to exercise jurisdiction to nullify the marriage (Article 27 of the Marriage Act 1974 and Article 72, paragraph (3) of the Compilation of Islamic Law). The courts will also refuse to exercise jurisdiction if the families of the spouses do not have sufficient grounds in their petitions for the nullity. Sufficient grounds for families of the spouses to file petitions for nullity are that a marriage was not performed before an authorised authority, was not performed before a valid guardian (*wali nikah*) of the female spouse in an Islamic marriage, or was not witnessed by two witnesses (Article 26, paragraph (1) of the Marriage Act 1974). Further grounds for nullity of marriage based on Islam are stated in Articles 70 to 72 of the Compilation of Islamic Law.

Unlike the divorce between Indonesian or mixed marriage couples outside Indonesia that is governed by Article 41 of the Population Administration Act 2006 as amended in 2013 and by Article 66, paragraph (4) and Article 73, paragraph (3) of the Religious Judicature Act 1989, the nullity of marriage outside Indonesia is not dealt with in any Indonesian law. The Population Administration Act 2006 as amended in 2013 also does not have provisions concerning the registration of foreign nullity decrees. The Act only governs the registration of nullity decrees issued by Indonesian courts (Article 39). This fact suggests that only Indonesian courts have jurisdiction over the nullity of Indonesian or mixed marriages where the couples are domiciled outside Indonesia.

As discussed, the courts that have jurisdiction over nullity of marriage are religious courts for couples whose marriages were performed under Islamic law, and district courts for couples whose marriages were celebrated in accordance with the rites of another religion. Unlike with divorce, so far there have been no cases of foreign couples domiciled in Indonesia applying for the nullity of their marriage before the Indonesian court. Several mixed marriage couples have applied for nullity of marriage in Indonesian courts, even where the foreign spouses do not reside in Indonesia. Regarding Indonesian or mixed marriage couples domiciled outside Indonesia, there is no provision in Indonesian law that governs the nullity of couples' marriages. Therefore, only Indonesian courts have jurisdiction over the nullity of a marriage between Indonesians or mixed couples domiciled outside Indonesia, insofar as the relevant marriages have been registered in the marriage registry offices in Indonesia. If the couples nullify their marriages in foreign courts after having registered their marriages in Indonesia, the nullity of their marriages may not be recognised in Indonesia because the civil registry offices in Indonesia only registers nullity decrees issued by Indonesian courts.

Legal separation no longer exists in the Indonesian legal system following the enactment of the Marriage Act 1974. The Marriage Act 1974 supersedes the previous marriage law of the Indonesian Civil Code (BW) recognising legal separation. The Population

[84] Not published. See also R Alfianti, 'Pembatalan Perkawinan Poligami Beda Kewarganegaraan Tanpa Izin Isteri Disertai Dengan Pemalsuan Identitas (Studi Kasus Putusan Pengadilan Agama Depok Nomor 324/Pdt.G/2006/PA.Dpk)' (Master thesis, Universitas Indonesia, 2011) 60–70.

Administration Act 2006 as amended in 2013 also does not govern the registration of legal separation in the Indonesian Civil Registry. That means Indonesian courts will refuse to exercise jurisdiction over matters of legal separation because it no longer exists in the Indonesian legal system.

c. Matters Relating to the Well-being of the Child

Article 1, No 1 of Act No 23 of 2002 as amended by Act No 35 of 2014 concerning child protection (the Child Protection Act 2002 as amended in 2014), defines a 'child' as a person under the age of 18 years old and includes an unborn child. Article 26, paragraph (1) of the Child Protection Act 2002 as amended in 2014, governs the responsibility of parents to care for, maintain, educate and protect their children; to ensure the growth and development of their children in accordance with their capabilities, talents and interests; and to prevent under-age marriage. The responsibility of parents stipulated in this provision is also referred to as 'parental authority'. Pursuant to Article 30 of the same Act, parental authority may be revoked by a court, if one or both of the parents neglect their responsibilities. The court may grant parental authority to one of the parents or to one of the children's blood relatives or may transfer the authority to an individual or organisation that will act as guardian (*wali*) (Article 31). The revocation of parental authority because of the neglect of parental responsibility is also governed by Article 49 of the Marriage Act 1974. The revocation of parental authority does not abolish parents' obligation to provide maintenance for their children (Article 49, paragraph (2)).

In the case of marital disputes between parents, Article 14, paragraph (2) of the Child Protection Act 2002 as amended in 2014 stipulates that:

> If the separation of the child from his parents mentioned in paragraph (1) occurs, the child is always entitled to:
>
> a. meet directly and maintain continuous contact with both of his parents;
> b. be cared, raised, educated and protected by both of his parents;
> c. receive maintenance from both of his parents; and
> d. receive other child rights.

The Elucidation of Article 14 of the Act explains that a child's separation from parents is a consequence, among other matters, of divorce. Article 41 of the Marriage Act 1974 further states:

> The consequences of divorce are as follows:
>
> a. Both the mother and father remain responsible for the sustenance and education of their children. In a dispute concerning custody of the children, the court shall decide the matter;
> b. The father is responsible for all expenses of the children's sustenance and education. If the father is in fact unable to fulfil his obligations, the court may decide that the mother shall share in such responsibility.

Article 105 of the Compilation of Islamic Law also provides:

> In the case of divorce:
>
> a. The mother has custody of a child who is not yet *mumayyiz* or has not attained the age of twelve years old;

b. A child who has attained the age of twelve years old may choose who between his parents, will have custody right to him;
c. The father is responsible for the maintenance of the children.

In the case that children are born in a mixed marriage, Article 29, paragraph (2) of the Child Protection Act 2002 as amended in 2014 stipulates that, 'In the case of the divorce of a mixed marriage couple, their children shall be entitled to choose to, or may be ordered by the court to be under the custodianship of their mother or their father.'

Thus, the well-being of children in the case of marital disputes or the dissolution of marriages due to divorce typically concerns the maintenance (child support) and custody of children. Under Indonesian law, both the father and mother maintain parental authority, including to raise, educate, protect and guard the property of their children, even though divorced (Article 14, paragraph (2) of the Child Protection Act 2002 as amended in 2014). In principle, the father is responsible for the maintenance of children in the case of divorce. Only if the father is unable to fulfil his obligations, does the mother have a shared responsibility for child support (Article 41, paragraph (2) of the Marriage Act 1974 and Article 105 c. of the Compilation of Islamic Law). Since the issue of child maintenance is part of a divorce proceeding, the court that has jurisdiction over the maintenance of the children is the same court that exercises jurisdiction over divorce. The rules to determine the jurisdiction of court over divorce also apply to the maintenance of children and have been outlined in section I.B.iv.b on Divorce, Nullity and Separation.

If the father does not comply with a court order for child support or is unwilling to pay, the mother or the child's family may bring a civil suit against him. Indonesian scholars characterise alimony and child support as an obligation arising by operation of law.[85] Accordingly, the breach of alimony and child support is governed by the law of obligation. Pursuant to Articles 196 and 197 of the Revised Indonesian Code (HIR), the claimant can bring a civil lawsuit against the father in the court that issued the divorce decree and maintenance order. In other words, the court that has jurisdiction over child support is the court that issued the divorce decree. The abovementioned principle of court also applies to child custody as a result of the dissolution of marriage due to divorce. Since the issue of child custody is part of a divorce proceeding, the court that has jurisdiction over the child custody is the court that exercises jurisdiction over the divorce. Indonesian courts also have jurisdiction over maintenance and custody of children in the case of mixed marriage and foreign couples domiciled in Indonesia. The jurisdiction of Indonesian courts over such matters is premised on the habitual residence of a child in Indonesia and the protection of the best interest of the child. The 2015 Academic Paper of the Indonesian Private International Law Bill recommends that the child's habitual residence be used to determine the law applicable to matters pertaining to the welfare of the child.[86] Although the Academic Paper is silent on the court's jurisdiction over matters relating to the well-being of the child, in the author's opinion the habitual residence of the child can also be applied to determine the court's jurisdiction over such matters.

[85] TT Tutik, *Hukum Perdata Dalam Sistem Hukum Nasional* (Kencana, 2018) 239; Marilang, *Hukum Perikatan, Perikatan yang Lahir dari Perjanjian* (Indonesia Prime, 2017) 81.
[86] Supancana, *Naskah Akademik* (n 3) 213.

The use of habitual residence to determine jurisdiction in matters relating to the well-being of the child was apparent in *Purnima Ralhan v Jonathan I. Kine*. The parties were American citizens who were married in Philadelphia in 1997 and had lived in Jakarta since 2000. Their daughter, Lara Rose, was born in Jakarta in 2001 and had US citizenship. In September 2007, Ms Ralhan reported her husband to the Jakarta Police Office for domestic violence. In her report, she alleged that Mr Kine had assaulted her in front of their daughter and that the incident had caused deep trauma to the child. In addition, Ms Ralhan told the police that her husband had threatened her life. Following her report, Ms Ralhan requested the South Jakarta District Court to grant protection for her and her daughter from her husband's violence. Based on Articles 10, 28, and 29 of Act No 23 of 2004 concerning the elimination of domestic violence (the Elimination of Domestic Violence Act 2004), the Court ruled that police and other relevant institutions should provide protection to Ms Ralhan, her daughter and her parents who also lived in Jakarta. The Court temporarily revoked Mr Kine's parental authority over their daughter and granted the parental authority to Ms Ralhan and Lara's maternal grandparents. The Indonesian Supreme Court in extraordinary appeal affirmed the ruling.[87] Based on the Court ruling, in 2008 Ms Ralhan filed a petition for divorce in the South Jakarta District Court. In her divorce petition she asked the court to order her husband to pay Lara Rose's maintenance until the latter finished university. In his response to his wife claim, Mr Kine objected to the jurisdiction of the South Jakarta District Court, because the parties were foreign nationals and their marriage had been celebrated in the US. Mr Kine asked the Court to reinstate his parental authority over Lara Rose. The Court rejected Mr Kine's objection to jurisdiction and maintained that it was right to settle the parties' dispute in Indonesia. In the Court's opinion, it would take longer for the parties to settle their dispute if they had to return to the US as that would require them to obtain a bona fide residence in Philadelphia to file a suit in a court there. In its provisional judgment, the Court denied Mr Kine's objection to jurisdiction and decided to exercise its jurisdiction over Ms Ralhan's petition for divorce along with her application for Lara Rose's child support and custody.[88] Although the Court's provisional judgment did not mention the child's habitual residence as the reason of its jurisdiction, it was evident that the Court took into consideration the family's habitual residence in the South Jakarta district when exercising its jurisdiction over the case.

In summary, the court that has jurisdiction over matters relating to the well-being of the child in cases of marital dispute or dissolution of marriage due to divorce will be the same court that exercised jurisdiction over the divorce. This is because issues of child maintenance and custody are regarded as part of a divorce proceeding. The court also has jurisdiction over questions of the maintenance and custody of the children of mixed marriages and foreign marriages, where the parents are domiciled in Indonesia. The jurisdiction of Indonesian courts over the latter situations may be based on the habitual residence of the foreign child in Indonesia and the need to protect the best interests of the child.

[87] District Court of South Jakarta Decision 394/Pdt.P/2007 /PN.Jak.Sel (21 January 2008); affd Supreme Court Extraordinary Appeal 76PK/PDT/2009 (26 November 2009).

[88] District Court of South Jakarta Decision 47/Pdt.G/2008/PN.Jak.Sel (not published); affd High Court of Jakarta Decision 141/PDT/2009/PT. DKI (unpublished); affd Supreme Court Decision 2640 K/Pdt/2009 (unpublished).

v. Law of Corporations and Insolvency

By Act No 37 of 2004 concerning bankruptcy and the suspension of obligations for the payment of debts (the Bankruptcy and Suspension of Debt Payment Act 2004), corporate insolvency occurs after a declaration of bankruptcy by the commercial court. As a consequence of being declared bankrupt, a corporate debtor is to offer a composition plan to its creditors in a meeting mediated by a receiver appointed by the court. If the corporate debtor does not offer a composition plan or its composition plan is rejected by its creditors, the corporate debtor will enter insolvency. Elucidation of Article 57, paragraph (1) of the Act states: '"Insolvency" shall mean the condition of being unable to pay debts.' After the corporate debtor enters insolvency, the receiver starts the liquidation process under supervision of a judge (Article 178).

Pursuant to Article 2, paragraph (1) of the Bankruptcy and Suspension of Debt Payment Act 2004, a corporate debtor which has two or more creditors and does not repay in full at least one debt that is due and payable, can be declared bankrupt by the court. The Elucidation of Article 2, paragraph (1) explains that by 'a debt which is due and payable' is meant the obligation to pay a debt that is due under a contract, due by reason of acceleration, due by reason of a sanction imposed by a regulatory body, or due by reason of a court judgment or arbitral award. Creditors that can file a bankruptcy petition under the Act are natural or legal persons having receivables under agreements or by operation of law that can be claimed against the corporate debtor before the court (Article 1, No 2). Those creditors may be secured, unsecured or preferred creditors (Elucidation of Article 2, paragraph (1)). The Act is silent about foreign or international creditors, but in practice foreign creditors can file a bankruptcy petition under the Act. For instance, in *Oxedon Enterprises Limited v PT. Beruangmas Perkasa*,[89] the creditor (Oxedon Enterprises Limited) was a BVI corporation and the debtor (PT. Beruangmas Perkasa) was an Indonesian corporation.

The bankruptcy petition leading to corporate insolvency, can be filed either by a corporate debtor, one of its creditors, or by a third party, provided that the corporate debtor has at least two creditors and it has not repaid in full at least one of its debts which is due and payable. The third party that is allowed by the Act to file the bankruptcy petition is the public prosecutor in the event that no other bankruptcy petition has been filed against a corporate debtor and the filing for the bankruptcy petition has as its objective the protection of the public interest. The 'public interest' according to the Elucidation of Article 2, paragraph (2) of the Act refers to situations where: (1) the corporate debtor has embezzled its assets; (2) the corporate debtor owes money to SOEs or an entity which collects money from the public;[90] (3) the corporate debtor has obtained a loan on the strength of having accumulated public monies[91] and is unable to repay such loan; (4) the corporate debtor has not shown good faith or is uncooperative in settling its debts. Pursuant to Article 2, paragraphs (3), (4), (5) of the Act, specific procedures and limitations to the filing of a bankruptcy petition apply for the following corporate debtors: (1) Bank Indonesia is the only institution authorised

[89] Commercial Court of Jakarta Decision 16/Pailit/2006/PN.JKT.PST. (13 June 2006).

[90] That is, non-banking financial institutions, such as cooperatives, pawnshops, pension funds, insurance firms and securities companies. that take in monies from members of the public.

[91] That is, the corporate debtor is a non-banking financial institution that has accumulated monies from members of the public and has obtained a loan on the strength of its accumulation of such monies.

to file a bankruptcy petition relating to a bank; (2) the Financial Services Authority is the only institution authorised to file a bankruptcy petition relating to a security company, the stock exchange, a guarantee clearing institution, or a central securities depository; (3) the Ministry of Finance is the only institution authorised to file a bankruptcy petition relating to an insurance or re-insurance company, pension funds, and SOEs whose capital is entirely owned by the Indonesian Government and which operate in the public interest. Consequently, the court will reject bankruptcy petitions against those specific corporate debtors if the petitions are filed by parties other than the aforementioned authorities.

Where a corporate debtor issued bonds managed by a bond trustee and the corporation fails to pay interest and does not return the principal upon maturity to members of the public who have bought or hold the bonds, the party who can file the petition for bankruptcy is the bond trustee. Pursuant to Article 51, paragraph (2) of the Capital Market Act 1995, the bond trustee (*wali amanat*) represents the interests of bondholders in and out of court without the need for specific powers-of-attorney from such creditors. It is, accordingly, the bond trustee and not the individual creditors (bondholders) who will file the petition for bankruptcy. Article 50 of the Capital Market Act 1995 requires the bond trustee to be registered with the Indonesian Financial Services Authority and to comply with certain government regulations. This means that foreign bond trustees not registered with the Indonesian Financial Services Authority cannot file bankruptcy petitions on behalf of foreign bondholders in the Indonesian commercial court, although they manage bonds issued by Indonesian corporations that are traded outside Indonesia. This limitation has caused problems for foreign creditors buying Indonesian bonds.[92] For example, in *PT. Indah Kiat Pulp & Paper Tbk v Bank America National Trust Company*[93] and *OCM Opportunities Fund II LP v PT Tri Polyta Indonesia Tbk*,[94] the Indonesian corporate debtors (PT Indah Kiat Pulp & Paper Tbk and PT Tri Polyta Indonesia Tbk) challenged the legal standing of the foreign bond trustees. The Bankruptcy and Suspension of Debt Payment Act 2004 does not have provisions to address this issue. Neither does the Indonesian Financial Services Authority address this issue. In the author's opinion, the only recourse for a foreign bond trustee which is not registered with the Indonesian Financial Services Authority is to bring a civil action for breach of the indenture agreement against an Indonesian bond issuer in the Indonesian civil court.

The court with jurisdiction over corporate insolvency in Indonesia is the commercial court (Article 1, No 7 of the Bankruptcy and Suspension of Debt Payment Act 2004). Pursuant to Elucidation of Article 27 of the Judicial Power Act 2009, the commercial court is a specialised court within the general system of district courts. Unlike the general district courts established in most cities or districts of Indonesia, commercial courts have only been established in a few districts, namely, within the Central Jakarta District Court, the Makassar District Court, the Medan District Court, the Surabaya District Court, and the Semarang District Court. Each commercial court has jurisdiction over different provinces. Pursuant to Presidential Decree No 97 of 1999, the jurisdiction of the Jakarta Commercial Court covers the provinces of Jakarta, West Java, South Sumatera, Lampung and West Kalimantan. The

[92] D Coles, 'Special Report Overview of Indonesia's Insolvency and Restructuring Regime' (*Conventus Law*, May 2016) www.conventuslaw.com/special-report/overview-of-indonesias-insolvency-and/ (accessed 2 May 2020).

[93] District Court of Bengkalis Decision 05/PDT.G./2003/PN-BKS (21 September 2004).

[94] Commercial Court of Jakarta Decision 18/PAILIT/2003/PN. NIAGA/JKT.PST. (17 July 2003); affd Supreme Court Decision 021 K/N/2003 (27 August 2003).

jurisdiction of the Makassar Commercial Court covers the provinces of South Sulawesi, Southeast Sulawesi, Central Sulawesi, North Sulawesi, Maluku and Papua. The jurisdiction of the Medan Commercial Court covers the provinces of North Sumatera, Riau, West Sumatera, Bengkulu, Jambi, and Aceh. The jurisdiction of the Surabaya Commercial Court covers the provinces of East Java, South Kalimantan, East Kalimantan, Central Kalimantan, Bali, West Flores, and East Flores. The jurisdiction of the Semarang Commercial Court covers the provinces of Central Java and Yogyakarta. Besides bankruptcy, commercial courts have jurisdiction over matters of intellectual property rights and bank liquidation. Unlike the decisions of general district courts that can be appealed to the High Courts and the Court of Cassation, the decisions of commercial courts can only be appealed to the Supreme Court (Article 11, paragraph (1) of the Bankruptcy and Suspension of Debt Payment Act 2004).

Article 3 of the 2004 Act governs the jurisdiction of commercial courts over corporate insolvency. Under the Article, the court having jurisdiction in a matter is the commercial court whose jurisdiction covers the province in which the corporate debtor has its legal seat. If the corporate debtor does not have a legal seat in Indonesia but conducts its business in Indonesia, the commercial court that has jurisdiction is the one whose jurisdiction covers the province in which the corporate debtor conducts its business or its Indonesian office is located. The legal seat of a corporate debtor for the purpose of determining the jurisdiction of a commercial court is the corporate seat as stated in its memorandum of association. Although not expressly in the Act, a commercial court also has jurisdiction over a corporate debtor which has a legal seat or conducts business in Indonesia, but which has assets outside Indonesia. Pursuant to Article 21 of the Act, a commercial court may declare bankruptcy in respect of all of the assets of a corporate debtor, including assets that are located outside Indonesia. Creditors of the bankrupt corporate debtor are not allowed to execute against the debtor's assets located outside Indonesia without accounting for the same in respect of assets put under bankruptcy in Indonesia (Articles 212 to 214).

Besides having jurisdiction to declare a corporate debtor bankrupt, a commercial court also has jurisdiction for the following:

(1) to appoint a receiver and a supervisory judge to manage and monitor the assets of the bankrupt corporate debtor (Article 15 of the Act);
(2) to issue a ruling of conservatory seizure against the assets of the bankrupt corporate debtor if requested by its creditors or related third parties (Article 10);
(3) to annul a legal act performed by the corporate debtor that was not compulsory and which the corporate debtor ought to have known before it was declared bankrupt would adversely affect the recourse of its creditors (*actio pauliana*) (Article 41);
(4) to affirm or reject a composition plan negotiated between the bankrupt corporate debtor and its creditors (Article 159);
(5) to annul the implementation of a composition plan because the corporate debtor breached the same (Article 172);
(6) to order rehabilitation requested by the corporate debtor wishing to restore its reputation through a declaration that it has fulfilled its obligations (Article 215).

Article 303 of the Act provides that a commercial court has jurisdiction over corporate insolvency, although arising out of debt under a contract containing an arbitration agreement, provided that the corporate debtor: (1) has two or more creditors and has not repaid in full at least one debt; and (2) is a debtor listed in Article 3 of the Act.

In brief, the court that has jurisdiction over corporate insolvency in Indonesia is the commercial court, which is the specialised court within the general system of district courts. The commercial court also has jurisdiction over a corporate debtor that does not have a legal seat in Indonesia insofar as the latter conducts business in Indonesia.

vi. Law of Personal Bankruptcy

Under the Bankruptcy and Suspension of Debt Payment Act 2004, bankruptcy is a simple declaration that a debtor with two or more creditors has not fully paid a debt which is due and payable (Article 2, paragraph (1)). The main purpose of the bankruptcy declaration is to impose a general attachment on all of the debtor's assets to satisfy the creditors' claims, so that the debtor no longer has the right to control and manage its assets. The debtor can appeal the court ruling of bankruptcy to the Supreme Court. If its appeal is rejected, the debtor is to propose a composition plan to creditors mediated by a receiver. If the composition plan is rejected by creditors, the debtor will enter insolvency. Under the Act, insolvency means the condition of being unable to pay debts (Elucidation of Article 57, paragraph (1)). When the debtor enters insolvency, the receiver starts the liquidation process on the debtor's assets under the supervision of a supervisory judge (Article 178). A debtor that is declared bankrupt and enters insolvency according to the Act could be a natural person as well as a corporation. A debtor may also be a non-corporate entity, such as a partnership, firm, or sole proprietorships (Article 1, No 11). As such, the Bankruptcy and Suspension of Debt Payment Act 2004 applies to all types of debtors and does not distinguish between individuals, non-legal entities and corporations. The bankruptcy and insolvency procedures in the Act apply to both individuals and corporations. The court that has jurisdiction over the bankruptcy of individuals and corporations is also the same, namely the commercial court. In summary, there is no distinction between corporations and individuals under the Indonesian bankruptcy law.

Article 3 of the Act that governs the jurisdiction of commercial courts over bankruptcy applies to individuals, non-legal entities and corporations. The court that has jurisdiction over personal bankruptcy and related matters is the commercial court whose jurisdiction covers the province wherein the debtor is domiciled. If the debtor has left Indonesia, the commercial court that has jurisdiction is the one whose jurisdiction covers the province where the debtor was last domiciled. If the debtor is a partner in a firm, the commercial court that has jurisdiction is the one whose jurisdiction covers the province where the firm has its legal seat. In the case the debtor does not have a legal seat or domicile in Indonesia but carries out a profession or business in Indonesian territory, the commercial court that has jurisdiction is the one whose jurisdiction covers the province wherein the debtor conducts business or has an office.

The commercial court also has jurisdiction to declare that the estate of a deceased person to be in bankruptcy, provided that there are two or more creditors who file a petition for bankruptcy and can prove: (1) that the deceased had debts that were not paid in full during the deceased's lifetime; or (2) that when the deceased passed away, the deceased's debts exceeded his or her assets (Article 207). The court that has jurisdiction over the bankruptcy of a deceased's estate is the commercial court whose jurisdiction covers the province of the deceased's last residence (Article 208). The petition for bankruptcy of a deceased's estate is filed in the relevant commercial court within 90 days of the death (Article 210).

The declaration of bankruptcy on the estate will separate the estate of the deceased from the property of the heirs (Article 209). The creditors who can file a petition for bankruptcy of the estate can be Indonesian as well as foreign nationals, as in *Michael Kong Kenneth Kitson v William Bong Kon Ho*.[95] Mr Kitson, a Singaporean national filed a petition in the Jakarta Commercial Court for the bankruptcy of the estate of Mr Ho, an Indonesian, who had died two years earlier. The Act is silent on the estate of a deceased person who no longer lived in Indonesia before death, but who has left assets in Indonesia. In the author's opinion, the abovementioned provisions should also apply to the assets of a deceased person who no longer lived in Indonesia, but left assets in Indonesia, provided that the deceased had two or more creditors and did not repay in full at least one debt which was due and payable during the deceased's lifetime. The commercial court that has jurisdiction over the matter should be the one whose jurisdiction covers the province of the last residence of the deceased person before moving overseas.

In relation to bankruptcy, a relevant commercial court also has jurisdiction to appoint a receiver and a supervisory judge:

(1) to manage and monitor the assets of the bankrupt debtor (Article 15 of the Act);
(2) to issue a ruling of conservatory seizure against the assets of the bankrupt debtor if requested by the creditors or related third parties (Article 10);
(3) to annul a legal act performed by the debtor that was not compulsory and which the debtor ought to have known before being declared bankrupt would adversely affect creditors (*actio pauliana*) (Article 41);
(4) to put the bankrupt debtor under house arrest or in a state detention facility upon the request of the supervisory judge, a receiver, or a creditor (Article 93);
(5) to affirm or reject a composition plan negotiated between the bankrupt debtor and creditors (Article 159);
(6) to annul a composition plan because the debtor breached the same (Article 172);
(7) to issue a rehabilitation requested by a debtor wishing to restore one's reputation by a declaration of having fulfilled one's obligations (Article 215).

An alternative to the bankruptcy procedure provided by the Act is the suspension of debt payment obligations. The suspension is intended to be a mechanism for restructuring the debts of a debtor. This procedure can be applied for either by a debtor who has more than one creditor, by a creditor, or by one of the government agencies listed in Article 2 of the Act. The debtor can be a natural person, corporation or non-corporate entity. A bond trustee registered with the Indonesian Financial Services Authority is also entitled to apply for the suspension of a debt payment obligation of a corporation that issues bonds. Pursuant to Article 51, paragraph (2) of the Capital Market Act 1995, a bond trustee (*wali amanat*) can represent the interests of bondholders without the need for specific powers-of-attorney from them. The court that has jurisdiction over the suspension of debt payment obligations is the commercial court stipulated in Article 3 of the Act. The court will determine the suspension of debt payment obligations based on the votes of unsecured and secured creditors (Article 228, paragraph (3)). After the application for suspension of debt payment is granted by the court, within 270 days the debtor shall obtain approval from its creditors

[95] Jakarta Commercial Court Decision 18/Pailit/2008/PN.NIAGA.JKT.PST (16 June 2008) (not published).

for its composition plan (Article 228, paragraph (6)). If the creditors do not approve the composition plan, the court will declare the debtor bankrupt. The court rulings on the matters related to the suspension of debt payments cannot be appealed, unlike under the bankruptcy procedure. A relevant commercial court also has jurisdiction to appoint an administrator and a supervisory judge to manage and monitor the assets of a distressed debtor (Article 225 of the Act), to end the suspension of debt payment obligation based on the request of a debtor who agrees to repay one's debts (Article 259), and to affirm or reject a composition plan negotiated between the distressed debtor and creditors (Article 285, paragraphs (1) and (2)). If the commercial court rejects a composition plan, the court has jurisdiction to declare a distressed debtor bankrupt (Article 285, paragraph (3)). Further, it can annul the implementation of the composition plan because the distressed debtor has breaches it and declare the distressed debtor bankrupt (Article 291)

As discussed, the bankruptcy procedure in the 2004 Act applies to both individuals and corporations. The court with jurisdiction over the bankruptcy of individuals and corporations is the same, namely the commercial court. In short, there is no difference between corporate and natural person debtors in terms of bankruptcy procedure under Indonesian bankruptcy law.

vii. Competition Law

Under the Act No 5 of 1999 concerning the prohibition of monopolistic practices and unfair competition (the Anti-Monopoly Act 1999), the institutions that are responsible for enforcing competition law in Indonesia are the Commission for the Supervision of Business Competition (the Indonesia Competition Commission) and the courts. The Indonesia Competition Commission is responsible for enforcing competition law and adjudicating cases relating to that law. Its decisions can take the form of administrative measures, rulings for the payment of damages by way of compensation, and the imposition of a fine (Article 47). The Commission's decision can be appealed to the District Court with a final appeal to the Supreme Court. In principle, the Indonesia Competition Commission has jurisdiction over business actors that have a presence in Indonesia, for instance, through subsidiaries or agents, or under the single economic entity doctrine. The Indonesia Competition Commission also has jurisdiction over foreign parties who enter into agreements to carry on business in Indonesia, even though the foreign parties have no presence in Indonesia. Pursuant to Article 1, No 5, business actors governed by the Anti-Monopoly Act 1999 are all businesses incorporated or having legal seats in Indonesia or which operate in Indonesia whether or not they are legal entities. Article 16 of the Act prohibits business actors from entering into agreements with foreign parties in which the conditions of the agreements may cause monopolistic practices or unfair business competition in Indonesia. In other words, in cases of unfair competition involving foreign elements, the Indonesia Competition Commission has jurisdiction over the Indonesian business actors and their foreign partners – regardless of whether or not the latter have a presence in Indonesia – insofar as they enter into business agreements which may result in monopolistic practices or unfair business competition in Indonesia. In addition, the Commission has jurisdiction over foreign parties (even when they have not entered into business agreements with Indonesian business actors or have no presence in Indonesia), if they meet the requirements of the single economic entity doctrine. The doctrine has been applied by the Commission to determine whether several separate foreign legal entities can constitute a single economic entity for competition law purposes. For example, a foreign holding company which neither operates or has established any agreement with business actors in Indonesia, will be within the Commission's jurisdiction, if it has subsidiaries that have entered into agreements with business actors in Indonesia and those agreements have given rise to anti-competitive effects in Indonesia. The subsidiary companies must be under the control of the foreign holding company with no economic independence from it.

In *Temasek Holdings Pte Ltd*, the Competition Commission exercised jurisdiction over Temasek Holdings, although it was a Singapore company, had no presence in Indonesia, and had not entered into any agreement with Indonesian business actors. The Commission found that Temasek Holdings' Singapore subsidiaries (namely, STT Communications Ltd and Singapore Telecommunications Ltd) held shares in PT Telekomunikasi Selular and PT Indosat, Indonesia's first and second largest mobile phone operators. STT Communications Ltd along with its subsidiaries (such as Asia Mobile Holding Company Pte. Ltd and Indonesia Communications Pte. Ltd) owned 41.94 per cent shares of PT Indosat, and Singapore Telecommunications Ltd owned 35 per cent shares of PT Telekomunikasi Selular. The arrangements meant that Temasek Holdings held cross-ownership in Indonesia's two largest mobile operator companies and could influence prices in Indonesia's telecommunications industry. PT Telekomunikasi Selular was a major player in the industry and had abused its dominant position by setting excessively high prices for cellular services in Indonesia. The Competition Commission found that PT Indosat and PT Telekomunikasi Selular were under the effective control of Temasek Holdings through the latter's Singapore subsidiaries and did not have economic independence from Temasek Holdings. In addition, the Commission found that the Temasek Holdings' subsidiaries were in a position to influence and control the management and business plans of PT Indosat and PT Telekomunikasi Selular. Therefore, in the Commission's opinion, for competition law purposes, Temasek Holdings and its subsidiaries were treated as a single economic entity in Indonesia.[96] Hence, the Commission had jurisdiction over Temasek Holdings, even though Temasek Holdings was technically a separate foreign legal entity from its subsidiaries.

The Indonesia Competition Commission imposed sanctions on the parties involved in the *Temasek Holdings* case because of their infringement of the Anti-Monopoly Act 1999. Under Article 44, paragraph (2) of the Act, the parties could appeal the Commission's judgment to a district court. The district court that has jurisdiction over a competition case is the court in the district of the business actor's legal seat (Article 1, No 19 of the Act). Since Temasek Holdings and its subsidiaries, apart from PT Indosat and PT Telekomunikasi Selular, did not have legal seats in Indonesia, the civil procedure codes were applied to determine the district court that had jurisdiction over Temasek Holdings and its subsidiaries. Supreme Court Regulation No 3 of 2005 as amended by Supreme Court Regulation No 3 of 2019 concerning the procedure for appealing against the judgment of the Commission in relation to the supervision of business competition, prescribed that civil procedure law applies to legal proceeding in the district court. Pursuant to Article 44, paragraph (2) and Article 1, paragraph (19) of the Anti-Monopoly Act 1999, and thus,

[96] Commission for the Supervision of Business Competition Decision 07/KPPU-L/2007 (19 November 2007) 607–612.

not following the principle of *actor sequitur forum rei*, the court that has jurisdiction over an appeal against the Commission's judgment is the court in the district of the business actor's legal seat. Since the appellants in this case were foreign companies that did not have legal seats in Indonesia, the court that had jurisdiction was the Central Jakarta District Court. When the Central Jakarta District Court dismissed their appeal, Temasek Holdings and its subsidiaries brought the case to the court of cassation and finally to the extraordinary appeal.[97]

In another case also involving foreign business actors, the Competition Commission exercised jurisdiction over Goldman Sachs (Singapore), Pte., a Singapore company, because Goldman Sachs had agreed to provide financial advice to PT Pertamina (Persero), an Indonesian SOE when PT Pertamina sold its two very large crude carriers (VLCCs) to Frontline Ltd (a Bermuda company). The Commission also exercised jurisdiction over Frontline, because it had a Sale and Purchase Agreement with PT Pertamina for the two VLCCs. Although neither Goldman Sachs not Frontline operated or had a presence in Indonesia, the Commission had jurisdiction because they had concluded business agreements with Indonesian business actors and those agreements could give rise to monopolistic practices and unfair business competition within Indonesia (Article 16 of the Anti-Monopoly Act 1999).[98] Goldman Sachs and Frontline appealed against the Commission's judgment in the Central Jakarta District Court in accordance with Indonesian civil procedure law.[99]

In conclusion, in cases of unfair competition involving foreign elements, the Indonesia Competition Commission has jurisdiction over foreign partners of Indonesian business actors, whether or not present in Indonesia, if they enter into business agreements with Indonesian business actors which may result in monopolistic practices and unfair business competition in Indonesia. In addition, the Commission also has jurisdiction over a foreign party that neither has a presence in Indonesia nor entered into a business agreements with Indonesian business actors, if the foreign party constitutes a single economic entity with parties that have agreements with business actors in Indonesia or which operate through wholly-controlled subsidiaries in Indonesia.

II. Jurisdiction in Shipping Claims

A. Jurisdiction of the Indonesian Court

Shipping claims in Indonesia refer to the maritime claims listed in the elucidation of Article 223, paragraph (1) of Act No 17 of 2008 concerning Shipping (the Shipping Act 2008).

[97] Commission for the Supervision of Business Competition Decision 07/KPPU-L/2007 (19 November 2007); affd District Court of Central Jakarta Decision 02/KPPU/2007/PN.JKT.PST (9 May 2008); affd Supreme Court Decision 496 K/Pdt.Sus/2008 (10 September 2008); affd Supreme Court Extraordinary Appeal 128 PK/PDT.SUS/2009 (5 May 2010).

[98] Commission for the Supervision of Business Competition Decision 07/KPPU-L/2004 (3 March 2005).

[99] District Court of Central Jakarta Decision 04/KPPU/2005/PN.JKT.PST. (25 May 2005); Supreme Court Decision 04 K/KPPU/2005 (29 November 2005); Supreme Court Extraordinary Appeal 01 PK/Pdt.Sus/2007 (12 May 2008).

The elucidation of Article 23 lists 22 types of maritime claims that can lead to the arrest of a ship. Those are claims relating to the following matters:

(1) loss or damage caused by the operation of a ship;
(2) loss of life or personal injury occurring, whether on land or water, in direct connection with the operation of a ship;
(3) damage to the environment, ship, or cargo as a result of salvage operations or a salvage agreement;
(4) damage or the threat of damage by a ship to the environment, coastline, or related interests, including the cost of measures taken to prevent damage to the environment, ship, and cargo, as well as the cost of reasonable measures of reinstating the environment;
(5) expenses of raising, removing or repairing a ship, including the cost of ship salvage and crew rescue;
(6) using, operating or chartering a vessel pursuant to a charterparty;
(7) carriage of goods or passengers on board a ship, whether pursuant to a charterparty or otherwise;
(8) loss of or damage to or in connection with goods (including luggage) carried on board a ship;
(9) general average;
(10) towage;
(11) pilotage;
(12) materials, provisions, bunkers, equipment (including containers) supplied, or services rendered to a ship for its operation, management, preservation or maintenance;
(13) construction, reconstruction, repair, conversion or equipping of a ship;
(14) port, canal, dock, harbour and other waterway dues and charges;
(15) wages and other sums due to the master, officers and members of the ship's crew in respect of their employment on a ship, including the cost of repatriation and social insurance contributions payable on their behalf;
(16) disbursements incurred in the interests of a ship on behalf of the owners;
(17) insurance premiums (including mutual insurance calls) in respect of a ship, payable by or on behalf of the shipowner or demise charterer;
(18) commissions, brokerages or agency fees payable in respect of a ship by or on behalf of the shipowner or demise charterer;
(19) disputes as to ownership or possession of a ship;
(20) disputes between co-owners of a ship as to its employment or earnings;
(21) mortgages, hypothecs, or charges of the same nature over a ship;
(22) disputes arising out of a contract for the sale of a ship.

Other claims may give rise to maritime liens as set out in Article 65, paragraph (2) of the Shipping Act 2008, namely, wages of the ship's crew; payment for injuries, losses, and damages caused by operation of the ship; payment for the salvage of the ship; and pilotage. These maritime liens can also result in ship arrest.[100]

[100] Art 65, para (1) governs debts and receivables secured by a ship, such as hypothecs. Art 65, para (2) provides the list of receivables that are prioritised over the secured debts mentioned in para (1). Among the prioritised debts and receivables are the wages of the ship's crew, payments for injuries, etc. The difference between the prioritised maritime liens listed in Art 65, para (2) and the shipping claims listed in Art 223 is that to enforce the maritime

The Shipping Act 2008 does not contain specific provisions concerning shipping claims involving foreign elements. The Act also does not have provisions concerning the court's jurisdiction in shipping claims. Some practitioners have argued that the court that has the jurisdiction must be the district court where the defendant resides or where the ship is located.[101] There is no maritime court in Indonesia that deals with shipping claims.[102] Shipping claims are litigated in the district courts as courts of first instance. Article 223 of the Shipping Act 2008 is the only provision to mention shipping claims that result in ship arrest. Paragraph (2) of the Article requires the government to draft a ministerial regulation that governs the procedure of ship arrest in connection with shipping claims. To date, the government has not issued such ministerial regulation. Therefore, it is difficult to know for sure which district court has jurisdiction in shipping claims in Indonesia, especially shipping claims involving foreign elements.

Despite the absence of a specific regulation governing the jurisdiction of the Indonesian court in shipping claims, parties might rely on Indonesian Civil Procedure Law to determine some jurisdictional issues. Based on Article 100 Rv, the presence of the shipowner in Indonesia is not required for an Indonesian court to have jurisdiction over shipping claims, as long as the shipowner owes an obligation to an Indonesian claimant. Because shipping claims may lead to the arrest of a ship, the jurisdiction of the Indonesian court over shipping claims is determined by the existence of the ship within Indonesian territory, irrespective of the ship's flag and the nationality of the parties.[103] If the ship is located outside Indonesian territory, the Indonesian court will not have jurisdiction in a shipping claim even if both claimant and defendant are in Indonesia, in accordance with Article 431 Rv, which provides that the orders of the Indonesian court are valid and enforceable within Indonesia only. Because a shipping claim that leads to ship arrest can be categorised as a mixed action against the defendant (shipowner) and the property (the ship), the court that has jurisdiction in the shipping claim is the court chosen by the claimant either in the district where the ship is located or in the district where the shipowner resides (Article 99, paragraph (10) Rv). In some shipping claim disputes, for example in *PT Asuransi Indrapura v PT Pelayaran Nasional Fajar Marindo Raya*[104] and *Trustrade Enterprises Pte Ltd v PT Bank Syariah Mandiri*,[105] the claimants brought their shipping claims to the district court of the shipowners' residence. These precedents could be used as pointers to the court's jurisdiction in shipping claims

liens in Art 65, para (2), a plaintiff must file a civil lawsuit to have the ship arrested. In contrast, the shipping claims in Art 223 do not require a plaintiff to file a civil lawsuit in order to get the ship arrested. In an Art 223 situation, all that would be needed would be to show evidence of a relevant maritime claim. Because Art 223 remains ineffective due to the lack of implementing regulations, to date the only way to get a ship arrested is by Art 65, para (2).

[101] Sahat Siahaan and others, 'Indonesia' in J Gosling and TJ Huzarski (eds), *The Shipping Law Review* 3rd edn (Law Business Research Ltd, 2016) 267.

[102] The Maritime Court in Indonesia (*Mahkamah Pelayaran*) does not litigate shipping disputes, but merely examines indications or allegations of error or negligence in the event of a ship accident. It is not a tribunal, but a panel of experts under the Ministry of Transportation (the Shipping Act).

[103] The Shipping Act and Regulations of Ministry of Transportation allow several types of foreign-flagged ships to operate in Indonesia with certain restrictions and requirements, particularly to conduct specific activities, such as oil and gas survey vessels, drilling vessels, offshore construction and support activities, dredging, salvage and underwater works.

[104] District Court of Jambi Decision 10/PDT.G/2013/PN.JBI. (31 July 2013).

[105] District Court of Central Jakarta Decision 23/PDT.G/2011/PN.JKT.PST (1 December 2011).

In summary, shipping claims that lead to ship arrest are governed by the Shipping Act 2008. But, the Shipping Act 2008 does not provide rules to determine the court's jurisdiction in shipping claims. Therefore, parties must rely on Indonesian Civil Procedure Law to determine jurisdiction in shipping claims. In some Indonesian cases, the courts that asserted jurisdiction were the courts in the districts where the defendants or shipowners had their residence. These precedents, together with Indonesian Civil Procedure Law, can be used as references to determine the court's jurisdiction over shipping claims.

B. The Process of Ship Arrest in Indonesia

Article 222 of the Shipping Act 2008 stipulates that ships implicated in criminal or civil cases are subject to arrest by the harbourmaster under a court order. Article 223, paragraph (1) of the Shipping Act 2008 mentions that the ship arrest in civil cases shall be based on maritime claims. The maritime claims that are the bases of ship arrest are listed in the elucidation of Article 223, paragraph (1). The maritime claims listed in the elucidation of Article 223 give rise to maritime liens. This means that those maritime claims may be used as the bases of ship arrest. A party may request an order from the court for the arrest of a ship with respect to a maritime claim without filing a civil lawsuit (Article 223). It is enough for the claimant to file a petition of ship arrest in a district court supported by evidence of a maritime claim. The judge will then issue an order for ship arrest. Therefore, ship arrest in this case is not the same as conservatory pre-judgment attachment to secure a judgment or an enforceable instrument, such as, mortgage or hypothec, because the conservatory attachment must be preceded by a civil lawsuit.

As a matter of fact, Articles 222 and 223 of the Shipping Act 2008 are ineffective due to the lack of implementing regulations. Article 223, paragraph (2) requires the government to draft a ministerial regulation that governs the procedure of ship arrest in relation to shipping claims. To date, the government has not issued any such regulation. Moreover, Indonesia is not a party to the 1952 Arrest Convention and, although it is a signatory to the 1999 International Convention on Arrest of Ships, Indonesia has not yet ratified the Convention. Consequently, there is currently no specific procedure for ship arrest under Indonesian law. Since there is no regulation that governs the process of ship arrest as mandated by Article 223 of the Shipping Act 2008, no record of a court order for the arrest of a ship can be found in Indonesian case law. Some law practitioners claim that Indonesian courts are reluctant to issue orders for ship arrest because of the lack of specific regulations for ship arrest.[106] In light of this situation, claimants usually combine the request of arrest and conservatory seizure (*saisie conservatoire*) of the ships in one civil lawsuit against shipowners.[107] Another practice is for a claimant to request that the harbourmaster postpone the issuance of a port

[106] Siahaan and others, 'Indonesia' (n 101) 271; Members of The Shiparrested.com Network, *Ship Arrests in Practice* 11th edn(2018) 192 http://shiparrested.com/wp-content/uploads/2016/07/Final-Ship-Arrests-in-Practice-11th-edition.pdf (accessed 20 April 2019). See also I Firman, 'Ship Arrest Process in Indonesia' (*Indra Firman & Associates*, 14 September 2016) http://indrafirman.com/en/2016/09/14/ship-arrest-process-in-indonesia/ (accessed 3 May 2019).

[107] District Court of Jambi Decision 10/PDT.G/2013/PN.JBI. (31 July 2013); District Court of Central Jakarta Decision 23/PDT.G/2011/PN.JKT.PST (1 December 2011).

clearance (*Surat Persetujuan Izin Berlayar* (SPIB)) for the relevant ship. The ship would then be unable to sail. The SPIB will be issued by the harbourmaster once the claimant and shipowner have settled their dispute as mediated by the harbourmaster.[108] These different practices in ship arrest are carried out as a consequence of the absence of a specific ship arrest procedure.

In short, although ship arrest is recognised in the Indonesian legal system, there is a lack of clarity regarding the process of ship arrest because the government has not issued any regulation on this matter despite being mandated to do so by the Shipping Act 2008. As a result, Indonesian courts are reluctant to issue orders for ship arrest. Further, claimants typically bring a civil lawsuit to the district court with a request for conservatory seizure of the relevant ship as well as its arrest. This is despite the fact that a civil lawsuit is not required under Article 223, paragraph (1) of the Shipping Act 2008.

III. Immunities from Jurisdiction

A. Sovereign Immunity

Immunity of foreign states from court jurisdiction has never been expressly regulated under Indonesian law. There is no specific law concerning the jurisdictional immunity of foreign states in Indonesia. In addition, Indonesia is not a signatory to the 2004 UN Convention on Jurisdictional Immunities of States and Their Property.[109] However, the Convention on the Settlement of Investment Disputes between States and Nationals of Other States (the ICSID Convention) was ratified by Indonesia under Act No 5 of 1968 concerning investment disputes settlement between states and foreign nationals (the Investment Disputes Settlement between States and Foreign Nationals Act 1968) and may indicate that Indonesia accepts the doctrine of restrictive immunity. By ratifying the ICSID Convention, Indonesia waives liability immunity[110] in ICSID arbitrations in investment disputes between Indonesia and foreign investors. Nevertheless, the ICSID Convention only applies to ICSID arbitrations. It does not apply to or concern itself with the jurisdiction of national courts over states. Another law in Indonesia that stipulates the court jurisdiction over a foreign state without addressing sovereign immunity, is Article 99, paragraph (18) Rv, which reads that 'In the case that the Indonesian Government represents the State, either as a plaintiff or a defendant, Jakarta is assumed as their residence.' This provision indicates that, in civil cases, the Indonesian state is not immune from court jurisdiction. Article 99, paragraph (18) Rv allows the Indonesian state to be sued in the Jakarta court and the Jakarta court to have jurisdiction over the Indonesian state. In relation to this Article, M Yahya Harahap, a former Indonesian Supreme Court Justice, has suggested that not only the Jakarta District

[108] Firman, 'Ship Arrest' (n 106); See also District Court of Central Jakarta Decision 451/PDT.G/2010/PN.JKT.PST (8 December 2011).

[109] At the time of writing, this Convention is not yet in force, as it has not reached the required number of ratification instruments.

[110] Article 55 of the ICSID Convention provides: 'Nothing in Article 54 shall be construed as derogating from the law in force in any Contracting State relating to immunity of that State or of any foreign State from execution.' Thus, ratification of the ICSDI Convention does not derogate from immunity against execution.

Court, but also other courts in other districts in which the Indonesian Government has its representatives, have jurisdiction over the Indonesian state when the state or its representative is a defendant in a civil case.[111] Therefore, there have been civil cases in which district courts in Indonesia have asserted jurisdiction over the Indonesian Government and its representatives when sued by private entities or individuals.[112] These cases, based on Article 99, paragraph (18) Rv, show that the Indonesian state and its representatives are not immune from the jurisdiction of Indonesian courts. Nevertheless, Article 99, paragraph (18) Rv only governs court jurisdiction over the Indonesian state. It is silent on the jurisdiction of Indonesian courts over foreign states.

To understand whether foreign states are immune from court jurisdiction in Indonesia, one must look at judicial practice, doctrine and case law. The report of the Third Session of the Asian-African Legal Consultative Committee (AALCC) held in Colombo in 1960 observed that Indonesia adhered to the doctrine of absolute immunity, although other countries in the AALCC were of the view that the immunity of foreign states did not extend to their commercial or private activities.[113] Until recently, Indonesia was perceived as following a doctrine of absolute immunity[114] and this has indeed been the position when private entities or individuals in civil cases have sued the Republic of Indonesia in foreign courts. For example, in *Republic of Indonesia, His Excellency Ambassador Soeratmin, Minister Counsellor Azhari Kasim v James Vinzon*,[115] Indonesia, as the defendant, maintained that it enjoyed sovereign immunity, although engaged in a commercial activity when entering into a maintenance agreement with James Vinzon who had been asked to maintain some facilities within the Indonesian embassy compound and in the ambassador's residence. The Philippine Supreme Court accepted Indonesia's defence, holding that Indonesia had been engaged in a sovereign activity when entering into a contract with Vinzon. The Republic of Indonesia entered into a contract with a private individual to maintain its embassy and its facilities and the maintenance contract was to support Indonesia's diplomatic mission. The Philippine Supreme Court concluded that it was an act *jure imperii*. Accordingly, the Republic of Indonesia was immune from the jurisdiction of the Philippine court. The Maintenance Agreement stated: 'Any legal action arising out of this Maintenance Agreement shall be settled according to the laws of the Philippines and by the proper court of Makati City, Philippines.' But the Philippine Supreme Court found that the clause was not a waiver of immunity, but a mere stipulation that, in the event that it consented to waiving immunity, Philippine law would be the applicable law and the court of Makati City the proper court. The Philippine Supreme Court's decision overturned the Makati Trial Court's decision which had ruled that, by the clause, Indonesia waived immunity and submitted itself to the jurisdiction of the Philippine court. Other commercial cases in which the Republic

[111] This is to implement the principle of simple, quick and economical judiciary required by Art 2, para (4) of Judicial Power Act 2009; Harahap, *Hukum Acara* (n 2) 136.

[112] Decisions of the courts that asserted their jurisdiction over the Government of the Republic of Indonesia or its representatives can be found in the directory of court decisions compiled by the Indonesian Supreme Court at https://putusan.mahkamahagung.go.id/.

[113] S Sucharitkul (Special Rapporteur), 'Fourth Report on Jurisdictional Immunities of States and Their Property' UN Doc A/CN.4/357 and Corr.1 (1982), 226.

[114] EK Bankas, *The State Immunity Controversy in International Law Private Suits Against Sovereign States in Domestic Courts* (Springer, 2005) 103, 202, 330.

[115] Supreme Court of Philippine Decision G.R. No 154705 (26 June 2003).

of Indonesia has asserted sovereign immunity by way of defence to foreign proceedings are *Juan Ysmael & Co., Inc. v Government of the Republic of Indonesia*,[116] *Velasco v Government of Indonesia*,[117] and *Phaneuf v Republic of Indonesia*.[118]

In contrast, the Indonesian courts apply a narrower conception of sovereign immunity. For example, in *Brazilian Embassy in Jakarta v Luis F.S.S Pereira*, the Brazilian Embassy was sued by Mr Pereira, an Indonesian local employee at the embassy, before the Industrial Relations Court in Central Jakarta, for breach of an employment contract. The Brazilian Embassy as the defendant asserted sovereign immunity and argued that it was not subject to Indonesian law or the Indonesian court's jurisdiction. The argument was advanced despite the employment contract providing that it was governed by Indonesian law and that any dispute arising out of the agreement was to be settled by the ruling of a labour dispute settlement body in Indonesia. The Central Jakarta Industrial Relations Court rejected the Brazilian Embassy's argument and ordered the embassy to pay compensation to Mr Pereira for the violation of his rights under Indonesian labour law.[119] The Supreme Court affirmed the decision, stating that foreign embassies in Indonesia were subject to Indonesian law when they entered into an employment contract with Indonesian nationals.[120] The judgment in this case was designated as a landmark decision in 2017 by the Supreme Court.[121] The legal principles established by the landmark decision are thus: (1) employment contracts between foreign country representatives and local staff or employees will always be governed by the Manpower Act 2003; and (2) diplomatic immunity under the Vienna Conventions on Diplomatic and Consular Relations will be treated as waived when foreign legal representatives enter into employment contracts with local staff or employees. In 2016 the Supreme Court issued Circular Letter No 4 of 2016 addressed to all lower courts, stating that the Industrial Relations courts have jurisdiction over disputes between foreign country representatives and local staff or employees arising out of their employment contracts. In consequence, foreign embassies in Indonesia are deemed to waive sovereign immunity when entering into employment contracts with Indonesian nationals and the Industrial Relations courts have jurisdiction in respect of such contracts. The landmark decision confirmed court judgments in similar cases, for example, *Erna Amiarsih v the Embassy of the Republic of India in Indonesia*,[122] the *Embassy of the Republic of Suriname in Indonesia v Maria Itania Setiawan and Anggreni Ekasari*,[123] and *Indra Taufiq Djafar v Office of the US Consulate in Medan and the US Embassy in Indonesia*.[124] In spite of court judgments that have rejected the diplomatic immunity defence, there has been uncertainty regarding enforcement of those judgments, as the Indonesian nationals who won their case did not receive compensation from the foreign embassies even after the judgments.

[116] Judicial Committee of the Privy Council on appeal from Hong Kong, 7 October 1954.

[117] 370 F.3d 392 (4th Cir. 2004).

[118] 106 F.3d 302. US Court of Appeals, 9th Cir., 7 February 1997.

[119] Central Jakarta Industrial Relations Court Decision 196/PHI.G/ 2012/PN.JKT.PST (18 February 2013).

[120] Supreme Court Decision 376 K/Pdt.Sus-PHI/2013 (29 October 2013).

[121] Tim Pokja Laporan Tahunan Mari, *Laporan Tahunan 2017 Mahkamah Agung Republik Indonesia* (Mahkamah Agung RI, 2018) 202.

[122] Central Jakarta Industrial Relations Court Decision 64/PHI.G/2014/PN Jkt Pst (27 October 2014).

[123] Central Jakarta Industrial Relations Court Decision 41/Pdt.Sus-PHI/2015/PN.Jkt.Pst (27 July 2015); Supreme Court Decision 696 K/Pdt.Sus-PHI/2016 (15 September 2016).

[124] Supreme Court Decision 673 K/Pdt.Sus/2012 (2 April 2013).

The Minister of Foreign Affairs added to this uncertainty by stating that the employment contract between foreign embassies and their Indonesian employees are not binding in absolute terms in the same way that contracts between Indonesian embassies and their local employees overseas are not.[125]

The issue of different approaches between the Indonesian Government and the courts in interpreting the immunities of states has not been resolved. Based on existing law, judicial practice and doctrine, four types of state immunity are known in Indonesia. First, there is no immunity for the Indonesian state when sued before an Indonesian court in civil cases (Article 99, paragraph (18) Rv). Second, there is absolute immunity when the Republic of Indonesia and its representatives are brought to foreign courts by private entities or individuals. Third, there may be a narrower immunity when foreign states or their representatives in Indonesia are sued in Indonesian courts. Fourth, there may be restrictive immunity in ICSID arbitration relating to Indonesia. The reasons for different applications of jurisdictional immunity in Indonesia is that the Indonesian Government applies the doctrine of absolute immunity to protect the interests of the Indonesian state in foreign courts. On the other hand, Indonesian courts apply a narrower conception of sovereign immunity, readily finding the same to be waived in employment contract cases, to protect the interests of Indonesian nationals who conduct commercial transactions with foreign states in Indonesia. The uncertainty in the application of jurisdictional immunities of states in Indonesia may be resolved when Indonesia passes a law that governs immunities of states or when Indonesia joins the 2004 UN Convention on Jurisdictional Immunities of States and Their Property.

B. State-Owned Enterprises (SOEs)

Although Indonesian law does not expressly govern the jurisdictional immunity of state-owned enterprises ('SOEs'), Indonesian judicial practice suggests that SOEs do not have immunity from the jurisdiction of Indonesian courts. As such, in practice, Indonesian courts have jurisdiction over SOEs. This judicial practice has been reinforced by a decision taken at the 2010 national work meeting of the Indonesian Supreme Court stating that courts can seize the assets of Indonesian SOEs in civil and commercial claims. Although Article 50 of Act No 1 of 2004 concerning the State Treasury (the State Treasure Act 2004) prohibits the seizure or execution of state assets, the Supreme Court was of the opinion that Article 50 did not cover the assets of SOEs.[126] The decision taken at the 2010 Supreme Court meeting resolves previous differing interpretations among Indonesian courts concerning attachments or execution of SOEs' assets. To date, the decision at the 2010 Supreme Court meeting has not been adopted in any regulation. However, the 2010 decision provides Indonesian courts with the authority to exercise jurisdiction over SOEs and their assets. The 2010 decision does not expressly mention foreign SOEs that are sued before Indonesian

[125] A Saputra, '3 Kedubes Asing Belum Laksanakan Putusan MA, Ini Kata Menlu RI' (*detikNews*, 28 December 2015) https://news.detik.com/berita/d-3105829/3-kedubes-asing-belum-laksanakan-putusan-ma-ini-kata-menluri (accessed 3 August 2019).

[126] Decision taken at the 2010 national work meeting of the Indonesian Supreme Court in Balikpapan, 11–14 October 2020, as summarised in Ali, 'Pengadilan Boleh Sita Harta BUMN' (*hukumonline*, 18 October 2010) www.hukumonline.com/berita/baca/lt4cbc1bcd43fa9/pengadilan-boleh-sita-harta-bumn?page=all (accessed 18 July 2020).

courts, but judicial practice with domestic SOEs is indicative that foreign SOEs will not be immune from the jurisdiction of Indonesian courts either. Indonesian courts will treat foreign and domestic SOEs in the same way.

There have been cases in which the Indonesian courts have exercised jurisdiction over Indonesian SOEs. For example, in *PT. Globex Indonesia v PT. Djakarta Lloyd* the Central Jakarta District Court exercised jurisdiction over PT. Djakarta Llyod PT. Djakarta Lloyd (which is 100 per cent owned by the Indonesian Government) when PT. Globex Indonesia filed a civil lawsuit against the latter for failure to pay on a promissory note. The Court decided in favour of PT. Globex Indonesia. To pay the debt owed to PT. Globex Indonesia, the Court ordered an executory attachment against PT. Djakarta Lloyd's assets.[127] PT. Djakarta Lloyd objected to the Court's order and argued that its assets belonged to the state by reason of Article 50 of the State Treasure Act 2004 and so could not be seized by the Court. The judges found that assets owned by PT. Djakarta Lloyd were not state property because as a matter of principle an SOE's assets were separate from those of the government. The Central Jakarta District Court therefore rejected PT. Djakarta Lloyd's objection.[128] Indonesian courts have also asserted jurisdiction over foreign SOEs. In *Temasek Holding (Private) Limited; et al v Komisi Pengawas Persaingan Usaha Republik Indonesia (KPPU)*, Indonesian courts exercised jurisdiction over Temasek Holding (Private) Limited ('Temasek') (which is 100 per cent owned by the Government of Singapore through its Ministry of Finance). Although the Central Jakarta District Court and Supreme Court did not refer to the issue of Temasek's immunity from the courts' jurisdiction in their judgments, the case illustrates that a foreign SOE does not enjoy immunity from the jurisdiction of Indonesian courts. The Indonesian courts ordered Temasek to pay a fine to the Indonesian Competition Commission for breaching Indonesian competition law. Temasek complied after the Indonesian Supreme Court denied its extra-ordinary appeal. Details of the case have been explained in section I.B.vii. Competition Law.

In summary, SOEs do not enjoy immunity from the jurisdiction of Indonesian courts. This principle is founded on judicial practice as confirmed by the Indonesian Supreme Court in 2010. This principle equally applies to foreign SOEs.

[127] District Court of Central Jakarta Decision 288/PDT.G/2008/PN.JKT.PST (25 March 2009); affd High Court of Jakarta Decision 323/PDT.2009/PT.DKI (19 November 2009).

[128] District Court of Central Jakarta Decision 428/PDT.BTH/2010/PN.JKT.PST (5 May 2011).

3

Choice of Law

I. Law of Obligations

A. Contracts

i. Governing Law of a Contract

In principle, the governing law of a contract with foreign elements is the law chosen by the parties to the contract. This principle is stated in Article 1338, paragraph (1) BW, which recognises the parties' freedom of contract, including the freedom to choose a governing law. Article 1338 BW stipulates that all valid agreements are binding as law between the parties. Accordingly, if the parties validly agree to make a certain law the governing law of their contract, their choice of law is binding on them. To be regarded valid, the parties' agreement must meet requirements set out in Article 1320 BW. First, the parties must mutually consent to the agreement. Second, the parties must have capacity to enter into an agreement. Third, the agreement must be based on a legitimate cause. Fourth, the subject matter of the agreement must be certain. Parties are not free to construct law to govern their agreement. They are free only to choose the law of a particular country or countries to govern their agreement.[1]

The parties' freedom to choose the law that governs their contract has been recognised in several Indonesian Acts. Article 72 of Act No 1 of 2009 concerning Aviation (the Aviation Act 2009) provides that security agreements, title reservation agreements and leasing agreements resulting in international interests in aircraft objects may be governed by law chosen by the parties to the agreements. The elucidation of Article 72 explains that the parties' choice of law is not restricted by any requirement that the law chosen has some connection with the parties or their agreement. Article 18, paragraph (2) of the Electronic Information and Transaction Act 2008 as amended in 2016 provides that the parties have the right to make a choice of law for their international electronic transaction. The elucidation of Article 18, paragraph (2) explains that the choice of law in the electronic transaction can only be made if there is a foreign element in the transaction and shall be implemented in accordance with the principles of private international law. Furthermore, Article 18, paragraph (3) of the same Act provides that if the parties do not make a choice of law for their international electronic transaction, the governing law of their transaction will be determined by the principles of private international law. Article 56, paragraph (2) of the Arbitration Act 1999 provides that the parties are entitled to choose an applicable law to settle their disputes. The elucidation of Article 56, paragraph (2) explains that if the parties

[1] S Gautama, *Pengantar Hukum Perdata Internasional Indonesia* (Binacipta, 1985) 169.

do not make a choice of law the applicable law shall be the law of the country of the arbitration. The Indonesian judiciary also recognises the parties' freedom to choose the law that governs their contract. For example, in the case of *Bank America National Trust Company; et al v PT. Indah Kiat Pulp & Paper Tbk.; et al*, the judges annulled the decisions made of the previous courts because the previous courts had not applied New York law, which was the law chosen by the parties, when adjudicating the case.[2]

The above-mentioned Acts and court decision demonstrate the existence of the principle of the parties' freedom of choice in respect of the law that governs their contract in the Indonesian legal system.

This freedom of choice is subject to limitations. First, the law chosen by the parties must not infringe Indonesian *ordre public*, mandatory rules, and public law (concepts discussed above in Chapter 1, section VIII on mandatory rules, *ordre public*, public law, and the evasion of law). Second, the law chosen by the parties must be the law of a country that has some connection with their contract, either because the place of the contract is in the country, or because the legal seats or residences of the parties are in the country, or because customary practice dictates the application of the law of the country to their contract.[3] For example, English law is usually chosen to govern marine insurance contracts in Indonesia, although neither the contracts nor the parties have connections with the UK.[4] Third, the law chosen by the parties only covers substantive law and does not include procedural law, which is always *lex fori*. Fourth, the law chosen by the parties only refers to a country's domestic or internal law, and not the country's private international law. Therefore, the parties' choice of law will not result in *renvoi*. Fifth, the law chosen by the parties only governs the implementation of their contract, not the validity of their contract.[5]

Bearing in mind the above limitations, the parties' choice of law gives them the freedom of choosing more than one legal system to govern their contract. Accordingly, the parties may choose different laws to govern different parts of their contract (*dépeçage*). For instance, in a loan agreement between an Indonesian and Singaporean, the parties may agree that the security clause is governed by Indonesian law, as the security is located in Indonesia, and the rest of the agreement is governed by Singaporean law, as the agreement is executed in Singapore. Indonesian scholars in general accept the *dépeçage* doctrine in international business contracts by which the parties in a contract subject different parts of their contract to different systems of law.[6] The freedom also allows the parties to agree to modify the law governing their contract. However, such modification of the governing law may not prejudice the formal validity of the contract and pre-existing rights of third parties.[7]

Indonesian scholars recognise two types of governing law of a contract.[8] First, governing law of a contract that is expressly chosen by the parties. This will usually be written in a specific choice of law provision within the contract. Second, governing law of a contract

[2] Supreme Court Extraordinary Appeal 445 PK/Pdt/2007 (19 August 2008).

[3] Though this requirement is sometimes dispensed with, see, eg, Art 72 of Act No 1 of 2009 concerning Aviation.

[4] Z Djoko Basuki and others, *Materi Pokok Hukum Perdata Internasional. Modul 6* (Universitas Terbuka, 2014) 37.

[5] Gautama, *Pengantar Hukum* (n 1) 170–171.

[6] S Gautama and H Wiknjosastro, 'Some Aspects of Indonesian Private International Law' (1990) 32 *Malaya Law Review* 430 www.jstor.org/stable/24865645 (accessed 26 May 2018).

[7] Gautama, *Pengantar Hukum* (n 1) 209.

[8] ibid, 181.

that is impliedly chosen by the parties. This implied governing law is indicated by the form and content of the contract, and the intention of the parties when making the contract. For example, where parties make contracts in the fields of Islamic banking, Islamic insurance, or other Islamic financing, the governing law of the contracts, in the absence of express provision otherwise, is *Sharia* or the Compilation of Islamic Law, rather than the Indonesian Civil Code.[9]

In conclusion, the governing law of a contract with foreign elements is the law chosen by the parties in the contract, either expressly or impliedly. However, the parties in the contract must adhere to some limitations in choosing the law that governs their contract.

ii. Determination of the Applicable Law

Indonesian scholars agree that the parties' choice of law, whether express or implied, determines the law applicable to their contract.[10] In the event that the parties do not make a choice of law for their contract, there are several legal doctrines that are known in Indonesia to determine the applicable law.

First, the doctrine of *lex loci contractus*. This doctrine states that the law applicable to a contract is the law of the place in which the parties make or execute their contract. Indonesian scholars agree that this doctrine is difficult to apply to modern international transactions.[11] The difficulty is in determining the place of contracting. Frequently, the parties will never meet in a certain place, for example because the contract will be made online.

Second, the doctrine of *lex loci solutionis*. This doctrine states that the law applicable to a contract is the law of the place in which the contract is performed. This doctrine is difficult to apply where a contract is performed in more than one place.

Third, the doctrine of the proper law of the contract. This doctrine states that the law applicable to a contract is the law of the place that has the most real and substantial connection with the contract. Where a contract has connection with several countries, it is necessary to determine which of those countries has the greatest connection to the contract; the law of that country will be the law applicable to the contract.

Fourth, the doctrine of the most characteristic performance. This doctrine states that the law applicable to a contract is the law of the party who makes the most characteristic performance. For example, in the case of a sales contract the delivery of the goods is considered the most characteristic performance. Therefore, the law of the seller that delivers the goods will be the law applicable to the sales contract. Sudargo Gautama, the leading scholar of Indonesian Private International Law, has recommended that this doctrine be applied to determine the law applicable to a contract in which the parties do not make a choice of law.[12] Professor Gautama's position is also adopted in the 1983, 1997 and 2015 Bills of

[9] YU Oppusunggu and GF Bell, 'Indonesia' in J Basedow and others (eds) *Encyclopedia of Private International Law*, vol 3 (Edward Elgar, 2017) 2170.

[10] Oppusunggu and Bell, 'Indonesia' (n 9) 2170; Basuki and others, *Materi pokok. Modul 6* (n 4) 26–30; S Gautama, *Hukum Perdata Internasional Indonesia Jilid III Bagian 2 Buku Ke Delapan* (Penerbit Alumni, 1987) 11.

[11] Basuki and others, *Materi pokok. Modul 6* (n 4) 51.

[12] Gautama, *Perdata Internasional Jilid III Bag 2* (n 10) 33.

Indonesian Private International Law. The Bills provide that the law applicable to a contract with foreign elements is the parties' choice of law, either made expressly or impliedly, provided that mandatory law does not govern otherwise. Where the parties do not make a choice of law for their contract, the law applicable to their contract is the law of the party who makes the most characteristic performance. Chapter III of the 2015 Bill provides that the law applicable to a sales agreement regarding movable property is the law of the country or the habitual residence of the seller; the law applicable to an insurance agreement is the law of the legal seat of the insurance company; the law applicable to a publishing contract is the law of the legal seat of the publishing company.

However, current judicial practice indicates that Indonesian judges do not always follow the above-mentioned doctrines to determine the law applicable to a contract with foreign elements. For example, in the case of *Bank America National Trust Company; et al v PT. Indah Kiat Pulp & Paper Tbk.; et al*, the parties had made an indenture agreement, loan agreement, and underwriting agreement to fund PT. Indah Kiat Pulp's business expansion. The parties agreed to the laws of the State of New York as the governing law of those agreements. Despite the parties' choice of law, the Bengkalis District Court in Indonesia applied Indonesian law to adjudicate the case. The defendants, who were the holders of the bonds issued by PT. Indah Kiat Pulp's subsidiary, argued that the case should be adjudicated under the laws of New York State, not Indonesian law. Despite the defendants' arguments, the Bengkalis District Court decided in favour of PT. Indah Kiat Pulp and annulled all agreements between the parties. The Riau High Court and Indonesian Supreme Court affirmed the Bengkalis District Court's judgment.[13] Only when the opponents of PT. Indah Kiat Pulp & Paper Tbk. applied for extraordinary appeal did the Indonesian judiciary recognise New York law as the law applicable to the parties' agreements. The judges in the extraordinary panel annulled the decisions made by the previous courts because those courts had not applied New York law.[14]

As explained, Indonesian scholars have proposed several legal doctrines which may determine the applicable law of a contract containing foreign elements. The Bills of Indonesian Private International Law engage with these doctrines. The Bills provide that the law applicable to a contract with foreign elements is the parties' choice of law, either made expressly or impliedly. Where the parties do not make a choice of law for their contract, the law applicable to their contract is the law of the party who makes the most characteristic performance. However, current judicial practice indicates that Indonesian judges do not always follow these doctrines. This has been demonstrated in several cases of international contract disputes brought before Indonesian courts. This uncertainty concerning the law applicable to a contract with foreign elements may be solved when the Bill of Indonesian Private International Law is passed to become an Act. The choice of law rules in the Bill will then be binding on all parties to international contracts and to all Indonesian judges that adjudicate the parties' disputes.

[13] District Court of Bengkalis Decision 05/PDT.G./2003/PN-BKS (21 September 2004); affd High Court of Riau Decision 40/PDT/2004/PTR (16 June 2005); affd Supreme Court Decision 381 K/Pdt/2006 (24 May 2006).

[14] Supreme Court Extraordinary Appeal 445 PK/Pdt/2007 (19 August 2008).

iii. Formal Validity

Pursuant to Article 18, paragraph (1) AB, the law applied to determine the formal validity of a contract is the law of the country where the contract is performed. If the contract has been made and performed in accordance with the legal formalities required in the country where performance takes place, the contract will be regarded as formally valid in Indonesia. For example, two persons of Indonesian nationality make and perform a sales and purchase contract in Singapore. If the contract is made in accordance with the legal formalities required by Singaporean law, it will be regarded as formally valid in Indonesia.

However, for certain matters additional legislation must be referred to. For example, Article 31 paragraph (1) of the Flag, Language, State Emblem, and National Anthem Act 2009 requires that the Indonesian language be used in all agreements involving Indonesian parties irrespective of the place where the agreements are made or performed. As such, if the agreements are made in written form, the agreements must be written in Indonesian. Article 31, paragraph (2) of the same Act further requires that such agreements also be written in the language of the foreign party and/or in English. Failure to comply with this formality will result in the agreements being deemed invalid by Indonesian courts, as in the case of *PT Bangun Karya Pratama Lestari/PT. BKPL v Nine AM Ltd* In this case, the West Jakarta District Court rendered invalid and annulled a loan agreement between PT BKPL (an Indonesian mining company/debtor) and Nine AM Ltd (PT BKPL's American creditor) that was executed only in English. The Court regarded the agreement as violating Article 31 of the 2009 Act. As a consequence of the annulment, the judge ordered PT. BKPL to make restitution of the loan to Nine AM Ltd. The judgment of the West Jakarta District Court was upheld by the Jakarta High Court and the Supreme Court.[15]

Pursuant to Article 17 AB, the formal validity of contracts concerning immovable property is determined by the law of the country where the immovable property is located. Article 17 AB stipulates that 'Concerning immovable property, the law of the country or place where the property is located applies.' Hence the law of the place where the immovable property is located determines both the formal and material validity of the contract. Article 17 AB prevails over Article 18, paragraph (1) AB. For example, if an Indonesian company takes a loan from a Singaporean bank and the company's factory in Indonesia is used as the security or collateral for the loan, the mortgage agreement must comply with all legal formalities of Indonesian law, instead of Singaporean law, because the contract relates to immovable property located in Indonesia.

iv. Material Validity

Indonesian courts apply Indonesian law to determine the material validity of international contracts involving Indonesian and foreign parties, irrespective of the country where the contract is performed or executed.

To be materially valid according to Indonesian law, a contract with foreign elements involving an Indonesian party must meet the four requirements stipulated in Article 1320

[15] District Court of West Jakarta Decision 451/Pdt.G/2012/PN.Jkt.Bar (17 June 2013); High Court of West Jakarta Decision 48/PDT/2014/PT.DKI (17 June 2013); Supreme Court Decision 601 K/Pdt/2015 (31 August 2015).

BW. First, the parties must consent to the contract. Consent is not valid if it is granted based on mistake or obtained by duress or fraud (Article 1321 BW). Second, the parties must have capacity to enter into the contract. The capacity of the parties to enter into a contract with foreign elements will be discussed further in the following section. Third, the contract must concern a certain subject matter. In other words, the parties must be able to determine the nature of the subject matter of their contract (Articles 1332 and 1333 BW). Fourth, the contract must have a legitimate cause. If a contract is without a cause, or concluded pursuant to an illegitimate cause, the contract will be invalid (Article 1335 BW). What are regarded as legitimate and illegitimate causes of a contract is determined solely by Indonesian law. These four elements (consent, capacity, specific subject matter, and legitimate cause) must be present in contracts involving Indonesian parties. If they are absent, the contract will not be valid and enforceable in Indonesia.

In short, Indonesian courts apply Indonesian law to determine the material validity of contracts with foreign elements involving an Indonesian party.

v. *Capacity*

The capacity of the parties to enter into a contract is one of the substantive requirements to make a valid contract. If the parties lack capacity, or are otherwise not competent to enter into their contract, their purported contract will be unenforceable (Article 1320 BW). Indonesian scholars agree that capacity to perform a legal act is part of personal law (personal statute), and the capacity of a person to enter into a contract is determined by the national law of the person (the nationality principle).[16]

This application of the nationality principle based on Article 16 AB, which stipulates, 'Statutory provisions governing the status and capacity of persons remain binding for Indonesian citizens during their stay abroad.' Although Article 16 AB governs the application of nationality principle only for Indonesians abroad, jurisprudence established since the Dutch colonial era, rules that the nationality principle also applies to the personal statute of foreigners in Indonesia.[17] Therefore, the capacity of foreigners to enter into a contract involving an Indonesian party is determined by the national law of the foreigners. In 1925, the *Raad van Justitie* of Medan held that the Japanese law allowing a married woman to conduct a legal act independently of her husband was applicable to a Japanese wife who lived in Medan and applied for bankruptcy. The woman applied for bankruptcy to avoid being put under the civil imprisonment (*gijzeling*) that was requested by her business partner. Article 110 of the Dutch East Indies Civil Code stipulated that, 'A wife may not appear in court without the assistance of her husband, even though she is married without sharing matrimonial property with her husband, and has an independent profession.'[18]

[16] S Gautama, *Hukum Perdata Internasional Indonesia Buku Ketujuh Jilid Ke-Tiga (Bagian Pertama)* (Penerbit Alumni, 1981) 31.

[17] Gautama, *Perdata Internasional Jilid III Bag 1* (n 16) 9; S Gautama, *Hukum Perdata Internasional Indonesia Jilid Dua Bagian Dua Buku Ketiga* (Penerbit Alumni, 1973) 100.

[18] Since BW or the Dutch East Indies Civil Code becomes Indonesian Civil Code after Indonesia's independence, the Indonesian Supreme Court has issued several circular letters to Indonesian courts concerning the implementation of BW after independence. In Supreme Court Circular Letter No 1115/P/3292/M/1963 dated 5 September 1963, the Supreme Court told all Indonesian courts that Art 110 and some other Articles of BW were no longer enforceable or were abolished. As such, after 1963, a wife may appear before the court with or without the assistance of her husband.

However, this Article was no bar to the woman's application. The court accepted the woman's application as valid based on her national law.[19]

An exception to the nationality principle applies to foreigners who domicile in Indonesia and originate from countries that apply the domicile principle. For them, capacity to enter into contracts in Indonesia is determined by Indonesian law. This is because Indonesian Private International Law applies the *Renvoi* (remission) principle as has been discussed in Chapter 1, section IV.D on Renvoi and transmission.

The law governing the capacity of a natural person to enter into a contract is provided in Articles 1329 to 1331 BW. Article 1329 stipulates that, 'Each person is capable to enter into agreements, unless he has been declared by law of being incapable.' Pursuant to Article 1330 BW, persons incapable of entering into agreements are: minors; persons under conservatorship; and married women in certain cases stipulated by law. Minors who are incapable of entering into agreements are those who are under 21 years old and have not previously been married (Article 330 BW). Regarding married women, Article 1330 BW has been superseded by Article 31 of the Marriage Act 1974. This provides that a husband and a wife have equal rights and position in society, and each of them has the right to perform legal actions.

With regard to corporations or legal persons, Indonesian Private International Law determines the status and capacity of a corporation based on the law of its statutory seat or the law of the place of its headquarters. This has been previously discussed in Chapter 1, sections V.A.ii, V.B.ii, V.C.ii on Corporations. If according to either the law of the corporation's statutory seat or the law of the country of its headquarters, the corporation has capacity to enter into a contract, the corporation will be regarded competent to make a contract with an Indonesian party.

To conclude, since according to Indonesian Private International Law the capacity to enter into a contract is part of personal law, the applicable law to determine the capacity of a natural person to enter into a contract is the law of its nationality. For a legal person or a corporation, the applicable law to determine its capacity to enter into a contract is the law of the corporation's statutory seat or the law of the country of the corporation's headquarter.

vi. Mandatory Rules

The doctrine of mandatory rules has been developed by Indonesian legal scholars, mostly in the field of contract. Sudargo Gautama has written that some laws are considered mandatory rules and therefore must be applied to a contract irrespective of the parties' choice of law. He explains that Indonesian agrarian law, customer protection law, employment law, and laws concerning export and import prohibitions, rental or lease, and exchange regulations, are categorised as mandatory rules because they relate to Indonesian social and economic interests.[20] He refers to the opinion of Kollewijn on this issue.[21] In addition, contracts in certain fields must always be governed by Indonesian law.

[19] S Gautama, *Hukum Perdata Internasional Indonesia Jilid Kedua (Bagian Pertama) Cetakan Ke-3* (Eresco Bandung, 1986) 31.

[20] Gautama, *Pengantar Hukum* (n 1) 170, 205.

[21] S Gautama, *Hukum Perdata Internasional Indonesia Jilid II Bagian 4 Buku Ke 5* (Penerbit Alumni, 1992) 238.

For example, Article 38 of Government Regulation No 35 of 2004, concerning upstream oil and gas business activities, requires that contracts for the production sharing of gas and oil between foreign contractors and the Indonesian Special Task Force for Upstream Oil and Gas Business Activities (SKK Migas) use Indonesian law as the applicable law of the contracts. Article 4 of Government Regulation No 42 of 2007, concerning franchise, requires that franchise agreements with foreign elements in Indonesia be made in writing and use Indonesian law as the applicable law.

The doctrine of mandatory law has been used by the Indonesian courts in several contract cases. The courts have used wide discretion to decide what law to deem mandatory. In *Yani Haryanto v E. D. & F. Man (Sugar) Ltd*, the Central Jakarta District Court held that the export-import agreement between E. D. & F. Man (Sugar) Ltd (British sugar exporter) and Yani Haryanto (Indonesian sugar importer) was invalid as it violated Presidential Decree No 43 of 1971.[22] Presidential Decree No 43 ordained that, to stabilise the price and stock of sugar in Indonesia, the Indonesian Bureau of Logistics (BULOG) was to become the sole importer and distributor of sugar in Indonesia. Therefore, no other entity, including Yani Haryanto, was permitted to make agreements to import sugar into Indonesia.

In another case, *PT Bangun Karya Pratama Lestari v Nine AM Ltd*, the West Jakarta District Court rendered invalid and annulled a loan agreement between PT Bangun Karya Pratama Lestari/BKPL (an Indonesian mining company/debtor) and Nine AM Ltd (its American creditor). The agreement had been executed in English only, so was deemed to violate Article 31 of the Flag, Language, State Emblem, and National Anthem Act 2009, which requires that all agreements involving Indonesian parties be written in Indonesian. As a consequence of the annulment, the judge ordered PT. BKPL to make restitution of the loan to Nine AM Ltd. The judgment of the West Jakarta District Court was upheld by the Jakarta High Court and the Supreme Court.[23] The judges' interpretation of the mandatory status of Article 31 of the Flag, Language, State Emblem, and National Anthem Act 2009 was not shared by the government, that is the Minister of Law and Human Rights, who allowed, based on the principle of freedom of contract, that private contracts could be made in English only.[24] In his letter No M.HH.UM.01.01-35 dated 28 December 2009, the Minister argued that the implementation of Article 31 of the 2009 Act was pending the issuance of the presidential regulation concerning the use of Indonesian, as stipulated by Article 40 of the Act.[25] However, the minister's letter is not legally binding, so the judgment of the Indonesian courts on the mandatory status of Article 31 of the 2009 Act prevails.

In both cases discussed above, it was Indonesian defendants as debtors who requested that the court annul their agreements with their foreign partners (creditors) for the reason

[22] District Court of Central Jakarta Decision 499/Pdt/G/VI/1988/PN.Jkt.Pst (29 June 1989); affd High Court of Jakarta Decision 486/Pdt/1989/PT.DKI 14 (14 October 1989); affd Supreme Court Decision 1205K/Pdt/1990 (4 December 1991.

[23] District Court of West Jakarta Decision 451/Pdt.G/2012/PN.Jkt.Bar (17 June 2013); High Court of Jakarta Decision 48/PDT/2014/PT.DKI (17 June 2013); Supreme Court Decision 601 K/Pdt/2015 (31 August 2015).

[24] Hukumonline, 'UU Bahasa Batalkan Kontrak Bisnis Internasional' (*hukumonline*, 12 October 2013) www.hukumonline.com/berita/baca/lt5258d22c06dfe/uu-bahasa-batalkan-kontrak-bisnis-internasional (accessed 17 January 2019).

[25] Hukumonline, 'Pernyataan Menkumham Bertolak Belakang dengan Suratnya' (*hukumonline*, 5 February 2010) www.hukumonline.com/berita/baca/lt4b6b97f03c20a/pernyataan-menkumham-bertolak-belakang-dengan-suratnya (accessed 17 January 2019).

that their agreements did not comply with the laws, the Presidential Decree No 43 of 1971 and the Flag, Language, State Emblem, and National Anthem Act 2009, respectively. The courts agreed with the Indonesian defendants that compliance with the Indonesian laws was mandatory. As the agreements failed to comply with the relevant laws, they suffered the consequence of annulment.

Indonesian courts have reached differing conclusions on the mandatory status of Article 1266 of the Indonesian Civil Code (*Burgerlijk Wetboek voor Nederlandsch-Indie* or BW). Article 1266 BW provides that:

> (1) The resolutive condition is deemed to be always included in a mutual agreement in the case one of the parties fails to comply with its obligation. In such case, the agreement is not automatically dissolved by law, but *the dissolution shall be requested to the court*.[26]
>
> (2) This request shall also be made, even though the resolutive condition due to the non-compliance of obligation is expressed in the agreement. If the resolutive condition is not expressed in the agreement, the judge shall be free, depending on the circumstances, to grant the defendant, at his request, a period to comply with his obligation, which period shall not exceed one month.

Although Article 1266 BW is mandatory, in practice parties both in domestic and international agreements often waive it. Indonesian courts also allow the termination of agreements by one party without a court order when the other party fails to comply with their obligations. In the case of *Ir. Ermansyah Jamin v PT. Perusahaan Listrik Negara/PLN (Persero)*, the South Jakarta District Court approved the waiver of Article 1266 BW in a Rental and Purchase Agreement and approved the dissolution of the Rental and Purchase Agreement by the owner of the property when the tenant of the property had failed to keep up payments to the owner of the property. The tenant did not accept the dissolution of the agreement by the owner and requested that the court allow continuation of the agreement. The Court rejected the tenant's arguments, approving the unilateral dissolution of the agreement and ordered the tenant to vacate and return the property to the owner. The Court also ordered the property's owner to return the 90 per cent of the instalment already paid by the tenant and keep the remaining 10 per cent once the tenant vacated the property.[27]

In another case, the court adopted a different interpretation of Article 1266 BW. In the case of *Tn Soegianto; Ny Ellies Soegianto v Tn Eka Gunawan; Ny Linda Soetanto*, the court did not allow the parties in an Asset Purchase Agreement to waive Article 1266 BW, although the seller and buyer in the agreement had agreed to waive the Article. When the seller purported to unilaterally dissolve the agreement because the buyer was ten months late completing the last instalment, the buyer sued the seller in the Bandung District Court and requested that the court order the seller to continue to comply with their agreement. The Court agreed with the buyer despite the parties' waiver of Article 1266 BW. The Court applied Article 1266 BW in this case to prevent unjust enrichment of the seller, who benefitted from a clause in the agreement allowing him to keep all the money already paid by the buyer in the case of termination of the contract. At the time that the seller dissolved the agreement, he had already received 75 per cent of the total amount due from the buyer.

[26] Emphasis added.
[27] District Court of South Jakarta Decision 338/Pdt.G/2014/PN.Jkt.Sel (3 December 2014).

Therefore, the Court applied Article 1266 BW and ordered the seller to continue selling the asset to the buyer.[28] Although these cases involved domestic contracts without foreign elements, the judgments of the courts can be applied to international contracts involving Indonesian and foreign parties.

With respect to industrial employment contracts in Indonesia, Article 1266 BW cannot be waived by the parties. That is, it is a mandatory provision of law. This follows from Articles 151, 155, and 170 of the Manpower Act 2003, which prohibit the termination of industrial employment contracts by the employers without permission from the Institute for the settlement of industrial relation disputes. Failure to obtain permission will render void the purported termination of the employment contract.

As discussed, the doctrine of mandatory rules has been developed by scholars and implemented by the courts. In implementing the doctrine, judges have employed wide discretion to determine what laws are deemed mandatory rules which must be applied to contracts irrespective of the parties' agreements. Judges might justify finding that a law is mandatory by reference to public policy and the interest of the state. Such was the case in *Yani Haryanto v E. D. & F. Man (Sugar) Ltd.* Similarly, judges decided that a law was mandatory in order to protect the weaker party to a contract in the case of *Tn Soegianto; Ny Ellies Soegianto v Tn Eka Gunawan; Ny Linda Soetanto.* In different circumstances, the mandatory status of a law could be waived for economic and efficiency reasons. For example, Article 1266 BW is often waived in commercial contracts to speed up the process of terminating contracts by non-defaulting parties without having to pass through costly and lengthy court procedures.

B. Specific Contracts

i. Consumer Contracts

A consumer contract with foreign elements involving an Indonesian party is governed by the law chosen by the parties to the contract. This principle is found in Article 18, paragraph (2) of the Electronic Information and Transaction Act 2008 as amended in 2016, which provides that the parties have the right to make a choice of law for their international electronic transaction. The elucidation of Article 18, paragraph (2) explains that the choice of law can be made only if there is a foreign element in the transaction and must be implemented in accordance with the principles of private international law. Furthermore, Article 18, paragraph (3) of the same Act provides that if the parties do not make a choice of law, the governing law of their transaction will be determined by the principles of private international law. This principle can also be applied to consumer contracts with foreign elements that are not conducted electronically based on Article 1338, paragraph (1) BW that recognises the parties' freedom of contract.

The Hague Principles on Choice of Law in International Commercial Contracts ('the Hague Principles'), developed and approved by the Hague Conference on Private

[28] District Court of Bandung Decision 168/Pdt.G/2008/PN.Bdg (7 January 2009); affd Supreme Court Decision 2821K/Pdt/2009 (18 March 2010); affd Supreme Court Extraordinary Appeal 738 PK/Pdt/2010 (2 May 2011).

International Law, do not govern consumer contracts. This is because one party in a consumer contract, namely the consumer, is not acting as a trader or professional in the contract, unlike in other types of commercial contracts.[29] The consumer is a natural person who is merely a user of the goods or services. In addition, the bargaining power of the consumer in consumer contracts is presumptively weaker,[30] because in practice most consumer contracts take the form of a standard contract in which the content, including the governing law of the contract, has been predetermined by one party, namely the commercial enterprise. To date, Indonesia has not adopted the Hague Principles. Despite this, Indonesian legal doctrine concerning consumer protection law is similar to the Hague Principles' approach to consumer contracts. Although in Indonesia contracting parties have the right to make a choice of law to govern their consumer contracts, their choice of law cannot set aside the Consumer Protection Act 1999. The Act is a mandatory law designed to protect consumers, so supersedes the parties' choice of law. In addition to the Consumer Protection Act 1999, there are other mandatory laws that govern the protection of consumers in various sectors, such as in phone and internet services (the Telecommunications Act No 36 of 1999); banking and financial services (regulations issued by the Indonesian Central Bank and Financial Services Authority); healthcare services (the Health Act No 36 of 2009; the Hospitals Act No 44 of 2009); medical services (the Medical Practices Act No 29 of 2004); legal services (the Advocates Act No 18 of 2003); and air transport services (the Aviation Act 2009).

In other words, the parties to a consumer contract with foreign elements may choose the law that governs their contract. However, their freedom of choice is limited by the Consumer Protection Act 1999 and other mandatory laws that govern the protection of consumers. If there is a conflict between the parties' choice of law and those mandatory laws, the mandatory laws prevail.

ii. Employment Contracts

The Manpower Act 2003 recognises two types of employment contract. First, an individual work agreement between an employee and an employer (Article 1, no 14). Second, a collective work agreement resulting from negotiation between a labour union and an entrepreneur or between several labour unions and several entrepreneurs (Article 1, no 21). The Manpower Act 2003 also recognises employment contracts between foreign workers and Indonesian companies (Chapter VIII of the Manpower Act 2003). The Act mentions three types of disputes that can arise from employment contracts, namely disputes over rights, interests, and termination of employment (Article 1, no 22). Pursuant to Article 56 of the Industrial Dispute Settlement Act 2004, all these disputes fall under the jurisdiction of the Industrial Relations Court, which is a special Court established within the district court in the capital cities of provinces in Indonesia. The only disputes which do not fall under the jurisdiction of this Court are disputes between foreign embassies or foreign country

[29] Hague Conference on Private International Law, *Principles on Choice of Law in International Commercial Contracts* (The Hague Conference on Private International Law Permanent Bureau, 2015) 29.

[30] ibid, 25.

representative offices in Indonesia and foreign workers who work as diplomatic or consular officers (Article 42, paragraph (3) of the Manpower Act 2003).

The Industrial Relations Court will always apply Indonesian law to settle disputes arising out of employment contracts in Indonesia, including disputes between Indonesian employees and foreign embassies that employ them. In 2017, the Supreme Court designated the judgment in *Brazilian Embassy in Jakarta v Luis F.S.S Pereira*[31] as a landmark decision.[32] In Indonesia, the objective of designating particular judgments as landmark decisions is, among others, to highlight principles whose consistent application would lead to greater legal certainty and thereby lead to a more stable jurisprudence.[33] The legal principles established by the landmark decision in the *Brazilian Embassy* case are as follows: (1) Employment contracts between foreign country representatives and local staff or employees are always governed by the Manpower Act 2003. (2) Diplomatic immunity under the Vienna Conventions on Diplomatic and Consular Relations are regarded as waived when foreign legal representatives enter into employment contracts with local staff or employees. The landmark decision confirms judgments in similar cases made by the Industrial Relations Court.

In the case of *Eriks Pte Ltd (Representative Office Indonesia) v May Lindawati*, Ms Lindawati had entered into an employment contract with Eriks Pte Ltd, whose legal seat was in Pasir Panjang Distripark, Singapore. The contract contained no express choice of law provision. Pursuant to the contract, Ms Lindawati worked as the Sales Secretary at Eriks Pte Ltd Representative Office Indonesia in Jakarta and received a monthly salary in Indonesian currency (*Rupiah*). However, she never received the religious/festivity holiday allowance to which she was entitled under Indonesian law.[34] When Ms Lindawati asked Eriks Pte Ltd's representative office in Indonesia to pay her religious holiday allowance, the company argued that Ms Lindawati was an employee of a Singaporean company that was governed under Singaporean law, and that Singaporean employment law did not require any religious holiday allowance. After four years working in the company without receiving religious holiday allowance, Ms Lindawati involved an advocate to represent her in her demand for the religious holiday allowance. As a result, Eriks Pte Ltd in Singapore fired her with a letter of termination dated 1 February 2010. Pursuant to the Industrial Dispute Settlement Act 2004, Ms Lindawati brought Eriks Pte Ltd's Indonesian office to the Industrial Relations Court in Central Jakarta and demanded that the company pay her severance package and overdue religious holiday allowance in accordance with Indonesian law. Eriks Pte Ltd's Indonesian office objected to Ms Lindawati's claim, arguing that the Indonesian office was not a party to Ms Lindawati's employment contract. According to them, Ms Lindawati was an employee of a Singaporean company that was governed by Singaporean law. Therefore, Ms Lindawati could not sue the Indonesian office.

[31] Supreme Court Decision 376 K/Pdt.Sus-PHI/2013 (29 October 2013).

[32] Tim Pokja Laporan Tahunan Mari, *Laporan Tahunan 2017 Mahkamah Agung Republik Indonesia* (Mahkamah Agung RI, 2018) 202.

[33] A Suadi, *Penyelesaian Sengketa Ekonomi Syariah: Penemuan dan Kaidah Hukum* (Prenada Media, 2018) 98–99.

[34] Under Indonesian law, the religious holiday allowance is a yearly mandatory allowance that must be paid by a company or a business owner to its employees who have continuously worked for the company for a certain period of time: Regulation of Minister of Manpower No PER.04/MEN/1994 of 1994 as amended by Regulation of Minister of Manpower No 6 of 2016 concerning religious holiday allowance for workers/labourers in company.

They pointed to, for example, the fact that the letter of termination was issued by Eriks Pte Ltd in Singapore. The Indonesian office further maintained that Ms Lindawati and Eriks Pte Ltd in Singapore had impliedly chosen Singaporean law as the law governing their employment contract. They argued that Ms Lindawati had agreed to work in accordance with the terms and conditions of employment determined by the company, as stipulated by Article 4 of the employment contract. Accordingly, the dispute should be settled under Singaporean law in a Singaporean court. The Industrial Relations Court in Central Jakarta dismissed the objection of Eriks Pte Ltd's Indonesian office and decided mostly in favour of Ms Lindawati.[35] Eriks Pte Ltd's Indonesian office appealed the decision to the Indonesian Supreme Court. The Supreme Court affirmed the lower court's decision and decided that the lower court was correct in applying Indonesian law to the case. The Supreme Court found that Eriks Pte Ltd's Indonesian office was the employer of Ms Lindawati, under Article 1. 5c of the Manpower Act 2003, and therefore Ms Lindawati was correct to bring a lawsuit against the Indonesian office in the Industrial Relations Court. Given that her employment was in Indonesia and with an Indonesian company, the Supreme Court could not find any connecting factor between the employment of Ms Lindawati and Singaporean law. The Court concluded that the lower court was correct to implement Indonesian employment law to the case. On this basis, the Supreme Court rejected the appeal brought by Eriks Pte Ltd's Indonesian office.[36]

Foreign workers who enter into employment contracts in Indonesia must obtain a work permit from the Indonesian Ministry of Manpower. Employers that employ foreign workers in Indonesia must also obtain a permit from the Ministry entitling them to employ foreigners (Article 42 of the Manpower Act 2003). Their employment contracts will be governed by Indonesian law and the foreign workers must comply with Indonesian employment law. An example of the application of these rules is found in the case between *Lau Chak Loong v PT Wira Pamungkas Pariwara (Young & Rubicam Indonesia)*,[37] which concerned a Malaysian individual employed by an Indonesian corporation subsidiary of a multinational company.

In conclusion, although the courts in the above-mentioned cases did not expressly classify Indonesian employment law as mandatory law, their decisions demonstrate that Indonesian law will always be the law applicable to employment contracts performed in Indonesia. In addition, disputes arising out of employment contracts in Indonesia must be brought to the Industrial Relations Court, which will only apply Indonesian law.

iii. Insurance Contracts

As previously discussed in section 12.1.1 on the governing law of contracts, in Indonesian practice English law is usually chosen to govern marine insurance contracts in Indonesia, although neither the contracts nor the parties are connected with the UK.[38]

[35] Central Jakarta Industrial Relations Court Decision 185/PHI.G/2010/PN.Jkt.Pst (9 November 2010).

[36] Supreme Court Decision 278 K/PDT.SUS/2011 (5 July 2011).

[37] Central Jakarta Industrial Relations Court Decision 274/Pdt.Sus-PHI/2015/PN.JKT.PST (14 April 2016); affd Supreme Court Decision 697 K/Pdt.Sus-PHI/2016 (15 September 2016).

[38] Basuki and others, *Materi pokok. Modul 6* (n 4) 37.

In the case of *PT. Pelayaran Manalagi v PT. Asuransi Harta Aman Pratama, Tbk*, the plaintiff, an Indonesian shipping company (PT. Pelayaran Manalagi), sued PT. Asuransi Harta Aman Pratama ('PT. AHAP'), an Indonesian insurance company, for breach of an insurance agreement. The plaintiff alleged that PT. AHAP had refused to pay an insurance claim filed by the plaintiff who had lost its vessel amid fire during transit. According to the plaintiff, the loss that it suffered was covered by the Marine Hull and Machinery Policy No 03.08.05.10.827. 00025 dated 24 October 2005. In accordance with the *actor sequitur forum rei* principle stipulated in Article 118 HIR, PT. Pelayaran Manalagi filed their lawsuit against PT. AHAP in the Central Jakarta District Court because PT. AHAP's legal seat was in Central Jakarta. The Central Jakarta District Court confirmed its jurisdiction over the case. In adjudicating the dispute, the Court applied the English law and practice that was the applicable law of the parties' marine insurance agreement (labelled Institute Time Clauses – Hulls). PT. AHAP objected to the jurisdiction of the Central Jakarta District Court, arguing that only the English courts had jurisdiction over the case because the applicable law of the parties' agreement was English law. On 29 July 2010, the Central Jakarta District Court issued a preliminary decision that dismissed PT. AHAP's objection to the Court's jurisdiction. On 21 October 2010, the Court made a final decision in favour of the plaintiff. The Jakarta High Court affirmed the decision of the Central Jakarta District Court.[39] PT. AHAP appealed those decisions to the Supreme Court. In the Supreme Court, PT. AHAP once again argued that the Central Jakarta District Court did not have jurisdiction over the case because the applicable law of the Institute Time Clauses – Hulls, the parties' insurance agreement, was English law. However, this time, PT. AHAP also presented evidence that the Institute Time Clauses – Hulls agreement was an integral part of the New Marine Policy Form (MAR 91), which gave exclusive jurisdiction to English courts. The MAR 91 stipulated that 'This insurance shall be subject to the exclusive jurisdiction of the English Courts, except as may be expressly provided herein to the contrary.' The Supreme Court accepted PT. AHAP's appeal and held that the English courts, not the Central Jakarta District Court, had jurisdiction over the case.[40] Hence the Court applied the provisions of the New Marine Policy Form (MAR 91) giving exclusive jurisdiction to English courts. The Supreme Court respected the English law and practice that was the applicable law of the parties' marine insurance agreement. In addition, this case is evidence of parties' preference for English law as the governing law of marine insurance contracts.

For other types of insurance contracts with foreign elements that involve Indonesian parties, the governing law is the law chosen by the parties. If the parties do not make a choice of law, the prevailing doctrine of the most characteristic performance adopted in the 1983, 1997 and 2015 Bills of Indonesian Private International Law should apply. That means the law of the place of an insurance company's statutory seat will govern the relevant contract. Applying the most characteristic performance doctrine will usually lead to the insurance company being treated as the party making the most characteristic performance in an insurance contract.

[39] District Court of Central Jakarta Decision 52/Pdt.G/2010/PN.Jkt.Pst. (21 October 2010); affd High Court of Jakarta Decision 297/PDT/2011/PT.DKI (24 November 2011).

[40] Supreme Court Decision 1935 K/Pdt/2012 (14 January 2013).

iv. Contracts for the Sale of Immovable Property

Article 17 AB determines the law applicable to contracts for the sale of immovable property. The Article stipulates that, 'Concerning immovable property, the law of the country or place where the property is situated applies.' As such, Article 17 AB applies the principle of *lex rei sitae* (the law where the property is situated). Hence if the immovable property is situated in Indonesia, Indonesian law will govern contracts for its sale. Indonesian law will also determine the validity and legal effect, of contracts for the sale of immovable property, and the formalities necessary for their creation. Indonesian law, as the *lex situs* of the land, also governs contracts for the sale of land and buildings and all objects attached to the land. As such, the validity of such contracts, their procedure and their effect will be governed by Indonesian law, whether or not the parties are Indonesian citizens or foreigners.

Note that Indonesian registered or Indonesian-flagged vessels with the minimum gross weight of 20 cubic meters are characterised as immovable property by Article 749, paragraph (3) of the Commercial Code. Accordingly, the principle of *lex rei sitae* in Article 17 AB applies to the vessels. Hence, contracts for the sale of such vessels will be governed by Indonesian law.

v. Contracts for Sale of Goods

In principle, the governing law of sale of goods contracts with foreign elements is the law chosen by the parties in the contract. This principle follows from Article 1338, paragraph (1) BW, which recognises parties' freedom of contract, including the freedom of choosing a governing law for their contract. Article 1338 BW stipulates that all valid agreements made are binding as law to the parties. Hence, the parties' choice of law will also bind the parties in their contracts for sale of goods.

Contracts for the international sale of goods involving Indonesian parties by common practice adopt certain trade usages to govern the obligations of the parties with respect to delivery of the goods. The International Commercial Terms (INCOTERMS) are commonly used in contracts. INCOTERMS, published by the International Chamber of Commerce, is comprised of a series of terms parties may wish to adopt. The parties will agree to incorporate a particular term or terms into their contract, such as FOB, CIF, FAS, and so on. The agreed commercial term may determine what acts the seller must do in delivering the item sold; what acts the buyer must do to accommodate the delivery; what costs of delivery each party must bear, and at what point in the delivery process the risk of loss passes from seller to buyer. The application of a commercial term of INCOTERMS reflects the parties' freedom of choosing a particular term or trade usage with respect to the delivery of goods, departing from the rules provided by the parties' national laws. Lastly, the prevailing academic opinion in Indonesia accepts the doctrine of *dépeçage* in international business contracts whereby the parties in a contract may subject different parts of their contract to different systems of law.[41]

[41] Gautama and Wiknjosastro 'Some Aspects' (n 6) 430.

Despite the parties' freedom to choose the governing law of their contract for sale of goods, the law chosen by the parties may not infringe Indonesian *ordre public*, mandatory rules, or public law. In the case of *Yani Haryanto v E. D. & F. Man (Sugar) Ltd*, the Central Jakarta District Court held that an export-import agreement between E. D. & F. Man (Sugar) Ltd and Yani Haryanto was invalid as it violated Presidential Decree No 43 of 1971.[42] Presidential Decree No 43 required that, to stabilise the price and stock of sugar in Indonesia, the Indonesian Bureau of Logistics (BULOG) became the sole importer and distributor of sugar in Indonesia. Therefore, no other entity, including Yani Haryanto, was permitted to make an agreement to import sugar into Indonesia. More generally, in the context of international contracts for sale of goods, public laws usually govern the taxation of the transaction, foreign exchange control, and customs. The parties in the contracts may not infringe these public laws.

Where the parties do not make a choice of law for their contract, either expressly or impliedly, the prevailing doctrine to determine the applicable law of the contract is the doctrine of the most characteristic performance.[43] This doctrine states that the law applicable to a contract is the law of the party who makes the most characteristic performance. For example, in the case of a sales contract, the delivery of the goods is considered the most characteristic performance. Therefore, the law of the seller that delivers the goods will be the law applicable to contracts for the sale of goods. This doctrine is also adopted in the 1983, 1997 and 2015 Bills of Indonesian Private International Law. The Bills provide that the law applicable to a contract with foreign elements is the parties' choice of law, either made expressly or impliedly, provided that mandatory law does not govern otherwise. If the parties do not make a choice of law for their contract, the law applicable to their contract is the law of the party who makes the most characteristic performance. With respect to the law of the party who makes the most characteristic performance, Chapter III of the 2015 Bill provides that the law applicable to a sales agreement on movable property is the law of the country or the habitual residence of the seller.

In summary, the governing law of contracts for the sale of goods with foreign elements is the law chosen by the parties in the contract. The law chosen by the parties shall not infringe Indonesian *ordre public*, mandatory rules, and public law. If the parties do not make a choice of law for their contract for sale of goods, either expressly or impliedly, the law of the seller who delivers the goods will be the law applicable to the contracts for sale of goods (the doctrine of the most characteristic performance).

vi. Contracts for the Hire of Goods

Pursuant to Article 17 AB, the law applicable to contracts for the hire of immovable property is the law of the country or place where the immovable property is situated. If the immovable property is situated in Indonesia, Indonesian law will govern the contracts for

[42] District Court of Central Jakarta Decision 499/Pdt/G/VI/1988/PN.Jkt.Pst (29 June 1989); affd High Court of Jakarta Decision 486/Pdt/1989/PT.DKI 14 (14 October 1989); affd Supreme Court Decision 1205K/Pdt/1990 (4 December 1991.

[43] Gautama, *Perdata Internasional Jilid III Bag 2* (n 10) 33; Basuki and others, *Materi pokok. Modul 6* (n 4) 54–55; IBR Supancana, *Naskah Akademik Rancangan Undang-Undang tentang Hukum Perdata Internasional (lanjutan)* (Badan Pembinaan Hukum Nasional Kementerian Hukum dan Hak Asasi Manusia RI, 2015) 47, 204 www.bphn.go.id/data/documents/na_ruu_ttg_hukum_perdata_internasional_(lanjutan).pdf (accessed 8 July 2018).

the hire of immovable property. Indonesian law will also determine the validity, legal effect, and formality of the contracts for the hire of immovable property. Regarding contracts for the hire of movable property with foreign elements in Indonesia, the governing law of the contracts is the law chosen by the parties provided that the choice of law does not infringe Indonesian *ordre public*, mandatory rules, and public law. In this respect, a mandatory law of particular significance is the Consumer Protection Act 1999.

vii. Contracts for the Carriage of Goods by Sea, Air, or Land

In a contract for the carriage of goods with foreign elements, the parties are a shipper and a carrier. The shipper makes a contract with a carrier that promises to transport goods to a consignee's location in a different country. In practice, contracts for the carriage of goods with foreign elements are usually in the form of standard contracts, in which the terms and conditions are set by the carriers. This includes the provision determining the governing law of the contract.

Where the parties do not make a choice of law for their contract, the prevailing doctrine to determine the applicable law of a contract for the carriage of goods with foreign elements is the doctrine of the most characteristic performance. This doctrine states that the law applicable to a contract is the law of the party who makes the most characteristic performance. For example, in the case of contracts for the carriage of goods, the delivery of the goods is considered the most characteristic performance. Therefore, the law of the carrier that delivers the goods will be the law applicable to the contracts for the carriage of goods. The doctrine of the most characteristic performance is also adopted by the 1983, 1997 and 2015 Bills of Indonesian Private International Law. The Bills provide that the law applicable to a contract with foreign elements is the parties' choice of law, made expressly or impliedly, provided that mandatory law does not govern otherwise. Where the parties do not make a choice of law, the law applicable to their contract is the law of the party who makes the most characteristic performance. With respect to the law of the party who makes the most characteristic performance, Chapter III of the 2015 Bill provides that the law applicable to contracts for the carriage of goods is the law of the country or the legal seat of the carrier.

viii. Negotiable Instruments (Including Bills of Exchange)

Rules governing the transfer of negotiable instruments issued in Indonesia are mandatory so must be complied with. The transfer of bills of exchange and order is governed under Chapter VI of the Indonesian Commercial Code. The transfer of checks and promissory notes is governed under the Chapter VII of the Indonesian Commercial Code. The transfer of Bills of Lading is governed under Articles 507 and 508 of Indonesian Commercial Code. Other negotiable instruments are not governed under the Commercial Code, but under different laws or regulations, which are similarly mandatory and must be complied with. For example, the transfer of stocks and bonds is governed under regulations issued by the Indonesian Financial Services Authorities. The transfer of warehouse receipts is governed under Act No 9 of 2006 as amended by Act No 9 of 2011 concerning the system of warehouse receipt. The regulations of the Indonesian Central Bank, Bank Indonesia, also govern all negotiable instruments involving banks in Indonesia.

In short, the types of negotiable instruments in Indonesia, and the regulations which apply to them, are determined by law. Negotiable instruments that are not known in the Indonesian legal system are not valid as negotiable instruments.

ix. Letters of Credit

In principle, the governing law of letters of credit is the law chosen by the parties in the letters of credit. In practice, letters of credit are usually made in the form of standard contracts in which the terms and conditions of the letters of credit are set by the issuing banks. This includes identification of the governing law. Banks usually adopt certain trade usages to govern the obligations of the parties in letters of credits. One of the trade usages most commonly used in letters of credit in Indonesia is the Uniform Customs and Practices for Documentary Credits ('UCP'), which has been developed and published by the International Chamber of Commerce. The use of UCP in letters of credit issued in Indonesia is also recommended, although not obligated, by Bank Indonesia, the Indonesian Central Bank, in its Circular Letter No 26/34/ULN dated 17 December 1993. Unlike in some other countries, Indonesia does not have national legislation or regulation concerning letters of credit for international sale transactions.

Judicial practice in Indonesia recognises the UCP as the governing law of letters of credit if the letter of credit in question expressly refers to the UCP as its governing law. Article 1 of the Uniform Customs and Practice for Documentary Credits, 2007 Revision, ICC Publication No 600, provides that the UCP is binding on all parties where the letters of credit expressly indicate that they are subject to the UCP. For example, in the cases of *Koperasi Pegawai PT. ASABRI (Persero) v Inham Refrigeration, B.V, et al* and *PT. Bank Permata, Tbk (d/h PT. Bank Universal Tbk) v Hudiono Liyanto*, the Indonesian courts applied the rules and principles contained in the UCP to settle the disputes related to the parties' letters of credit. In the case of *Koperasi Pegawai PT. ASABRI (Persero) v Inham Refrigeration, B.V, et al*, the courts in the appellate, cassation, and extraordinary appeal levels adopted the UCP principle concerning the separation of letters of credit from contracts for the sale of goods (the autonomy principle).[44] In the case of *PT. Bank Permata, Tbk (d/h PT. Bank Universal Tbk) v Hudiono Liyanto*, the Supreme Court and the lower courts reached different interpretations concerning the UCP principle of complying documents. The lower courts applied the strict compliance standard against the discrepancies found in the documents tendered by the seller to the bank,[45] whereas the Supreme Court applied the substantial compliance standard.[46] No court in the latter case addressed the issue of fraud raised by the plaintiff, because the UCP has no provisions concerning fraud. The courts did not apply Article 1328 BW, which provides that fraud is a ground for the annulment of a contract, because BW was not regarded as the governing law of the letters of credit.

[44] High Court of Jakarta Decision 100/Pdt/2000/PT.DKI (19 July 2000); affd Supreme Court Decision 3771 K/Pdt/2001 (13 May 2004); affd Supreme Court Extraordinary Appeal 125 PK/Pdt/2006 (28 September 2006).

[45] District Court of South Jakarta Decision 282/PDT.G/ 2001/PN.Jak.Sel. (15 January 2002); affd High Court of Jakarta Decision 533/PDT/2002/PT.DKI (12 March 2003).

[46] Supreme Court Decision 2925 K/PDT/2003 (15 April 2005).

x. *Contracts Involving the Transfer of Foreign Currency*

The law that governs contracts involving the transfer of foreign currency is the fiscal law of both the country that transfers, and the country that receives, the foreign currency. The fiscal law that relates to foreign currency is categorised as public law.[47] Thus, the parties cannot violate the law of foreign currency in either country. A contract involving the transfer of foreign currency, such as a transnational contract for the sale or purchase of goods, or an international credit agreement, may affect a country's exchange resources. Therefore, each country has and maintains exchange control regulations to protect its foreign exchange resources. Any contract that is contrary to the exchange control regulations, which are public law, will be invalid.

In conclusion, the law that governs the transfer of foreign currency will be the fiscal law of the parties' nationalities, whereas the law that governs the underlying contract, such as a sales contract or credit agreement, is the law chosen by the parties according to the principles of private international law. The Indonesian fiscal law that governs the aspects of the transfer of foreign currency in a contract is found in Act No 7 of 2011 concerning currency and several regulations of Bank Indonesia concerning currency.

xi. *Agency*

In principle, the law that governs the relationship between an agent and its principal and their respective rights and duties is the law chosen by them in their contract. However, the law chosen by the parties may not infringe Indonesian *ordre public*, mandatory rules, and public law. Accordingly, the parties' choice of law in an agency contract cannot set aside the Consumer Protection Act 1999 and the Anti-Monopoly Act 1999, because those Acts are mandatory law so supersede the parties' choice of law. In respect of agency contracts with foreign elements, public law usually governs customs, taxation, business licence, and so on.

The capacity of a party to act as an agent in Indonesia is determined by Indonesian law, namely the Regulation of Minister of Commerce No 11/M-DAG/PER/3/2006 concerning rules and procedure of the issuance of registration letters for agents or distributors of goods and/or services (the Minister of Commerce Regulation). Persons not registered in Indonesia in accordance with this regulation do not have capacity to perform as agents in Indonesia. The law determining the formal validity of agency contracts in Indonesia is Indonesian law (Article 18, paragraph (1) AB). To be binding on an Indonesian agent, pursuant to Article 8, paragraph (a) of the Minister of Commerce Regulation, an agency contract must be legalised by a public notary and confirmed by a letter of statement issued by an Indonesian Trade Attaché or an official of Indonesian Representative Office in the principal's country.

Where the parties do not make a choice of law for their agency contract, either expressly or impliedly, the prevailing doctrine to determine the applicable law is the doctrine of the most characteristic performance. This doctrine states that the law applicable to a contract is the law of the party who makes the most characteristic performance. In the case of an

[47] Gautama, *Pengantar Hukum* (n 1) 170, 205.

agency contract, the obligations of an agent are considered the most characteristic performance. Therefore, the law of the agent will be the law applicable to the agency contract. The doctrine of the most characteristic performance is also adopted in the 1983, 1997 and 2015 Bills of Indonesian Private International Law. With respect to the law of the party who makes the most characteristic performance, Chapter III of the 2015 Bill provides that the law applicable to an agency contract is the law of the country or the habitual residence or the legal seat of the agent.

In summary, the governing law of agency contracts with foreign elements is the law chosen by the parties in the contracts. The law chosen by the parties may not infringe Indonesian *ordre public*, mandatory rules, and public law. Where the parties do not make a choice of law for their agency contract, either expressly or impliedly, the law of the agent will be the law applicable to the agency contracts (the doctrine of the most characteristic performance).

C. Torts

i. Governing Law in Tort Generally

Indonesian Private International Law is silent as to the law governing tortious conduct with foreign elements. The prevailing doctrine applied in this respect is the principle of *lex loci delicti commissi* ('the law of the place where the tort was committed'). In its preference for this principle, Indonesia is influenced by the European continental legal system. According to European law, the *locus* is the place where the tortfeasor commits their tort, not the place where the impact of the tort is felt. For example, the place where the tortfeasor posts a defaming letter, the place where the tortfeasor delivers poisonous food, the place where the tortfeasor fires a gun, the place where the tortfeasor commits arson.[48] This doctrine is adopted in the 1983, 1997 and 2015 Bills of Indonesian Private International Law (none of which have been passed into law). Article 15 of the 1983 Bill provides that the law of the country where the tort was committed is the law that governs the tort. Article 19, paragraph (1) of the 1997 Bill provides that the law of the country where the tortious conduct took place determines whether that conduct is categorised as a tort, and if so the legal consequences. Paragraph (2) of the same Article provides that the *lex loci delicti commissi* principle is not applied exclusively; the legal effect of the tortious action can also be determined by the law of the country where the consequences of the tort are felt. The 2015 Bill does not regulate governing law in tort. It only explains that besides the principle of *lex loci delicti commissi*, there is another principle which may apply, namely the *lex fori* or the law of the court. Chapter XI of the 2015 Bill mentions that the *lex fori* is applied for practical reasons. In addition, the *lex fori* can protect citizens of the country in which the court is situated from being forced by the *lex locus* to pay higher damages than the damages recoverable under the *lex fori*.[49]

[48] Gautama, *Perdata Internasional Jilid III Bag 2* (n 10) 194–195.
[49] ibid, 132.

Despite this support for the principle of *lex loci delicti commissi*, the current practice of Indonesian courts is to apply *lex fori* ('the law of the court'). As described in the following sections, in making their judgments on torts, Indonesian civil courts often relate tort actions, such as nuisance, trespass to goods, defamation, or environmental damage, to Indonesian public laws, for example, nuisance ordinances, the penal code, press law or environmental law. This practice of relating torts to Indonesian public law may influence the courts in preferring the *lex fori* principle. Also relevant is the rule that condemnatory judgments made by Indonesian courts are valid and enforceable only in Indonesia (Article 431 Rv). This influences Indonesian courts to apply *lex fori* to tort cases with foreign elements because their judgments or decisions are expected to be enforced only in Indonesia.

ii. Specific Torts

a. Negligence

In the case of *Sigit Suciptoyono v Singapore Airlines Limited*, Mr Suciptoyono, an Indonesian national, brought a tort lawsuit against Singapore Airlines Limited ('Singapore Airlines'), a Singaporean corporation, in the Central Jakarta District Court in 2007. He sought damages for the negligence of the Singapore Airlines' pilots who had caused an accident in the Chiang Kai-shek International Airport, Taiwan in 2001. As a result of the accident, Mr Suciptoyono suffered injuries and loss of property and income. Singapore Airlines had a representative office in South Jakarta that confirmed Mr Suciptoyono's flight reservation and accepted his ticket payment. The South Jakarta District Court found that this connection to Indonesia justified the Court in exercising jurisdiction over the airliner. This exercise of jurisdiction was in accordance with Article 28, paragraph (1) of the 1929 Warsaw Convention and Article 33, paragraph (1) of the 1999 Montreal Convention. In his argument, Mr Suciptoyono claimed that the pilots on his flight from Taipei to Los Angeles made a mistake by taking off from a runway which had been closed for repairs. The plane collided with the construction equipment and caught fire. Because of the accident, Mr Suciptoyono suffered injuries and became disabled. His total financial loss in Indonesian Rupiah ('IDR') was IDR1,458,746,334, but Singapore Airlines only offered him compensation of US$25,000 (IDR 366,000,000). In addition to seeking the compensation of IDR1,458,746,334, he sought damages of IDR10 billion with interest of 2 per cent per month because of his long-term trauma and emotional distress. In its response to Mr Suciptoyono's claim, Singapore Airlines relied on Article 29, paragraph (1) of the 1929 Warsaw Convention, to which both Indonesia and Singapore are parties. This Article requires the claimant to bring a legal action within two years from the date of the accident, whereas Mr Suciptoyono had brought his lawsuit seven years after the collision. Further, Singapore Airlines argued that the terms of the contract between themselves and Mr Suciptoyono established that the contract was to be subject to the 1929 Warsaw Convention.

The Central Jakarta District Court held that Singapore Airlines had committed a tort by failing to perform its obligation to give fair and proper compensation to Mr Suciptoyono. The Court ordered Singapore Airlines to immediately pay compensation of IDR1 billion to

Mr Suciptoyono.[50] Singapore Airlines appealed the decision to the Jakarta High Court. The High Court upheld the lower court's decision and held that Singapore Airlines had committed a tort by failing to give fair and proper compensation to Mr Suciptoyono. The High Court corrected the compensation to be IDR1,504,487,124.[51] Singapore Airlines brought the decision of the Jakarta Hight Court to the court of cassation, arguing that the decision was incorrect in law as it failed to apply the two-year claim limit from the 1929 Warsaw Convention. Singapore Airlines also argued that the lower courts did not provide any legal justification for its assessment of the value of compensation awarded to Mr Suciptoyono. The Supreme Court, as the court of cassation, held that the decisions of the lower courts were correct, despite their failure to apply the 1929 Warsaw Convention. The Supreme Court also affirmed the decision of the Jakarta Hight Court that increased the amount of compensation owed to Mr Suciptoyono.[52]

In essence, the Indonesian courts held that Singapore Airlines committed a wrong because it did not perform its obligation to give fair and proper compensation to Mr Suciptoyono. That is, the relevant decisions were not based on the negligence of Singapore Airlines' pilot, but on the failure of Singapore Airlines to perform its obligation to compensate Mr Suciptoyono. The courts did not refer to any particular law, whether Indonesian or foreign, involving tort as the basis of their decisions. The courts simply found that Singapore Airlines did not perform an obligation to give fair and proper compensation to Mr Suciptoyono and therefore ordered Singapore Airlines to pay compensation. The decisions indicate that Indonesian courts will simply apply the *lex fori* (that is, Indonesian law) in negligence cases having a foreign element, notwithstanding the prevailing legal doctrine in Indonesia that supports the principle of *lex loci delicti commissi*.

b. Nuisance

Whereas nuisance in English law is divided into two kinds – private and public nuisance – nuisance in Indonesian law is mostly public in nature. Theoretically, *hinder* (nuisance in Dutch law) is a similar concept to private nuisance in English law. However, in practice, Indonesian courts often relate *hinder* to government permits to perform an activity, hold an event, or run a business that can potentially cause nuisance (harm, loss or disturbance). It is the court that determines the compensation owed to the claimant as a result of the material and immaterial damages caused by the nuisance.[53]

Since *hinder* in Indonesia is mostly public in nature and relates to administrative permits (nuisance permits), Indonesian law is the law that governs nuisance. Whereas *lex fori* or the law of the Indonesian courts determines the civil damages granted to the claimants.

[50] District Court of South Jakarta Decision 908/Pdt.G/2007/PN.Jak.Sel. (5 February 2008).

[51] High Court of Jakarta Decision 611/PDT/2008/PT.DKI (2 February 2009).

[52] Supreme Court Decision 1517 K/Pdt/2009 (18 April 2011).

[53] M Santy, 'Gangguan Ketenangan Hidup (Hinder dan Nuisance): Analisis Perbandingan Perbuatan Melawan Hukum Indonesia dan Inggris' (Universitas Indonesia Library, 2017) 15–18 www.lib.ui.ac.id/naskah-ringkas/2019-11/S66236-Meyliana%20Santy (accessed 6 June 2020).

c. Wrongful Interference with Goods

Indonesian statutes and regulations are silent on wrongful interference with goods in the context of private international law. Therefore, one must look at judicial practice in Indonesia to determine the law governing wrongful interference with goods. Indonesian judicial practice is often to categorise wrongful interference with goods as a crime governed by the Indonesian Penal Code (*Wetboek van Strafrecht voor Indonesia* 1915).[54] Unlike BW, which does not have specific provisions concerning wrongful interference with goods, the Indonesian Penal Code expressly governs wrongful interference with goods in Article 406, paragraph (1), which stipulates that,

> A person who deliberately and unlawfully destroys, damages, renders useless or mislays property that fully or partially belongs to another person, shall be sentenced by a maximum imprisonment of two years and eight months or a maximum fine of four thousand and five hundred rupiahs.

The same sentencing is also applied to wrongful interference with an animal that fully or partially belongs to another person (Article 406, paragraph (2)). Based on the above provision, wrongful interference with goods, including animals, must be intentional and result in material damage to the goods. Immaterial damage is insufficient. This is to distinguish wrongful interference with goods from nuisance or *hinder*, which may also result in immaterial damage, such as distress or inconvenience.

Article 1365 BW stipulates that, 'Every unlawful act that causes damage to another person obliges the doer to compensate such damage.' Hence, where a person has suffered wrongful interference with their goods, the Indonesian legal system allows the victims to bring a tort lawsuit against the tortfeasors, separate from any criminal action taken by the state. Indonesian law will govern the wrongful interference as *lex fori* because wrongful interference with goods is often tried first as a crime, before a civil action is initiated in respect of the same wrongful interference.

Hence, following judicial practice in Indonesia the law that governs wrongful interference with goods containing foreign elements will be *lex fori*, or Indonesian law.

d. Defamation

In the case of *H.M. Soeharto v Time Inc Asia; et al*, H.M. Soeharto ('Soeharto'), who was an Indonesian former president, filed a defamation lawsuit against Time Inc Asia et al ('Time') over an article published in *TIME Magazine*, Asian edition, dated 24 May 1999, Vol 153 No 20, and the issue's cover page. In the article, the Time's journalists reported that a total of US$9 billion linked to Soeharto and his families had been shifted from a bank in Switzerland to another bank in Austria. The article also alleged that Soeharto's businesses paid less than 10 per cent of their real tax obligations. The cover page of the magazine was titled 'SUHARTO INC.: How Indonesia's long-time boss built a family fortune'. Soeharto filed his defamation lawsuit against Time in the Central Jakarta District Court in 1999.

[54] S Hasanah, 'Ulasan lengkap: Akibat Hukum Jika Merusak Barang Orang Lain Tanpa Sengaja' (*hukumonline*, 15 September 2016) www.hukumonline.com/klinik/detail/ulasan/lt539a466693874/akibat-hukum-jika-merusak-barang-orang-lain-tanpa-sengaja/ (accessed 6 June 2020).

Time objected to the jurisdiction of the Court, but the Court dismissed Time's objection and held that it had jurisdiction over the parties.[55]

Although the defamation took place in the US where Time published the *TIME Magazine* and had its central office, the judges did not apply American law. Nor did the judges apply Hong Kong law, the law of the place where the Asian edition of *TIME Magazine* was distributed throughout Asia by Time Inc Asia. Instead, the judges applied Articles 1372 to 1380 BW, which govern the tort of defamation in Indonesia. Article 1372, paragraph (1) BW stipulates that, 'The civil claim for defamation is to get compensation of damages and to reinstate the [claimant's] good name and honour.' To determine that the defamation claimed by Soeharto existed, the judges referred to Article 310 of Indonesian Penal Code. Pursuant to Article 310, paragraph (1) of the Penal Code, defamation is an action to intentionally harm a person's honour or reputation by charging them with a certain matter and deliberately publicising the matter. Conduct does not amount to defamation if carried out in the general public interest or out of necessity. After hearing from several expert witnesses, and considering the available facts, the judges found that Time's article was in the general public interest in light of the Indonesian public prosecutor's investigation of Soeharto's alleged corruption. Hence, the Central Jakarta District Court concluded that Time's article and its cover page were not categorised as defamation under Article 310, paragraph (3) of the Penal Code. Accordingly, Soeharto was not entitled to claim for damages provided by Article 1372 BW.[56] The Jakarta Hight Court upheld the decision of the Central Jakarta District Court,[57] but the court of cassation overturned the lower court decisions and ordered Time to pay damages to Soeharto.[58]

Time filed an extraordinary appeal against the court of cassation's decision in the Supreme Court. The Court accepted Time's extraordinary appeal and established a panel of justices to deal with the case. Besides applying Articles 1372 to 1380 BW and Article 310 of the Indonesian Penal Code, the justices in the extraordinary appeal panel also applied Act No 21 of 1982 concerning basic press (the Basic Press Act 1982) and Act No 40 of 1999 concerning the press (the Press Act 1999). The justices found that Time had complied with Article 15 of the Basic Press Act 1982 and Article 5 of the Press Act 1999, which required Time to provide a right of reply and right of correction to Soeharto. Soeharto through his lawyers had given his reply to Time's article and Time had published Soeharto's reply and correction along with the disputed article. As such, Time had performed its journalistic duties. The justices in the extraordinary appeal agreed with the decision made by the Central Jakarta District Court and concluded that Time did not commit defamation based on Article 310, paragraph (3) of the Penal Code and Article 1376 BW. The extraordinary appeal court annulled the previous decision made by the court of cassation.[59] This case demonstrates that the Indonesian courts relate the tort of defamation to public law, namely the Penal Code and Press Acts. In this case, the courts did not apply *lex loci delicti commissi*, New York or Hong Kong law, but applied Indonesian law as *lex fori*.

[55] District Court of Central Jakarta Decision 338/PDT.G/1999/PN.JKT.PST (6 June 2000).
[56] District Court of Central Jakarta Decision 338/PDT.G/1999/PN.JKT.PST. (6 June 2000).
[57] High Court of Jakarta Decision 551/PDT/2000/PT.DKI (16 March 2001).
[58] Supreme court Decision 3215 K/PDT/2001 (30 August 2007).
[59] Supreme Court Extraordinary Appeal 273 PK/Pdt/2008 (16 April 2009).

In the case of *Richard Bruce Ness v Jane Perlez and the New York Times Company*, the parties were not Indonesian nationals. Mr Ness was an American citizen who was domiciled in Jakarta and president director of an Indonesian mining company; Ms Perlez was an Australian journalist who when living in Jakarta had written articles about Mr Ness and his company; and the New York Times Company was an American legal entity established and with legal seat in New York. Mr Ness brought a tort lawsuit against Ms Perlez, who had written three articles deemed harmful to Mr Ness's reputation. He also sued the New York Times Company, which had published Ms Perlez' articles. The articles stated that Mr Ness, as the president director of PT. Newmont Minahasa Raya, an Indonesian company, was responsible for serious mining pollution at Buyat Bay, North Sulawesi, Indonesia. The defendants raised the motion of *forum non conveniens* against the jurisdiction of the Indonesian court based on the fact that Ms Perlez no longer lived in Indonesia and had moved to Islamabad, Pakistan, sometime before Mr Ness brought his lawsuit. In addition, the New York Times Company did not have any representative in Indonesia. The defendants also argued that the judgment made by the Central Jakarta District Court would not be enforceable in the territories of the defendants, as there were no treaties on the recognition and enforcement of judgments between Indonesia and their countries of residence.

Judges in the Central Jakarta District Court agreed with the defendant's motion of *forum non conveniens* and refused to exercise jurisdiction over the case.[60] When Mr Ness filed the same lawsuit again, but with one additional defendant who was an Indonesian and had residence in Central Jakarta, the Central Jakarta District Court agreed to exercise its jurisdiction over this case. The judges in the latter case acknowledged that all parties in the case, except Ms Perlez's translator, were foreigners; hence, the Court had to choose the law to govern this tort case. First, the judges stated that the choice must be fair to all the parties. With this in mind, the judges decided to apply the universal journalistic standard code of ethics and the Press Act 1999. They did not apply New York law to the case, although it was the law of the place of the defamation as the New York Times Company had published the article in New York. The court decided that the defendants had performed their journalistic duties in accordance with the journalistic standard and the Press Act 1999, and therefore did not commit the tort of defamation as governed in BW.[61]

This latter case, once again, shows the Indonesian courts applying *lex fori* instead of *lex locus delicti commisi*, though the plaintiff and defendants were foreigners and the place of defamation was outside Indonesia.

e. Environmental Damage and Pollution

To date, no case of transboundary environmental damage and pollution has been adjudicated by the Indonesian courts.

The Montara oil spill in 2009 resulted from a blowout at the Montara wellhead platform in Australia. This blowout caused an uncontrolled release of oil and gas into the Timor Sea for 74 days. As a result of the pollution caused by the oil spill, the seaweed farmers and

[60] District Court of Central Jakarta Decision 181/PDT.G/2007/PN.JKT.PST. (8 October 2007).

[61] District Court of Central Jakarta Decision 408/Pdt.G/2007/PN.Jkt.Pst. (25 March 2009).

fishermen who lived in West Timor, Indonesia, suffered financial loss, health problems, and property damage. In addition to the damages suffered by the West Timor population, the oil spill caused damage to the marine environment in the Timor Sea.[62] The Montara wellhead platform was located in Australian water and was operated by an Australian corporation, PTTEP Australasia (Ashmore Cartier) Pty Ltd ('PTTEPAA'), which was a subsidiary of PTT Exploration and Production Public Company Limited ('PTTEP'), a Thai corporation. In May 2017, the Indonesian Government, represented by the Ministry of Environment and Forestry and the Office of the Attorney General, filed a tort lawsuit against those companies in the Central Jakarta District Court (case No 241/Pdt.G/2017/PN.Jkt.Pst.) They sought compensation of IDR27.5 trillion for the damage suffered in West Timor. The government based their lawsuit on Articles 87 and 88 of Act No 32 of 2009 concerning the protection and management of the environment (the Environmental Protection Act 2009) and Article 1365 BW, which governs torts in general.[63] Unfortunately, in February 2018, the government had to withdraw its lawsuit. The government had written the name of the Australian company incorrectly in its lawsuit; hence, the company refused to participate in the trial.[64]

In the meantime, the Indonesian Government through the Coordinating Ministry of Maritime Affairs used diplomatic channels to discuss the dispute with the Thai Government. The Indonesian Minister of Maritime Affairs, Luhut Panjaitan, and the Prime Minister of Thailand, Prayuth Chan-O-Cha, met with PTTEP representatives to discuss the possibility of an out-of-court settlement. However, PTTEP, which was the subsidiary of the Thai state-owned PTT Public Company Limited, offered to pay only US$5 million in compensation. The Indonesian Government rejected this offer.[65] After the failed diplomatic negotiation, in 2019 the Indonesian Government planned to file a tort lawsuit against the same companies, but with their corrected names.[66] To date the new tort lawsuit has not been filed in the Jakarta courts. While the Indonesian Government was attempting to file a tort lawsuit against the foreign companies, in 2016 approximately 15,000 seaweed farmers in West Timor launched a class-action against the Australian company that operated the Montara wellhead platform, PTTEPAA, to seek compensation for financial loss and property damage. In December 2019, the Federal Court of Australia in Sydney concluded the hearings and was expected to

[62] 'Montara Oil Spill' (*Wikipedia*, 7 April 2020) https://en.wikipedia.org/wiki/Montara_oil_spill#Environmental_effects (accessed 9 June 2020).

[63] D Amnifu, 'Lawsuit against Thai firm to protect environment' (*The Jakarta Post*, 8 May 2017) https://icel.or.id/berita/icel-dalam-berita/kasus-tumpahan-minyak-montara-10-tahun-satu-gugatan/ (accessed 9 June 2020).

[64] A Triyono, 'Kasus Montara, Pemerintah Cabut Gugatan Ke PTTEP' (*Kontan.co.id*, 6 February 2018) https://nasional.kontan.co.id/news/kasus-montara-pemerintah-cabut-gugatan-ke-pttep (accessed 9 June 2020); Heriyanto, 'Gugatan Pemerintah Soal Montara Salah Alamat, Ada Apa?' (*BeritaSatu.com*, 26 August 2017) www.beritasatu.com/nasional/449337-gugatan-pemerintah-soal-montara-salah-alamat-ada-apa (accessed 9 June 2020).

[65] Indonesian Center for Environmental Law, 'Case of Montara Oil Spill: 10 Years, One Lawsuit' (*ICEL*, 23 October 2019) https://icel.or.id/en/news/icel-in-the-news/case-of-montara-oil-spill-10-years-one-lawsuit/ (accessed 9 June 2020); Indonesian Center for Environmental Law, 'Kasus Tumpahan Minyak Montara: 10 Tahun, Satu Gugatan' (*ICEL*, 23 October 2019) https://icel.or.id/berita/icel-dalam-berita/kasus-tumpahan-minyak-montara-10-tahun-satu-gugatan/ (accessed 9 June 2020).

[66] Y Viodeogo, 'KLHK Tetap Gugat PTTEP AA' (*kabar24*, 22 August 2019) https://kabar24.bisnis.com/read/20190822/16/1139562/klhk-tetap-gugat-pttep-aa (accessed 9 June 2020); A Septiadi, 'Akan Digugat Lagi Atas Tumpahan Minyak Di Montara, PTT PCL Nilai Gugatan Salah Alamat' (*Kontan.co.id*, 1 May 2018) https://nasional.kontan.co.id/news/akan-digugat-lagi-atas-tumpahan-minyak-di-montara-ptt-pcl-nilai-gugatan-salah-alamat (accessed 9 June 2020).

deliver its judgment in 2020.[67] At the time of writing, the judgment is not yet available. In the author's opinion, the Indonesian Government has not filed the new tort lawsuit against PTTEPAA and PTTEP in the Jakarta court because the judgment of the Australian Federal Court is underway. If the Australian judgment is in favour of the West Timor farmers, the farmers will be able to enforce the court judgment in Australia, where PTTEPAA is operating. In contrast, pursuant to Article 431 Rv, condemnatory judgments made by Indonesian courts will not be enforceable in Australia, where the company and most of their assets are located. An Indonesian judgment could only be enforced on the company's assets in Indonesia, if there are any such assets.

The Montara oil spill case demonstrates that the Indonesian (Central Jakarta District) court might apply *lex fori* or Indonesian law in this case, because the Indonesian Government based its tort lawsuit on Indonesian law (the Environmental Protection Act 2009 and BW) and the effect of the tort committed by the Australian company was felt in Indonesian territory. It was unlikely that the Indonesian court would apply *lex locus delicti commisi* (Australian law), which was the law of the place where the companies committed their tort.

In the case of transboundary smoke pollution originating from Indonesia and crossing to neighbouring countries, there has never been a tort lawsuit brought by the citizens of Indonesia's neighbouring countries against the polluting companies in Indonesian courts. This is despite the fact that transboundary smoke pollution originating from Indonesia's forests has become regular occurrence since the late 1990's.[68] In the author's opinion, were the citizens or governments of other countries to file tort lawsuits against polluting companies that operate in Indonesian forests, the Indonesian courts most likely would apply Indonesian law to govern the transboundary pollution. That is because the court will refer to the Environmental Protection Act 2009 and its implementing regulations to determine the damage caused by the transboundary pollution. In addition, the judgments of Indonesian courts will be enforceable only within Indonesia; thus, Indonesian law is more appropriate to govern the case.

D. Unjust Enrichment

Unlike the New Netherlands Civil Code (*Nieuw Burgerlijk Wetboek*), which in 1992 introduced a specific provision on unjust enrichment in Article 6:212, the only provisions in the Indonesian Civil Code or BW on undue performance or undue payment concern *condictio indebiti* (the obligation to make restitution where one has received something not due to him). Rules governing undue performance are provided in Articles 1359 to 1364 BW under the Book of Obligations (Book III). Article 1359, paragraph (1) BW provides that every payment implies a debt; what has been paid without being due may be reclaimed. Anyone who has inadvertently or knowingly accepted something that was not due to them is obliged to return it to the person from whom it was received

[67] M Blackburn, 'Montara oil spill class action' (*Maurice Blackburn*) www.mauriceblackburn.com.au/class-actions/current-class-actions/montara-oil-spill-class-action/ (accessed 9 June 2020).

[68] P Listiningrum, 'Transboundary Civil Litigation for Victims of Southeast Asian Haze Pollution: Access to Justice and the Non-Discrimination Principle' (2018) 8 *Transnational Environmental Law* 119 doi:10.1017/S2047102518000298 (accessed 9 June 2020).

(Article 1360 BW). Someone who mistakenly believes themselves to be a debtor and for that reason makes a payment is entitled to reclaim the payment from the person they believed to be their creditor (Article 1361, paragraph (1) BW). A person who in bad faith has received something not owed to them must return it with interests and proceeds, effective as of the day of payment, including compensation for costs and damages, and with interest with respect to depreciation in the value of the goods (Article 1362, paragraph (1) BW). Anyone who in good faith has sold goods received as payment for a debt that was not due to them may remedy the situation by giving the purchase price to the debtor (Article 1363, paragraph (1) BW).

One difference between the actions of unjust enrichment and undue performance is that undue performance results in a restitution claim by the performer against the recipient, whereas unjust enrichment results in a claim of compensation of damage by the performer against the recipient. Consider an example. Last week, Mr A thought that he owed Bank X US$100,000. Forgetting that he had paid his debt to Bank X several months ago, Mr A transferred US$100,000 to the bank. This is an example of undue performance under the Dutch and Indonesian Civil Codes, by which Mr A has performed an obligation that is not owed to Bank X. The law gives him a right to demand restitution from Bank X, and the law imposes an obligation on Bank X as a recipient to return the undue payment. In a different example, a builder of a house thought that she had acquired the right of ownership of the building site, but afterwards the sale of the land is nullified by law so that the seller of the land is legally considered to still be the owner of the land. As such, the owner of the land becomes the owner of the house built on his land. Unlike in the case of undue performance, the builder of the house did not wrongfully think that she had to perform an obligation to the owner of the land. The builder never intended to deliver any performance to the owner of the land, because the builder wanted to build a house for herself on her own land. This case is an example of unjust enrichment under the New Netherlands Civil Code, by which the owner of the land has been unjustifiably enriched at the expense of the house builder. The law gives the builder of the house the right to claim compensation from the owner of land, but only of the amount of the enrichment that has been enjoyed by the owner of land. The compensation can never exceed the advantage which the recipient has gained.[69]

Since Indonesian law only governs undue performance and not unjust enrichment, this section will only discuss undue performance. In BW, undue performance is classified as an obligation created by operation of law as a result of a lawful act (Article 1353). Therefore, undue performance is an obligation, although it is created neither by contract nor by tort. Indonesian Private International Law is silent on the law that governs undue performance involving foreign elements. The 1983, 1997 and 2015 Bills of Indonesian Private International Law also do not contain provisions on undue performance. Neither the doctrine of the most characteristic performance nor the doctrine of *lex loci* can be applied to determine the law that governs undue performance, because undue performance is neither contractual nor tortious.

Therefore, in the absence of applicable statutory provisions or legal doctrine, it is the court itself that must determine the law that governs undue performance involving foreign

[69] Dutch Civil Law, 'Obligatory claims and obligations' (*Dutch Civil Law*) www.dutchcivillaw.com/content/dutchcivillaw033.htm (accessed 11 June 2020).

elements. *Lex fori* or the law of the court will determine whether an action is characterised as undue performance and if so the legal effect of the action. That is because a court judgment on this matter is categorised as a condemnatory judgment, so is not enforceable outside Indonesia. Therefore, as the judgment is expected to be enforced only in Indonesia, *lex fori* is most appropriate to govern the case of undue performance.

E. Trusts and Charitable Foundations

As previously explained in Chapter 2, section I.B.i.d on trusts and charitable foundations, English trusts do not create ownership rights or personal liabilities in Indonesia. Therefore, Indonesian courts that deal with trust agreements will not recognise the existence and validity of trust agreements and will not adjudicate trust cases.

Regarding charitable foundations, Indonesian courts apply the principle of *locus regit actum* stipulated in Article 18, paragraph (1) of *Algemene Bepalingen van Wetgeving voor Nederlandsch Indie* ('AB') to determine the existence and validity of charitable foundations as legal persons. Article 18 stipulates, 'Formality of a legal action is determined by the court in accordance with the law of the country or place where the action is performed.' As such, the court will refer to the procedural law (formality) of the country in which the foundations are established to determine their existence and validity as legal persons. For example, if the law of the country in which a foundation is established requires the foundation to be established by a notarial deed or to be registered in a certain office, but the foundation does not comply with the formal requirement, then the Indonesian court can hold that the foundation does not exist and cannot operate as a charitable foundation. If it is found that the purported foundation is in fact a non-existent legal entity, it is the individuals who run the foundation that will bear responsibilities to third parties for any transactions made by the foundation. The foundation itself will not have any legal liabilities because of its non-existence.

In general, there are three doctrines in Private International Law which may determine the applicable law for the personal status and capacity of a legal entity, including charitable foundations. First, the doctrine of incorporation, stating that the applicable law is the law of the place where the entity is incorporated. Second, the doctrine of statutory seat, stating that the applicable law is the law of the legal seat of the entity as written in its memorandum of association. Third, the doctrine of central management, stating that the applicable law is the law of the place in which the entity's central or effective management is situated.[70] In Indonesia, the first and second doctrines are combined because, in practice, the place or country where the corporation has its statutory seat is usually the place under whose law it is incorporated.[71] Consequently, Indonesia applies only two doctrines to determine the applicable law for personal status and capacity of a legal entity: first, the combination of the doctrines of incorporation and statutory seat; and, second, the doctrine of central management. Articles 30, 36, and 42 of the Basic Agrarian Act 1960 adopt the combination of the doctrines of incorporation and statutory seat to determine

[70] Gautama, *Perdata Internasional Jilid III Bag 1* (n 16) 212, 229.
[71] Supancana, *Naskah Akademik* (n 43) 47.

the rights to land for legal entities in Indonesia. The Investment Act 2007 adopts the combination of doctrines of incorporation and statutory seat (Article 5) and the doctrine of central management (Article 17) for corporations to invest in Indonesia. Based on the doctrines adopted in Indonesia, the applicable law to determine the personal status and capacity of a charitable foundation is the law of the country where the foundation's statutory seat is located or the law of the country where its central management is situated. As such, an Indonesian court will determine the capacity of a foreign foundation to make agreements with Indonesian individuals or entities based on the law of the country where the foundation's statutory seat is located or based on the law of the country where its central management is situated. The rights and obligations of individuals in the organ of a foreign foundation is also determined by the law of its statutory seat or the law of the country where its central management is situated. In addition, the laws also apply to the insolvency status of a foundation.

However, a foundation's right to the land or immovables in Indonesia is determined by the *lex rei sitae* principle. Pursuant to Article 17 AB, the *lex situs* of the immovable property will govern the right to, the transfer, and the lien of immovable property by a foreign foundation in Indonesia. The *lex situs* also governs the validity of the transfer, as well as the procedure and the effect of the transfer of the immovable property. Accordingly, the Basic Agrarian Act 1960 determines the rights and obligations of a foreign foundation to land in Indonesia, as well as determines the procedure and effect of the transfer of land in Indonesia. The Indonesian law will also determine the foundation's rights and obligations to other kinds of immovable properties as well as the transfer of the immovables and its effect in Indonesia.

The law applicable to the agreements or contracts made between foreign foundations and Indonesian individuals or entities is determined by the choice of law made by the parties. If the parties do not make a choice of law in their agreements, the legal doctrines on this matter will apply to determine the law applicable to their agreements. Section III.A above on contracts has discussed the doctrines of applicable law for contracts in Indonesia.

As demonstrated, there is no discussion on the law applicable to trusts in Indonesia because trust agreements do not exist and are not valid in the Indonesian legal system. Regarding charitable foundations, the applicable law to determine their personal status and capacity is the law of the country where its statutory seat is located or the law of the country where its central management is situated.

II. Law of Property

A. Immovable Property

Article 17 AB determines the law applicable to immovable property. The Article stipulates that, 'Concerning immovable property, the law of the country or place where the property is situated applies.' As such, Article 17 AB applies the principle of *lex rei sitae* (the law where the property is situated). If the immovable property is situated in Indonesia, Indonesian law will govern matters such as the right to transfer and alienate of the property. Indonesian law will also determine the validity, legal effect, and formality requirements of the transfer of immovable property.

Although no express provision states the law applicable to characterising a property as movable or immovable, as a consequence of the *lex rei sitae* principle the applicable law for the characterisation of a property will be the law where the property is situated. For example, land and all objects attached to or built on it, such as buildings and plants or crops in Indonesia, are characterised as immovable property under Article 506 BW. Accordingly, the rights to the land and buildings or crops attached to the land are governed by the 1960 Basic Agrarian Act and its implementing regulations. The succession to the land will be governed by the 1960 Basic Agrarian Act and other Indonesian laws concerning succession to property. The transfer or conveyance of the land will also be governed by Indonesian law, namely the 1960 Basic Agrarian Act and its implementing regulations. The material and formal validity of the transfer, as well as the procedure and the effect of the land transfer, are also governed by Indonesian law, whether or not the parties are Indonesian citizens or foreigners. Indonesian law, as the *lex situs* of the land, also governs the creation of encumbrance rights attaching to the land and buildings attached to the land. As such, the validity of a land mortgage, its procedure, and its effect will be governed by the Mortgage on Land and Its Related Objects Act 1996, as well as its implementing regulations.

In the case of Indonesian registered or Indonesian-flagged vessels with the minimum gross weight of 20 cubic meters, Article 749, paragraph (3) of the Commercial Code characterises the vessels as immovable property. Accordingly, the principle of *lex rei sitae* in Article 17 AB applies to the vessels. That means the validity, transfer, security interest (hypothec), and all other aspects of the vessels will be governed by Indonesian law. With regard to the security interest or hypothec of the vessels to take effect, the principal agreement related to the hypothec must be made in Indonesia (Article 1173 BW) and the hypothec deed must be recorded in the Register of Ships Parent Registration in Indonesia (Article 60, paragraph (2) of the Shipping Act 2008), although the creditor in the principal agreement does not have their legal seat or domicile in Indonesia.

In summary, based on Article 17 AB, Indonesian Private International Law applies the principle of *lex rei sitae* to immovable property. The *lex situs* of the immovable property will govern the characterisation, rights to, transfer, succession, and lien of immovable property. The *lex situs* also governs the validity of the transfer, as well as the procedure and the effect of the transfer of immovable property.

B. Transfer of Movable Property

Where the principle of *lex rei sitae* (law of the site) in Article 17 AB applies to immovable property, the principle of *mobilia sequuntur personam* applies to movable property. That is, movables follow the personal statute (personal law) of their owners or holders. The principle of *mobilia sequuntur personam* was adopted in the Dutch colonial jurisprudence to govern movable property that was owned by and transferred among different groups of inhabitants (indigenous, European, and foreign oriental) in the Dutch East Indies.[72] The principle continues to be implemented after independence. Recently, there have been

[72] Oppusunggu and Bell, 'Indonesia' (n 9) 2170.

attempts to reformulate the rules on movable property in the 1983, 1997 and 2015 Bills of Indonesian Private International Law. Instead of applying the principle of *mobilia sequuntur personam*, the Bills suggest the application of *lex rei sitae* to determine the law applicable for movable property. As such, under the Bills, the principle of *lex rei sitae* is applied to determine the applicable law for both movable and immovable properties (Article 16 of the 1983 Bill, Article 20 of the 1997 Bill, and Part IV of the 2015 Bill). The application of the *lex rei sitae* principle to both movable and immovable properties is also suggested by Sudargo Gautama in his writings.[73]

The current law does not expressly identify the law applicable to property in transit or in shipments. However, Article 8 of the Shipping Act 2008 prohibits foreign vessels from transporting goods on Indonesian waters, allowing only Indonesian-flagged vessels to operate in domestic sea freight. It follows from this that Indonesian law applies to all property in transit within Indonesian waters. As foreign vessels are prohibited from transporting goods on Indonesian waters, foreign law becomes inapplicable to property in transit within Indonesian waters. Accordingly, although the property in transit belongs to a foreign national, the law applicable to the property in transit is always Indonesian law. Indonesian law is also silent on the law applicable to property in transit outside Indonesia that belongs to an Indonesian national. The only references to this matter are in the Bills of Indonesian Private International Law, which have not been passed into law by the Indonesian Parliament. The Bills provide that the law applicable to movable property shipped from one country to another is to be the law chosen by the parties. If the parties do not make a choice of law, the law applicable to the movable property is the law of the country where the property is situated (*lex rei sitae*). Where the property is located on high seas or in international water, the law applicable to the property is the law of the forum (*lex fori*) (Article 21 of the 1997 Bill and Chapter IV of the 2015 Bill).

With regard to the validity of security rights over movable property, the applicable law will follow the law of the principal agreement. For example, the validity of lien is determined by the law that governs the related credit agreement. The applicable law also governs the transfer of the security rights. With regard to security rights over an aircraft, the applicable law is the law chosen by the parties in the principal agreements to which the security rights relate (Article 72 of the Aviation Act 2009). Since Indonesia is a party to the Convention on International Interests in Mobile Equipment and The Protocol to The Convention on International Interests in Mobile Equipment on Matters Specific to Aircraft Equipment, both of which were ratified by Presidential Regulation No 8 of 2007, the rules of Indonesian Private International Law determine the law applicable to international security rights over aircraft (Article 5, paragraph (3) of the Convention on International Interests in Mobile Equipment).

In conclusion, the principle of *mobilia sequuntur personam* generally applies to determine the law applicable to movable property. With regard to security rights over movable property, the law applicable to the security rights follows the law of the principal agreements related to the security rights.

[73] Gautama, *Perdata Internasional Jilid III Bag 1* (n 16) 315.

C. Expropriation

The law applicable to expropriation in Indonesia is Indonesian law. This principle is stated in Article 7 of the Investment Act 2007. Article 7 provides that:

> (1) The Government shall take no measures of nationalisation against or taking over the property rights of investors, unless provided for by law.
> (2) In the case that the Government takes measures of nationalisation against or taking over the property rights as mentioned in paragraph (1), the Government shall pay compensation in which the amount shall be determined by market value.
> (3) If both parties fail to reach an agreement of compensation or damages as intended by paragraph (2), the settlement shall be made through arbitration.

Although Article 7, paragraphs (1) and (2) of the Investment Act 2007 do not expressly use the term 'expropriation', the phrase 'taking over the property rights of investors' has been interpreted as meaning expropriation of property by the United Nations Conference on Trade and Development (UNCTAD).[74] The term 'expropriation' can be found in international investment agreements made between the Indonesian Government and other governments, for example in the ASEAN Comprehensive Investment Agreement.[75] In those international investment agreements, expropriation is meant to include nationalisation.

In the case of *Churchill Mining and Planet Mining Pty Ltd v Republic of Indonesia*,[76] the local government of the East Kutai Regency on the island of Kalimantan revoked the mining licences that had been issued to the East Kutai Coal Project (EKCP). The EKCP was a joint venture investment established by Churchill Mining PLC, a British company, Planet Mining Pty Ltd, an Australian company, and an Indonesian group of companies, the Ridlatama companies. The revocation of the mining licences in 2010 was based on the recommendation of the Indonesian Ministry of Forestry. The Ministry alleged that the mining licences had been obtained through the use of forged documents made by the Ridlatama companies. As a consequence of the fraudulent mining licences, the Ministry of Forestry argued that the EKCP had falsely acquired a concession to operate in a protected forest zone that should not be exploited without a permit validly issued by the Ministry. Based on the Bilateral Investment Treaties, one signed by the Indonesian and UK Governments, and the other signed by the Indonesian and Australian Governments, the two foreign investor companies brought the Indonesian Government to the International Centre for the Settlement of Investment Disputes (ICSID) on several grounds, one of which was indirect expropriation by the Indonesian Government. They argued that the unilateral revocation by the Indonesian Government of mining licences in which the investors held interests constituted indirect expropriation. The ICSID decided in favour of the Indonesian Government. This case demonstrates that Indonesian law governs the indirect expropriation of foreign investors' property in Indonesia.

[74] UNCTAD, Expropriation – UNCTAD Series on Issues in International Investment Agreements II (UNCTAD/DIAE/IA/2011/7, (New York and Geneva, 2012) available from https://unctad.org/en/Docs/unctaddiaeia2011d7_en.pdf 5–7.

[75] See Investment Policy Hub UNCTAD, 'Indonesia' (*International Investment Agreements Navigator*) https://investmentpolicy.unctad.org/international-investment-agreements/countries/97/indonesia (accessed 12 May 2020).

[76] *Churchill Mining PLC and Planet Mining Pty Ltd v Republic of Indonesia*, ICSID Case No ARB/12/14 and 12/40, Procedural Order No 4 (18 March 2019).

Indonesian law also governs the divestment of shares owned by foreign companies investing in Indonesia. This ensures that the Indonesian Government or Indonesian companies can gain majority shareholding in a company previously owned by foreign investors. For example, in the case of the divestment of PT Freeport Indonesia (PT FI) in 2018, the Freeport McMoran Inc, an American parent company, owned 90.64 per cent of PT FI. Freeport McMoran Inc was required to divest or sell their shares in PT FI to the Indonesian Government or an Indonesian state-owned company, so that the Indonesian party could become the majority shareholder of PT FI. The divestment of shares owned by foreign investors in Indonesian joint-venture mining companies is governed by Indonesian law, namely Article 112 of Act No 4 of 2009 concerning mineral and coal mining, Article 97 of Government Regulation No 1 of 2017 concerning business activities in mineral and coal mining, and related implementing ministerial regulations.

As is clear from the above discussion, the law applicable to expropriation, either direct or indirect, is Indonesian law.

D. Succession to Property

i. General Considerations

Succession is part of personal law (personal statute) and accordingly the law applicable to succession is the law of the nationality of the deceased, not the law of the deceased's domicile. This doctrine is based on Article 16 AB, which implements the nationality principle.[77] Although Article 16 AB governs the application of the nationality principle only for Indonesians, jurisprudence established since the Dutch colonial era rules that the nationality principle also applies to the personal statute of foreigners in Indonesia.[78] Therefore, in general, succession to a foreigner's property in Indonesia will be determined by the law of the foreigner's nationality. There is an exception where the foreigner originates from a country that applies the domicile principle. In such a case, succession to the foreigner's property will be determined by Indonesian law, if they domicile in Indonesia. This is because Indonesian Private International Law applies the *Renvoi* (remission) principle as has been discussed in Chapter 1, section IV.D on Renvoi and transmission. There is no distinction between the law governing movable and immovable property of the deceased. All property of the deceased is governed by the national law of the deceased.[79] Accordingly, the principle of *lex rei sitae* in Article 17 AB does not apply to the immovable property of the deceased. For example, an Indonesian deceased man has an illegitimate daughter in Indonesia. The deceased man leaves behind immovable property in Australia. His illegitimate daughter is not entitled to inherit his properties both in Indonesia and in Australia, because Indonesian law (Article 43, paragraph (1) of the Marriage Act 1974) does not entitle an illegitimate child to inherit from her unmarried father. This is despite the fact that Australia, in which the immovable property is located, gives both illegitimate and legitimate children the same inheritance rights.

[77] Oppusunggu and Bell, 'Indonesia' (n 9) 2172; Gautama, *Perdata Internasional Jilid III Bag 1* (n 16) 236.
[78] Gautama, *Perdata Internasional Jilid III Bag 1* (n 16) 9; Gautama, *Perdata Internasional Jilid II Bag 2* (n 17) 100.
[79] Gautama, *Perdata Internasional Jilid III Bag 1* (n 16) 236.

Indonesian personal law on succession is based on three laws that govern private relationships among different groups of the Indonesian population. First, the Compilation of Islamic Law governs succession to the property of a deceased Muslim, including where the deceased had heirs who embrace religions other than Islam. Second, the BW governs succession to the property of a deceased non-Muslim, including where the deceased had heirs who embrace Islam. Third, *Adat* law governs succession to the property of members of the population who live in *Adat*-based communities. As a consequence, if an Indonesian Muslim who had lived in Australia died in Australia the succession of his estate left in Indonesia would be governed by the Compilation of Islamic Law. If the Indonesian Muslim died in the Netherlands, a country that applies the nationality principle, the Dutch authorities must refer to the Compilation of Islamic Law to settle the deceased's succession issues.

In summary, under Indonesian Private International Law, the law applicable to succession is the national law of the deceased. The national law of the deceased governs all property of the deceased, because there is no distinction between the law that governs movable property and the law that governs immovable property of the deceased.

ii. Administration of a Deceased's Estate

The estate of a deceased Indonesian person will not be distributed to the heirs until the heirs obtain a letter of statement to inherit (*Surat Keterangan Mewaris*). The letter will identify the legitimate heirs of the deceased and the portion of the estate accorded to each heir under Indonesian law. The letter of statement to inherit also states whether there is a will made by the deceased during their life, to separate the assets mentioned in the will from the rest of the estate. Pursuant to Letter of the Directorate of Land Registration No DPT/12/63/12/69 of 1969 and Article 111, paragraph (1) C of Regulation of the State Minister of Agrarian Affairs No 3 of 1997 concerning implementation of Government Regulation No 24 of 1997 concerning land registration, there are three public officials or offices that deal with the issuance of letters of statement to inherit for Indonesian heirs. First, for heirs categorised as Indonesian natives/indigenous, the letter of statement to inherit is made by the Indonesian heirs themselves, with two witnesses, and then confirmed by the head of the village (*lurah*) and sub-district (*camat*) in which the deceased last resided. Second, for heirs categorised as Indonesian Chinese, the letter must be in the form of a notarial deed made by a public notary in the district of the deceased's last residence. Third, for heirs categorised as Indonesian oriental other than Chinese, such as Arabs and Indians, the letter must be issued by the Office of Administration of Estates (*Balai Harta Peninggalan*) in the region of the deceased's last residence. In making the letter of statement to inherit, be it in a notarial deed or letter, the heirs must check whether there is a will made by the deceased. The heirs can enquire with the Central Register of Wills of the Directorate General of General Administration of Law, the Ministry of Law and Human Rights, as explained in the section II.D.iv on wills below. The existence of any will must be included in the letter of statement to inherit. This avoids legal disputes between the heirs and the beneficiaries of the will. This procedure also applies to heirs with foreign citizenship. After the heirs obtain the letter, they may start the process of converting the ownership of the estate from the deceased's name to their names. Any debts owed by the deceased, and tax related to the deceased's assets, must be paid by the heirs to the relevant parties before the heirs are able to transfer the ownership of the estate from the deceased's name to their names.

The above-mentioned procedure is also required for the administration of an estate of an Indonesian deceased person that is located outside Indonesia. The deceased's heirs must show their letters of statement to inherit to the foreign authorities responsible for administering the deceased's estates and follow the legal formalities required by the law of that country.

Where the deceased was a foreigner who left an estate in an Indonesian territory, and the deceased's heirs do not live in Indonesia, the estate will be administered by the Office of Administration of Estates (*Balai Harta Peninggalan*) in the region of the deceased's last residence (Article 463 BW and *Staatsblad* No 166 of 1872 concerning instruction for Office of Administration of Estate in Indonesia). The heirs of the deceased may claim the estate in Indonesia only if they have an equivalent of the letter of statement to inherit issued by the authorities in the country of the deceased.[80]

As demonstrated, the administration of an estate of a deceased Indonesian is handled by three different authorities depending on the population group that the deceased belonged to: Indonesian Chinese, Indonesian natives, or Indonesian oriental other than Chinese.

iii. Intestacy

In the case of intestacy, the property or estate of the deceased will be administered and distributed according to rules laid down by the law. The principles applicable to the intestacy are the same as those previously explained in the section II.D.i on general considerations.

iv. Wills

The law applicable to the formal validity of a will is the law of the place or country where the will is made (*locus regit actum* principle). This doctrine is derived from Article 945, paragraph (1) BW, which provides that an Indonesian citizen in a foreign country cannot make a will in any manner other than by an authentic deed and by following the applicable formalities in the country in which the deed is made. Article 1868 BW explains that an authentic deed is a legal document made in accordance with the local law, by or before public officials who are authorised to make or witness wills. Further, the will must be made in the country in which the assets it distributes are located. For example, an Indonesian who wishes to make a will concerning his property in Singapore must make his will in Singapore. As discussed previously in section II.D.i, Indonesian succession law does not distinguish between the law applicable to movable and immovable property. Hence the principle of *locus regit actum* applies to the formal validity of wills or testaments concerning both movable and immovable property.

In addition to complying with the legal formalities of the foreign country, an Indonesian national must comply with the substantive requirements of Indonesian succession law when making a will in a foreign country. This is because the material validity of a will is

[80] I Devita, 'Pembuatan Wasiat Oleh Orang Asing' (*Irmadevita.com*, 5 December 2018) https://irmadevita.com/2012/pembuatan-wasiat-oleh-orang-asing/ (accessed 17 May 2020).

determined by the national law of the person who makes a will. If a will complies with the formalities required by a foreign country but does not comply with the substantive requirements of Indonesian succession law, the will is not valid according to Indonesian law and will not be enforced by the Indonesian courts. The substantive requirements of a will are found in the BW if the testator is not a Muslim and in the Islamic Compilation Law if the testator is a Muslim. One requirement is that a will made abroad shall not override the legitime (*legitima portio*) set by Indonesian law (Article 913 BW and Article 173 of the Compilation of Islamic Law). Pursuant to Article 11 of Regulation of Minister of Law and Human Rights No 60 of 2016, the will made abroad must be reported by the testator, the beneficiary, or the testator's legal representative, via a notary in Indonesia, to the Central Register of Wills of the Directorate General of General Administration of Law, the Ministry of Law and Human Rights, one month after the will was made abroad. If the will made abroad is not reported in accordance with this regulation, the testator will be regarded as dying intestate and the estate will be distributed according to the rules laid down by the BW if the deceased was a non-Muslim or by the Compilation of Islamic Law if the deceased was a Muslim. If the will made abroad is reported to the Central Register of Wills, on the testator's death the property mentioned in the will is separated from the estate before the estate is distributed to the heirs. In the case of *Erlina and Ahmad Yuni Nasution, S.H. v Yulia Yusriani Mualim*, the Indonesian courts considered a will made by an Indonesian testator in Singapore. The courts found that the will complied with the formalities required by Singaporean law, but was nonetheless null and void because it had been vacated by the action of two of the testator's heirs.[81] That is, Singaporean formalities were complied with, but not Indonesian substantive requirements. In the case of *Leo Bonady, et al v Lelly Iskandar, et al*, the Indonesian courts found that a will made by an Indonesian testator in Singapore was valid in accordance with both the formalities of Singaporean law and substance of Indonesian law.[82] In both cases the parties also brought their dispute to the Singaporean court, and the Singaporean court took into consideration Indonesian substantive law when adjudicating the two cases.

Finally, there is the case where a foreigner with assets in Indonesia seeks to make a will distributing those assets. In such a case, the form of the will must comply with the formalities and procedures mandated by Indonesian law (*locus regit actum* principle), but the content of the will must comply with the substantive requirements governed by the national law of the testator (the nationality principle). Formalities are governed in Article 4 of *Staatsblad* No 559 of 1924, which provides that the will must be in the form of a general testament, made by or before a public notary and witnessed by two witnesses. The notary will report the wills of foreigners to the Central Register of Wills of the Directorate General of General Administration of Law, the Ministry of Law and Human Rights (Article 16 of Act No 30 of 2004 as amended by Act No 2 of 2014 concerning notary office and Article 11 of Regulation of Minister of Law and Human Rights No 60 of 2016). If either Indonesian

[81] District Court of Medan Decision 348/Pdt.G/2009/PN.Mdn (22 June 2010); affd High Court of East Kalimantan Decision 94/PDT/2010/ PT.KT.SMDA (3 March 2011); affd Supreme Court Decision 2562 K/Pdt/2011 (13 March 2012).

[82] District Court of North East Jakarta Decision 158/69/1979 G (not published); affd High Court of Jakarta Decision 241/1979 (unpublished); affd Supreme Court Decision 148/PK/Perd/1982 (unpublished).

formality rules or the substantive requirements of the testator's national law are not complied with, Indonesian courts will declare the wills null and void.

In conclusion, the law applicable to the formal validity of wills is the law of the place or country where the wills are made (*locus regit actum* principle). The law applicable to the material validity of wills is the national law of the testator (the nationality principle).

III. Intellectual Property

Indonesian intellectual property law does not contain any specific choice-of-law provisions concerning the law applicable to intellectual property involving foreign elements. In the absence of specific provision, it is safe to assume that Indonesian intellectual property law follows the traditional rules, namely *lex loci protectionis* and the territoriality principle, to determine intellectual property matters such as the existence, validity, content, ownership, duration, transfer, and protection of intellectual property rights, and remedies where intellectual property rights are violated.

Lex loci protectionis in intellectual property law means that the law applicable to determine matters related to registered intellectual property rights is the law of each state of registration; and, for unregistered intellectual property rights, the law of each state where protection is sought or granted.[83] The territoriality principle in intellectual property law means that the existence of an intellectual property right and the prerogatives afforded to the right-holder are determined by the law of the state, and limited to the territory of the state, which grants the right. For example, the validity of a patent registered and protected in Indonesia only exists in Indonesia. If the holder sought to enforce the patent in Singapore, they would find that the Singaporean courts would not recognise the patent. In dealing with intellectual property cases, Indonesian courts, namely the Commercial Court[84] and Supreme Court, must apply the aforementioned principles. For example, in a patent infringement case in which the patent has never been registered in Indonesia, the Indonesian court will not adjudicate the case. The patent does not deserve the *lex loci protectionis* and lacks validity within Indonesian territory. By contrast, if the patent has been registered – meaning that it is protected in Indonesia – the Indonesian court will adjudicate the case, applying Indonesian law.

Certain types of foreign intellectual property require registration to be protected in Indonesia, for example, patents. Indonesian courts may refuse to hear cases related to these rights if they have not been registered in Indonesia. This follows from both the territoriality and *lex loci protectionis* principles. Other types of foreign intellectual property do not require registration in Indonesia, for instance copyright, well-known trademarks, and trade secrets. Indonesian courts must apply *lex loci protectionis* when adjudicating cases involving rights of this type. In effect, this means they will apply Indonesian law. In accordance with the territoriality principle, judgments given in respect of unregistered intellectual

[83] Intellectual property that shall be registered in Indonesia to get protection are patent, trade-mark, geographical indication, industrial design, layout design of integrated circuit, and plant variety. Other intellectual property that is not required to be registered is copyright, trade secret, and well-known trade-mark.

[84] Indonesian commercial court is part of district court that specialises in commercial cases, namely bankruptcy, intellectual property rights, and bank liquidation.

property are only valid within Indonesian territory. In claims involving the infringement of a trade secret not required to be registered in Indonesia, Indonesian courts also apply Indonesian tort and/or criminal laws. Hence, they apply both the law of the forum (*lex fori*) and *lex loci protectionis*.

A case concerning an unregistered intellectual property right is *Prada S.A. v Fahmi Babra*,[85] which involved the PRADA trademark. Prada S.A. were the Italian owners of the PRADA trademark, but had not registered the trademark in Indonesia. They brought a case against Fahmi Babra, who had registered the PRADA trademark in Indonesia. In adjudicating their claim, the Central Jakarta Commercial Court applied Act No 14 of 1997 concerning trademarks (the Trademark Act 1997) as both the *lex loci protectionis* and *lex fori* in the case. The Trademark Act required a trademark to be registered in Indonesia to be valid. Therefore, the judges of the court found that Fahmi Babra was the valid holder of the PRADA trademark in Indonesia. This finding was in accordance with the *first to file* principle adopted by the Indonesian trademark law. In addition, based on the available evidence presented by the parties, the Court dismissed the claim that PRADA was a well-known trademark. The Indonesian Supreme Court upheld the judgment of the Central Jakarta Commercial Court. Finally, Prada S.A. filed an extraordinary appeal to the Indonesian Supreme Court. In the extraordinary appeal, the Supreme Court was presented with new evidence by Prada S.A. to show that Fahmi Babra had registered the PRADA trademark in bad faith and that the PRADA trademark was well-known in many countries including Indonesia. Applying *lex loci protectionis*, the judges in the extraordinary appeal referred to Article 4, paragraph (1) of the Trademark Act 1997, which required good faith for registration of a trademark, and Article 56, paragraph (1), which allowed annulment of a trademark registered in bad faith. Based on their findings, the judges in the extraordinary appeal found that Fahmi Babra was not acting in good faith when he registered the PRADA trademark in Indonesia. In addition, based on the new evidence, the court found that the PRADA trademark was a well-known trademark as qualified by Article 6, paragraph (3) of the Trademark Act 1997. Therefore, the court annulled the PRADA trademark registered by Fahmi Babra. This case demonstrates the application of *lex loci protectionis* by Indonesian courts in cases involving intellectual property not requiring registration in Indonesia.

Foreign copyright protection requires registration in Indonesia unless the works are created in countries that have bilateral or multilateral agreements on copyright protection with Indonesia. This principle is stipulated in the Berne Convention for the Protection of Literary and Artistic Works, to which Indonesia is a party. The initial title to a copyrighted work is always determined by the law of the state in which the work is created; once the initial title to the work is established, the work will be protected under Indonesian copyright law. This means that the Indonesian copyright law become the *lex loci protectionis* for that copyrighted work in Indonesian courts.

For contractual obligations related to intellectual property, such as licensing agreements or sale of intellectual property, Indonesian courts enforce the parties' choice of law

[85] Commercial Court of Central Jakarta Decision 200/PDT.G/1998/PN.JKT.PST (8 January 1999); affd Supreme Court Decision 2413 K/Pdt/1999 (26 April 2001); affd Supreme Court Extraordinary Appeal 274 PK/Pdt/2003 (14 December 2007).

with regard to their contractual obligations, while proprietary matters are governed by Indonesian law as the *lex loci protectionis* or *lex fori*.

In summary, Indonesian intellectual property law does not have specific choice-of-law provisions concerning the law applicable to intellectual property involving foreign elements. In the absence of specific provisions, Indonesian intellectual property law may implement the traditional rules, namely, *lex loci protectionis*, territoriality principle, and *lex fori*, for different types of intellectual property, depending on whether or not a particular intellectual property requires registration to be protected.

IV. Family Law

A. Marriage

i. Formal Validity

Under Indonesian Private International Law, the formal validity of a legal action such as marriage is determined by the principle of *locus regit actum*. Article 18, paragraph (1) AB stipulates that the '[f]ormality of a legal action is determined by the court in accordance with the law of the country or place where the action is performed'. This principle was adopted in the specific context of marriage by Article 83 of BW, concerning marriage abroad. The Marriage Act 1974 has since superseded the marriage provisions of Book I of BW. Article 56, paragraph (1) of the Marriage Act 1974 reiterates the applicability of the *locus regit actum* principle, stipulating that:

> A marriage performed outside Indonesia between two Indonesian citizens or between an Indonesian and a foreign citizen is valid if performed according to the law of the country where the marriage is performed, and as regards the Indonesian citizens, provided that such marriage does not violate this Act.

Indonesian scholars agree that the above provision contains two rules.[86] The first part of the provision requires a marriage to comply with formality rules of the country where the marriage is performed. The second half of the provision requires Indonesian citizens to comply with the substantive requirements of Marriage Act 1974 when performing a marriage abroad. The first rule implements Article 18, paragraph (1) AB (the *locus regit actum* principle), and the second rule implements Article 16 AB (the nationality principle). Matters that are categorised as formality and as substance have been discussed earlier in Chapter 1, section VI on Substance and Procedure.

For an example of the implementation of Article 56, paragraph (1) of the Marriage Act 1974, consider a marriage by an Indonesian couple in Australia. Such a marriage must comply both with Australia formality requirements, such as registration and witnesses, and the substantive Indonesian requirements, such as the capacity of the couple to marry as dictated by the Marriage Act 1974. If the marriage does not comply with the formalities

[86] Gautama, *Perdata Internasional Jilid III Bag 1* (n 16) 126; ZD Basuki and others, *Materi Pokok Hukum Perdata Internasional. Modul 2* (Universitas Terbuka, 2014) 12–13; Supancana, *Naskah Akademik* (n 43) 30.

of the *lex loci celebrationis* (Australian law), it will not be valid in Australia, Indonesia, or anywhere else, irrespective of the domicile of the couple. This principle also applies to foreigners marrying in Indonesian territory. They must comply with the formal requirements of Indonesian marriage law, while abiding by substantive marriage requirements of their national law. Formality requirements for marriages performed by foreigners in Indonesia are governed by Article 37, paragraph (2) of Presidential Regulation No 96 of 2018 concerning requirements and procedure for population registration and civil registry. Article 37, paragraph (2)g requires foreigners to register their marriage with the Office of Civil Registry in Indonesia. To register their marriage, the foreigner must obtain a marriage permit from the embassy of their country in Indonesia. The marriage permit issued by foreign embassies in Indonesia is usually called 'Certificate of No Impediment to Marriage' or 'Certificate of Legal Capacity to Marry'. This certificate is important for the Indonesian authorities who officiate the marriages of foreigners to determine that their marriage will not breach the national law or the *ordre public* of their countries of origin. The Indonesian authorities, including the Civil Registry Office, may refuse to officiate and register the marriages of foreigners who cannot obtain the certificate from their embassies.

In the case No 253/1978 G (14 January 1979), an Indonesian wife filed a petition for nullity of her marriage performed in Hong Kong in 1969, in the North-East Jakarta District Court. She and her husband, Indonesian Muslims, married in Hong Kong. They followed Islamic requirements but did not comply with the formalities demanded by Hong Kong marriage law. Their marriage was not officiated, nor was it registered at the Office of Marriage Register of Hong Kong, as required by Hong Kong marriage law. Instead, their marriage was solemnised by a Muslim marriage officiant (*qadi*) at the Muslim Universal Love Society, which was not a valid location to officiate a marriage in Hong Kong. The *qadi* who solemnised the couple's marriage was not an authorised marriage officiant under Hong Kong law. Since the marriage was not valid for registration in Hong Kong, the couple did not register their marriage at a Marriage Registry Office in Indonesia, as required by Article 56, paragraph (2) of the Marriage Act 1974. In her petition for nullity in the North-East Jakarta District Court, the wife used the non-compliance with legal formalities in Hong Kong as a ground for the nullity of her marriage. Surprisingly, the judge refused to nullify the couple's marriage. According to the judge, he could not unravel a sacred marriage that had been performed under the law of a religion embraced by majority of the Indonesian population, which contained divine values. The judge cited *ordre public* as the reason for his refusal to nullify the marriage. The court decision in this case was heavily criticised by Indonesian legal scholars.[87] Scholars maintained that the decision breached Article 56 of the Marriage Act 1974, and Charles Himawan, a Professor of Law, stated that the judge should not abuse the *ordre public* doctrine to set aside the law of the country of marriage.[88]

Prior to 2006, Article 56, paragraph (2) of the Marriage Act 1974 stipulated that 'Within one year of the couple's return to Indonesia, their marriage certificate shall be registered at the office of marriage registry in the district of their residence.' This Article provided another

[87] ZD Basuki and others, *Materi Pokok Hukum Perdata Internasional. Modul 5* (Universitas Terbuka, 2014) 20–21.

[88] TMP Allagan, 'International mixed marriage in Indonesia and ASEAN: international mixed marriage and its recognition in Indonesia towards one ASEAN community' (PhD thesis, University of Groningen, 2019) 109.

formal requirement that must be adhered to by Indonesian or mixed marriage couples who performed their marriages outside Indonesia. In 2006, this provision was superseded by Article 37 of the Population Administration Act 2006, which provides,

> (1) Marriage of an Indonesian citizen outside Indonesia shall be registered with an authorised official in the foreign country and reported to the representative office of the Republic of Indonesia in the foreign country.
> (2) If the country referred to in paragraph (1) does not provide for the registration of marriage for foreigners, the registration shall be performed by the representative office of the Republic of Indonesia in the foreign country.
> (3) The representative office of the Republic of Indonesia shall register the marriage in the Register of Marriage Certificates and issue an Excerpt of Marriage Certificate.
> (4) The registration of marriage referred to in paragraphs (1) and (2) shall be reported by the couple to the registry office at the district of their residence within thirty days of their return to Indonesia.

Failure to comply with the above provisions is penalised with an administrative fine, as dictated in Article 90, paragraph (1)b of the Population Administration Act 2006 as amended in 2013. In the author's opinion, the provisions of Articles 37 and 90 should apply *mutatis mutandis* to the foreign spouse of a mixed couple performing marriage outside Indonesia, to make their marriage to their Indonesian spouse valid under Indonesian law and to avoid a 'limping marriage', ie a marriage deemed valid by the law of their country, but deemed invalid in Indonesia.

In 2015, the Indonesian Supreme Court issued Circular Letter No 3 of 2015. This circular letter, issued to all courts in Indonesia and concerning the guidelines governing court actions, the Supreme Court mentioned that a marriage performed outside Indonesia is invalid if it is not registered in a marriage registry office in Indonesia.[89]

To summarise, the formal validity of a marriage under Indonesian law is determined by the law of the country where the marriage is performed. The principle of *locus regit actum* applies to all marriages performed by either Indonesians or foreigners irrespective of their nationalities and domicile. In addition, the registration of a marriage performed outside Indonesia, in an Indonesian marriage registry office, is essential to determine the existence of the marriage under Indonesian law. This registration should be done by all spouses of both Indonesian couples and mixed marriage couples.

ii. Capacity

Indonesian practice uses the terms 'substantive requirements' or 'non-impediments to marriage' as equivalents to the concept 'capacity for marriage'.[90] Capacity to marry is translated as *hoedanigheden en voorwaarden, die vereischt worden om een huwelijk te kunnen aangaan* (capacity and conditions required to enter into a marriage) in the title of Part I of Chapter IV, Book I of BW. Until 1974, the BW regulated the capacity to marry, but it

[89] Supreme Court of the Republic of Indonesia, *Rumusan Hukum Rapat Pleno Kamar Mahkamah Agung Republik Indonesia Tahun 2015. Surat Edaran Nomor 03 Tahun 2015 Tentang Pemberlakuan Rumusan Hasil Rapat Pleno Kamar Mahkamah Agung Tahun 2015 Sebagai Pedoman Pelaksanaan Tugas Bagi Pengadilan*, 4.

[90] Gautama, *Perdata Internasional Jilid III Bag 1* (n 16) 123; Basuki and others, *Materi pokok. Modul 5* (n 87) 112.

has now been superseded in this respect by the Marriage Act 1974. The BW instituted a number of requirements to have capacity for marriage. These included being single, being of minimum age, the consent of the parties, the consent of the parents, absence of certain consanguinity or affinity, and passing the waiting period after the dissolution of a previous marriage (Articles 27–49 BW). The Marriage Act 1974 mirrors the BW to an extent, as in Chapter II adopts the capacities to and conditions for marriage found in Book I of BW. However, unlike the BW, which governs a marriage only within its civil (ie non-religious) relations (Article 26 BW) and considers a civil marriage as legally binding, the Marriage Act 1974 introduces religious requirements for marriage (Article 2, paragraph (1)). Thus, to have capacity to marry in Indonesia, a person must comply with both religious and civil requirements. In addition, the Marriage Act 1974 contains provisions governing the capacity to marry more than one wife, which was not addressed in BW. This matter will be dealt with in section IV.A.iv below.

Indonesian scholars agree that capacity to marry is part of personal law (personal statute) and therefore the law applicable to capacity to marry is the law of the person's nationality, not the law of the person's domicile.[91] This doctrine is based on Article 16 AB, which stipulates that 'Statutory provisions governing the status and capacity of persons remain binding for Indonesian citizens during their stay abroad.' Although Article 16 AB only governs the application of the nationality principle to Indonesians abroad, jurisprudence since the Dutch colonial era establishes that the nationality principle also applies to foreigners in Indonesia. Therefore, the capacity of foreigners to marry in Indonesia will be determined by the law of their nationalities. For example, although Indonesian law contains no impediment to Muslim men marrying more than one wife (polygamous marriage), if a Muslim man is a national of a country that prohibits polygamous marriage, then although he domiciles in Indonesia he cannot marry more than one wife.

There is an exception where a foreigner domiciled in Indonesia originates from a country that applies the domicile principle. In this case, Indonesian private international law applies the *Renvoi* (remission) principle, with the effect that the foreigner's capacity to marry in Indonesia is determined by Indonesian law.[92] Jurisprudence and administrative practices since the Dutch colonial era have applied this *Renvoi* principle concerning capacity to marry for foreigners having domicile in Indonesia. In 1922, the attorney general of the Dutch East Indies issued a circular letter dated 9 March 1922 to the Civil Registry offices. The circular letter sought to deal with the question of the capacity of foreigners to marry in the Dutch East Indies and whether adult foreigners under 30 years old had to obtain parental consent to marry in accordance with Articles 42 to 48 BW. Article 42 BW in principle requires adults under 30 years old to obtain the consent of their parents to enter into a marriage, and Article 48 BW provides that Articles 42 to 47 BW may be exempted if either or both parents are not available in Indonesia. In his circular letter, the attorney general instructed the Marriage Registrars of Civil Registry to apply Articles 42 to 48 BW to determine the issues of capacity to marry and parental consent of foreigners who came from countries with the domicile principle. He also instructed the Marriage Registrars of

[91] Gautama, *Perdata Internasional Jilid III Bag 1* (n 16) 9; Gautama, *Perdata Internasional Jilid II Bag 2* (n 17) 100.
[92] The *Renvoi* principle in Indonesian private international law is discussed at ch 1, section IV.D.

Civil Registry to apply the national law of foreigners who came from countries with the nationality principle, to determine the issues of their capacity and the need for parental consent to marry in the Dutch East Indies. The circular letter provided specifically for cases of German and French citizens who sought to marry in the Dutch East Indies, stating that the applicable law to determine their capacity to marry was German and French law, respectively. In the case of British citizens, the circular letter suggested the application of the Articles 42 to 48 BW to determine their capacity and requirements to marry.[93] Based on Article II of the Transitional Provisions of the Indonesian Constitution 1945,[94] the attorney general's circular letter of 9 March 1922 remains valid after independence as no new regulation supersedes it.

Although Indonesian private international law applies the nationality principle to the marriage of foreigners in Indonesia, so that requirements for marriages in Indonesia are based on the couple's national law, foreigners are required to comply with certain substantive requirements in Indonesian marriage law that are fundamental for Indonesian *ordre public*. These fundamental requirements cannot be waived by the foreigners' national law. There is no law that expressly determines which capacity or substantive requirements are fundamental for Indonesian *ordre public*. However judicial and administrative practices indicate that religious requirements related to marriage are *ordre public* in Indonesia, even for citizens of countries that only recognise civil marriage. Article 37, paragraph (2)a of Presidential Regulation No 96 of 2018 concerning requirements and procedure of population registration and civil registry, provides that marriages by foreigners in Indonesia can only be registered in Indonesian registry offices if they are religious marriages or solemnised by religious authorities. On the other hand, although required by the Marriage Act 1974, parental consent to marriage of adults under 21 years old is not *ordre public*. Therefore, the websites of Indonesian embassies and foreign embassies in Indonesia include religious marriage in the list of marriage requirements for foreigners in Indonesia, but rarely include parental consent.[95]

In the case of a mixed marriage (ie a marriage between a foreigner and an Indonesian) in Indonesia, capacity to marry is governed by the Marriage Act 1974. Article 59, paragraph (2) of the Marriage Act 1974 provides that '[a] mixed marriage performed in Indonesia shall be held in accordance with this Act'. As such, regardless of the nationality of the foreigner, capacity to marry an Indonesian national in Indonesia is determined by the Marriage Act 1974 and other relevant Indonesian marriage law.

As stated earlier, the nationality principle of Article 16 AB applies to determine the capacity of Indonesian nationals to marry outside Indonesia, both with fellow Indonesians and

[93] Gautama, *Pengantar Hukum* (n 1) 101–103; Gautama, *Perdata Internasional Jilid II Bag 2* (n 17) 102.

[94] It provides that 'All existing state institutions and regulations remain effective, as long as the new ones have not yet been provided under this Constitution.'

[95] See Australian Embassy Indonesia, 'Marriage in Indonesia' (Australian Embassy Indonesia) https://indonesia.embassy.gov.au/jakt/MarriageInd.html (accessed 10 April 2020); Embassy of The Republic of Indonesia in Manila, The Republic of The Philippines, Accredited to The Republic of Marshall Islands and The Republic of Palau, 'Certificate Of Legal Capacity To Marry' (Kementerian Luar Negeri Repulik Indonesia) https://kemlu.go.id/manila/en/pages/certificate_of_legal_capacity_to_marry/486/etc-menu (accessed 10 April 2020); Embassy of Republic of Indonesia Ottawa and Permanent Representative to ICAO Canada, 'Marriage & Divorce' (Kementerian Luar Negeri Repulik Indonesia) https://kemlu.go.id/ottawa/en/pages/perkawinan___perceraian/680/about-service (accessed 10 April 2020); MAECI, 'Stato Civile' (Ambasciata d'Italia, 1 August 2019) https://ambjakarta.esteri.it/ambasciata_jakarta/it/informazioni_e_servizi/servizi_consolari/stato_civile (accessed 10 April 2020).

with foreigners. In other words, Indonesian law governing the capacity to marry remains binding on Indonesian nationals when they are abroad. For example, where an Indonesian national performs a marriage in a country that only recognises civil marriage, or where an Indonesian Muslim performs a marriage in a country that does not provide authorities to solemnise Islamic marriage, according to Indonesian law the Indonesian national lacks capacity to marry and consequently, his or her marriage abroad is deemed invalid.

In relation to the Islamic requirements for Indonesian Muslims abroad to have capacity to marry, the Minister of Foreign Affairs and the Minister of Religious Affairs issued Joint Ministerial Decree No 589, 182/OT/X/99/01 of 1999. This decree was intended to facilitate marriages of Indonesian Muslims in countries that do not provide authorities to solemnise Islamic marriage. The decree assigns Indonesian public servants to solemnise marriages of Indonesian couples in accordance with Islamic rites in the Indonesian Embassies or Indonesian representative offices located in countries that lack Islamic authorities. Since marriage under the joint ministerial decree is solemnised inside the Indonesian embassies or representative offices, the marriage is characterised as a domestic marriage that must comply with all requirements of the Marriage Act 1974. The joint ministerial decree only provides for marriage between Indonesian nationals who are Muslims. The decree does not apply to mixed marriage couples, though both partners may be Muslim. For Indonesian nationals who are not Muslims, the Indonesian Government provides no facility to solemnise their religious marriage in the Indonesian embassies or representative offices. Even in the case of Muslim Indonesian nationals, not all Indonesian embassies have personnel assigned to implement the joint ministerial decree. If the Indonesian embassies in a particular country cannot implement the joint ministerial decree, Indonesian Muslims who wish to perform a religious marriage in those countries must attempt to comply with the religious requirements by themselves, otherwise their marriage will be deemed invalid by Indonesian law.

In summary, foreigners' capacity to marry in Indonesia is determined by their national law, or by Indonesian law in the case of *Renvoi* or transmission. In applying the national law of the foreigners to their capacity to marry, Indonesian *ordre public* must be respected. If the foreigner is performing a mixed marriage with an Indonesian national within Indonesia, the foreigner's capacity to marry in Indonesia is determined not by their national law but by Indonesian law, namely the Marriage Act 1974 and other relevant Indonesian marriage law. Finally, capacity to marry for Indonesian nationals outside Indonesia is determined by Indonesian marriage law.

iii. Consent of the Parties

Under Indonesian law, parties from whom consent to a marriage is required are: the would-be spouses; parents or guardians; and, in a polygamous marriage, existing wives. Lack of the consent from any of these parties will render a marriage invalid.

Consent of the prospective spouses to their marriage is part of substantive requirements of marriage. Therefore, it is governed under the personal statutes of the would-be spouses. Pursuant to Article 16 AB, personal statute under Indonesian Private International Law is determined by the law of the nationality of the parties. Accordingly, the consent of the would-be spouses to their marriage is determined by the law of their nationalities. The requirement that prospective spouses consent to their marriage is found in Article 6, paragraph (1) of the

Marriage Act 1974 and Article 16, paragraph (1) of Compilation of Islamic Law. Legal scholars maintain that consent is vitiated by duress, pressure, threat, and coercion of the will. The consent requirement is also not satisfied where there is misrepresentation about the would-be spouses' identities, characters, backgrounds, etc. This misrepresentation could be caused by mistake or fraud. Under Indonesian law, a husband or a wife can file a petition for nullity of a marriage that was performed without consent (Article 27 of the Marriage Act 1974 and Article 72 of the Compilation of Islamic Law). Because consent of the prospective spouses is categorised as a substantive requirement under the personal statutes of the parties, the existence and definition of consent is determined by the national law of each spouse. For example, an Indonesian authority who officiates or solemnises a marriage of a Dutch bride and groom in Indonesia will determine the existence of the spouses' consent based on Dutch law. Supposing that Dutch national law dictates that consent must be expressed, the Indonesian authority will require the Dutch bride and groom to present their express consent to validate their marriage, either verbally or in writing, although Indonesian law itself does not require consent of the parties to be expressed. Only if the foreigners have domicile in Indonesia and originate from countries that apply the domicile principle is the relevance of their consent to marriage determined by Indonesian law. This is because Indonesian Private International Law applies the *Renvoi* (remission) principle as previously discussed in Chapter 1, section IV.D on Renvoi and transmission.

A foreigner and an Indonesian who seek to be joined in a mixed marriage in Indonesia will find the law to determine their consent to marriage in the Marriage Act 1974. Article 59, paragraph (2) of the Marriage Act 1974 provides that, 'A mixed marriage performed in Indonesia shall be held in accordance with this Act.' As such, regardless of the nationality of the foreigner, his or her consent to marriage in Indonesia to an Indonesian national, will be determined by the Marriage Act 1974 and other relevant Indonesian marriage law. The nationality principle of Article 16 AB also applies to determine the consent of Indonesian nationals who seek to marry outside Indonesia, either with fellow Indonesians or with foreigners. In other words, Indonesian law governing the consent of parties remains binding for Indonesian nationals during their stay abroad.

With regard to the consent of parents or guardians, Indonesian scholars agree that this is a substantive, not formal, requirement of marriage.[96] Therefore, pursuant to Article 16 AB, it is governed by the national law of the parties. For example, an adult Indonesian national under 21 years old who is married outside Indonesia must obtain written parental consent, or if this is not available, written consent from other family members of direct parental lineage, guardians, or caregivers (Article 6, paragraphs (2) to (4) of the Marriage Act 1974 and Article 6, paragraph (2)c of the Marriage Regulation 1975). This parental consent is required even if in the particular country there is no such requirement. If the Indonesian youth performs a marriage outside Indonesia without written parental consent, their marriage will be voidable under Indonesian law. Written parental consent is also required where a foreigner under 21 years old seeks to perform a mixed marriage with an Indonesian national in Indonesia (Article 59, paragraph (2) of the Marriage Act 1974). Where two foreigners wish to be married in Indonesia, and neither is required by their national law to obtain parental consent, the basic rule is that Indonesian law will not impose any requirement of parental consent. This is because Indonesian jurisprudence applies the nationality

[96] Gautama, *Perdata Internasional Jilid III Bag 1* (n 16) 120.

principle to the personal statute of foreigners in Indonesia. By the same token, Indonesian law will require that any minimum age requirements found in the foreigners' national laws are satisfied. However, because of the *Renvoi* principle, where the foreigner has domicile in Indonesia and originates from a country that applies the domicile principle, Indonesian law concerning parental consent will be applied.

Following the Shafi'i school of Islamic law, Indonesian marriage law requires a Muslim bride to obtain her father's consent or, if he is not available, the consent of her patrilineal male relatives (Part 3 of Chapter IV Compilation of Islamic Law). The bride's father or patrilineal male relatives are called *wali* (guardian) in Islamic marriage law. Besides giving consent to the bride's marriage, the role of the *wali* is to marry the bride to the groom during the wedding ceremony. Since the *wali*'s consent is part of the religious requirements for marriage, and religious marriage is *ordre public* in Indonesia, the requirement applies to Islamic marriages performed by an Indonesian couple both inside and outside Indonesia, by a Muslim foreigner in Indonesia, and by a mixed marriage couple. If the bride cannot obtain the consent of her father or her male relatives, she can request a religious court to issue a ruling that appoints a *qadi* to give consent to her marriage and to marry her to the groom in her wedding ceremony. A *qadi* is an official appointed by the government to function as a *wali* for a Muslim bride, in addition to other functions as dictated by the Compilation of Islamic Law. Although the point is not expressly governed by Indonesian marriage law, a foreign bride performing an Islamic marriage in Indonesia should be able to request a religious court in Indonesia to appoint a *qadi* to act as a *wali* for her marriage.

Indonesian law recognises polygamous marriage. For a polygamous marriage to be valid, various parties must consent, for instance, the parents of prospective spouses under 21 years old; the *wali* for the Muslim bride; and the prior wives. These requirements are discussed more fully in section IV.A.iv.

As demonstrated above, for a marriage to be valid in Indonesian law the consent of various parties may be required. In principle, their consent is determined by the national law of the parties, based on the nationality principle adopted in Indonesian Private International Law. The Indonesian law concerning consent of the parties always applies to the Indonesians wherever they are, to the mixed marriages between Indonesian nationals and foreigners, and to the marriages of foreigners having domicile in Indonesia and originate from countries that apply the domicile principle.

iv. Polygamous Marriages

Polygamous marriages are legal in Indonesia with some conditions. The legality of polygamous marriages is governed in the Marriage Act 1974. Article 3 of the Act stipulates that:

> (1) In principle, a man can be married to only one woman. A woman shall be married to only one man.
> (2) Each marriage shall be registered in accordance with the applicable regulations.

The General Elucidation of the Act writes that:

> The Act adheres to the principle of monogamy. Only if desired by the parties, because their law and religion permit, a husband can marry more than one wife. However, the marriage of a husband with more than one wife, although desired by the parties, shall be allowed only if it meets certain conditions and is decreed by the court.

Based on the above provisions, polygamous marriages can be performed in Indonesia only with certain conditions. First, only men can perform polygamous marriages. Second, both their national law and religion must allow polygamous marriage. Third, the number of wives in polygamous marriages is determined by the parties' national law and religion. For example, according to *Sharia* or Islamic law, the maximum number of wives in a polygamous marriage is four. Fourth, polygamous marriages can be performed only if validated by a court ruling. Fifth, the court will issue the ruling only after obtaining the consent of the prior wife or wives. Sixth, the court sees evidence that the prior wife or wives cannot perform their function as a wife; or are disabled; or cannot conceive. The court can waive the requirement of consent only if the wife or wives are incapable of giving her or their consent, or have been missing for at least two years and presumed dead (Articles 4 and 5 of the Marriage Act 1974 and Articles 40 to 43 of the Marriage Regulation 1975). Because the requirements of polygamous marriages in Indonesia are related to the national and religious law of the parties, the requirements are substantive and part of the parties' personal statute. As such, where there is an international element to the marriages, the capacity to be married polygamously is determined by both the national law and religion of the parties, as dictated by the nationality principle adopted in Article 16 AB. However, in the author's opinion, the requirement to obtain a court ruling approving the polygamous marriage is a formal, not substantive, requirement. As explained in section IV.A.ii, the substantive requirements for marriage, including a polygamous marriage, require that the persons entering into the marriage have attained a specified age; the consent of the parties to the marriage; the consent of the parents; the absence of prohibited degrees of consanguinity or affinity; the lapse of any specified waiting period after dissolution of a marriage; and compliance with religious rules. Obtaining a court ruling is not mentioned as a substantive requirement in the BW or the Marriage Act 1974. A court ruling in respect of a polygamous marriage is only mentioned in the General Elucidation of the Marriage Act 1974. It is not governed by the provisions of the Marriage Act 1974 or the Marriage Regulation 1975. Therefore, the court ruling can only be a formal requirement. It follows that, pursuant to Article 17 AB, the necessity of a court ruling in the case of a polygamous marriage entered into by an Indonesian male abroad should be determined by the law of the country in which the polygamous marriage is performed (*locus regit actum*).

Pursuant to the nationality principle of Article 16 AB, Indonesians performing polygamous marriages outside Indonesia must comply with the requirements of polygamous marriage of the Marriage Act 1974, the Marriage Regulation 1975, and the Compilation of Islamic Law for Muslims. For example, an Indonesian man having domicile outside Indonesia intends to perform a polygamous marriage in the country of his domicile. His prior wife is an Indonesian national. In this case, he must obtain the consent of his prior wife, although he domiciles and performs his polygamous marriage in a country that does not require the consent of prior wives. If he does not comply with this requirement, his polygamous marriage made outside Indonesia is invalid under Indonesian law. The nationality principle also applies to foreigners performing polygamous marriages in Indonesia. That is, the capacity of foreigners to perform polygamous marriages in Indonesia is determined by the law of their nationalities. For example, although Indonesian law does not prevent a Muslim man from marrying more than one woman, if a Muslim man is a national of a country that prohibits polygamous marriage he will be prevented from marrying more than one wife in Indonesia. In the case of a foreigner having domicile in Indonesia who originates from a country that applies the domicile principle, capacity to partake in a polygamous marriage in Indonesia is determined by Indonesian law. This is because Indonesian private international law applies the *Renvoi* (remission) principle, as has been discussed in Chapter 1, section IV.D on Renvoi and transmission. However, there is in practice an additional formal requirement for a foreigner to marry in Indonesia; that is, the foreigner must obtain a Certificate of No Impediment to Marriage from their embassy in Indonesia. Without this certificate, the Indonesian authority may refuse to officiate and register his polygamous marriage in Indonesia.

Pursuant to the principle of *locus regit actum* of Article 18 AB, a foreigner, irrespective of his nationality and domicile, who has capacity to perform polygamous marriage in Indonesia must comply with all formal requirements of polygamous marriage, including but not limited to filing a request to a court to issue a ruling that allows him to marry more than one wife in Indonesia (Article 4 of the Marriage Act 1974 and Article 41 of the Marriage Regulation 1975). If the court denies the foreigner's application for polygamous marriage, he cannot perform the marriage. The court ruling is mandatory for all polygamous marriages. It cannot be substituted by the Certificate of No Impediment to Marriage issued by the foreigner's embassy in Indonesia.

In summary, polygamous marriages are legal in Indonesia with some conditions. Capacity to marry polygamously is determined by both the national law and religion of the parties. The formal requirements of a polygamous marriage, such as obtaining a court ruling and the registration of the marriage, are determined by the law of the place of polygamous marriage (*locus regit actum*).

v. Same-sex Marriages and Civil Unions

Article 1 of the Marriage Act 1974 stipulates that, 'Marriage is a physical and spiritual bond between a man and a woman as husband and wife, with the purpose of establishing a happy and lasting family founded on the belief in God Almighty.' Article 2, paragraph (1) of the same Act provides that, 'A marriage is lawful if performed in accordance with the rules of religion and belief of each party.' As such, the fundamental principles of marriages in Indonesia are: first, a marriage is only between a man and a woman – or a man and women in the case of polygamous marriages – and second, a marriage exists based on the rules of religion and belief of each party. These principles are *ordre public* in Indonesia. Accordingly, same-sex marriages are regarded as against *ordre public* in Indonesia. Such marriages are not between parties of the opposite sex as required by Article 1 of the Marriage Act 1974. In addition, same-sex marriages are not accepted by the religions officially recognised in Indonesia. Therefore, same-sex marriages cannot be performed in accordance with religious rules as required by Article 2, paragraph (1) of the Marriage Act 1974. The 2015 Academic Paper of Indonesian Private International Law Bill reiterated that same-sex marriages are contrary to *ordre public* in Indonesia.[97]

[97] Supancana, *Naskah Akademik* (n 43) 18.

Indonesian law is silent about marriages performed by people whose gender identity does not correspond with their sex assigned at birth, for instance the cases of marriages performed by transgender and intersex individuals. In practice, this kind of marriage can be potentially characterised as same-sex marriage that violates Article 1 of the Marriage Act 1974. In the view of the religions recognised in Indonesia, although the individuals have officially changed their sex identity in their civil status, they do not become the opposite sex. Thus, though according to their civil sex identity they have an opposite-sex marriage, religion classes the marriage as same-sex, making such marriages void regardless of the nationalities and domicile of the parties and the law of the place of their marriages. It shall be noted, however, that although the religious authorities in Indonesia do not accept marriages performed by individuals who changed their sex identity, the Indonesian Government recognises and registers the new sex of those who change their sex in accordance with the Population Administration Act 2006 as amended in 2013. Article 56, paragraph (1) of the Act and its elucidation provides that the registration of a newly changed sex by a civil registry official is based on an application made by a resident after the resident obtains a court ruling on the matter that is final and binding. The new sex decreed by the court is registered in the civil registry offices and recorded on the residents' birth certificates and other civil documents (Article 58 of Presidential Regulation No 96 of 2018 concerning requirements and procedure of population registration and civil registry and Article 15, paragraphs (1) and (3) of Regulation of Minister of Internal Affairs No 108 of 2019 concerning implementing regulation of the Presidential Regulation No 96 of 2018).

In the case of *Alterina Hofan v Jane Deviyanti H*, Alterina Hofan, who was assigned female at birth, changed his legal sex to become male and in 2006 registered his new legal sex at the civil registry office in the city of Jayapura where he was born in 1977. Based on the registration, Alterina Hofan, who changed his name to Alter Hofan, applied to other government offices to change the sex identity written in his other civil documents. After being recognised as a man in his civil documents, Alter Hofan, 31 years old, married Jane Deviyanti, 22 years old, in Las Vegas, the US in September 2008 and obtained State Nevada Marriage Certificate No 20080909000685000 dated 9 September 2008. When they returned to Jakarta in 2009, the couple reported their marriage to the civil registry office in Jakarta in Marriage Report No 203/Perkawinan LN/08/2009, registered under Registration No 339/KHS/II/2008/2009. Ms Deviyanti's parents, who disapproved of the marriage, reported Mr Hofan to the Jakarta police and accused him of committing identity forgery in his civil documents to lure their daughter. The police and public prosecutor brought Mr Hofan to the criminal court of the South Jakarta District in 2010. The public prosecutor accused Mr Hofan of forging his sex identity in his civil documents because he changed his sex identity without first obtaining a court ruling as required by the Administration Act 2006 as amended in 2013. Mr Hofan corrected his error during his criminal trial, and obtained a court ruling No 12/Pdt.P/2010/PN.Jpr. (29 March 2010) from the Jayapura District Court that declared him a man. Based on the expert witness reports and medical observation that concluded that Mr Hofan was male and suffered from Klinefelter syndrome, the judges in the South Jakarta District Court held that Mr Hofan did not commit any crime, although he changed his sex identity without following the procedure required by the law.[98]

[98] District Court of South Jakarta Decision 583/Pid.B/2010/PN.Jkt.Sel (23 November 2010).

The Supreme Court upheld the judgment of the South Jakarta District Court.[99] As such, Mr, Hofan was freed from all the charges in 2011. Ms Deviyanti stayed faithful to Mr Hofan during his criminal trial. But in 2012, she sued Mr Hofan for tort and filed a petition to nullify their marriage in the South Jakarta District Court. In this latter case the judges acknowledged that Mr Hofan was legally a male person but found that he was nonetheless female by nature. They based their findings on Mr Hofan's DNA evidence and Ms Deviyanti's testimony. The Court decided to annul the marriage that had been registered in the civil registry office in Jakarta under Registration No 339/KHS/II/2008/2009, because in the Court's opinion the couple's marriage was a same-sex marriage in violation of Article 1 of the Marriage Act 1974.[100] The Supreme Court upheld the judgment of the South Jakarta District Court.[101] This case demonstrates that in Indonesia, a marriage performed by a transgender or intersex person will be characterised as a same-sex marriage, although the state has recognised the newly changed sex of the person. Accordingly, such marriages are voidable.

Civil unions, involving both opposite-sex couples and same-sex couples, do not exist in the Indonesian legal system. Accordingly, any rights and obligations of the parties in the civil unions do not exist under Indonesian law.

B. Matrimonial Causes

i. Divorce, Nullity and Separation

Matrimonial causes include divorce, nullity of marriage, and separation. Indonesian scholars agree that matrimonial causes are part of personal law (personal statute)[102] and therefore, the law applicable to matrimonial causes is the law of the nationality of the person, not the law of the person's domicile. This doctrine is based on Article 16 AB that stipulates, 'Statutory provisions governing the status and capacity of persons remain binding for Indonesian citizens during their stay abroad.' In other words, the nationality principle conveyed in Article 16 AB applies to matrimonial causes and to other fields of personal law. The following paragraphs will explain the rules in Indonesian Private International Law that determine the law applicable to each of the matrimonial causes. The parties in matrimonial causes in the context of Indonesian private international law could be Indonesian couples having domicile outside Indonesia, mixed marriage couples having domicile in Indonesia and outside Indonesia, and foreign couples having domicile in Indonesia.

Regarding the divorce of a couple where both spouses have the same nationality, the law applicable to the divorce is the law of the couple's nationality. For example, consider the case where an Indonesian couple having domicile in the Netherlands is divorcing in the Netherlands. To be valid in Indonesia, the couple's divorce in the Netherlands must comply with the substantive requirements provided in the Marriage Act 1974 and the

[99] Supreme Court Decision 704 K/Pid/2011 (31 May 2011).

[100] District Court of South Jakarta Decision 481/Pdt.G/2012/PN.Jkt.Sel (6 March 2013).

[101] Supreme Court Decision 1103 K/Pdt/2014 (29 October 2014).

[102] Gautama, *Perdata Internasional Jilid III Bag 1* (n 16) 21, 24; ZD Basuki and others, *Materi Pokok Hukum Perdata Internasional. Modul 3* (Universitas Terbuka, 2014) 12, 27.

Marriage Regulation 1975. If their marriage was performed under Islamic law, their divorce in the Netherlands must also comply with the requirements contained in the Compilation of Islamic Law. For instance, if the wife is an Indonesian Muslim, she has to comply with the *iddah* (waiting period) required in the Compilation of Islamic Law before her divorce in the Netherlands can take effect. The nationality principle also applies to the divorce of a foreign couple having domicile in Indonesia in which both spouses have the same nationality. An Indonesian court that exercises its jurisdiction over the divorce will apply the national law of the foreign couple. Although Article 16 AB only applies the nationality principle to Indonesians abroad, jurisprudence established since the Dutch colonial era rules that the nationality principle also applies to the personal statute of foreigners in Indonesia.[103] Therefore, for foreign couples who domicile in Indonesia and originate from countries that implement the nationality principle, the couple's divorce in Indonesia will be adjudicated under their national law. For instance, in 1953 the West-South Jakarta District Court applied the German Civil Code (BGB) to adjudicate the divorce of a German couple domiciled in Jakarta.[104] As explained earlier in Chapter 2, section I.B.iv.b on divorce, nullity and separation, even though the couple's divorce will be adjudicated under the national law of the foreign couple, an Indonesian judge will not grant the divorce if the grounds for the couple's divorce are not known in Indonesia. Examples of grounds for divorce that are not known in Indonesia are divorce by mutual consent (divorce without motive) and divorce because of the change of one's income.

In addition to the nationality principle, Indonesian private international law applies the *Renvoi* (remission) principle as previously discussed in Chapter 1, section IV.D on Renvoi and transmission. Because of *Renvoi*, when an Indonesian judge applies the national law of a foreign couple divorcing in Indonesia, the judge will refer to the private international law of the foreign couple's nationality. If this national law applies the domicile principle, the applicable law will remit or refer back to Indonesian law as the law of their domicile. Accordingly, the judge will adjudicate the divorce under Indonesian substantive law. Indonesian courts have applied the *renvoi* principle in this way in cases involving couples domiciled in Indonesia that were nationals of England,[105] the US,[106] and South Africa.[107]

Where divorcing spouses have different nationalities, the choice of law rules stated in the previous paragraphs cannot apply. In other words, the above-mentioned rules only apply to divorcing couples whose nationalities are the same. For a couple who have different nationalities, the law applicable to their divorce cannot be the law of their respective nationalities, because each national law may provide different rules and requirements for a divorce. The different rules and requirements of divorce in each spouse's national law can result in a limping divorce in which one spouse's divorce is regarded valid by its country but

[103] Gautama, *Perdata Internasional Jilid III Bag 1* (n 16) 9.

[104] ibid, 176.

[105] District Court of South Jakarta Decision 112/Pdt.G/1987 (not published).

[106] District Court of South Jakarta Decision 47/Pdt.G/2008/PN.Jak.Sel (not published) as cited on p 9 of the District Court of Denpasar Decision 172/Pdt.G/2014/PN.Dps. (6 May 2014); High Court of Jakarta Decision 141/PDT/2009/PT.DKI (not published) as cited on p 9 of the District Court of Denpasar Decision 172/Pdt.G/2014/PN.Dps. (6 May 2014); Supreme Court Decision 2640 K/Pdt/2009 is not published, but the legal opinion in the decision is cited on p 9 of the District Court of Denpasar Decision 172/Pdt.G/2014/PN.Dps (6 May 2014) (published).

[107] District Court of Denpasar Decision 172/Pdt.G/2014/PN.Dps. (6 May 2014).

is regarded invalid by the country of the other spouse. Therefore, Indonesian and Dutch scholars agree that the nationality principle does not apply to the divorce of a couple with different nationalities.[108] In other words, the law applicable to the couple's divorce shall not be the national law of each spouse as dictated by Article 16 AB and jurisprudence. In this regard, Indonesian scholars, Sudargo Gautama and his disciples often refer to the opinion of Professor R D Kollewijn, a leading Dutch scholar in interpersonal law, who supported the French jurisprudence on divorce cases between spouses with different nationalities.[109] The Dutch scholars supported French court judgments that abandoned the nationality principle, for example the famous case of *Rivière v Roumiantzeff*.[110] In this case, the French court had to decide on the validity of the divorce between Ms Lydya Roumiantzeff and her former husband, Mr Dimitri Petrov, because Mr Robert Rivière, a French citizen, who was currently Ms Roumiantzeff's husband, sought annulment of his marriage to Ms Roumiantzeff. Ms Roumiantzeff was French by naturalisation and her first husband, Mr Petrov, was a Russian national who had settled in Ecuador. The couple had divorced by mutual consent in Ecuador. Mr Rivière claimed that divorce by mutual consent was not known under French law, and consequently the divorce never took place. Although French private international law followed the nationality principle, in this case the French court applied the law of the couple's domicile, Ecuadorian law, to determine the validity of Ms Roumiantzeff's and Mr Petro's divorce. In the *Lewandowski* case,[111] the French court also applied the law of the couple's domicile to the divorce of a couple in which the spouses were of different nationalities. The French jurisprudence applying the law of the domicile (the domicile principle) to the divorce of a couple with different nationalities has been adopted in scholarly writings on Indonesian Private International Law.[112]

The 1983, 1997, and 2015 Bills of Indonesian Private International Law accept the scholarly opinion concerning the rules of choice of law in divorce. The Bills provide three rules of choice of law to determine the law applicable to divorce. First, the law applicable to the divorce of a where both spouses have the same nationality is the national law of the couple. Second, the law applicable to the divorce of a couple where the spouses are of different nationalities but domicile in the same place is the law of their domicile. Third, the law applicable to the divorce of a couple where the spouses are of different nationalities and domicile in different countries is the law of the forum (*lex fori*) that adjudicates the couple's divorce.

Zulfa Basuki, a scholar in Indonesian family law, maintains that regardless of the choice of law or the law applicable to a divorce, the Indonesian courts must refuse grounds for divorce that are not known in Indonesian law. That is, Indonesian courts cannot issue divorce decrees if the grounds for divorce presented by the spouses are not known in Indonesia. In her opinion, the application of grounds for divorce not known in Indonesian law infringes Indonesian *ordre public*.[113] She refers to the decision of the Jakarta Special District Court

[108] Gautama, *Perdata Internasional Jilid III Bag 1* (n 16) 23.

[109] Gautama, *Perdata Internasional Jilid II Bag 1* (n 19) 141; Basuki and others, *Materi pokok. Modul 3. Modul 3* (n 102) 30.

[110] Cour de cassation, chambre civile 1, 17 avril 1953, Arrêt Rivière.

[111] Cour de cassation, 15 mars 1955, Arrêt Lewandowski.

[112] Gautama, *Perdata Internasional Jilid II Bag 1* (n 19) 141; Basuki and others, *Materi pokok. Modul 3* (n 102) 30; Supancana, *Naskah Akademik* (n 43) 209.

[113] Basuki and others, *Materi pokok. Modul 3* (n 102) 31.

dated 5 December 1955 (unpublished) that declined a petition for divorce based on mutual consent that was filed by a Chinese national couple domiciled in Indonesia. The Court stated that the grounds for divorce are limited to those provided by the BW – the law applicable to divorce at the time of the case. According to the Court, the BW provisions concerning the grounds for divorce shall not be set aside by the *lex causae* of the case, because they are related to Indonesian *ordre public*. Since mutual consent was not listed as one of the grounds for divorce under BW, the Court declined the couple's petition for divorce.[114]

As a conclusion, Indonesian private international law provides four rules of choice of law for divorce. First, the law applicable to the divorce of a couple where both spouses have the same nationality is the national law of the couple. Second, the *renvoi* (remission) principle applies to divorce cases of foreign couples who domicile in Indonesia and originate from countries that apply the domicile principle. Third, the law applicable to the divorce of a couple where both spouses are of different nationalities but domicile in the same place is the law of their domicile. Fourth, the law applicable to the divorce of a couple where both spouses are of different nationalities and domicile in different countries is the law of the forum (*lex fori*) that adjudicates the couple's divorce.

Concerning the nullity of marriage, Indonesian private international law has not established specific choice of law rules. Indonesian private international law categorises nullity of marriage as part of personal statute; thus, the nationality principle applies. In other words, the nullity of a marriage is governed by the law of the nationality of the couple, not the law of the place of their marriage. This principle was upheld by the Dutch East Indies Supreme Court (*Hooggerechtshof*). In 1932, *Hooggerechtshof* held that the nullity of the marriage of a Swiss couple domiciled in the Dutch East Indies had to be based on the grounds known in Swiss law, and not be based on the grounds known in the Dutch law, although the Swiss couple had performed their marriage in Bandung, Dutch East Indies, in 1929.[115] The 1983, 1997, and 2015 Bills of Indonesian Private International Law sought to further develop the choice of law rules for nullity of marriage. Though they have not been passed into law by the Indonesian Parliament, they contain two rules which may be the basis for future legal change. The first rule provides that the law that governs the nullity of a marriage is the same as the law that governs the material validity of the marriage. Thus, when an Italian husband whose wife is an Indonesian files a petition for nullity of his marriage in an Indonesian court, the law applicable to the nullity of his marriage should be the law that governs the material validity of his marriage, namely Italian law. The second rule provides that the law that governs the nullity of marriage because of a lack of consent to the marriage due to duress, mistake, or fraud, is the law of the place of the marriage (*lex loci celebrationis*).

Following Article 59, paragraph (2) of the Marriage Act 1974, Indonesian courts apply the Marriage Act 1974 and other Indonesian marriage law when deciding on the marriage nullity of mixed marriage couples who performed their marriages in Indonesia. Article 59, paragraph (2) of the Marriage Act 1974 provides that, 'A mixed marriage performed in Indonesia shall be held in accordance with this Act.' In the case of *Ludwig Franz Willibald Maria Josepf Leonhard Erbgraf von Waldburg-Wolfegg-Waldsee v Yesisca Iskandar; et al*,[116]

[114] Gautama, *Perdata Internasional Jilid III Bag 1* (n 16) 177.

[115] Gautama, *Perdata Internasional Jilid III Bag 1* (n 16) 24; Gautama, *Perdata Internasional Jilid II Bag 1* (n 19) 40–41.

[116] District Court of South Jakarta Decision 586/Pdt.G/2014/PN.Jkt.Sel (15 October 2015).

Ludwig, Hereditary Prince of Waldburg-Wolfegg and Waldsee, a German national living in Germany, filed a petition in October 2014 in the South Jakarta District Court for nullity of his marriage to Ms Iskandar, an Indonesian actress. The couple had performed their purported marriage in a church in South Jakarta in early 2014 and had registered this marriage at the South Jakarta civil registry office. The Court applied Indonesian law to adjudicate Prince Ludwig's claim for marriage nullity. The judges decided in his favour, finding that the marriage did not meet the religious requirements of the Marriage Act 1974. In this case, the South Jakarta District Court clearly did not apply the nationality principle as they had in 1932 in the case of the Swiss couple. Had the judges of the South Jakarta District Court applied the nationality principle, the failure to comply with religious requirements would not have been an applicable ground of nullity, because Prince Ludwig's national law (ie German) does not require a marriage to comply with religious requirements.

As previously discussed in Chapter 2, section I.B.iv.b on divorce, nullity and separation, the Population Administration Act 2006 as amended in 2013 only recognises nullity decrees issued by Indonesian courts (Article 39). Therefore, Indonesian and mixed marriage couples who perform their marriages abroad must file their petition for marriage nullity with an Indonesian court. As a result, the law applicable to marriage nullity for such couples is the law of the forum (*lex fori*). This is because Indonesian courts apply Indonesian marriage law to adjudicate the nullity of marriages of Indonesian couples and mixed marriage couples who performed marriages abroad. The courts apply neither the law of the place of the marriage nor the national law of the parties. For example, in the case of *Alterina Hofan v Jane Deviyanti H*,[117] the South Jakarta District Court applied the Marriage Act 1974 when adjudicating the nullity of the marriage of Alterina Hofan and Jane Deviyanti H, who performed their marriage in Las Vegas.

As discussed above, theoretically, Indonesian private international law categorises nullity of marriage as part of personal statute; thus, it should be governed by the law of the nationality of the parties. However, in practice, Indonesian courts apply Indonesian law to the nullity of marriages of mixed marriage couples, and the marriages of Indonesian couples who perform their marriages outside Indonesia. To date, Indonesian courts do not exercise their jurisdiction over the nullity of marriages of foreign couples having domicile in Indonesia. Therefore, there is no issue of choice of law to the nullity of marriage of foreign couples in Indonesia.

Legal separation no longer exists in the Indonesian legal system, following the enactment of the Marriage Act 1974. The Marriage Act 1974 supersedes the previous marriage law contained in the BW, which recognised legal separation. The Population Administration Act 2006 as amended in 2013 also does not govern the registration of legal separation in Indonesian Civil Registry. As Indonesian courts will not adjudicate a petition for legal separation, the issue of choice of law for legal separation does not exist in Indonesia.

ii. Presumption of Death

'Presumption of death' is not a ground for dissolution of marriage under Indonesian law. The grounds for dissolution or termination of a marriage in Indonesia are death, divorce, and court decree (Article 38 of the Marriage Act 1974).

[117] District Court of South Jakarta Decision 481/Pdt.G/2012/PN.Jkt.Sel (6 March 2013).

Though the term 'presumption of death' is not found in the Marriage Act 1974, 'desertion' as a ground for divorce[118] will apply in some situations that in other jurisdictions would come under the heading 'presumption of death'. 'Desertion' is defined in three places: the Elucidation of Article 39, paragraph (2)b. of the Marriage Act 1974; Article 19 b. of the Marriage Regulation 1975; and Article 116 b. of Compilation of Islamic Law. The ground of 'desertion' is established where one of the parties to the marriage has deserted the other for two years consecutively, without the other's consent and with no valid reason, so long as the desertion is not due to circumstances beyond his or her control. As a consequence, in the case where a person whose spouse has gone missing and is presumed dead wishes to dissolve their marriage so that they can remarry, they must file a petition for divorce with the ground of desertion. For example, consider an Indonesian woman married to a foreign man in a mixed marriage. The man goes missing. Eventually, he is missing for so long that, under the law of his nationality, he is presumed dead. Based on Indonesian marriage law, the Indonesian wife cannot remarry simply because her husband is presumed dead under his national law. She must obtain a divorce decree from a court, which will dissolve her marriage to her missing husband. To obtain the divorce decree from the court she must file a petition for divorce on the grounds that her husband has deserted her for two years consecutively. If she attempts to remarry without this divorce decree, the new marriage will be deemed invalid. This rule applies *mutatis mutandis* to the Indonesian husband whose foreign wife is missing.

To date, there is no established and settled jurisprudence or doctrine of Indonesian private international law concerning the presumption of death. Theoretically, the correct position appears to be that presumption of death is determined by the national law of the missing spouse, because presumption of death is part of personal statute so comes under the nationality principle. Likewise, the capacity of the surviving spouse to remarry with another person is determined by the national law of the surviving spouse, because the capacity to marry is also part of personal statute so comes under the nationality principle. Therefore, it will not be enough, for example, for a wife to show that her husband is presumed dead under his national law; she must also show that *her* national law permits her to remarry.

Indonesian law more generally does recognise the concept of 'presumed death'. Under the Population Administration Act 2006 as amended in 2013, Indonesian citizens may be classified as presumed dead, in which case this status will be registered in the civil registry offices (Article 44, paragraph (4) and Article 45, paragraphs (3), (5), (6)). However, Indonesian marriage law takes no cognisance of this status. The registration of a person as presumed dead is not by itself a valid ground for remarriage for their surviving spouses.

If the missing person is found to be alive after their spouse has remarried following the issuance of a divorce decree, the missing person's living status will not affect the legality of his or her spouse's new marriage.

iii. Financial Relief

Under the Marriage Act 1974, where a couple divorces the courts may grant financial relief to the wife and children. The Act does not expressly govern financial relief on the basis of

[118] Elucidation of Art 39, para (2) of the Marriage Act 1974; see also the Marriage Regulation 1975.

nullity of marriage. That is, it neither provides for financial relief following a petition for nullity, nor prohibits it. Relief is only available to the wife and children because Indonesian marriage law positions a husband as the head of a family who must be responsible for the welfare of his family (Article 34, paragraph (1) of the Marriage Act 1974).

An application for financial relief must be submitted along with the divorce petition in the court that has jurisdiction over the divorce. Because the application for financial relief is part of the divorce petition, Indonesian courts cannot grant financial relief individually and separately from the divorce petition. A wife is not guaranteed to receive financial relief alongside a divorce decree; the court may or may not award financial relief (Article 41 c. of the Marriage Act 1974). However, the courts will always grant financial relief to the couple's children. If the husband cannot afford to maintain the children, the court may order the wife to contribute financially (Article 41 b. of the Marriage Act 1974). During the process of divorce, a wife can apply for the court to award provisional relief. That is, the court may order the husband to pay financial relief to the wife during the divorce process, before a final decision is reached (Article 24, paragraph (2) a. of the Marriage Regulation 1975).

Indonesian Private International Law is silent on the law applicable to financial relief. However, since the financial relief application is part of the divorce petition, it follows that the law applicable to divorce is also applicable to financial relief. Therefore, the following propositions can be stated. First, the law applicable to financial relief in the divorce of a couple of the same nationality is the couple's national law. Second, the *renvoi* (remission) principle applies to financial relief in the divorce of a foreign couple who domiciles in Indonesia and originates from a country that applies the domicile principle. Third, the law applicable to financial relief in the divorce of a couple where the spouses have different nationalities but domicile in a same place is the law of their domicile. Fourth, the law applicable to the financial relief in the divorce of a couple where the spouses are of different nationalities and domicile in different countries is the law of the forum (*lex fori*) that adjudicates the couple's divorce.

C. Children

i. Parental Responsibility

Parental responsibility in Indonesia is governed by the Marriage Act 1974, the Compilation of Islamic Law, the Child Protection Act 2002 as amended in 2014, the Elimination of Domestic Violence Act 2004, and the landmark ruling of the Constitutional Court No 46/PUU-VIII/2010 (17 February 2012). Article 1, No 1 of the Child Protection Act 2002, as amended in 2014, defines a 'child' as a person under the age of 18 years old, including an unborn person. Article 26, paragraph (1) of the same Act governs the obligations and responsibilities of parents. It provides that parents have obligations and responsibilities to care for, to maintain, to educate, and to protect their children; to ensure the growth and development of their children in accordance with their capabilities, talents and interests; and to prevent underage marriages. These parental obligations and responsibilities are coupled with parental authority under Article 1, No 11 of the same Act. Parental authority includes the authority of parents to represent their children in any legal acts in and out of court and to protect any property that belongs to their children (Article 47, paragraph (2) and Article 48 of the Marriage Act 1974). Article 47 of the Marriage Act 1974 stipulates that a child under 18 years old and unmarried is under parental authority insofar as the parental authority is not revoked by a court order. Article 45 of the Marriage Act 1974 provides that both parents have obligations to sustain and educate their children until their children marry or become independent. Parental obligation and authority remain effective even though the marriage between the parents has been dissolved (Article 41, 45, paragraph (2)) or annulled (Article 28, paragraph (2) of the same Act). Where children are separated from their parents because their parents are, for example, divorced, work overseas, or are imprisoned, the parental obligation and authority remains effective (Article 14, paragraph (2) of the Child Protection Act 2002 as amended in 2014).

The Marriage Act 1974 uses the word 'obligations' where the Child Protection Act 2002, as amended in 2014, uses 'responsibility'. Both 'obligations' and 'responsibility' refer to the same concept. Under the Marriage Act 1974, a father's parental obligations can only be enforced by a legitimate child (ie a child conceived in a valid marriage or conceived before his parents' marriage but born after his parents are legally married to each other). Article 43 of the Marriage Act 1974 provides that a child born outside marriage (a 'natural child') has civil relations only with the child's mother and the mother's family. The same rule is also adopted in Articles 99 to 102 Compilation of Islamic Law. Civil relations between parents and children under the 1974 Act means the mutual rights and obligations under civil law between parents and children (Chapter X of the Marriage Act 1974). If a child does not have civil relations with its father, the father has no rights over, or obligations towards, the child. The father will not have parental authority over the child, as parental authority exists along with parental obligations. The situation is different with mothers. A mother always has parental obligations towards, or responsibility for, her child. This applies in the case of all children. It makes no difference, for example, that the child was born as a result of rape or an incestuous relationship. As such, the man who fathers the natural child simply has no responsibility toward the child, but the woman who gives birth to the child does.

A natural child cannot claim parental obligations or responsibility from their biological father until the father legitimises the child. With the legitimation, the child becomes a legitimate child under Indonesian law with all the rights of a legitimate child, including claiming the responsibility of his father and inheritance from his father. Neither the Marriage Act 1974 nor the Compilation of Islamic Law provide for the legitimation of natural children. These two laws only govern the status and rights of legitimate children. The legitimation of natural children is governed under Article 50 of the Population Administration Act 2006 as amended in 2013. Article 50, paragraph (2) provides that a natural child can be legitimated only after the child's father and mother perform a valid marriage in accordance with the law and religious rules. The requirement that the child's biological father and mother perform a regular marriage before legitimising their child is satisfied by compliance with Article 2 of the Marriage Act 1974, which concerns the substantive and formal validity of a marriage. The legitimation must be reported to the Office of Population and Civil Registration in the couple's relevant district within 30 days of the issuance of the parents' marriage certificate (Article 50, paragraph (1)). The Office will register and issue a deed of child legitimation based on the report (Article 50, paragraph (3)).

Besides legitimation, a natural child can also claim parental responsibility from their biological father upon an acknowledgment of paternity by the father. Like legitimation, acknowledgment of paternity of a natural child is not addressed in the Marriage Act 1974 or Compilation of Islamic law. Instead, it is governed in the BW. Article 280 BW provides that the acknowledgment of paternity of a natural child creates civil relations between the child and his father. Such acknowledgment cannot be given to a natural child without the approval of the child's mother (Article 284 BW). The acknowledgment of paternity is usually given in cases where there is some ambiguity in the validity of the marriage. This may be a deficiency in the period of cohabitation, some prolonged absence by the husband, or any other irregularity in the marriage and birth of the child. The acknowledgment of paternity under BW is further regulated in Article 49 of the Population Administration Act 2006 as amended in 2013. Article 49, paragraph (2) provides that an acknowledgment of paternity can only be given to a child whose parents are married in accordance with religious rules. That is, an acknowledgment of paternity can be given to a child whose parents' marriage is not valid in accordance with the state law (irregular marriage), but not to a child whose parents are unmarried, or whose marriage is invalid, under religious rules. The acknowledgment of paternity must be reported to the Office of Population and Civil Registration in the couple's relevant district within 30 days of the date of the issuance of the letter of acknowledgment that is made by the father and approved by the mother of the child (Article 49, paragraph (1)). The Office will register and issue a deed of acknowledgment of paternity based on the report (Article 49, paragraph (3)).

Besides a legitimate child and a child acknowledged by his or her mother, an adopted child can also establish civil relations with their adoptive mother and father, which means that the adoptive parents will have parental responsibility for and parental authority over the adopted child (Article 1, No 9 of the Child Protection Act 2002 as amended in 2014 and Article 171 h. of the Compilation of Islamic Law).

In 2010, in the case of *Hj. Aisyah Mochtar alias Machica binti H. Mochtar Ibrahim and Muhammad Iqbal Ramadhan bin Moerdiono* ('Ms Mochtar case'), Ms Mochtar, the mother of Muhammad, filed a petition for a judicial review of Article 43, paragraph (1) of the Marriage Act 1974 in the Indonesian Constitutional Court. She claimed that the rule that, 'A child born outside marriage has civil relations only with his mother and his mother's family', was unconstitutional because it violated Article 28, paragraph (2) of the Indonesian Constitution, which stipulates, 'Every child shall have the right to live, to grow and to develop, and shall have the right to protection from violence and discrimination.' Ms Mochtar's marriage in 1993 to Mr Moerdiono, who fathered Muhammad, complied with Islamic requirements but was not valid according to the state law because they had not obtained consent to polygamous marriage from Mr Moerdiono's prior wife (Article 5, paragraph (1)a. of the Marriage Act 1974). Therefore, the state did not issue a marriage certificate to Ms Mochtar and consequently Muhammad, who was born in 1996, had civil relations only with Ms Mochtar, not with Mr Moerdiono. Before the Court, Ms Mochtar argued that her son, Muhammad, was discriminated against because, following Article 43, paragraph (1) of the Marriage Act 1974, his father's name could not be written in his birth certificate; hence, the state had revoked her son's right to be sustained by his father. Muhammad's father, Mr Moerdiono, was freed from his parental obligations to Muhammad. The Constitutional Court judges gave their opinion that:

> [...] relationship between a child and a man who fathers the child shall not be based solely on a wedlock, but can also be based on an evidence of blood relation between the child and the man as his father. Therefore, regardless of its marriage procedure/administration, a child born to it shall get legal protection. If not, who suffers is the child born out of wedlock, even though the child is

not guilty because he is not responsible for his birth. A child who was born without a legal father often suffers discrimination and stigma in the society. Law shall give legal certainty and protect the rights of children, including a child born in a marriage which its validity is disputed.

In their ruling,[119] the judges of the Constitutional Court declared that Article 43, paragraph (1) of the Marriage Act 1974 was unconstitutional if it was meant to dismiss the child's civil relations with a man who can be proven to be the child's father. Therefore, in its judicial review, the Constitutional Court ruled that Article 43, paragraph (1) should be read:

A child born outside marriage has civil relation with his mother and his mother's family as well as with a man who based on science and technology and/or other evidences by law, has blood relation to be his father, including with the man's family.

Based on the Constitutional Court's judicial review of Article 43, paragraph (1) of the Marriage Act 1974, one may conclude that children born as a result of rape, incestuous and adulterous relations shall have civil relation with the men who, based on science and technology and/or other evidences, could be proven to have fathered the children. However, in its ruling, the Constitutional Court did not elaborate the legal effects of the civil relation. It did not explain whether the civil relation between an illegitimate child and a man who fathered the child would only create maintenance obligations to the child, or also create parental authority over and parental responsibility for the child.

To date, the Marriage Act 1974 has not been amended in accordance with the above-mentioned judicial review and neither have other related Acts and regulations, such as the Compilation of Islamic Law, the Marriage Regulation 1975, and the Population Administration Act 2006 as amended in 2013. There has been some resistance against the implementation of the Constitutional Court's ruling by several religious courts whose Muslim judges considered the judicial review as not being in line with Islamic teaching concerning the purity of the family line (*hifz al-nasl*).[120] This teaching only recognises family lineage or filiation on the basis of a valid marriage (*nasab*). Some Muslim judges and academics argue that only *nasab* could grant men parental responsibility for and authority over their children, including passing inheritance and being legal guardians (*wali nikah*) for their daughters in Islamic marriage.[121] In 2013, the Indonesian Supreme Court instructed all Indonesian judges, including the judges of religious courts, to implement the Constitutional Court's judicial review of Article 43, paragraph (1) of the Marriage Act 1974. According to the Supreme Court, natural or illegitimate children born outside valid marriage shall receive maintenance from their biological fathers and the fathers' families, although those children are not entitled to inheritance from their fathers.[122] The Head

[119] Constitutional Court Decision 46/PUU-VIII/2010 (17 February 2012).

[120] AI Islami, 'Dialektika Status Dan Hak Keperdataan Anak Luar Kawin' (*Mahkamah Agung Republik Indonesia Pengadilan Agama Sidoarjo*, 14 January 2020) https://pa-sidoarjo.go.id/informasi-pengadilan/241-dialektika-status-dan-hak-keperdataan-anak-luar-kawin#ftnref2 (accessed 27 June 2020).

[121] N Hak, 'Kedudukan dan Hak Anak Luar Nikah Pasca Putusan Mahkamah Konstitusi Nomor 46/Puu-VIII/2010 Tentang Status Anak Luar Nikah (Studi Persepsi Hakim Pengadilan Agama Se-Wilayah Pengadilan Tinggi Agama Bengkulu)' (Doctoral thesis, Universitas Islam Negeri (UIN) Raden Intan Lampung, 2018) 42–43.

[122] detikNews, 'MA Perintahkan Hakim Laksanakan Putusan MK Soal Hak Anak Hasil Zina' (*detiknews*, 4 February 2013) https://news.detik.com/berita/d-2160080/ma-perintahkan-hakim-laksanakan-putusan-mk-soal-hak-anak-hasil-zina (accessed 27 June 2020).

of Legal Bureau and Public Relations of the Supreme Court, Ridwan Mansur, stated that the maintenance obligation to natural or illegitimate children was imperative and enforceable under the Child Protection Act 2002 as amended in 2014 and the Elimination of Domestic Violence Act 2004. A petition for maintenance responsibility against Muslim parents should be filed in religious courts, and the same petition against non-Muslim parents should be filed in district courts.[123] It can be concluded from the Supreme Court's instructions that the civil relations between natural children and their biological fathers, as written in the revised Article 43, paragraph (1) of the Marriage Act 1974, only raises maintenance obligations. It does not raise full parental responsibility and authority for biological fathers, unless they legitimise or acknowledge or adopt their natural children. This interpretation has been accepted by a majority of Muslim jurists, including the Indonesian Ulema Council that in 2012 issued *fatwā* (Islamic non-binding legal opinion) No 11 of 2012, which contained provisions similar to the Supreme Court's instructions.

Indonesian private international law is silent on the law that governs parental responsibility involving foreign elements. Sudargo Gautama in his book explains different varieties of doctrines that are available to determine the governing law of parental responsibility. Some doctrines state that civil relations between parents and their legitimate children is governed by the national law of the father, whereas civil relations between parents and their illegitimate children is governed by the national law of each parent.[124] The 1983, 1997, and 2015 Bills of Indonesian Private International Law provide that civil relations between parents and their legitimate children (and hence the parental responsibility of parents towards their children) is governed by the national law of the father, whereas civil relations between a mother and a child born outside marriage is governed by the national law of the mother. Based on the 2013 instruction of the Supreme Court, the law that governs parental responsibility for a natural or illegitimate child – outside the maintenance obligation – is the national law of the mother. Only after the illegitimate child is legitimised or acknowledged or adopted by their father does the national law of the father govern parental responsibility for the child. The law that governs parental responsibility for a legitimate child should always be the national law of the father.

For example, an Indonesian man and woman legally marry in Australia. Their marriage is in accordance with Australian law, but not Indonesian law. Following their marriage, they have a child together. When they return to Indonesia, their marriage is deemed invalid because it does not comply with Indonesian law. Their child is categorised as a child born outside marriage; that is, the child is illegitimate. Accordingly, parental responsibility for the child is governed by the national law of the mother, ie Indonesian law. Based on Indonesian law, only the mother has parental responsibility for and authority over the child. The father does not have parental responsibility over the child except for the maintenance obligation. The picture is the same where the female partner is Indonesian and the male partner is foreign. For instance, an Indonesian woman is married to a man with Saudi Arabian nationality. Their marriage is valid according to Saudi Arabian law and Islamic law,

[123] detikNews, 'Pria Hidung Belang Tak Beri Nafkah Anak Hasil Zina Bisa Dipenjara!' (*detiknews*, 4 February 2013) https://news.detik.com/berita/d-2160115/pria-hidung-belang-tak-beri-nafkah-anak-hasil-zina-bisa-dipenjara (accessed 27 June 2020).

[124] Gautama, *Perdata Internasional Jilid III Bag 1* (n 16) 54–60.

but not valid according to Indonesian state law. The couple have a child from the marriage, who obtains Saudi Arabian citizenship because he was born in a valid marriage according to Saudi Arabian law. When the family move their domicile to Indonesia, their marriage is deemed invalid under Indonesian law. Accordingly, their child is categorised as a child born outside marriage. That is, the child is illegitimate under Indonesian law. Hence, parental responsibility for the child is governed by the national law of the mother, ie Indonesian law. Based on Indonesian law, only the mother has parental responsibility for and authority over the child in Indonesia. The father does not have parental responsibility over the child in Indonesia, except for the maintenance obligation. He, of course, has parental responsibility for his child, but in his country, not in Indonesia. Next, consider the case where the child's parents are not validly married under any nation's laws. For example, an unmarried Italian man and Indonesian woman cohabitate. They have a child together. Their child is categorised as an illegitimate child according to Indonesian law. Parental responsibility for the child is governed by the national law of the mother, ie Indonesian law. Based on Indonesian law, only the mother has parental responsibility for and authority over the child in Indonesia. The Italian father does not have parental responsibility over the child in Indonesia, except for the maintenance obligation, although he may have parental responsibility for his child in Italy.

In conclusion, the law that governs parental responsibility for a legitimate child is the national law of the child's father, and the law that governs parental responsibility for a natural or illegitimate child is the national law of the child's mother.

ii. Guardianship and Custody

The Marriage Act 1974, the Compilation of Islamic Law, the Child Protection Act 2002 as amended in 2014, Government Regulation No 44 of 2017 concerning implementation of child custody, and Government Regulation No 29 of 2019 concerning requirements and procedure of guardian appointment all have provisions concerning guardianship and custody. However, none provide choice of law rules which determine the law applicable to guardianship and custody in cases involving foreign elements. For example, a child was born in a valid marriage between an Indonesian mother and an Australian father. The family domicile in Indonesia. Following the Citizenship Act 2006, the child has dual nationalities, Indonesian and Australian. If the parents are experiencing a custody dispute, an Indonesian judge must decide which law to apply to adjudicate the custody issue. The above-mentioned Acts and regulations do not provide choice of law rules to determine the law that will govern the custody dispute. That is, they do not dictate whether the dispute should be governed by the law of the domicile of the parties, or the national law of the parties, or the national law of the habitual residence of the child. The same applies to guardianship. Where the parental authority of a mixed-couple is revoked or the parents pass away leaving a child, the Act and regulations do not provide choice of law rules to determine the law that governs the guardianship of a child with dual nationalities.

Therefore, one may refer to the 1983, 1997, and 2015 Bills of Indonesian Private International Law for guidance on the law that governs guardianship and custody in cases involving foreign elements. The Bills provide that the child's national law determines the applicable law for: (i) guardianship of a minor child; (ii) the reasons for the guardianship; and (iii) the guardian's obligations to the child. However, the authority of a guardian over the child's immovable property is to be governed by the law of the country wherein the immovable property is located.[125] With regard to custody, the law of the child's habitual residence governs the revocation of custody for a parent or both of the parents.[126]

In the case of *Purnima Ralhan v Jonathan I. Kine*, the parties were American citizens who were married in the US in 1997 and had lived in Jakarta since 2000. Their daughter, Lara Rose, was born in Jakarta in 2001 and had American citizenship. In September 2007, Ms Ralhan reported her husband to the Jakarta Police Office for domestic violence. In her report, she alleged that Mr Kine had assaulted her in front of their daughter and that the incident had caused deep trauma to the child. In addition, Ms Ralhan told the police that her husband had threatened her life. Following her report to the Jakarta police, Ms Ralhan requested that the South Jakarta District Court grant protection for her and her daughter from her husband. Based on Articles 10, 28, and 29 of the Elimination of Domestic Violence Act 2004, the Court ruled that police and other relevant institutions must give protection to Ms Ralhan, her daughter and her parents who also lived in Jakarta. The Court also temporarily revoked Mr Kine's custody over their daughter and transferred custody to Ms Ralhan and Lara's maternal grandparents, who also lived in Jakarta. The Indonesian Supreme Court in extraordinary appeal affirmed the ruling of the South Jakarta District Court.[127] In this case, it is apparent that the Court applied the law of the child's habitual residence, ie the law of Indonesia, when deciding the issue of custody. The Court based its decision on the Elimination of Domestic Violence Act 2004, although Mr Kine had argued that the Court should apply the national law of the parties, who were all American citizens. The decision in this custody case supported the provisions adopted in the Bills of Indonesian Private International Law that apply the law of the child's habitual residence to the revocation of child custody.

Notwithstanding the provisions concerning guardianship and custody in current Indonesian law, and the choice of law rules provided in the Bills, the courts must take into account the wishes and consent of children who have reached adolescence when making decisions on guardianship and custody, so as to make decisions in the best interests of the children.

iii. Maintenance

Based on the Indonesian Supreme Court instruction to all Indonesian judges in 2013 that interpreted the Constitutional Court's judicial review of Article 43, paragraph (1) of the Marriage Act 1974, natural or illegitimate children born outside valid marriage are to receive maintenance from their biological fathers and the fathers' families, whether their father acknowledges paternity or not.[128] The Head of Legal Bureau and Public Relations of the Supreme Court, Ridwan Mansur, stated that the maintenance obligation to natural or illegitimate children was imperative and enforceable under the Child Protection Act 2002 as amended in 2014, and the Elimination of Domestic Violence Act 2004.

[125] Art 30 of the 1983 Bill, Art 36 of the 1997 Bill, and Ch V, Pt 4 of the Bill.

[126] Art 31 of the 1983 Bill, Art 37 of the 1997 Bill, and Ch V, Pt 4 of the Bill.

[127] District Court of South Jakarta Decision 394/Pdt.P/2007 /PN.Jak.Sel (21 January 2008); affd Supreme Court Extraordinary Appeal 76PK/PDT/2009 (26 November 2009).

[128] See n 122.

A petition for maintenance responsibility made against Muslim parents must be filed in the religious courts; the same petition against non-Muslim parents must be filed in the district courts.[129] Therefore, the maintenance obligation can be claimed by all children from their parents, whether the children are natural, legitimate, or the result of rape or an incestuous relationship, and whether the parents are legally married, unmarried, or adoptive. Unlike other types of parental obligations, that can be claimed only by legitimate or acknowledged or adopted children, the maintenance obligation of parents can be claimed by or on behalf of all children irrespective of the marital status of their parents.

The Supreme Court, through its Head of Legal Bureau and Public Relations of the Supreme Court, in 2013 reiterated that the maintenance obligation owed to natural or illegitimate children was imperative and enforceable under the Child Protection Act 2002 as amended in 2014 and the Elimination of Domestic Violence Act 2004.[130] Pursuant to the Elucidation of Article 13, paragraph (1)c. of the Child Protection Act 2002 as amended in 2014, if parents deliberately ignore the obligation to maintain or to take care of their children, their conduct is classified as abandonment. Abandonment of children is an offence under Article 77 of the Child Protection Act 2002 as amended in 2014 and Article 49 of the Elimination of Domestic Violence Act 2004. Revocation of parental authority does not abolish the parents' obligation to provide maintenance for their children (Article 32 b. of the Child Protection Act 2002 as amended in 2014 and Article 49, paragraph (2) of the Marriage Act 1974). In the case that children are separated from their parents because their parents are divorced, or work overseas, or are imprisoned, or for any other reason, Article 14, paragraph (2)g. of the Child Protection Act 2002 as amended in 2014 stipulates that the children are always entitled to receive maintenance from both of their parents. The Child Protection Act 2002 as amended in 2014 does not differentiate parents based on their marital status in the matters of parental obligations. In this respect it is unlike the Marriage Act 1974, the Compilation of Islamic Law, and the Population Administration Act 2006 as amended in 2013. Article 1, No 4 of the 2002 Act defines 'parent' as a biological father and/or mother, or stepfather and/or stepmother, or adoptive father and/or mother. The Child Protection Act also does not differentiate children based on the marital status of their parents like in the other Acts.

Indonesian private international law is silent as to the law that governs parental maintenance obligations in cases involving foreign elements. Sudargo Gautama in his book cited a doctrine under which maintenance obligations in respect of children, regardless of the marital status of the parents, is determined by the law of the place where the child is habitually resident. Sudargo Gautama wrote that he agreed with the habitual residence principle.[131] The 1983, 1997, and 2015 Bills of Indonesian Private International Law also adopt the habitual residence principle to determine the maintenance obligations owed to children. Article 32 of the 1983 Bill and Article 38 of the 1997 Bill provide that maintenance obligations are governed by the law of the country of habitual residence of the children. The 2015 Bill similarly provides that maintenance obligations are governed by the law of the country of habitual residence of the child, so that the child is protected in a country where they live de facto (Chapter V, Part 4).

[129] See n 123.
[130] ibid.
[131] Gautama, *Perdata Internasional Jilid III Bag 1* (n 16) 73.

Based on the 2013 instruction of the Supreme Court to judges in Indonesia that interpreted the Constitutional Court's decision in the Ms Mochtar case and the provisions in the Bills of Indonesian Private International Law, parental maintenance obligations in cases involving foreign elements where the child is habitually resident in Indonesia should be governed by the Child Protection Act 2002 as amended in 2014. Since this Act intends to protect the welfare of children living and residing in Indonesia, whether they are Indonesians or foreigners, and irrespective of the marital status of their parents, it supersedes other Acts and regulations, and supersedes also the national law of the parents in matters of maintenance obligations. This Act was referred to by the Indonesian Supreme Court when instructing Indonesian judges to implement the Constitutional Court's judicial review on Article 43, paragraph (1) of the Marriage Act 1974. Therefore, for example, where a Saudi Arabian man fathers an illegitimate child in Indonesia outside marriage, based on the law of the child's habitual residence in Indonesia (the Child Protection Act 2002 as amended in 2014) he can be ordered to provide maintenance to the child although according to his national law, which is based on *Sharia*, he does not have any civil obligation to the illegitimate child.

In summary, the law that governs parental maintenance obligation involving foreign elements in Indonesia should be the Child Protection Act 2002 as amended in 2014.

iv. Legitimacy, Legitimation and Adoption

Legitimacy is the status of a child born to parents who are legally married to each other. The 1983, 1997, and 2015 Bills of Indonesian Private International Law provide that the national law of the husband of the child's mother when the child is born determines the legitimacy of the child. The national law of the husband should therefore be the law applicable to a petition for denying the legitimacy of a child. Where the husband of the child's mother is dead when the child is born, the legitimacy of the child is determined by the national law of the dead husband. If the man's marriage to the child's mother is invalid according to Indonesian law, Indonesian authorities will not apply his national law to determine the legitimacy of the child. Indonesian law will apply, and the child will be categorised as an illegitimate child who has civil relations only with the mother. The Bills of Private International Law do not expressly determine the law that governs the legitimation of a child. However, it is sensible to conclude that legitimation will be governed in the same way as legitimacy. That is, the national law of the man who is legally married to the mother who gives birth to the child also governs the legitimation of a child. For example, an unmarried American man and Indonesian woman have a child together. Their child is categorised as a child born outside marriage. Two years after the child's birth, the couple are legally married to each other in accordance with the national law of each of them. The American husband proceeds, in his own state, with the procedure to legitimise his child. Once the legitimation is valid in accordance with his national law, the legitimation is deemed valid in Indonesia also.

In the case of adoption, the adopted child establishes civil relations with his adoptive parent or parents, though they are not blood relations. Accordingly, the adoptive parents have parental responsibility for and authority over the adopted child. Provisions governing adoption with foreign elements in Indonesia are found scattered in different Acts and regulations. Examples are: the Child Protection Act 2002 as amended in 2014; Government Regulation No 54 of 2007 concerning procedures of adoption (the Government Regulation No 54 of 2007); and Regulation of the Social Minister No 110/HUK/2009 of 2009 concerning requirements of child adoption (Regulation of Social Minister 2009). These regulations provide substantive and procedural requirements for adoption. Pursuant to Article 7 of Government Regulation No 54 of 2007, three categories of adoption are recognised in Indonesia: (i) adoptions of Indonesian citizens by Indonesian citizens; (ii) adoptions of Indonesian citizens by non-Indonesian citizens; and (iii) adoptions of foreign citizens by Indonesian citizens. Hence, Indonesian law does not expressly govern the adoption of foreign citizens by foreign citizens in Indonesian territory. If a court has to rule on a petition for this type of adoption, the court may exercise discretion to determine the law applicable to this type of adoption, provided that the court agrees to exercise its jurisdiction over the petition. The last known case of this type of adoption is the 1989 case of a Vietnamese child refugee who was adopted by a couple with Canadian citizenship. The Canadian couple worked as volunteers in the Galang refugee camp, Indonesia, for almost two years and wished to adopt a twelve-year-old Vietnamese girl who lived in the camp. The judge in the Tanjung Pinang District Court decided that the Court had jurisdiction over the parties because of their residence in the district. In deciding this case, the judge did not apply Indonesian law, because none of the parties were Indonesian citizens. Instead, the judge applied Canadian law. The judge's reason was that the Canadian law had the most significant relationship to the case because the child would be taken to Canada by the prospective adoptive parents who were Canadian nationals. Based on the Canadian law, the judge granted the adoption.[132]

The general principles of child adoption under Indonesian law are: (i) adoption may only be implemented in the best interests of the child and carried out based on local customs and law; (ii) adoption shall not sever the blood relationship between the adopted child and his natural parents; (iii) adoption shall be recorded in the child's birth certificate without erasing the original identity of the child; (iv) prospective adoptive parents must be of the same religion as the prospective adopted child, and in the case that the child's religion is unknown, his religion is deemed the same as the religion embraced by the majority of the local community; (v) adoption of an Indonesian child by foreign nationals shall only be carried out as a last recourse (Articles 39 and 40 of the Child Protection Act 2002 as amended in 2014, and Articles 2 and 3 of the Regulation of Social Minister 2009). Prospective adoptive parents of an Indonesian adopted child must write a letter of statement on Indonesian stamped duty paper that if they take the Indonesian child to their country of origin after the adoption, they agree to report the development of the child to the Indonesian Embassy in their country every year until the child is 18 years old, to contact the Indonesian Embassy about any future areas of residence, and to be visited by a representative from the Indonesian Embassy to monitor the child's development until the child is 18 years old (the Regulation of Social Minister 2009). Although an Indonesian adopted

[132] Tanjung Pinang District Court Decision 205/Pdt.P./P/N/FPAT (20 May 1989) (not published); see TMP Allagan, 'Intercountry Adoption in Indonesia' (2019) 15 *Indonesian Journal of International Law* 214, 232–234 http://ijil.ui.ac.id/index.php/home/article/view/725/pdf_603 (accessed 27 June 2020).

child can acquire citizenship of the country of his adoptive parents, based on Article 5 of the Citizenship Act 2006, an Indonesian child under five years old who is legally adopted by foreign parents retains Indonesian citizenship until the child turns 18 or is married, whichever is earlier. Therefore, in this case, it is in the best interests of the young adopted child to be monitored and visited by a representative of the Indonesian Embassy in the country of his adoptive parents, because by law the child is still an Indonesian citizen. However, if the child is older than five when legally adopted by foreign parents, the child will lose Indonesian citizenship on acquiring the citizenship of the adoptive parents. This is because the Citizenship Act 2006 only recognises dual citizenship of children where one of the child's parents holds Indonesian citizenship. Therefore, once the Indonesian adopted child is no longer an Indonesian citizen and becomes a citizen of a foreign country, the monitoring of the child and visitation by the Indonesian Embassy must be conducted in full compliance with the law of the foreign country where the child resides.

Failure to comply with the substantive and procedural requirements for adoption stipulated will result in the Indonesian adopted child being unable to immigrate to the adoptive parents' country of origin, and to obtain the citizenship of the adoptive parents.

None of the above-mentioned Acts and regulations govern adoptions of foreign children by foreign citizens that take place within Indonesian territory, as happened in the case of the child refugee of the Galang refugee camp. In regard to this issue and other matters that are not governed by the current adoption laws, one may refer to the 1983, 1997, and 2015 Bills of Private International Law, which provide choice of law rules to determine the law applicable to aspects of intercountry adoption. The Bills provide that in the case where the adoptive parents and the adopted child have different nationalities, the capacity to adopt, the requirements of adoption, and the legal effects of adoption are determined by the law of the country in which the child has habitual residence. The rights and obligations between the adopted child and their natural parents are also determined by the law of the country in which the child has habitual residence.

Since none of the Bills of Private International Law have been passed into law by the Indonesian Parliament, their choice of law rules concerning intercountry adoption can be applied insofar as this does not offend the existing adoption laws.

v. Wrongful Removal of Children

Although there have been some cases of international wrongful removal of Indonesian children by one of the child's parents, such wrongful removal is not governed by Indonesian private law. Indonesia is not a party to the 1980 Hague Convention on the Civil Aspects of International Child Abduction.

In the absence of provisions specifically governing the international wrongful removal of children, Indonesian courts often adjudicate cases of wrongful removal as if they were cases of child custody. An example is found in the case No 210/Pdt/G/1992/PN.JKT. Sel, between an Indonesian husband and a German wife who had lived in Germany and had two sons who were born in 1986 and in 1988 respectively. In 1992 the mother filed for divorce in a German court, and the German court granted her temporary custody of the two children while the couple's divorce was being finalised. During the divorce process, the Indonesian father abducted their two children and brought them to Jakarta, Indonesia. He filed a petition for divorce and sole custody of the couple's children in the

South Jakarta District Court. He also applied for a citizenship conversion for his children to become Indonesian nationals. Responding to her husband's legal proceeding in the Jakarta Court, the German wife claimed that there had been an interlocutory judgment by a German court that granted temporary custody of their two children to her. The judges in the South Jakarta District Court refused to recognise the provisional custody ruling made by the German court and took jurisdiction over the dispute. In their judgment, they granted a divorce to the couple. The judges considered that both parents were capable to care for and raise their children, and therefore granted both parents custody of their children. The custody of the elder son, who was six years old, was granted to the Indonesian father and the custody of the younger son, who was four years old, was granted to the German mother.[133] This case demonstrates that the Indonesian Court did not consider the case as an issue of wrongful removal of children by the father. The Court merely saw the case as custody dispute.

Another case where wrongful removal of a child was dealt with as a custody issue was between a French husband and an Indonesian wife, adjudicated in the Indonesian court in the district of Tangerang. In this case, the couple were legally married in Jakarta in 1994. They had a son born in 1995 in Jakarta. Pursuant to Indonesian citizenship law at the time, their son only had French nationality, derived from his father's nationality. The family lived in Tangerang, Indonesia. Because of conflict in the marriage, the husband moved out from the family's house. In 1999, the husband took the couple's son to France for holiday but did not return the child to his mother in Indonesia. Instead, he left the child, who was four years old, with his French grandparents. The child's mother filed petitions for custody of the child in the Tangerang District Court, Indonesia, and in the Rouen High Court, France. Both the courts in Indonesia[134] and France granted the custody of the couple's child to the mother, but the child was retained in France by his father and his father's family. The French father, who was already divorced from the child's mother, appealed the ruling of the Tangerang District Court to the Bandung High Court, in Indonesia. The Bandung High Court reversed the lower court's ruling and granted the custody of the child to the French father, because of the child's French nationality.[135] In its judgment, the High Court also explained that granting the custody of the child to his father was in the child's interests, because the child required a specific medical treatment which was available in France and which the French father could afford to provide. In this case, like in the case discussed immediately above, the Indonesian courts did not take the issue of the wrongful removal of child into their consideration. The courts made their decision solely on the basis of the custody issue.

In a case between an Indonesian wife and an Australian husband, in which the husband took the couple's son to Australia without the consent of his wife, the Family Court of Australia in Sydney issued Court Order No 3121 of 13 July 2012, ordering the Australian father to return the child to Indonesia because Indonesia was the country of the child's

[133] District Court of South Jakarta Decision 210/Pdt/G/1992/PN.JKT.Sel (not published); see Supancana, *Naskah Akademik* (n 43) 50, 53.

[134] District Court of Tangerang Decision No 125/Pdt/G/1999/PN.TNG (not published); see Supancana, *Naskah Akademik* (n 43) 58–62.

[135] High Court of Bandung Decision 481/PDT/1999/PT.BDG. (not published); see Supancana, *Naskah Akademik* (n 43) 58–62; PP Penasthika, L Arijati, and AG Anggriana, 'International Child Abduction: Bagaimana Indonesia Meresponnya?' (2018) 48 *Jurnal Hukum & Pembangunan* 521, 531.

habitual residence. In addition, the Family Court of Australia granted custody of the child to the child's mother. Australia is a party to the 1980 Hague Convention on the Civil Aspects of International Child Abduction. After the child was returned to his mother, the Australian father filed a petition for custody of the child and applied for revocation of the mother's parental authority over their son in the South Jakarta District Court. Contrary to the earlier ruling of the Australian Family Court, in 2012 the judge of the South Jakarta District Court ruled in favour of the Australian father. The judge revoked the Indonesian mother's parental authority over the child and granted custody of the child to the Australian father, because the judge, on the basis of statements from a number of witnesses, considered that the mother was not a responsible parent.[136] The mother challenged the ruling of the South Jakarta District Court in the Supreme Court, requesting the Supreme Court to reinstate her custody in accordance with the ruling of the Australian Family Court. In 2013, the Supreme Court found in favour of the Indonesian mother and annulled the ruling of the South Jakarta District Court.[137] As with the previous cases discussed in this section, the Indonesian courts in this case did not take the issue of wrongful removal of the child into their consideration. Unlike the Australian Family Court, the Indonesian courts made their decision only on the custody issue.

Since the wrongful removal of children is not recognised in Indonesian family law, there are no provisions concerning choice of law rules to determine the law that governs international wrongful removal of children. The 1983 and 1997 Bills of Indonesian Private International Law also do not have provisions concerning the international wrongful removal of children. The 2015 Academic Paper of Indonesian Private International Law Bill discussed the international wrongful removal of children, but did not suggest Indonesia's accession to the 1980 Hague Convention on the Civil Aspects of International Child Abduction until Indonesian family law is reformed and Indonesian judges, lawyers and law enforcement agencies are trained and ready to implement the Convention.[138]

D. Mental Incapacity

The 1847 BW uses the term '*onbekwaamheid*' for mental incapacity. Article 433 BW provides that persons with *onbekwaamheid* are adults who are in a perpetual state of idiocy, insanity or madness, or spend thriftiness. Article 433 BW further provides that such persons shall be placed under conservatorship, even if they gain mental capacity from time to time. As such, a person with mental incapacity is also called a person under conservatorship. Mental incapacity can only be claimed before a court after the court examines evidence and listens to the person, the person's family, and witnesses.

Each blood relative is authorised to apply for conservatorship on behalf of one of their relatives on the grounds of mental incapacity. An individual who feels unable to take proper care of their affairs due to limited mental capacity may also request to be

[136] District Court of South Jakarta Decision 700/Pdt.P/2012/PN.JKT. Sel. (not published); see Penasthika, Arijati, and Anggriana, 'International Child Abduction' (n 135) 532.

[137] Supreme Court Decision 3/Pen/Pdt/2013 (not published); see Penasthika, Arijati, and Anggriana, 'International Child Abduction' (n 135) 533.

[138] Supancana, *Naskah Akademik* (n 43) 69.

placed under conservatorship (Article 434 BW). A public prosecutor can also apply for conservatorship for a person who is in a state of idiocy, insanity or madness, but not spend thriftiness, if the person does not have a spouse or a blood relative in Indonesia (Article 435 BW). This provision is applicable to a foreigner with mental incapacity whose spouse or family is not in Indonesia. In considering the petition for conservatorship, the judge will examine the witnesses and evidence, and listen to the blood relatives of the person with mental incapacity (Article 438 BW). In addition, the judge will summon the person for whom the conservatorship is sought and examine them. If they cannot attend the court proceedings, the examination will be held in the person's residence by personnel appointed by the judge, and in the presence of the court clerk and personnel of the public prosecutor's office. Alternatively, the examination will be carried out by local government personnel, who must send the minutes of the examination to the court (Article 439 BW). The court must issue its ruling on the petition for conservatorship in a session open to the public (Article 442 BW). The court that has jurisdiction over the petition for conservatorship is the court in the district of the person for whom conservatorship is sought (Article 436 BW). After the court rules that a person is to be placed under conservatorship due to mental incapacity, that person is no longer capable of performing certain legal actions as dictated by BW. Namely: parental authority (Article 319a); guardianship (Article 379); making testament (Article 895); making contract (Article 1330, paragraph (2)); and giving testimony or serving as a witness (Article 1912). Persons with mental incapacity are capable of performing marriage, insofar as their marriages are not prevented by the court based on the petition for marriage prevention filed by the parties mentioned in Article 14 of the Marriage Act 1974.

Indonesian Private International Law is silent on the matter of mental capacity, but based on its general principles, mental capacity is part of personal statute so must be determined by the national law of the person (the nationality principle). As such, Indonesian law will determine the status of mental capacity of an Indonesian national in relation to their legal actions in Indonesia, although they domicile outside Indonesia. Indonesian law also determines the scope of legal actions that can or cannot be performed by the Indonesian national in Indonesia. It also determines when the person's mental incapacity ceases. These principles are illustrated in case No 258/Pdt.P/2007/PN Jaksel, in which the South Jakarta District Court in 2007 recognised an Australian judgment made by the Administrative Tribunal of Western Australia.[139] The Australian Tribunal had held that the applicant's elderly father, who was an Indonesian citizen who lived and owned properties in Australia as well as in Indonesia, was legally incompetent to manage his properties. Therefore, the Australian Tribunal put the applicant's father under an administrator. The Australian Tribunal reached its judgment based on, among other things, an assessment made by a specialist geriatric, medical doctor in Western Australia. The applicant, who lived in Indonesia, presented the Australian judgment that declared her father was incompetent to the South Jakarta District Court to apply for conservatorship of her elderly father and his properties. The Court accepted the applicant's petition and ruled that she was her father's conservator. The applicant's father appealed both the rulings of the South Jakarta

[139] District Court of South Jakarta Decision 258/Pdt.P/2007/PN Jaksel (not published).

District Court and the Administrative Tribunal of Western Australia in their respective countries.[140] In his appeal to the Indonesian Supreme Court, the appellant argued that the South Jakarta District Court had to examine and hear from him before ruling on his mental incapacity and placing him under conservatorship (Article 439 BW). In addition, he argued that a foreign judgment was not enforceable in Indonesia (Article 436 Rv). The Supreme Court concluded that the South Jakarta District Court's failure to examine and hear from the appellant before making its ruling was not in conformity with Article 439 BW. For this reason, in March 2008 the Supreme Court annulled the South Jakarta District Court's ruling. The Supreme Court held that the appellant was not under conservatorship, meaning that he was not suffering mental incapacity. As such, the Supreme Court held that he was fully capable of performing any legal actions.[141]

This case demonstrates that Indonesian law is applied to determine the mental capacity of an Indonesian national, although the Indonesian national domiciles abroad. Nevertheless, neither the BW nor Indonesian civil procedure codes provide procedure for implementing Article 439 BW, which requires the judges or other relevant authorities to examine the person who is sought to be placed under conservatorship and whose residence is outside Indonesia. In the author's opinion, to implement Article 439 BW, Indonesian courts can follow the procedure concerning service of process outside Indonesia and the procedure of taking evidence abroad. These procedures are outlined above in Chapter 2, section I.A.iii on service of process outside Indonesia and Chapter 1, section VII.C on taking evidence abroad.

The nationality principle also applies to determine the mental capacity of foreigners in Indonesia. Indonesian judges apply the national law of the foreigners to determine their mental incapacity and conservatorship, as well as the scope of legal actions that they can or cannot perform. However, based on the *Renovi* (remission) principle, if the foreigners having domicile in Indonesia originate from countries that apply the domicile principle, their mental capacity, conservatorship and the scope of their permitted legal actions will be determined by Indonesian law.

V. Law of Corporations and Insolvency and Law of Bankruptcy

A. Capacity, Agency and Internal Management

In general, private international law contains three doctrines used to identify the applicable law for determining the capacity of a legal entity, including corporations. First, the doctrine of incorporation, under which the applicable law to determine the capacity of a legal entity is the law of the place where that entity is incorporated. Second, the doctrine of

[140] Hukumonline, 'MA Batalkan Penetapan Pengampuan Prof. Sudargo' (*hukumonline*, 29 March 2008) www.hukumonline.com/berita/baca/hol18857/ma-batalkan-penetapan-pengampuan-prof-sudargo (accessed 11 February 2019); Anthony, 'Ketika Profesor Digugat Sang Putri Salah Satu Rumah Sudargo di Jakarta' (*Gatra*, 7 April 2008) http://arsip.gatra.com/2008-04-07/majalah/artikel.php?pil=23&id=113936 (accessed 12 February 2019).

[141] Anthony, 'Ketika Profesor Digugat' (n 140).

statutory seat, under which the applicable law is the law of the legal seat of the entity, found in its memorandum of association. Third, the doctrine of central management, where the applicable law is the law of the place in which the entity's central or effective management is situated.[142] In Indonesia, the first and second doctrines are effectively interchangeable because the place or country where the corporation has its statutory seat is usually the place under whose law it is incorporated.[143] Consequently, Indonesia applies only two doctrines to determine the applicable law for deciding the capacity of a legal entity: first, a combination of the doctrines of incorporation and statutory seat; second, the doctrine of central management. Articles 30, 36, and 42 of the Basic Agrarian Act 1960 adopt the combination of the doctrines of incorporation and statutory seat to determine the rights to land for legal entities in Indonesia. The Investment Act 2007 adopts the combination of doctrines of incorporation and statutory seat (Article 5) and the doctrine of central management (Article 17) for corporations investing in Indonesia. Hence, in all cases the law applied to determine the capacity of a foreign corporation will be the law of the country where its statutory seat is located or the law of the country where its central management is situated. This law will apply to govern both the capacity of the corporation to interact with Indonesian individuals and entities, and the dissolution of the corporation.

The rights, obligations and liabilities of individuals in the internal management of a foreign corporation are determined in the first place by the corporation's Memorandum of Association. The Memorandum of Association also determines whether an agent of the foreign corporation has the authority or power to represent the corporation in making a contract with an Indonesian individual or entity. If the corporation's Memorandum of Association does not govern these matters, the law that governs the capacity of the corporation will apply to these matters.[144]

B. Bankruptcy and Insolvency

i. *Effect of Bankruptcy and Insolvency on Assignments of Property*

Under the Bankruptcy and Suspension of Debt Payment Act 2004, bankruptcy is a simple declaration that a debtor with two or more creditors has not fully paid a debt which is due and payable (Article 2, paragraph (1)). The main purpose of the bankruptcy declaration is to impose a general attachment on the debtor's property to satisfy the creditors' claims, so that the debtor no longer has the right to control and manage its property. The debtor can appeal the court ruling on its bankruptcy to the Supreme Court. If its appeal is rejected by the Supreme Court, the debtor must offer a composition plan to its creditors mediated by a receiver. If this composition plan is rejected by the creditors, the debtor will enter insolvency. Under the Act, insolvency means the condition of being unable to pay debts (Elucidation of Article 57 paragraph (1)). When the debtor enters insolvency, the receiver starts the liquidation process of the debtor's property under the supervision of a supervisory judge (Article 178). A debtor that is declared bankrupt and enters insolvency could

[142] Gautama, *Perdata Internasional Jilid III Bag 1* (n 16) 212, 229.
[143] Supancana, *Naskah Akademik* (n 43) 47.
[144] Gautama, *Perdata Internasional Jilid III Bag 1* (n 16) 220–221.

be a natural person or corporation. A debtor could also be a non-corporate entity, such as a partnership, firm, or sole proprietorship (Article 1, No 11). As such, the Bankruptcy and Suspension of Debt Payment Act 2004 applies to all types of debtors and does not distinguish between individuals or non-legal entities and corporations.

The Bankruptcy and Suspension of Debt Payment Act 2004 is silent on the law that governs the effect of bankruptcy and insolvency on assignments of property located outside Indonesian territory. Since Indonesia does not recognise cross-border insolvency, insolvency or bankruptcy judgments by Indonesian courts are not enforceable against property located outside Indonesia. As such, assignments of property located outside Indonesia are not governed by Indonesian law but are governed by the law of the country in which the property is located. Because of this, pursuant to Articles 212 to 214 of the Act, the creditors of the bankrupt or insolvent debtors are not permitted to assign to third parties the bankruptcy property located outside Indonesia without compensating it in the bankruptcy assets. This issue is discussed further in section V.C cross-border insolvency. In summary for now, Indonesian judgments on bankruptcy and insolvency cover the debtor's property that is located outside Indonesia, although the assignment of the property to a third party is governed by the law of the country where the property is located.

ii. Effect of Bankruptcy and Insolvency on Discharge of Debts

The general regime contained in the Bankruptcy and Suspension of Debt Payment Act 2004 does not distinguish between the effect of bankruptcy and insolvency on corporations and natural persons (individuals). Under the Act, once the closing distribution list is final and binding, creditors repossess the right to claim the debtor's property to cover their unpaid claims.[145] Bankruptcy and insolvency do not discharge a debtor's indebtedness. As a result, if the debtor in future meets the requirements of Article 2 of the Act, they can be sued again for bankruptcy by the same creditors for the outstanding debts unpaid after the previous liquidation.[146] However, there is a special regime governing the effect of bankruptcy and insolvency in the case of corporate debts. Article 142, paragraph (1)d of the Corporations Act 2007 provides that a corporation shall dissolve, if upon the commercial court terminating its bankruptcy, the corporation does not have sufficient property to pay the cost of the bankruptcy. The 2007 Act also provides that a corporation dissolves if its property becomes insolvent under the Bankruptcy and Suspension of Debt Payment Act 2004 (Article 142, paragraph (1)e). Hence, on insolvency, a corporation is dissolved and consequently is discharged of its outstanding debts. A corporate debtor could file a petition for its own bankruptcy, provided that it has at least two creditors and it does not repay in full at least one debt which is due and payable (Article 2, paragraph (1) of the Bankruptcy and Suspension of Debt Payment Act 2004). In this way, a corporation may pursue its dissolution and the cancellation of its outstanding debts.

Since Indonesia does not recognise cross-border insolvency, foreign bankruptcy and insolvency judgments will not discharge debts owed to creditors in Indonesia. For instance,

[145] Art 204 of the Bankruptcy and Suspension of Debt Payment Act 2004.

[146] K Toha and S Retnaningsih, 'Legal Policy Granting Status of Fresh Start to the Individual Bankrupt Debtor in Developing the Bankruptcy Law in Indonesia' (2020) 9(2) *Academic Journal of Interdisciplinary Studies* 157, 158.

consider a foreign debtor that does not have its legal seat in Indonesia but operates its business within Indonesian territory, and has creditors in Indonesia as well as elsewhere. The creditors file petitions for bankruptcy or insolvency in a foreign court against the debtor, and that court declares the debtor bankrupt or insolvent. As a result, the creditor's property in the country of that court is liquidated. It may be that the bankruptcy law in that country allows the discharge of the debtor's debts (debt cancellation). However, Indonesia will not recognise the foreign court judgment on the discharge of the debtor's debts, because Indonesia does not recognise cross-border insolvency. As a result, the creditors that still have outstanding debts remain entitled to the payment of their outstanding debts in Indonesian courts. Indonesian courts have jurisdiction over the debtor although the debtor has been discharged of its debts by a foreign judgment because, first, Indonesia does not recognise foreign judgments and cross-border insolvency, and second, the debtor operates its business within Indonesian territory.

To conclude, in Indonesian law, bankruptcy and insolvency in general do not discharge a debtor's debts, following the Bankruptcy and Suspension of Debt Payment Act 2004. However, the Corporations Act 2007 provides different rules concerning the effect of bankruptcy and insolvency on the discharge of corporate debts. If the bankruptcy or insolvency leads to the dissolution of the corporation, the corporation is discharged of its debts. Since Indonesia does not recognise cross-border insolvency, foreign bankruptcy and insolvency judgments will not discharge the debts of foreign individuals and corporate debtors owed to creditors in Indonesia. Although a debtor has been discharged of its debts by a foreign judgment, its creditors remain entitled to the payment of their outstanding debts in Indonesian courts.

C. Cross-Border Insolvency

Indonesia does not adopt the United Nations Commission on International Trade Law (UNCITRAL) Model Law on Cross-Border Insolvency, and is not a party to any treaty concerning cross-border insolvency. Although the Bankruptcy and Suspension of Debt Payment Act 2004 does not expressly address cross-border insolvency, several provisions govern insolvency involving foreign elements. Article 212 of the Act stipulates that:

> The Creditors that after the bankruptcy declaration, take the bankruptcy assets located outside Indonesian territory to satisfy part or all of their claims, and the assets are not collaterals that give them priority right, shall compensate it in the bankruptcy assets.

Article 213, paragraph (1) of the Act stipulates that:

> The creditors that assign to a third party, part or all of their claims to the bankrupt debtor, with the intention that the third party will take the bankruptcy assets located outside Indonesian territory based on priority right, shall compensate it in the bankruptcy assets.

Article 214, paragraph (1) of the Act stipulates that:

> Any person that assigns to a third party, part or all of its claim to enable the third party to set off its debt to the bankrupt debtor outside Indonesian territory, shall compensate it in the bankruptcy assets.

These three provisions indicate that Indonesian insolvency and bankruptcy judgments apply to debtors' assets located outside Indonesia, although the judgments are only enforceable within Indonesian territory, as dictated by Article 431 Rv.

Pursuant to the General Elucidation of the Bankruptcy and Suspension of Debt Payment Act 2004, the applicable law for insolvency involving foreign elements is Indonesian law. The Act applies the integration principle, under which both the substantive and procedural law for matters of insolvency and bankruptcy are the national law of the court. Therefore, foreign judgments on insolvency and bankruptcy made on the basis of foreign laws will not be recognised or enforced by Indonesian courts, which only apply Indonesian law to matters of insolvency or bankruptcy.

VI. Competition Law

Indonesian competition law consists of the Anti-Monopoly Act 1999 and its implementing regulations. The Anti-Monopoly Act 1999 does not provide choice of law rules to determine the applicable law for anti-competitive conduct involving foreign elements. Article 16 of the Act addresses foreign elements in anti-competitive conduct, providing that 'Business actors shall be prohibited from entering into agreements with foreign parties in which the conditions of the agreements may cause monopolistic practices and or unfair business competition.' The Anti-Monopoly Act 1999 governs all businesses incorporated, having legal seats, or operating in Indonesia, whether or not they are legal entities (Article 1, No 5).

Indonesian competition law is enforced by the Commission for the Supervision of Business Competition (the Indonesia Competition Commission) and the courts. The Indonesia Competition Commission is responsible for enforcing competition law and adjudicates competition cases. Its decision could be in the form of administrative measures, a ruling of compensation for damages, and/or imposition of a fine (Article 47). The Commission's decision can be appealed to the District Court, with a final appeal to the Supreme Court. The Indonesia Competition Commission always applies the Anti-Monopoly Act 1999 to competition cases with foreign elements. As will be explained in Chapter 4, section I.B.vi competition law, the Commission's and the courts' judgments on competition are categorised as condemnatory judgments, which are not enforceable outside Indonesia (Article 431 Rv). Therefore, applying the Anti-Monopoly Act 1999 to competition cases involving foreign elements is appropriate, as the judgments made by the Indonesia Competition Commission and Indonesian courts are expected to be enforced only in Indonesia.

In the case of *Temasek Holdings Pte. Ltd; et al*, the Indonesia Competition Commission applied the Anti-Monopoly Act 1999 to a competition case involving several Singaporean corporations, namely, Temasek Holdings, Pte. Ltd ('Temasek Holdings) and its subsidiary companies, such as Singapore Telecommunications Ltd, Singapore Telecom Mobile Pte. Ltd, and Singapore Technologies Telemedia Pte. Ltd. The Singaporean holding company and its subsidiaries held stakes in PT Telekomunikasi Selular and in PT Indosat, Indonesia's first and second biggest mobile operators. Temasek Holdings' cross ownership structure created a price leadership in Indonesia's telecommunications industry. In its decision, the Indonesia Competition Commission stated that Temasek Holdings and its subsidiary companies violated Article 27 of the Anti-Monopoly Act 1999, which resulted in lower competitiveness and excessive pricing. The sanction imposed by the Indonesia Competition Commission to Temasek Holdings and its subsidiary companies, was based on the Anti-Monopoly Act 1999, namely an order to give up ownership in either PT Telekomunikasi Selular or PT Indosat, and payment of a fine. Temasek Holdings appealed the judgment of the Commission, but the Central Jakarta District Court, the Supreme Court and the Supreme Court for extraordinary appeal denied Temasek Holdings' appeal.[147] Finally, Temasek Holdings and its subsidiary companies, including PT Telekomunikasi Selular, paid the fine to the Indonesia Competition Commission.

In conclusion, the law applicable to anti-competitive conducts involving foreign elements is the Anti-Monopoly Act 1999. Applying the Anti-Monopoly Act 1999 to competition cases involving foreign elements is the most appropriate, as the condemnatory judgments made by the Indonesia Competition Commission and Indonesian courts are expected to be enforced only in Indonesia.

[147] Commission for the Supervision of Business Competition Decision 07/KPPU-L/2007 (19 November 2007); affd District Court of Central Jakarta Decision 02/KPPU/2007/PN.JKT.PST (9 May 2008); affd Supreme Court Decision 496 K/Pdt.Sus/2008 (10 September 2008); affd Supreme Court Extraordinary Appeal 128 PK/PDT. SUS/2009 (5 May 2010).

4

Recognition and Enforcement of Foreign Judgments

I. Recognition

A. General Principles

In principle, foreign judgments are not recognised and cannot be enforced in Indonesia. Although this principle is not expressly written in any specific law, it can be inferred from Article 22a AB which provides that court judgments, their enforcement, and authentic deeds are restricted by international law principles. Sudargo Gautama considered this principle and decided that Article 22a AB was in line with the principle of judicial sovereignty of a state. However, he wrote that in practice, there has been moderation in this principle by which the court is given the freedom to recognise foreign declaratory and constitutive judgments in Indonesia, subject to Indonesian public policy.[1] A judgment is declaratory in nature if it is to confirm a legal status or position. Examples are: status as legal heir of a deceased person; the ownership of a property; the validity of a contract; or the validity of a marriage. Whereas a judgment is constitutive in nature if it is to create a new legal condition which abolishes an existing legal condition. For instance, annulment of a contract, a divorce ruling or appointment of a guardian. The reason for the recognition of foreign declaratory and constitutive judgments in Indonesia is that these judgments merely require Indonesian courts passively to acknowledge the existence of the judgments and do not require Indonesian courts actively to execute the judgments.[2] Sudargo Gautama wrote that the courts merely affirm rights and obligations between the parties in foreign declaratory and constitutive judgments and in the case of foreign judgments concerning the personal status of persons, such decisions only require an adjustment of the persons' civil registered status in Indonesian civil registry office.[3]

With regard to foreign condemnatory judgments, the principle of not recognising them in Indonesia remains applicable. A judgment is condemnatory in nature if its purpose is to punish or order the losing party to perform a certain action, such as to pay damages or relinquish a right. However, in practice, a condemnatory judgment may serve as prima facie evidence in a fresh action on the same matter brought before an Indonesian court.

[1] S Gautama, 'International Civil Procedure in Indonesia' (1996) 6 *Asian Yearbook of International Law* 87, 98.

[2] A Chong, 'Principle 1 General Principle' in A Chong (ed), *Asian Principles for the Recognition and Enforcement of Foreign Judgments* (Asian Business Law Institute, 2020) 15; YU Oppusunggu, 'Indonesia' in A Chong (ed), Recognition and Enforcement of Foreign Judgments in Asia (Asian Business Law Institute, 2017) 103.

[3] S Gautama, 'International Civil Procedure in Indonesia' (1996) 6 *Asian Yearbook of International Law* 87, 99.

In adjudicating such a case, the court may use its discretion to accept the foreign condemnatory judgment as prima facie evidence or take it as an authentic deed,[4] although the court will not treat the same as a *res judicata*. In other words, the court is practically free to determine, on a case-by-case basis, whether or not a foreign judgment is accepted as prima facie evidence of a state of affairs. The only condemnatory judgment that is exempted from this principle and which is thus recognised in Indonesia is a foreign judgment on maritime general average as stipulated by Article 724 of the Commercial Code. The exemption is found in Article 436, paragraph (1) Rv, which provides: 'All judgments delivered by foreign courts are unenforceable in Indonesian territory, except in the matters mentioned in Article 724 of the Commercial Code and in other regulations.' Since there is no other regulation in this matter, the only foreign condemnatory judgment that can be fully recognised and enforced in Indonesia, according to Article 436 Rv, is a judgment on maritime general average stipulated in Article 724 of Commercial Code.

It is also worth noting that a foreign judgment may consists of a part which is declaratory and another part which is condemnatory. In that situation, the declaratory part of the judgment, for example, the validity of a contract, can be recognised in Indonesia, while the condemnatory part of the judgment which orders the defendant to pay damages, will not be recognised. The plaintiff must bring a fresh action before an Indonesian court to obtain damages and adduce the foreign judgment to that court as prima facie evidence that damages are due and owing.

i. Recognition under Bilateral, Multilateral Treaties, and Conventions

Indonesia is not a party to any treaty or convention on the recognition of foreign judgments. No treaty or convention to which Indonesia is a party requires Indonesia to recognise foreign judgments. For example, the 1978 Bilateral Treaty on Judicial Co-Operation between Indonesia and Thailand does not address the matter of reciprocal recognition of judgments made in Indonesia and Thailand. Indonesian Private International Law also does not embrace the doctrines of comity and obligation that require states to recognise and enforce foreign judgments. It recognises and enforces foreign judgments only on the basis of reciprocity.[5] In the absence of reciprocal treaties or conventions, and without the comity and obligation doctrines, the recognition of foreign judgments in Indonesia is dictated by legal doctrine developed by Indonesian legal scholars. Sudargo Gautama asserts that recognition should be given to foreign declaratory and constitutive judgments insofar as this does not offend Indonesia's law and public policy.[6] His opinion is also accepted in the 2015 Academic Paper of Indonesian Private International Law Bill.[7] According to this doctrine, a foreign

[4] MY Harahap, *Hukum Acara Perdata Tentang Gugatan, Persidangan, Penyitaan, Pembuktian, dan Putusan Pengadilan* 16th edn (Sinar Grafika, 2016)136.

[5] S Gautama, 'Recognition and Enforcement of Foreign Judgments and Arbitral Awards in The Asean Region' (1990) 32(1) *Malaya Law Review* 172, 172–173; Harahap, *Hukum Acara* (n 4) 136.

[6] S Gautama, *Hukum Perdata Internasional Indonesia Jilid III Bagian 2 Buku Ke Delapan* (Penerbit Alumni, 1987) 282; S Gautama, *Essays in Indonesian Law* (Citra Aditya Bakti, 1991) 451.

[7] IBR Supancana, *Naskah Akademik Rancangan Undang-Undang tentang Hukum Perdata Internasional (lanjutan)* (Badan Pembinaan Hukum Nasional Kementerian Hukum dan Hak Asasi Manusia RI, 2015) 85 www.bphn.go.id/data/documents/na_ruu_ttg_hukum_perdata_internasional_(lanjutan).pdf (accessed 8 July 2018).

declaratory or constitutive judgment (for instance, a ruling on divorce or annulment of a marriage) can be recognised, and consequently be enforced, by registering the judgment in the Office of Civil Registry in Indonesia in accordance with the Population Administration Act 2006 as amended in 2013. By recognising a foreign declarative or constitutive judgment, the Indonesian court accepts the judgment's merit, and the parties do not need to bring another cause of action to the Indonesian court in respect of the same issue. However, in the Indonesian legal system legal doctrine is not a binding source of law. As a consequence, although Indonesian judges are usually guided by doctrine, in practice they are free to decide whether or not to recognise foreign declaratory and constitutive judgments For example, in the case No 258/Pdt.P/2007/PN Jaksel, the South Jakarta District Court recognised an Australian constitutive judgment made by the Administrative Tribunal of Western Australia, but in the cassation level, the Supreme Court did not recognise it and annulled the South Jakarta District Court's decision.

The practice of the recognition of foreign judgments by Indonesian courts will be explained further in the following parts.

ii. Indirect Jurisdiction

In principle, no law in Indonesia obliges Indonesian courts to recognise foreign judgments. Decisions on recognition are always left to the discretion of the individual court. If an Indonesian court does intend to recognise a foreign judgment, it will determine the jurisdiction of the foreign court over the subject matter solely by reference to Indonesian law. If the court finds that, under Indonesian law (HIR or Rv), the foreign court does not have jurisdiction over the case (for instance, because the Indonesian party is not a resident in the forum of the foreign court) then the Indonesian court will not recognise the foreign judgment.

Indonesian jurisprudence and doctrine are silent on indirect jurisdiction as, in principle, Indonesian courts are not obliged to recognise foreign judgments. Therefore, an Indonesian court is free to apply Indonesian law to determine whether the foreign court has jurisdiction.

iii. Reciprocity

In principle, reciprocity is one of the requirements for the recognition and enforcement of foreign judgments in Indonesia,[8] besides the conformity of foreign judgments to Indonesian public policy. However, even though to date no reciprocal treaty or convention between Indonesia and other states addresses the recognition of foreign judgments, there is a growing practice of recognising foreign declaratory and constitutive judgments in Indonesia, subject to Indonesian public policy. As explained above, the reason for the recognition of foreign declaratory and constitutive judgments despite no reciprocal treaty or convention, is that the judgments merely require Indonesian courts to passively acknowledge the

[8] Gautama, 'Recognition and Enforcement' (n 5); Harahap, *Hukum Acara* (n 4) 136.

existence of the judgments and do not require Indonesian courts to actively execute the judgments.[9] This practice has been supported by Indonesian scholars.[10]

iv. Grounds for Refusing Recognition

The only doctrine providing a general ground for the refusal to recognise foreign declaratory and constitutive judgments is public policy. A foreign judgment which is contrary to Indonesian public policy will not be recognised in Indonesia. For example, a foreign judgment that holds a same-sex marriage valid would not be recognised, as it contradicts the Indonesian public policy that regards marriage as a union between a man and a woman.[11] A foreign judgment on rights to land in Indonesia also cannot be recognised in Indonesia. Land in Indonesia bears on the public interest, as stated in Article 33 of Indonesian Constitution. It stipulates that, 'Land and water and the natural resources contained therein shall be controlled by the State and used for the greatest prosperity of people.' Therefore, all judgments relating to land in Indonesia must be made by Indonesian courts only. Other grounds for refusing the recognition of foreign judgments are determined by Indonesian courts on a case-by-case basis. Therefore, each individual court sitting in a particular case, may have its own grounds for refusing the recognition of foreign declaratory and constitutive judgments.

v. Recognition for the Purposes of Establishing Res Judicata and Issue Estoppel

Indonesian Private International Law does not recognise the doctrine of *res judicata*, which prevents a party from re-litigating an issue or a cause of action that has already been conclusively decided by a foreign court. According to the *res judicata* doctrine, even when the foreign judgment is subject to an appeal this will not render the judgment unenforceable, although the recognition could be pending the outcome of the appeal.[12] Since the doctrine of *res judicata* is unknown in Indonesian Private International Law, so too is the doctrine of estoppel.

This situation is demonstrated in the case No 258/Pdt.P/2007/PN Jaksel concerning the recognition of a foreign declaratory judgment of mental incapacity. The South Jakarta District Court in 2007 recognised an Australian judgment made by the Administrative Tribunal of Western Australia that was presented by the applicant to the South Jakarta Court.[13] The Australian Tribunal held that the applicant's elderly father, who was an Indonesian citizen but lived and owned properties in Australia as well as in Indonesia, was legally incompetent to manage his properties, and therefore the Australian Tribunal

[9] Chong, 'Principle 1' (n 2) 15; Oppusunggu, 'Indonesia' (n 2) 103.

[10] Gautama, *Perdata Internasional Jilid III Bag 2* (n 6); Gautama, *Essays in Indonesian Law* (n 6); Supancana, *Naskah Akademik* (n 7) 85.

[11] Art 1 of the 1974 Marriage Act; See also Supancana, *Naskah Akademik* (n 7) 18, 34.

[12] AJ Mayss, *Principles of Conflict of Laws* 3rd edn (Cavendish Publishing Limited, 1999) 95.

[13] District Court of South Jakarta Decision 258/Pdt.P/2007/PN Jaksel (not published).

put him under an administrator. The Australian Tribunal reached its judgment based on, among other things, an assessment made by a specialist geriatric, medical doctor in Western Australia. The applicant, who lived in Indonesia, presented this Australian judgment to the South Jakarta District Court, in order to apply for conservatorship of her elderly father and his properties. The Court accepted the applicant's petition and ruled that she was her father's conservator. The applicant's father appealed both of the rulings of the South Jakarta District Court and the Administrative Tribunal of Western Australia in their respective countries.[14] In his appeal to the Indonesian Supreme Court, the appellant argued that a foreign judgment was not enforceable in Indonesia (Article 436 Rv) and that the South Jakarta District Court had to examine and hear from him before delivering the ruling of mental incapacity and conservatorship (Article 439 BW). The Supreme Court concluded that because the South Jakarta District Court never examined and heard from the appellant before ruling against him, its ruling was not in conformity with Article 439 BW. Accordingly, in March 2008 the Supreme Court annulled the South Jakarta District Court's ruling.[15] This case shows that the recognition of the foreign judgment was not for the purpose of establishing *res judicata*. Although at first the Australian judgment was recognised by the lower court, the appellant was not estopped by the Indonesian Supreme Court from litigating the same issue that had been decided by the Australian court. In addition, the Supreme Court annulled the recognition of Australian judgment without waiting for the outcome of the appeal process in the Australian Appellate Court.

In the case of *Karaha Bodas Company, L.L.C. v Perusahaan Pertambangan Minyak Dan Gas Bumi Negara*,[16] the US District Court for the Southern District of Texas invited the Indonesian company Perusahaan Pertambangan Minyak Dan Gas Bumi Negara (Pertamina) to respond to the *res judicata* question. The Texas District Court raised the question of whether the *res judicata* rule should bar Pertamina's lawsuit against Karaha Bodas Company (KBC) in the Indonesian courts, after the Texas District Court had already delivered its final judgment in the case and an appeal to the Court of Appeals, Fifth Circuit, was underway. Pertamina declined to respond to the *res judicata* question, including the question on the effect of the Texas District Court judgment in Indonesia, where KBC sought its enforcement. On the other hand, KBC was able to present affidavits that the courts and laws of Canada, Hong Kong, and Singapore applied the principle of *res judicata* to give effect to the Texas District Court judgment. KBC sought enforcement of an arbitral award that had been confirmed by the Texas Court in those countries, besides in Indonesia. This case offers more evidence that the *res judicata* principle does not exist in Indonesian Private International Law.

[14] Hukumonline, 'MA Batalkan Penetapan Pengampuan Prof. Sudargo' (*hukumonline*, 29 March 2008) www.hukumonline.com/berita/baca/hol18857/ma-batalkan-penetapan-pengampuan-prof-sudargo (accessed 11 February 2019); Anthony, 'Ketika Profesor Digugat Sang Putri Salah Satu Rumah Sudargo di Jakarta' (*Gatra*, 7 April 2008) http://arsip.gatra.com/2008-04-07/majalah/artikel.php?pil=23&id=113936 (accessed 12 February 2019).

[15] ibid.

[16] US District Court for the Southern District of Texas Decision 264 F. Supp. 2d 470 (26 April 2002). Details of this case have been explained in the ch 2, section I.A.ii.c above.

Although Indonesian Private International Law does not recognise the principles of *res judicata* and estoppel in relation to foreign judgments, Article 1917 of the BW recognises these principles for domestic judgments.[17] Article 1917 BW provides that:

(1) The authority of a judicial decision does not extend beyond the subject of the judgment.
(2) To invoke this authority, it is required that the thing that is claimed be the same, that the claim be based on the same cause and be made by and against the same parties in the same relationship.

Some court decisions implement the principles of *res judicata* and estoppel established in Article 1917 BW. However, the BW is a domestic Civil Code that governs domestic civil matters, not international civil matters. The principles of *res judicata* and estoppel in Article 1917 BW therefore do not extend to judgments and decisions of foreign courts.

In the end, although the Indonesian courts may recognise a foreign judgment, this recognition does not estop the parties from relitigating the issue or cause of action in the higher courts. As such, recognition of foreign judgments does not establish *res judicata*.

vi. Interlocutory Judgments

An interlocutory judgment is not a final decision. It is a temporary decision or provisional ruling in a cause of action. It is not subject to appeal on its own, but can be appealed together with the final decision (Article 190, paragraph (1) HIR). To be recognised in Indonesia, a foreign judgment must be final.[18] Therefore, an interlocutory judgment that is not a final judgment cannot be recognised. This principle also applies to foreign interlocutory judgments, as demonstrated in the case No 210/Pdt/G/1992/PN.JKT.Sel.[19] In this case, the judge had to decide on a custody and child abduction dispute between a German mother and an Indonesian father. The couple had two sons, and the family had previously lived in Germany. In 1992, when the couple experienced conflict, the mother filed for divorce in a German court, and the German court granted temporary custody of the two children to her while the couple's divorce was being finalised. During the divorce process, the Indonesian father abducted their children and brought them to Jakarta, Indonesia.[20] He filed for divorce and sole custody for his children in the South Jakarta District Court. He also applied for citizenship conversion for his children to become Indonesian nationals. Responding to her husband's legal proceeding in the Jakarta Court, the German wife claimed that there had been an interlocutory judgment by a German court that granted temporary custody of their two children to her. Therefore, she requested that the Jakarta Court order her husband to return custody of their children to her in accordance with the provisional ruling made by the German court. In the trial, the judges in the Jakarta Court could accept the divorce petition, but refused to recognise the custody provisional ruling made by the German court. They based their refusal on Article 436 Rv and the counterclaim by the Indonesian father, who argued that he was not present in Germany and was not notified by the German court during the custody hearing. In judging this case,

[17] Harahap, *Hukum Acara* (n 4) 439–448.
[18] Oppusunggu, 'Indonesia' (n 2) 98.
[19] Not published. See also Supancana, *Naskah Akademik* (n 7) 50.
[20] Indonesia is not a party to the 1980 Hague Convention on the Civil Aspects of International Child Abduction.

the judges applied the Indonesian Marriage Act. They considered the fact that both the parents were capable of performing their parental obligations, as stipulated in the Marriage Act 1974, although they would be divorced. In their final judgment, the South Jakarta District Court granted the divorce to the couple and gave each of them custody of one child; the elder son was in his father's custody and the younger one in his mother's.[21]

This principle applies equally to anti-suit injunctions issued by foreign courts. Examples are found in *PT. Indah Kiat Pulp & Paper Tbk. v Bank America National Trust Company; et al*; and *Perusahaan Pertambangan Minyak dan Gas Bumi Negara (Pertamina) v Karaha Bodas Company LLC*. In these two cases, the Indonesian courts in the districts of Bengkalis and Central Jakarta issued their own anti-suit injunctions against the foreign parties and decided in favour of the Indonesian parties, although the foreign courts in New York and Texas had already issued an anti-suit injunction against the Indonesian parties.[22]

The cases above show that the Indonesian courts do not recognise, and are not bound by, foreign interlocutory judgments.

B. Special Rules

i. Law of Obligations

a. Judgments Relating to Specific Contracts

As previously stated, declaratory or constitutive judgments relating to contracts, such as the validity and annulment of contracts, may be recognised in Indonesia. On the other hand, condemnatory judgments relating to contracts, for instance awards of damages, will not be recognised in Indonesia. This principle is based on Indonesian legal doctrines and Article 436 Rv. In addition, foreign judgments concerning contracts that involve the public interest – such as employment contracts, consumer contracts, and contracts for sale of lands – are not recognised in Indonesia. This principle is intended to protect the public interest and public policy in Indonesia.[23] Disputes relating to these types of contracts must be brought to and settled by Indonesian courts under Indonesian law.

b. Judgments Relating to Specific Torts

Judgments relating to torts, whether general or specific torts, generally require enforcement, as the judgments provide remedies to the injured parties in the form of compensatory damages, injunctions, or restitution. This means that foreign judgments relating to torts are condemnatory in nature. Therefore, in accordance with legal doctrine and Article 436 Rv, they cannot be recognised in Indonesia, even if the domicile of defendants or the location of their assets is in Indonesia.

[21] Supancana, *Naskah Akademik* (n 7) 53.
[22] See ch 2, section I.A.ii.c Anti-suit injunctions above for detailed discussion of the two cases.
[23] S Gautama, *Pengantar Hukum Perdata Internasional Indonesia* (Binacipta, 1985) 170.

c. Judgments Relating to Unjust Enrichment

Judgments relating to unjust enrichment or undue performance, including undue payment, generally require enforcement, as the judgments provide remedies to the claimant in the form of restitution. Hence, foreign judgments relating to unjust enrichment are condemnatory in nature. Therefore, in accordance with Indonesian doctrines and Article 436 Rv, they cannot be recognised in Indonesia, although the domicile of defendants or location of their assets is in Indonesia.

d. Judgments Relating to Trusts and Charitable Foundations

As previously discussed in Chapter 2, section I.B.i.d on trusts and charitable foundations, the institution of trusts does not exist in the Indonesian legal system. Thus, foreign judgments relating to trusts will not be recognised in Indonesia. Unlike trusts, charitable foundations exist in the Indonesian legal system. Declaratory or constitutive judgments regarding the existence and validity of charitable foundations as well as the rights of all parties in the foundations may therefore be recognised in Indonesia. However, condemnatory judgments relating to charitable foundations that punish the parties, for instance by ordering them to pay damages or to relinquish a right, cannot be recognised in Indonesia. This outcome is in accordance with Article 436 Rv and legal doctrines in Indonesia.

ii. Law of Property

a. Judgments Relating to Immovable Property

Immovable property generally requires registration in Indonesia and is governed under Indonesian law in line with the principle of *lex rei sitae* of Article 17 AB. As discussed in section I.A.iv, rights and obligations pertaining to land in Indonesia always involve public policy and bear on the public interest. Therefore, all judgments relating to land in Indonesia must be made by Indonesian courts under Indonesian law. Foreign declaratory or constitutive judgments concerning other types of immovable property[24] may be recognised in Indonesia if they are in conformity with Indonesian law. This outcome is in accordance with the principle of *lex rei sitae* of Article 17 AB. As in other matters, foreign condemnatory judgments relating to immovable property are not recognised in Indonesia.

b. Judgments Relating to Intangible Property

Like immovable property, intangible property such as intellectual properties, commercial papers, and secured debts requires registration in Indonesia and, consequently, is governed under Indonesian law. Therefore, the status of the property is determined solely

[24] The Indonesian legal system categorises immovable properties based on their nature, their purposes, and by operation of law. Immovable properties because of their nature are, eg, land, buildings, flats, trees including their fruits and plantations. Immovable properties based on their purposes are, eg, machines in factories and furniture attached to buildings. Immovable properties by operation of law are, eg, Indonesian-flagged vessels with the minimum gross weight of 20 cubic meters (Art 314 of Commercial Code) and all rights, including security interests, arising out of immovable properties.

by Indonesian law. Accordingly, foreign declaratory or constitutive judgments relating to intangible property may be recognised in Indonesia so long as they are in conformity with Indonesian law. As in all other areas, foreign condemnatory judgments relating to intangible property are not recognised in Indonesia.

c. Judgments Relating to Succession to Property

Judgments concerning the succession to property or estate are declaratory if they are made to confirm the status and ownership of the estate, but condemnatory if they are to revoke the rights to the estate. In any case, estates located in Indonesia are governed under Indonesian law following the *lex rei sitae* principle.[25] Therefore, foreign declaratory or constitutive judgments relating to an estate will be recognised in Indonesia, but only if they are in conformity with Indonesian law. Foreign condemnatory judgments relating to estate are not recognised in Indonesia, in accordance with Article 436 Rv and Indonesian doctrines.

iii. Intellectual Property

Indonesian law is silent on the cross-border recognition and enforcement of judgments on intellectual property (IP) related matters. Indonesia is also not a party to any treaty or convention on the recognition and enforcement of IP-related judgments. Although Indonesia is a party to several international conventions on IP – namely, the TRIPS Agreement and some WIPO-administered treaties – none of these govern the cross-border recognition and enforcement of IP judgments. Indonesian IP law applies the territoriality principle, or *lex loci protectionis*, to determine the existence, content, and infringement of IP rights. This means that only Indonesian law and Indonesian authorities can determine the validity of an IP right in Indonesia, including the prerogatives of the IP right-holder and the infringement of the right. The national treatment principle found in IP international conventions, to which Indonesia is a member, also supports the application of the territoriality principle.[26] Together with Articles 436 and 431 Rv, these principles make foreign IP judgments to which Articles 436 and 431 Rv apply (ie condemnatory judgments) unrecognisable and unenforceable in Indonesia, and Indonesian judgments unrecognisable and unenforceable outside Indonesia. By contrast, foreign declaratory and constitutive judgments, to which Articles 436 and 431 Rv do not apply, may be recognised in Indonesia insofar as they do not offend Indonesia's public policy. In the case of IP judgments, the foreign declaratory or constitutive judgment must also be given by a court of the state in which the IP right exists and is protected or registered, because it is conceptually impossible for infringement of an IP right registered or protected in a certain country to occur in another country.[27]

[25] Supancana, *Naskah Akademik* (n 7) 3, 45, 46.

[26] Y Oestreicher, 'Recognition and Enforcement Of Foreign Intellectual Property Judgments: Analysis And Guidelines For A New International Convention' (S.J.D. thesis, Duke University School of Law, 2004).

[27] Co-Rapporteurs of HCCH draft Convention and the Permanent Bureau, *Treatment of Intellectual Property-Related Judgments under the November 2017 draft Convention* (Background document of May 2018, HCCH 2018) 9 https://assets.hcch.net/docs/0c2a7a4d-17ed-43b1-9b98-6bdb452f28a7.pdf (accessed 26 March 2019).

To illustrate, imagine that a legal suit was brought by an Indonesian indigenous group to a Japanese court to challenge a patent right granted by the Japanese Patent Office to a Japanese cosmetic company. The Indonesian party argues that the patent right granted to the Japanese company was not valid because the patented cosmetic appropriated the traditional herbal ingredients commonly used by the indigenous group. The Japanese court agrees with the Indonesian party and revokes the patent right granted to the Japanese company. In such a case, the judgment of the Japanese court that revoked the patent right of the Japanese company can be recognised in Indonesia as the judgment is constitutive in nature. The judgment was also made by the court in a country, namely Japan, in which the patent right was registered and protected. If the judgment includes damages/compensation awarded to the Indonesian party, the part of the judgment that awards the damages will not be recognised in Indonesia, as it is categorised as a condemnatory judgment.

In short, foreign judgments that determine the validity, rights of an IP holder, and infringement of IP rights may be recognised in Indonesia if the judgment is declaratory or constitutive in nature. To be recognised, the judgment must be made by a court in a country in which the IP right is registered or protected and, as illustrated in the above case study, the judgment must have relation to an Indonesian party. However, since Indonesian IP law applies the territoriality principle, and Indonesia is not a party to any treaty or convention on the recognition and enforcement of foreign judgments, subject to the public policy constraint it is up to Indonesian courts to recognise or not to recognise declaratory and constitutive IP judgments.

iv. Family Law

a. Decrees of Marriage

In Indonesian doctrine, decrees of marriage are categorised as declaratory judgments, and foreign declaratory judgments are generally recognised in Indonesia. This recognition is subject to the general constraint that those decrees must not be contrary to Indonesian public policy. For instance, a foreign decree of same-sex marriage is not recognised in Indonesia as it contradicts Indonesian public policy.[28] In addition, to be recognised in Indonesia, the foreign marriage decree must be registered in accordance with Article 37 of the Population Administration Act 2006 as amended in 2013.

b. Decrees of Divorce, Separation and Nullity

In Indonesian doctrine, a decree of divorce is categorised as a constitutive judgment. Therefore, a foreign decree of divorce is generally recognised in Indonesia, insofar as the decree is not challenged by one of the spouses in an Indonesian court. If a foreign divorce decree is challenged by one of the spouses, an Indonesian court must take the claim and adjudicate the divorce case itself, which means that it does not recognise the foreign divorce decree. This is because, as explained earlier, the doctrines of *res judicata* and *lis alibi pendens* do not exist in Indonesian Private International Law. For example, in the case No 1456/Pdt.G/2006/PA.JS,[29]

[28] Supancana, *Naskah Akademik* (n 7) 18, 34.

[29] Not published. See also A Pratiwi, 'Aspek-aspek Hukum Acara Perdata Internasional dalam Perceraian di Indonesia' (Undergraduate thesis, Universitas Indonesia, 2011) 5, 86–89.

between an Indonesian husband and a French wife, the husband refused to accept a divorce decree made by the *Tribunal de Grande Instance de Versailles*, France on 22 December 2005. The Tribunal in Versailles granted the divorce based on the petition made by the French wife. On 23 November 2006, eleven months after the judgment, the Indonesian husband filed a new divorce petition based on Islamic law to the South Jakarta Religious Court because the spouses were Muslims. Based on Islamic law, he wished to declare Islamic divorce, or *talaq*, to his wife in front of the Court and demanded the custody of their two children. The Religious Court of First Instance refused to take the case because the Court recognised the Versailles judgment and declared that the husband was already divorced accordingly. The husband appealed the decision to the Jakarta High Religious Court with the case registered under No 40/Pdt.G/2008/PTA.JK.[30] In this case, the appellate Court disagreed with the lower court's judgment. It declared that the couple were still married and accepted the husband's petition to pronounce the Islamic divorce, or *talaq*, to his wife in front of the Court. The divorce was finalised after the *talaq* declaration by the Indonesian husband to his French wife.[31]

The above case shows that a foreign divorce decree will not be recognised in Indonesia if one of the spouses challenges the decree. But where both spouses accept a foreign divorce decree, the decree will be recognised in Indonesia, as stipulated in the Supreme Court jurisprudence No 1037K/Sip/73 dated 23 March 1976.[32] To be recognised in Indonesia, the foreign divorce decree must be registered in accordance with Article 41 of the Population Administration Act 2006 as amended in 2013. The recognition and registration of foreign divorce decrees are given and provided only for decrees granted by courts. In other words, the divorce decree must have been obtained through judicial proceedings. It cannot be obtained from other proceedings, such as religious acts. This requirement is necessitated by Article 39 and the General Elucidation No 4.e. of the Marriage Act 1974 and Article 65 of the Religious Judicature Act 1989, which require that a divorce be decreed only before a court. In addition, foreign divorce judgments must be based on one of the grounds for divorce listed in Article 19 of the Marriage Regulation 1975 and Article 116 of the Compilation of Islamic Law. Otherwise, the divorce will be invalid and not be recognised in Indonesia.[33] It should be noted, however, that the recognition of foreign divorce decrees does not extend to orders relating to pecuniary obligations, custody of children, or division of marital property, which are categorised as condemnatory in nature.[34]

The situation may be different where the foreign divorce decree concerns a Muslim Indonesian or Muslim mixed marriage couple. Some scholars argue that such a decree cannot be recognised in Indonesia, as recognition would contradict Article 66, paragraph (4) and Article 73, paragraph (3) of the Religious Judicature Act 1989. These Articles, which

[30] ibid, 89.

[31] In the Indonesian legal system, *talaq*, or Islamic divorce, is performed in front of a religious court by the husband (petitioner) who petitions his wife (respondent) for witnessing his *talaq* declaration in front of the court. The court must approve the *talaq* in a court ruling.

[32] Not published. See also M Yasmin, 'Akibat Perkawinan Campuran Terhadap Anak dan Harta Benda yang Diperoleh Sebelum dan Sesudah Perkawinan (Studi Banding Indonesia-Malaysia)' (Undergraduate thesis, Universitas Indonesia, 2011) 21, 23.

[33] S Gautama and H Wiknjosastro, 'Some Aspects of Indonesian Private International Law' (1990) 32 *Malaya Law Review* 417 www.jstor.org/stable/24865645 (accessed 26 May 2018); S Gautama, *Hukum Perdata Internasional Indonesia Buku Ketujuh Jilid Ke-Tiga (Bagian Pertama)* (Penerbit Alumni, 1981) 172; ZD Basuki and others, *Materi Pokok Hukum Perdata Internasional. Modul 5* (Universitas Terbuka, 2014) 31.

[34] Gautama, *Perdata Internasional Jilid III Bag 2* (n 6) 224.

specifically concern Muslim couples, provide that in the case where the petitioner and respondent are domiciled outside Indonesia, the petition for divorce shall be filed in the court in the district in which the couple registered their marriage, or in the Central Jakarta Religious Court. As such, divorce decrees for Muslim couples can be made only by the courts mentioned in the Religious Judicature Act 1989. However, in practice there are judges in the religious courts who suggest that divorce decrees obtained by Muslim spouses from foreign courts may be recognised and registered in Indonesia. There is no need for the couples to bring another cause of action with the same merit to the Indonesian courts.[35] This assertion applies only if both the husband and wife agree with the jurisdiction of the foreign court over their divorce, and the grounds for their divorce abroad are legal under Indonesian law. The practice of recognising foreign divorce judgments despite the provisions of Religious Judicature Act 1989 is based on the legal doctrine of *lex posterior derogat legi priori* (a later law repeals an earlier law) in combination with the doctrine that categorises a divorce decree as a constitutive judgment. Those that adopt the doctrine of *lex posterior derogat legi priori* assert that Article 41 of the Population Administration Act 2006 as amended in 2013 supersedes Article 66, paragraph (4) and Article 73, paragraph (30) of the Religious Judicature Act 1989, and that therefore the divorce of an Indonesian Muslim couple abroad is recognised in Indonesia although it was not decreed by a religious court in Indonesia.[36] The doctrine that categorises foreign divorce decrees as constitutive judgments maintains that because divorce decrees are not intended to condemn or punish certain parties, but only to create a new legal condition, the decrees are constitutive in nature. Therefore, divorce decrees are outside the scope of Article 436 Rv that prohibits the enforcement of foreign condemnatory judgments in Indonesia.[37]

With the enactment of the Marriage Act 1974, decrees of legal separation no longer exist in the Indonesian legal system. The Marriage Act 1974 supersedes the previous marriage law of BW, which recognised legal separation. In consequence, foreign separation decrees will not be recognised in Indonesia. The Population Administration Act 2006 as amended in 2013 also does not have provisions concerning the registrability of legal separation in the Indonesian Civil Registry. This means that a couple that obtains foreign legal separation decrees cannot register their legal separation in Indonesia, and thus their separation is not valid in Indonesia.

With regard to the annulment of marriage, this institution exists in the Indonesian legal system and is governed by Chapter IV of the Marriage Act 1974 and Article 71 of the Compilation of Islamic Law, which is applicable to cases in the Religious Court. Marriage nullity can be obtained only through a court judgment (Article 25 of the Marriage Act 1974). To be recognised by the state, a decree of nullity must be registered in accordance with Article 39 of the Population Administration Act 2006, as amended in 2013. Article 39, unlike the similar provision applying to the registration of divorce decrees, does not distinguish between domestic and foreign decrees. This raises the question of whether Article 39

[35] This opinion was given by Justice Tamah, a judge at the South Jakarta Religious Court during an interview with Astrid Pratiwi for her thesis. See Pratiwi, 'Aspek-aspek' (n 29) 118, 119; The same opinion was also presented by Justice Mohamad Thoha, a judge at the Ponorogo Religious Court in his writing titled: Hukum Perceraian di luar negeri, on http://pa-ponorogo.net. Posted on 12 September 2008, but is no longer accessible on the internet.

[36] Yasmin, 'Akibat Perkawinan Campuran' (n 32).

[37] Pratiwi, 'Aspek-aspek' (n 29) 75–78.

of the Population Administration Act 2006 as amended in 2013 is only applicable to the registration of domestic nullity decrees or also to foreign nullity decrees. According to legal doctrine, foreign decrees of nullity are categorised as constitutive judgments, and therefore should be recognised in Indonesia insofar as the decree is final and binding and accepted by both spouses. Nevertheless, it is not clear how the couple may register its decree of nullity in Indonesia, as Article 39 of the Population Administration Act 2006 as amended in 2013 does not provide specific rules for the registration of foreign decrees of nullity. In the case that a foreign nullity decree is challenged by one of the spouses in Indonesia, an Indonesian court must take the claim and adjudicate the nullity case itself, which means that it does not recognise the foreign nullity decree. As stated earlier, the doctrine of *res judicata* does not exist in Indonesian Private International Law, which allows the Indonesian court not to recognise foreign nullity decrees that are challenged by one of the spouses in front of Indonesian courts.

In summary, foreign divorce decrees are generally recognised in Indonesia insofar as the decrees are not challenged by one of the spouses in front of an Indonesian court. A foreign divorce decree obtained by an Indonesian can be registered in Indonesia in accordance with Article 41 of the Population Administration Act 2006 as amended in 2013. Legal separation does not exist in Indonesia, thus foreign decrees of legal separation will not be recognised, and cannot be registered, in Indonesia. With regard to foreign decrees of nullity of marriage, theoretically they are recognised in Indonesia like foreign decrees of divorce. However, since the Population Administration Act 2006 as amended in 2013 does not provide rules for registering foreign nullity decrees, it may be up to the Indonesian civil registry offices to register or not to register the foreign nullity decrees.

c. Judgments on Matters Relating to the Well-Being of the Child

Foreign judgments on matters relating to the well-being of a child are categorised as condemnatory judgments when the judgments give custody of a child to one of the parents, or when the judgments order parents to provide financial relief for their children.[38] As explained earlier, a judgment is condemnatory when it punishes a party, for example ordering them to provide payment or relinquish a right. Following Article 436 Rv and doctrine, foreign condemnatory judgments cannot be recognised in Indonesia.[39] The previous chapter presents a case concerning a foreign custody judgment that the Indonesian court refused to recognise.[40] Because Indonesia is not a party to any conventions concerning parental obligations, family maintenance, and civil aspects of child abduction, foreign judgments that order parents to pay maintenance obligation or to relinquish a parent's custody to a child are not recognised in Indonesia. A foreign judgment that gives an illegitimate child status as a descendant of an Indonesian man is categorised as declaratory in nature. Therefore, the judgment can be recognised in Indonesia, especially after the 2012 Constitutional Court's judicial review of Article 43, paragraph (1) of the Marriage Act 1974 that results in the establishment of civil relations between illegitimate children and their biological fathers.

[38] Gautama, *Perdata Internasional Jilid III Bag 2* (n 6) 224, 289.

[39] ibid, 282.

[40] In the case of District Court of South Jakarta Decision 210/Pdt/G/1992/PN.JKT.Sel (not published), Indonesian judges in the Jakarta court kept processing a custody dispute between an Indonesian husband and a German wife, although a German court already processed the same custody dispute and issued a provisional ruling earlier. See also Supancana, *Naskah Akademik* (n 7) 50.

But, the part of the same foreign judgment that orders the Indonesian man to pay maintenance obligation to his illegitimate child will not be recognised in Indonesia because the part of the judgment is categorised as condemnatory in nature.

In short, judgments on matters relating to the well-being of a child are not recognisable because such judgments are generally condemnatory, such as ordering a parent to provide payment or to relinquish his or her custody of a child. Foreign judgments that give illegitimate children status as descendants of an Indonesian father can be recognised, but the parts of such judgments that order the Indonesian father to pay a maintenance obligation to his child cannot be recognised in Indonesia.

v. Law of Bankruptcy and Law of Corporations and Insolvency

The Bankruptcy and Suspension of Debt Payment Act 2004 does not distinguish corporate insolvency from personal bankruptcy. Article 2, paragraph (1) of the Act provides that,

> A debtor who has two or more creditors and fails to pay at least one debt which has matured and become payable, can be declared bankrupt through a court decision, either by the debtor's own petition or by the request of one or more of the debtor's creditors.

Unlike in some other countries where the term bankruptcy applies only to individuals, the terms 'bankruptcy', 'insolvency', and 'suspension of obligation for debt payments' in Indonesia are applied to both individuals and corporations. Article 1 of the Act defines bankruptcy as general confiscation of all assets of a bankrupt debtor that will be managed and liquidated by a curator under the supervision of a supervisory judge. The Elucidation of Article 57, paragraph (1) describes insolvency as the condition of being unable to pay debts. The suspension of obligation for debt payments in the Bankruptcy Act 2004 is a procedure taken either by the debtor or creditor before a bankruptcy petition to allow the debtor to restructure its debt. Foreign judgments concerning insolvency, bankruptcy, and suspension of obligation for debt payments are categorised by doctrine as constitutive judgments. Therefore, such judgments can be recognised in Indonesia.[41] This principle is also applied in Presidential Regulation No 8 of 2007 concerning Ratification of the Convention on International Interests in Mobile Equipment (Cape Town Convention) and Aircraft Equipment Protocol. The presidential regulation declares that Indonesian courts shall cooperate with foreign courts and foreign administrators in carrying remedies on the insolvency of debtors, namely returning aircraft objects to the creditors' possession. However, this particular provision regarding cooperation with foreign courts and foreign administrators in airline insolvency has never been tested, as foreign creditors prefer the mechanism of Irrevocable De-Registration and Export Request Authorisation (IDERA) provided by the Cape Town Convention and Aircraft Equipment Protocol. In Indonesia, the repossession of aircrafts through the IDERA mechanism by foreign creditors is usually taken before the insolvency proceeding begins[42] and does not require any court action or court order (Article 75 of the Aviation Act).

[41] Gautama, *Perdata Internasional Jilid III Bag 2* (n 6) 285.

[42] See the case of Batavia Air bankruptcy as reported in A Qodir, 'Banyak Pesawat Batavia Ditarik Pemilik Sebelum Dinyatakan Pailit' (*Tribunnews.com*, 31 January 2013) www.tribunnews.com/nasional/2013/01/31/banyak-pesawat-batavia-ditarik-pemilik-sebelum-dinyatakan-pailit (accessed 16 March 2019).

It is essential to note that the recognition of foreign judgments concerning insolvency, bankruptcy, and suspension of obligation for debt payments does not extend to the status of the debtor's assets in Indonesia. The recognition of judgments will not affect the debtor's rights to their assets in Indonesia, as the right to properties situated in Indonesia is governed by Indonesian law, in accordance with Article 17 AB.[43] In addition, Article 99, paragraphs (8) and (9) Rv stipulate that Indonesian courts have jurisdiction over cases that involve immovable properties located in Indonesia. This means that when foreign creditors need to administer, manage, or liquidate the debtor's assets that are located in Indonesia, the foreign creditors must first present an insolvency or bankruptcy petition in the Indonesian courts.

In conclusion, foreign judgments regarding insolvency, bankruptcy, and suspension of obligation for debt payments are categorised as constitutive judgments and can therefore be recognised in Indonesia. However, recognition does not affect the debtor's rights to their assets situated in Indonesia. Foreign creditors who need to administer, manage, or liquidate the debtor's assets that are located in Indonesia must file an insolvency or bankruptcy petition in Indonesian courts, in accordance with Article 17 AB, Article 99 Rv, and Article 436 Rv.

vi. Competition Law

Foreign judgments in the field of competition law, either made by foreign competition regulators or by foreign courts, will not be recognised in Indonesia if they are categorised as condemnatory judgments. For instance, orders to pay compensation and damages to plaintiffs in competition cases are categorised as condemnatory judgments so are not recognised in Indonesia. In addition, a foreign interim injunctive relief in the field of competition law will not be recognised because interim injunction is not a final and binding judgment. To be recognised in Indonesia, a foreign judgment must be final and binding. As in other areas, foreign declaratory and constitutive judgments in the field of competition law are recognised in Indonesia based on the prevailing legal doctrine. For example, a foreign judgment that nullifies an agreement considered to be anti-competitive is categorised as a constitutive judgment and thus may be recognised in Indonesia.

II. Enforcement of Judgments

A. Means of Enforcing Judgments in Indonesia

In principle, foreign judgments are not enforceable in Indonesia. The basis of this principle is Article 436 Rv, which provides:

> (1) All judgements made by foreign courts are unenforceable in Indonesian territory, except in the matters mentioned in Article 724 of Commercial Code and in other regulations.
> (2) Those [other] matters can be brought again in front of and judged by Indonesian courts.

[43] Concerning immovable property, the law of the country or place where the property is located, applies. (Art 17 AB).

(3) For matters exempted by paragraph (1), foreign judgments can be enforced only after an exequatur is requested and is granted by an Indonesian court in the district where the judgment shall be enforced.
(4) The merit of the case shall not be re-examined when requesting and granting the aforementioned exequatur.

Based upon Article 436 Rv, foreign judgments related to Article 724 of the Commercial Code are enforceable in Indonesia. Article 724 paragraph (5) of the Commercial Code grants foreign authorities power to make judgments in maritime general average that involve Indonesian parties. Under Article 436, paragraphs (3) and (4), if the cargo owners or ship owners are domiciled in Indonesia, the judgments can be brought before Indonesian courts to obtain an exequatur or execution order without review of their merits. As the only law that governs the recognition and enforcement of foreign judgments in Indonesia, Article 436 Rv does not say whether the judgment on general average must be a final judgment (ie a judgment which can no longer be appealed or reviewed) to be executed in Indonesia. However, the Indonesian Civil Procedural Law[44] that allows execution of a judgment that is still being appealed to a higher court is only applicable to a judgment rendered by a domestic court, not by a foreign court. Therefore, in the author's opinion, it is up to the Indonesian enforcing court to execute (or not) a foreign judgment in general average that is still being appealed in the rendering country. To date, there are no other regulations that allow foreign judgments to be enforced in Indonesia. In addition, Indonesia is not a party to any treaty or convention on the recognition and enforcement of judgments. In the absence of treaties and conventions, the enforcement of foreign judgments cannot be sought in Indonesia. The claim must be re-litigated before an Indonesian court in order to obtain a court order of enforcement. In adjudicating the claim, an Indonesian court may use its discretion to accept the foreign judgment as prima facie evidence, or take the foreign judgment as an authentic deed that has value as impeccable evidence during the re-litigation.[45] However, the Indonesian court may also choose to give no regard to foreign judgments because, in principle, foreign judgments are unenforceable in Indonesia.

Article 436 Rv applies only to condemnatory judgments, with constitutive and declaratory judgments falling outside its scope. This means that the latter judgments can be recognised and enforced in Indonesia by following certain procedures that will be explained in the following sub-chapter.

B. Procedures for Enforcing Judgments

Based upon Article 436 Rv and the fact that Indonesia is not a party to any treaty or convention on the enforcement of judgments, foreign condemnatory judgments are not enforceable

[44] Art 180, para (1) *Het Herziene Indonesisch Reglement* (Renewed Indonesian Code); Art 191, para (1) *Rechtsreglement Buitengewesten* (Code of Procedure for Areas Outside Java and Madura), Arts 54–57 *Reglement op de Rechtvordering* (Code of Civil Procedure), *Surat Edaran Mahkamah Agung* (Supreme Court Circular Letter) No 3 of 2000 concerning *putusan serta merta (uitvoerbaar bij vooraad) dan provisionil* (immediate and provisional judgments), and *Surat Edaran Mahkamah Agung* No 4 of 2001 concerning *permasalahan putusan serta merta (uitvoerbaar bij voorraad) dan provisionil* (issues of judgments with immediate execution and provisional judgments).

[45] Gautama, 'Recognition and Enforcement' (n 5); R Subekti, *Arbitrase Perdagangan* (Binacipta, 1981) 28; Harahap, *Hukum Acara* (n 4) 136.

in Indonesia. The only exception to this principle is the enforcement of foreign judgments in maritime general average that involve Indonesian parties. If the cargo owners or ship owners are domiciled in Indonesia, the judgments can be brought before the Indonesian courts to obtain an exequatur or execution order without review of the merits of the foreign judgments. The execution of the judgments will follow the provisions of Indonesian Civil Procedure Codes.[46]

Since Article 436 Rv applies only to condemnatory judgments, foreign declaratory and constitutive judgments can be recognised and enforced in Indonesia insofar as they do not offend Indonesia's public policy. Declaratory and constitutive judgments confirm a legal status or create a new legal condition for the parties, as in the cases of ownership of a property, adoption, or divorce. Therefore, to enforce foreign declaratory and constitutive judgments, interested parties may register the relevant judgment in an Indonesian civil registry office. This will change their legal status in accordance with the foreign judgments.[47]

To be enforceable in Indonesia, a foreign judgment and its supporting documents, such as certificates, must be legalised by the Ministry of Justice and Ministry of Foreign Affairs of the country in which the judgment is made, and by the Indonesian Diplomatic Office in that country. Afterwards, the foreign judgment has to be translated into Indonesian by a sworn translator.[48] After following the procedure, a foreign condemnatory judgment in maritime general average can be used to obtain an exequatur from an Indonesian court, and a foreign declaratory or constitutive judgment can be registered in a civil registry office.

[46] 1941 *Het Herziene Indonesisch Reglement* (Renewed Indonesian Code/HIR); 1927 Rechtsreglement Buitengewesten (Civil Procedure Code for Indigenous Outside Java and Madura/Rbg); 1847 *Reglement op de Burgerlijke Rechtsvordering* (Civil Procedure Code/Rv).

[47] Gautama, *Perdata Internasional Jilid III Bag 2* (n 6) 282–283.

[48] Annex of Regulation of Foreign Minister No 09/A/KP/XII/2006/01 dated 28 December 2006, point 70. See also Dit. Hukum and Perjanjian Sosial Budaya, 'Ketentuan Nasional' (Rogatory Online Monitoring) 'Rogatory Online Monitoring' http://rogatori.kemlu.go.id/nasional (accessed 17 December 2018).

5

Arbitration

Arbitration is now the preferred method for resolving commercial disputes in many countries, including Indonesia. Many private as well as government agreements and contracts use arbitration as their dispute settlement mechanism.[1] There are several reasons for this, namely the parties' ability to appoint arbitrators who are experts in their fields; the confidentiality of arbitration;[2] the lack of provision for appeals, making the decision final and binding; and the relative speed of the dispute resolution process in comparison with the ordinary judicial process. Increased interest in the use of arbitration can also be attributed to the nature of the award itself, which can be enforced internationally. In Indonesia, arbitration is often chosen because of the corruption, collusion and nepotism known in the judicial process.[3]

The main domestic arbitration institution in Indonesia is the Indonesian National Arbitration Board ('BANI'). The establishment of BANI was prompted by discussions about the need for 'private justice' in the form of an autonomous and independent commercial dispute resolution agency. On 3 December 1977, the Indonesian Chamber of Commerce and Industry ('KADIN') formed BANI as an institution that specifically provided fair and fast resolution in trade, industry and financial disputes both national and international in nature.[4] BANI was, and is, intended to resolve these commercial disputes without the need to go to court. Recently however, BANI has seemingly split into two entities; the original entity created in 1977 (BANI Mampang) and a new entity formed in 2016 that calls itself *BANI Pembaharuan* (BANI Sovereign). These two entities battled it out across the Indonesian court system to determine which has the legitimacy to call itself 'BANI', causing conflict and disunity in the process. This disorder was ended by the Supreme Court in decision No 232K/TUN/2018, which won BANI Mampang the sole right to use the name BANI, making it the BANI version of the Indonesian Chamber of Commerce. In addition to BANI, special arbitration bodies handle various types of disputes; among them are the Indonesia Capital Market Arbitration Board for capital market disputes ('BAPMI'), and the National Syariah Arbitration Board for Islamic banking matters ('BASYARNAS').

[1] In 2018, there were 62 parties which involved Indonesian companies at the Singapore International Arbitration Center ('SIAC'). That number jumped dramatically from previous years. In comparison, in 2017 there were only 32 parties that involved Indonesian companies in SIAC. The number 62 places Indonesia as the number 5 country with the most cases in SIAC, after the US, India, Malaysia and China. In fact, that number does not include cases involving Indonesian companies in the International Chamber of Commerce ('ICC'), the London Court of International Arbitration ('LCIA'), and the Hong Kong International Arbitration Center ('HKIAC').

[2] RMGP Soemartono, 'Finalitas Putusan Arbitrase Internasional: Analisis Pasal 52 Konvensi "ICSID"' (1997) 4(3) *Era Hukum. Jurnal Ilmiah Hukum* 60, 61; P Abdurrasyid, *Suatu Pengantar Arbitrase dan Alternatif Penyelesaian Sengketa* (Fikahati Aneska, 2002), 53.

[3] RI Tektona, 'Arbitrase sebagai Alternatif Solusi Penyelesaian Sengketa Bisnis di Luar Pengadilan' (2011) 6(1) *Pandecta* 86, 90.

[4] G Soemartono, *Arbitrase dan Mediasi di Indonesia* (Gramedia Pustaka Utama, 2006) 97.

Indonesia is a member of several international conventions related to arbitration, including the United Nations Convention on the Recognition and Enforcement of Foreign Arbitral Awards 1958 (the 1958 New York Convention) which was acceded to on 7 October 1981 through Presidential Decree No 34 of 1981. This was followed by the Supreme Court Regulation No 1 of 1990, an implementing regulation concerning the procedure for enforcing foreign arbitral awards (the Supreme Court Regulation No 1 of 1990). Since public international law is non self-executing in Indonesia, the theory of transformation is used so that international law (in this case international treaties) can be applied in the Indonesian domestic legal system. As a civil law country, international agreements such as the 1958 New York Convention need to be transformed into the form of national legislation such as laws or presidential regulations.[5] In addition, Indonesia has also ratified the Washington Convention on the Settlement of Investment Disputes between States and Nationals of Other States 1965 (the ICSID Convention) through the Investment Disputes Settlement between States and Foreign Nationals Act 1968. The Indonesian legal basis for the settlement of disputes through arbitration is the Arbitration Act 1999, which supersedes arbitration provisions contained in the Indonesian Civil Procedure Codes,[6] which was inherited from the Dutch colonial period. Although the Arbitration Act 1999 does not adopt the UNCITRAL Model Law on International Commercial Arbitration 1985,[7] it does address most of the crucial aspects of arbitration, such the power of courts to assist arbitration proceedings and the procedure and requirements for enforcing international arbitral awards.

This chapter begins by reviewing the international aspect of the Arbitration Act 1999. It then discusses the laws and practice of international arbitration in Indonesia which is divided into two parts, namely international commercial arbitration and investment treaty arbitration.

The Arbitration Act 1999 consists of 11 Chapters and 82 Articles. While the Act does not explain the difference in definition between national and international arbitration, it plainly distinguishes between the two, with most of its Articles regulating the conduct of national (domestic) arbitration and just a small number involving (but not regulating) international arbitration.[8] Notably, the Arbitration Act 1999 specifically includes the word 'international' to indicate that an arbitral award is not domestic. While the 1958 New York Convention and the Supreme Court Regulation No 1 of 1990 use the term 'foreign' arbitral award, the Arbitration Act 1999 uses the term 'international' to denote the same concept. As stated

[5] Art 9 of Act No 24 of 2000 concerning International Agreement.

[6] Art 81 of the Arbitration Act 1999 states that in the time this Act comes into force, the provisions concerning arbitration as referred to in Arts 615–651 of the *Reglement op de Burgerlijke Rechtsvordering, Staatsblad* 1847:52, Art 377 of *Het Herziene Indonesisch Reglement, Staatsblad* 1941: 44 and Art 705 of *Rechtsreglement Buitengewesten, Staatsblad* 1927: 227, are declared invalid.

[7] AFM Gerungan, L Alizia and R Sitorus, 'Indonesia' in J Tirado (ed), *International Arbitration* 1st edn (Global Legal Group, 2015) 163.

[8] The Arbitration Act 1999, Chapter VI of the second part is under the heading 'International Arbitration', contains 5 Articles, namely Arts 66 to 70. The five articles also regulate the implementation of international arbitration decisions in Indonesia, namely the authority of the court in the application for the implementation of foreign arbitral awards (Art 65); the requirements for the application of the decision (Art 66), the requirement for the registration of judgments (Art 67); the closing of the appeal against the verdict of the district court that granted the request for the implementation of a foreign arbitration award (Art 68); and the authority of the head of the district court (Art 70).

earlier, the Act does not expressly address the distinction between domestic and international arbitration and only governs the conduct of domestic arbitration; nevertheless, several Articles indicate that the Act is receptive to international arbitration proceedings. In particular, references to the 'international' element can be found in the definition of international arbitration awards in Article 1, paragraph (9) of the Arbitration Act 1999. This Article defines an international arbitration award as an award imposed by an arbitration or an individual arbitrator outside of the jurisdiction of the Republic of Indonesia, or an award of an arbitration institution or individual arbitrator that under the provisions of the laws of the Republic of Indonesia is considered to be an international arbitral award. To date, the latter half of this formulation has no effect, as no Indonesian legal provision outside of Article 1, paragraph (9) of the Arbitration Act 1999 regulates when an arbitral award will be considered international rather than domestic. Hence, it is suggested that an elaboration addressing this point be made in the elucidation section of the Act, to avoid confusion and legal uncertainty. In addition, Article 34, paragraph (1) states that dispute settlement through arbitration can be performed through a national or international institution based on an agreement among the parties. Article 34, paragraph (2) states that such disputes referred to in paragraph (1) shall be conducted in accordance with the rules and procedures of the chosen institution, unless the parties stipulate otherwise. The above provisions indicate that the Arbitration Act 1999 recognises the freedom of the parties to refer their disputes to either a national or international arbitration institution. Therefore, although the Act does not expressly draw any distinction between domestic and international arbitration, it is in principle receptive to international arbitration. Before moving on, it should be emphasised that Article 1, paragraph (9) does not specifically limit the meaning of international arbitration and only limits the meaning of international arbitration awards. Many suggest the Law should be revised.[9] Apart from being out of date with arbitral developments, the failure to clearly distinguish national and international arbitration may produce legal uncertainty. Definition of 'international arbitration awards' is not enough to make clear the meaning of the distinct and broader concept of 'international arbitration'. The meaning of both international and national arbitration should be clarified by definition.

The definition contained in Article 1, paragraph (9) makes clear that 'international arbitration award' can only have two alternative meanings. Namely, any award made outside of the territory of Indonesia (for example in Singapore or London); or any award issued by a permanent or ad hoc institution which under Indonesian law is considered as an international arbitral award. Any other award must be classified as a domestic arbitral award. The first alternative is relatively clear, namely an arbitral award (which is institutionalised or ad hoc) insofar as it is made outside of the jurisdiction of Indonesia is considered an international arbitral award. Problems arise when considering the second alternative. Though the explanation of this Article's provisions states that the definition given in this Article is clear,[10] the phrase 'which according to the laws of the Republic of Indonesia is considered

[9] For example, the Indonesian National Arbitration Board (BANI) continues to push for the revision of the Arbitration Act 1999. See also H Adolf, 'Urgensi Pembentukan Undang-Undang tentang Arbitrase Internasional' (2016) 10(2) *Fiat Justicia* 317, 329; M Situmorang, 'Pelaksanaan Putusan Arbitrase Nasional di Indonesia' (2017) 17(4) *Jurnal Penelitian Hukum De Jure* 309, 319.

[10] See the Elucidation of the Arbitration Act 1999.

an international arbitration decision' has the potential to yield to multiple interpretations. The case *PT Lirik Petroleum v PT Pertamina* can serve as an example of how Indonesian judges interpret the meaning of 'international' in this context.[11] The case concerned a dispute between PT Lirik Petroleum, an Indonesian oil and gas company and PT Pertamina, an Indonesian state-owned entity in the oil and gas sector, regarding Pertamina's refusal of Lirik's commercialisation application over a number of oil and gas fields in Indonesia. Lirik filed for arbitration with the International Chamber of Commerce ('ICC'), as the choice of forum in the underlying agreement between the parties named the Enhanced Oil Recovery ('EOR') Contract, with the arbitration venue in Jakarta. In its final award dated 27 February 2009, the ICC tribunal decided in favour of Lirik and ordered Pertamina to indemnify Lirik as well as to pay the arbitration costs.[12] The arbitral award was registered at the Central Jakarta District Court for enforcement. Pertamina immediately applied for annulment of the award at the same Court. The Central Jakarta District Court rejected the annulment application to which Pertamina responded by filing an appeal against the decision. One of the problems this case raised was whether the ICC award made in Jakarta could be considered a domestic arbitration. Based on Article 1, paragraph (9) above, Pertamina argued that the award was domestic because it had been issued in Indonesia, and therefore the registration of the award should be conducted in accordance with the provisions applicable for the domestic award.[13] However, PT Lirik argued the dispute showed international aspects, namely the choice of forum (ICC arbitration); the currency used in the contract (US dollar); and the intention of Pertamina at the signing of the EOR agreement to use an arbitration institution that was not a national arbitration body. In its decision, the Central Jakarta District Court stated that the ICC award made in Indonesia was an international arbitration award. The Supreme Court ruling also upheld the District Court's ruling notwithstanding the fact that the arbitration was seated in Indonesia and that the existence of 'foreign factors' in the case was due to the fact that an overseas arbitration institution had administered the arbitration.[14] This dispute illustrates how the significance of the distinction between international and domestic arbitral awards, and how uncertainty in the legal definition of international arbitral awards raises problems in Indonesia. The decision in *PT Lirik Petroleum v PT Pertamina* can be contrasted with the awards in the cases of *PT Aero Systems v Hewlett Packard*, and *PT Kurnia Sentosa Kahuripan v Hanampi Sejahtera*, where in classifying the arbitration awards the court did not take the foreign elements into consideration. Indeed, the court rigidly applied territorial factors, providing that since the decision was imposed on Indonesia the award was domestic.[15]

[11] *PT Lirik Petroleum v PT Pertamina*, ICC Case No 14387/JB/JEM, Partial Award, (22 September 2008) and Final Award (27 February 2009).

[12] T Sukirno and R Hirdarisvita, 'Indonesia' in Baker & McKenzie and N Thevenin (eds), *The Baker & McKenzie International Arbitration Yearbook: 2010–2011* (JurisNet, LLC, 2011) 55.

[13] Art 59 of the Arbitration Act 1999 stipulates that the domestic arbitral award must be registered within 30 days after the award is rendered.

[14] District Court of Central Jakarta Decision 01/Pembatalan Arbitrase/2009/PN.JKT.PST (3 September 2009); Supreme Court Decision 904K/PDT.SUS/2009 (9 June 2010); Supreme Court Extraordinary Appeal 56 PK/PDT.SUS/2011 (23 August 2011).

[15] BANI Decision No 641/XII/ARB-BANI/2014 (27 January 2016); BANI Decision No 628/XI/ARB-BANI/2014 (15 February 2016).

Note that the approach used in the Arbitration Act 1999 was not based on criteria that have been generally accepted by the international community as contained in the UNCITRAL Model Law on International Commercial Arbitration. The Model Law establishes a standard to serve as a basis for the harmonisation of national arbitration laws, on the basis that such harmonisation increases consistency and predictability in international arbitration, and therefore the fairness and efficiency of the settlement of international commercial disputes.[16] Despite this, Indonesia is one of four countries that has not adopted the Model Law.[17] Harmonisation with the Model Law is needed to ensure legal certainty in conducting international arbitration proceedings in Indonesia.

I. International Commercial Arbitration

A. Jurisdiction of the Arbitral Tribunal

The basis of the jurisdiction of arbitral tribunals differs from the basis of the jurisdiction of domestic courts. The court's jurisdiction is based on state power in the judiciary, while the jurisdiction of an arbitral tribunal originates from the agreement of the parties.[18] The 1958 New York Convention acknowledges the freedom of the parties to choose their own jurisdiction or arbitration forum as a way of resolving disputes that may have arisen among them. The agreement to choose the arbitration jurisdiction, overriding the general court forum, must be in written form and in respect of a defined legal relationship.[19] The autonomy of the parties is binding, therefore the parties as well as the court must respect this freedom, except insofar as such freedom is contrary to public policy or mandatory law (see below). The freedom to choose an ad hoc or institutional arbitration to resolve disputes is also recognised in Indonesia. Dispute resolution institutions outside of the court have been recognised for some time. The provisions of Article 134 HIR/160 Rbg[20] explicitly stated that if a dispute is in a case that is not included in the power of the district court, then at any time during the examination of that case it may be requested that the court declare its lack of jurisdiction. Today, the Arbitration Act 1999 recognises the competence principle under which district courts lack jurisdiction to hear disputes between parties bound by an arbitration agreement.[21] The agreement must contain an arbitration clause in writing, or in a separate agreement made after a dispute arises.[22] The arbitration clause should state, among

[16] DJA Cairns, 'The Spanish Application of the UNCITRAL Model Law on International Commercial Arbitration' (2006) 22(4) *Arbitration International* 573, 573–596.

[17] The other 3 states are Laos, Myanmar and Vietnam.

[18] SA Nugroho, *Penyelesaian Sengketa Arbitrase dan Penerapan Hukumnya* (Prenada Media 2016) 104.

[19] Art 2 of the 1958 New York Convention. See also SL Anindita, 'Hukum yang Dipergunakan dalam Kontrak Dagang Internasional' (2008) 5 *Indonesian Journal of International Law* 537, 544; TL Tuegeh-Longdong, *Asas Ketertiban Umum dan Konvensi New York 1958: sebuah tinjauan atas pelaksanaan Konvensi New York 1958 pada putusan-putusan Mahkamah Agung RI dan Pengadilan Asing* (PT Citra Aditya Bakti, 1998) 20.

[20] Art 134 HIR/160 Rbg states that 'If the dispute is a case that is not within the jurisdiction of the district court, then at any time in the examination of the case, it can be requested that the judge declare that he is not authorized and the obligation must also be acknowledged because of his position.'

[21] The Arbitration Act 1999, Art 3.

[22] ibid, Art 1, para (3).

other information, the parties' intention to settle any dispute through arbitration, the rules governing arbitration, and the seat of arbitration. The existence of a written arbitration agreement negates the right of the parties to submit the dispute to the district court.[23] Hence, the courts must dismiss and avoid interference in any dispute that is to be settled by arbitration, except in certain circumstances specified in the Arbitration Act 1999.[24] This rule is known as the limited court intervention principle,[25] and is one of the key principles of the 2006 UNCITRAL Model Law on International Commercial Arbitration. The prohibition of court interference is meant to assert that arbitration is an independent institution which the court must respect.[26]

The case between *PT Garuda Indonesia v Birgen Air Singapore*[27] is one example in which the court has rightly stated that the parties' choice of forum must be respected and binding. In the leasing contract, the parties agreed to resolve any dispute through arbitration in Jakarta. When a dispute occurred in 2012, PT Garuda Indonesia sued Birgen Air in an arbitration tribunal based in Singapura. The Singapore Court of Appeal declined jurisdiction on the basis of its initial finding that the seat of arbitration was in Indonesia. The Court pointed out that an arbitration hearing held outside of the seat of arbitration does not and cannot in itself change the legal seat of arbitration. As an example of a law overriding arbitration agreement, it is worth mentioning a decision of the Supreme Court in the bankruptcy case between *PT Putra Putri Fortuna Windu, et al v PT Environmental Network Indonesia, et al.*[28] In this case, although the parties had agreed that all disputes, including those relating to bankruptcy, had to be settled through arbitration, the Indonesian Supreme Court refused and set aside the applicability of the arbitration agreement. In doing so, the Court relied on the Bankruptcy and Suspension of Debt Payment Act 2004, which gives the Commercial Court absolute jurisdiction over bankruptcy issues in Indonesia as long as the underlying debt that is the ground for the bankruptcy application is due and payable under Article 2(1) of the Bankruptcy Act 2004.[29]

As stated above, courts in Indonesia are not allowed under any circumstances to entertain objections to arbitration while an arbitration agreement exists. However, the practice of the Indonesian courts is evidently otherwise.[30] In the case *Perusahaan Listrik Negara ('PLN') v Paiton*,[31] the Central Jakarta District Court decided to disregard the arbitration clause in the Power Purchase Agreement between the parties. PLN argued that the agreement was contrary to law, morality and public order, and hence it was null and void. Further,

[23] ibid, Art 11, para (1); See also B Sutiyoso, *Penyelesaian Sengketa Bisnis* (Citra Media, 2006) 18.

[24] The Arbitration Act 1999, Art 11, para (2).

[25] Soemartono, *Arbitrase dan Mediasi* (n 4) 70–71; See also Art 134 HIR.

[26] B Sutiyoso, 'Akibat Pemilihan Forum dalam Kontrak yang Memuat Klausula Arbitrase', (2012) 24 *Mimbar Hukum* 159, 167.

[27] *PT Garuda Indonesia v Birgen Air*, [2002] 1 SLR(R) 401.

[28] Supreme Court Extraordinary Appeal 13 PK/N/1999 (12 May 1999).

[29] Art 303 of the Bankruptcy Act 2004; the field of business competition is also an issue of absolute authority. In the Indonesian legal system, the Business Competition Supervisory Committee has the authority to handle business competition disputes. Whereas the commercial court has the authority to hear bankruptcy and intellectual property rights disputes.

[30] GA Bermann, 'Interpretation and Application of the New York Convention by National Courts' in M Schauer and B Verschraegen (eds), *General Reports of the XIXth Congress of the International Academy of Comparative Law, Rapports Généraux du XIXème Congrès de l'Académie Internationale de Droit Comparé, Ius Comparatum- Global Studies in Comparative Law* 1st edn (Springer, 2017) 44.

[31] District Court of Central Jakarta Interlocutory Decision No 517/Pdt.G/1999/PNJKT.PST (13 December 1999).

PLN also argued that, since the arbitration clause in the agreement was also null and void, the District Court had jurisdiction to hear the dispute. The Court decided that the existence of an arbitration clause was inappropriate and hence unjustified as an exception to the jurisdiction of the Court.[32] Unfortunately, the Court did not elaborate further as to what makes an exception to the Court's jurisdiction inappropriate. In *Perusahaan Listrik Negara ('PLN') v Paiton*, the judge took the opinion that the main agreement with the arbitration clause constitutes a single unit. Hence, if the main agreement is annulled, the arbitration clause will also become invalid.[33] Yet this directly contradicts Article 10(h) of the Arbitration Act 1999, which clearly stipulates that agreements to resolve disputes through arbitration, or an arbitration clause within a broader agreement, can be carried out even if the main agreement is null and void.

Claimants may also seek to avoid an arbitration agreement which avoids the jurisdiction of the courts by arguing that the dispute does not concern a breach of contract but is instead a tort claim. Tort claims fall outside of the scope of such arbitration agreements, falling instead under the jurisdiction of the courts. If such an argument is successful, the dispute then falls under the category of an unlawful act pursuant to Article 1365 BW, whereby every unlawful act causing losses to another person obligates the person who is responsible for such losses to pay compensation. In practice, an unlawful act has been interpreted broadly to mean violations of statutory law as well as unwritten norms of law. This concept and interpretation are left to the courts to decide, which leads to debate over how to distinguish a tort from a breach of contract. In such an event, the defendants may challenge the jurisdiction of the court under Article 134 HIR. By classifying the claim as tort (not arbitrable), the courts take jurisdiction over the dispute, thus terminating the jurisdiction of arbitral tribunals in that matter. In practice, there are still several instances in which the district court adopts this approach in order to deny the absolute jurisdiction of arbitration, by examining and adjudicating disputes submitted by parties bound to an arbitration clause. For example, in *PT Perusahaan Dagang Tempo (PT Tempo) v PT Roche Indonesia*,[34] the South Jakarta District Court decided to hear a dispute even though an arbitration agreement existed. The Court argued that the dispute arose from a tort action, and therefore should not be settled through arbitration.

However, the Supreme Court has not been receptive to such arguments. The Indonesian Supreme Court seems to have taken the opinion that in cases bound by an arbitration agreement the arbitration institution has the absolute authority.[35] The Court's interference in certain matters can only be carried out to facilitate the arbitration process, for example to obtain the executorial power of an arbitral award.[36] To support this opinion, in 2005 the Supreme Court issued guidelines affirming that district courts' lack of jurisdiction to hear any disputes between parties bound by an arbitration agreement, even

[32] G Soemartono, 'Interpretation and Application of the New York Convention in Indonesia', in GA Bermann (ed), *Recognition and Enforcement of Foreign Arbitral Awards, The Interpretation and Application of the New York Convention by National Courts* (Springer, 2017) 483.

[33] District Court of Central Jakarta Interlocutory Decision No 517/Pdt.G/1999/PNJKT.PST (13 December 1999).

[34] District Court of South Jakarta Interlocutory Decision No 454/Pdt.G/1999/PN/Jak.Sel (25 January 2000).

[35] Sutiyoso, *Penyelesaian Sengketa Bisnis* (n 23), 26.

[36] Ibid See also Soemartono, *Arbitrase dan Mediasi* (n 4) 71; Rajagukguk, *Arbitrase dalam Putusan* (n 2) 13–14.

if the claims are based on an unlawful act as defined by Article 1365 BW.[37] The guidelines were applied in the case of *Government of the Regency of Pasir, v Samtan Co. Ltd, PT Kideco Jaya Agung, and Samchully Pharmaceutical Co. Ltd.* The Tanah Grogot District Court, Tanah Grogot Appellate Court and the Supreme Court dismissed the Regency of Pasir's unlawful act lawsuit on the basis that Indonesian courts have no jurisdiction to hear a case in which both parties are bound by an arbitration clause.[38] Another example is the case of *PT Pertamina v PT Lirik*. After the Supreme Court dismissed Pertamina's appeal and affirmed the judgment of the Central Jakarta District Court, Pertamina sued Lirik, the ICC, the ICC tribunal and Lirik's counsel on the grounds of unlawful act/tort. In essence, Pertamina claimed that the way the ICC Tribunal adjudicated the dispute and the registration of the arbitral award were violations of the civil responsibility of the defendants, conducted without good faith. The defendants refuted this claim by arguing that the arbitration clause in the EOR Contracts eliminated the jurisdiction of the South Jakarta District Court in this matter, and that by agreeing to use the ICC Arbitration Rules the parties had agreed to grant the tribunal and the ICC immunity from any lawsuit. On 5 August 2010, the District Court of South Jakarta decided that it had no jurisdiction to hear the case.[39] Both cases offer evidence of Indonesia's ever-increasing awareness of the jurisdiction of arbitral panels.

In addition, a dispute can be settled through an arbitration if it is of a commercial nature and involves the rights of the disputed parties.[40] An indication of what constitutes disputes of a commercial nature can be found in Article 66 of the Arbitration Act 1999, which states that '[i]nternational arbitration awards as contemplated in [the] item above, are limited to awards which under the provision of Indonesian law fall within the scope of commercial law'. The Elucidation of Article 66(b) of the same Act assists in determining what fields are deemed to be of a commercial nature. These include, among others, commerce, banking, finance, investment, industry and intellectual property rights. This list above is not comprehensive; other fields not mentioned there may still be arbitrable. A guideline as to types of disputes that cannot be referred to arbitration can be found in Article 5, paragraph (2) of the Arbitration Act. This provides a negative formulation regarding disputes that are considered unable to be resolved through arbitration, namely disputes which according to laws and regulations cannot be settled, as regulated in the Civil Code of Book III of the eighteenth Chapter of Article 1851 to 1854. The classic examples of disputes that are not arbitrable are those relating to family law and criminal offences.[41] In practice, disputes that cannot be submitted to arbitration are, among others: criminal cases; industrial

[37] Sukirno, Kadir, and Hirdarisvita, Baker & McKenzie, *The Baker & McKenzie International Arbitration Yearbook* (n 12) 260.

[38] District Court of Tanah Grogot Decision No 07/Pdt.G/2003/PN.TG (23 December 2003); High Court of Tanah Grogot Decision No 47/Pdt/2004/PT.KT.SMDA (18 May 2004); Supreme Court Decision No 790/K/Pdt/2006 (5 February 2007).

[39] District Court of South Jakarta Decision No 1388/Pdt.G/2009/PN.Jkt.Sel.Tahun 2009 (19 August 2010); District Court of South Jakarta Decision was annulled by High Court of Jakarta Decision No 04/PDT/2011/PT.DKI (14 July 2011). However, the Supreme Court justified the decision of South Jakarta District Court through the Supreme Court Decision No 203 K/Pdt/2012 (29 June 2012).

[40] The Arbitration Act 1999, Art 5, para (1).

[41] T Bakker, S Siahaan, and U Naibaho, 'Indonesia' in JH Carter (ed), *The International Arbitration Review* 9th edn (Law Business Research, 2018) 243.

relationship cases (manpower); administrative cases; bankruptcy cases; and other related family matters (divorce and adoption). Specifically for bankruptcy cases, as explained earlier, the Commercial Court may still try the parties regardless of any agreement to settle disputes through arbitration. The Commercial Court is authorised to accept and settle bankruptcy cases in accordance with the provisions of Article 303 of the Bankruptcy Law. The Commercial Court is not only empowered to try bankruptcy cases despite the existence of an arbitration agreement; it cannot reject a bankruptcy case on the grounds that there is an arbitration clause in the agreement. However, it should be understood that a bankruptcy application must be based on debt in line with the conditions stated in Article 2, paragraph (1) of the Bankruptcy Law. Therefore, even though the arbitration agreement does not remove the authority to settle a bankruptcy case by the Commercial Court, the party submitting must still pay attention to the conditions of bankruptcy above.

To create legal certainty, there is a need to create clear guidelines regarding what types of disputes are included and are not included in the scope of arbitration.

B. Choice of Law

Indonesia is among the many countries whose national laws recognise the principle of freedom of contract, including the freedom to agree on which law will govern the contract, through Article 1338 BW.[42] This freedom is restated in the Article 56, paragraph (2) of the Arbitration Act 1999. However, this freedom is not absolute but is subject to certain limitations. According to Article 56, the agreement must not violate public policy;[43] can only be in the field of contract law; may not be an evasion of law; may not alter the law applying to land transactions or rights over immovable property; may not regard provisions of civil law with a public aspect (such as one's citizenship status, family law, inheritance issues, etc); and may not violate mandatory rules.

Public policy includes domestic laws and regulations.[44] The parties' choice of law may be challenged if it violates Indonesian law or is contrary to public policy. The scope of public policy in Indonesia is very broad. An example of the meaning of public policy can be seen in the case *E.D. & F. Man (Sugar) Ltd v Yani Haryanto*. The dispute arose out of an agreement for the provision of sugar from the seller (E.D. & F. Man) to the buyer (Yani Haryanto). At the time, only *Badan Urusan Logistik* ('BULOG') (Government Logistics Bureau) was permitted to import (or authorise the import of) sugar, through Presidential Decree No 43 of 1971. Yani Haryanto was not permitted to make an agreement to import sugar to Indonesia. The Central Jakarta District Court held that the export import agreement was a violation of public order. The Court is of the opinion that freedom of contract must not extend to conflict with public order.[45]

Mandatory rules are fundamental or mandatory binding rules of law. They are laws that purport to apply irrespective of a contract's proper law or the procedural regime

[42] Art 1338, para (1) of the Civil Code states that, 'All agreements made legally apply as laws for those who make the agreements.'

[43] H Adolf, *Dasar-dasar Hukum Kontrak Internasional* rev edn (Refika Aditama, 2007) 176.

[44] S Gautama, *Hukum Perdata Internasional Indonesia, Jilid III Bagian 2 Buku Ke-8* (Alumni, 2002) 5.

[45] District Court of Central Jakarta Decision No 499/Pdt/G/VI/1988/PN.Jkt.Pst (29 June 1989).

selected by the parties. Usually these rules are issued by a country to protect various social and economic interests. Certain mandatory laws in Indonesia apply to Indonesian parties or to certain types of contracts and cannot be circumvented by the selection of foreign governing law. The state has control over certain transactions, such as those relating to transfers of security interests in land, seagoing vessels, and shares in private Indonesian companies, which can only be governed by Indonesian law. Other laws require Indonesian law to govern various contracts relating to infrastructure and resource projects. Otherwise, parties are free to mutually designate the substantive law that will govern the interpretation and performance of their contracts.[46] Nevertheless, some contracts, such as franchise agreements and construction services contracts, must be governed under Indonesian law. There is an international private law doctrine called *lex rei sitae*, meaning 'the law where the property is situated'. Even though there is no strict requirement under land law to use Indonesian law in a real estate transaction, it is clear that under *lex rei sitae*, transactions in respect of properties in Indonesia should be governed by Indonesian law. The choice of language in an international contract also deserves serious attention under the topic of mandatory laws. Indonesia is among several countries that obliges the use of the national language in certain legal documents,[47] otherwise the contract may be categorised as a violation of law. Indonesia requires the use of the Indonesian language (Bahasa) in any agreement or contract to which an Indonesia citizen is a party in whole or in part. This rule is regulated in the Flag, Language, State Emblem, and National Anthem Act 2009,[48] which states that Bahasa must be used in official state documents,[49] as well as decrees, securities, diplomas, certificates, identity documents, sale and purchase deeds, agreement letters, and court decisions.[50] Furthermore, Bahasa is to be used in a memorandum, agreement or contract that involves Indonesian government institutions, Indonesian private entities, or Indonesian citizens.[51] As such, any contract with any governing law, as long as it involves an Indonesian party, must be drafted in Bahasa, in addition to the language chosen by the parties.[52] However, it is also important to note that the Flag, Language, State Emblem, and National Anthem Act 2009 does not expressly impose any sanctions or legal consequences in the event that an Indonesian language version of a contract is not available. This arrangement differs from the provisions concerning flags, national anthems and national symbols which are accompanied by criminal sanction and fines.

A dispute of language in a contract occurred in the case of *PT Bangun Karya Pratama Lestari v Nine AM. Ltd*.[53] The parties made a Loan Agreement on 23 April 2010.

[46] K Mills, 'Indonesia' [2018] *International Bar Association* 5–6.

[47] A Kusumadara, *Kontrak Bisnis Internasional Elemen-Elemen Penting dalam Penyusunannya* (Sinar Grafika, 2013) 86.

[48] The Flag, Language, State Emblem, and National Anthem Act 2009 consists of 74 Articles divided into five main regulations concerning: (i) national flags (Arts 4–24); (ii) national language (Arts 25–45); (iii) state symbols (Arts 46–57); (iv) national anthem (Arts 58–64); and (v) criminal provisions for violations of provisions concerning national flags, national symbols and national anthem (Arts 66–71).

[49] The Flag, Language, State Emblem, and National Anthem Act 2009, Art 27.

[50] The Elucidation of Article 27 of the Flag, Language, State Emblem, and National Anthem Act 2009.

[51] The Flag, Language, State Emblem, and National Anthem Act 2009, Art 31, para (1).

[52] ibid, Art 31, para (2).

[53] District Court of West Jakarta Decision 451/Pdt.G/2012/PN.JKT.BAR.Tahun 2012 (17 June 2013).

After making several loan payments, PT Bangun Karya Pratama Lestari ('BKPL') filed a lawsuit in the West Jakarta District Court stating that the loan agreement did not meet formal requirements and violated the Flag, Language, State Emblem, and National Anthem Act 2009, and thus was null and void. Nine AM. Ltd denied that the agreement violated the 2009 Act, putting forward two main arguments. First, the parties had signed the same agreement and the use of English had never been debated. Second, the parties were subject to the obligation of *pacta sunt servanda* when they entered and agreed to be bound by the loan agreement. In June 2013, the District Court of West Jakarta issued a decision declaring that the Loan Agreement not drafted in Bahasa was null and void.[54] The Court found that the absence of an Indonesian language version of the Agreement had violated Article 31, paragraph 1 of the Flag, Language, State Emblem, and National Anthem Act 2009. By referring to the illegal cause argument, the Court declared the contract to be null and void by considering Article 1335 BW, which provides that an agreement without reason, or which has been made for a false or forbidden reason, shall have no effect; and Article 1337 which provides that a cause is forbidden if it is forbidden by the law or if it is contrary to good morals or public order. In August 2015, the Supreme Court rejected the cassation requested by Nine AM. Ltd,[55] and favoured the decision of the District Court of West Jakarta and the Appellate Court of Jakarta.[56] This is the first case regarding the mandatory requirements for using Bahasa in an agreement to reach the Supreme Court. The case shows that the choice and use of language in making agreements must comply with the principles and rules of the law. Despite the verdict in *PT Bangun Karya Pratama Lestari v Nine AM. Ltd*, a number of parties have argued that Article 31 should not immediately annul a contract that does not use Indonesian language. The word 'mandatory' in Article 31 of the Flag, Language, State Emblem, and National Anthem Act 2009 is not appropriate to be considered a norm of command, because the provision does not contain sanctions. The term mandatory must be translated as a requirement to use Indonesian, without the consequences of annulling a contract not made in Indonesian. That is, the courts should not read into Article 31 a sanction of annulment which is not stated expressly. Article 31 does not justify the cancellation of agreements not made in Indonesian.

C. Recognition and Enforcement of Arbitral Awards

Indonesia acceded to the 1958 New York Convention on 7 October 1981 through Presidential Decree No 34 of 1981. To regulate the procedure for implementing foreign arbitration awards, the Indonesian Supreme Court issued Regulation No 1 of 1990 concerning the Procedure for the Enforcement of Foreign Arbitral Awards. Other than the 1958 New York Convention, Indonesia has not signed any treaty or convention on the recognition and enforcement of arbitral awards. Pursuant to the reciprocal principle contained in Article 1, Paragraph (3) of the 1958 New York Convention, only arbitral awards made in the territory of another contracting state can be recognised and enforced in Indonesia.

[54] ibid.
[55] Supreme Court Decision 601 K/PDT/2015 (31 August 2015).
[56] District Court of West Jakarta Decision 451/Pdt.G/2012.PN.Jkt (17 June 2013) and High Court of Jakarta Decision 48/PDT/2014/PT.DKI (7 May 2014).

In addition, Indonesia will apply the 1958 New York Convention only to disputes arising out of legal relationships, whether contractual or not, that are considered as commercial in nature under Indonesian law. Following the ratification of the 1958 New York Convention, it is to be hoped there will be no more significant problems regarding the recognition and enforcement of international arbitral awards in Indonesia. This is because the Convention stipulates that the execution of foreign arbitral awards from participating countries of the Convention should not be more difficult than the execution of domestic arbitration awards.[57] Although the national courts in Indonesia will normally honour the recognition and enforcement of an international arbitral awards in the same way as a court judgment, the practice varies. A notable case relating to the application or, more accurately, non-application of the 1958 New York Convention is *PT Nizwar v Navigation Maritime Bulgare*.[58] This controversial landmark case directly addressed the question of the legal status of the 1958 New York Convention.[59] In this case, the Indonesian Supreme Court held that a London arbitral award, being a foreign award, was not enforceable in Indonesia, notwithstanding that Indonesia had by this time ratified the 1958 New York Convention. The Court stated that in accordance with Indonesian practice, the government must still promulgate implementing regulations concerning the enforcement of foreign arbitral awards, including whether a request to enforce a foreign award should be made to a district court (and if so, which district court) or whether such requests should be made directly to the Supreme Court. Without implementing regulations, Indonesian courts cannot enforce foreign arbitral awards. This issue is likely to have been resolved at the latest by the promulgation of the Arbitration Act 1999, which clarifies that applications for the enforcement of foreign arbitral awards is to be made to the Central Jakarta District Court.[60]

Under the Arbitration Act 1999, the Central Jakarta District Court is the only court with jurisdiction to address the recognition and enforcement of international arbitral awards in Indonesia.[61] The first step towards enforcement is to register the foreign arbitral award with the Central Jakarta District Court. A party can only apply for an exequatur after the award is registered. The Act specifies that the award can be registered by either the arbitrator or their representative.[62] At present, this provision requires revision, since it leaves no room for parties to submit and register the arbitration award in the district court on their own. In practice, however, the Central Jakarta District Court has deviated from the strict language of the article by allowing the winning or even the losing parties to register an award.[63] In *Noble Americas Corp v PT Wahana Adhireksa Wiraswasta*, the Central Jakarta District Court allowed Noble America Corp as the winning party to register the award rendered by the Cocoa Merchants Association of America. A similar decision was reached in *Oceanis Shipping Limited v R. Adji A. Suryo di Puro*.[64] In *Karaha Bodas Co. v Perusahaan*

[57] 1958 New York Convention, Art 3.

[58] Supreme Court Decision 2944/K/Pdt/1983 (20 August 1984).

[59] DD Agusman, *Treaties Under Indonesian Law: A Comparative Study* (PT Remaja Rosdakarya, 2014) 401.

[60] The Arbitration Act 1999, Art 65.

[61] ibid.

[62] ibid, Art 67, para (1).

[63] T Budidjaja, *Public Policy as Grounds for Refusal of Recognition and Enforcement of Foreign Arbitral Awards in Indonesia* (PT Tatanusa, 2002) 28.

[64] G Soemartono and J Lumbantobing, 'Indonesia: Indonesian Arbitration Law and Practice in Light of the UNCITRAL Model Law' in GF Bell (ed), *The UNCITRAL Model Law and Asian Arbitration Laws, Implementation and Comparison* (Cambridge University Press, 2018) 341; See also GR Kartakusuma, 'Indonesia' in D Campbell (ed),

Pertambangan Minyak dan Gas Bumi Negara, an award rendered in Geneva was registered by Pertamina, the losing party. These cases show that the relevant article should not only give authority to the arbitrator or his power of attorney to register a request for the implementation of an international arbitration award, but also to both the winning and losing parties. Furthermore, unlike the registration of domestic awards,[65] the 1999 Arbitration Act does not provide a time limit for the registration of foreign arbitral awards, a position recently affirmed by the Supreme Court in PT Pertamina EP, *PT Pertamina (Persero) v PT Lirik Petroleum*.[66]

For the successful registration of an international arbitral award, the following documents must be submitted to the court: (a) the original or an authentic copy of the award, and its official Indonesian translation; (b) the original or an authentic copy of the arbitration agreement or the underlying agreement on which the award is based, as well as its official Indonesian translation; and (c) a statement from the diplomatic representative of Indonesia in the country where the award was made, stating that the country is bound to an agreement with Indonesia (either through a bilateral or multilateral treaty) on the recognition and execution of international arbitration awards.[67] Regarding the last of these documents, namely the statement concerning the bilateral or multilateral treaty with the country where the award was made, one might note the controversial case of the *Trading Corporation of Pakistan Limited v PT Bakrie and Brothers*.[68] The purchase contract made by the parties required that arbitration in London be the choice of forum in any future disputes. Following arbitration of a dispute, the award went in favour of Trading Corp of Pakistan. PT Bakrie challenged the enforcement of the arbitral award in Indonesia on the grounds that Pakistan and Indonesia had no Bilateral Investment Treaty. The Supreme Court referred to Article 1, paragraph (3) of Presidential Decree No 34 of 1981 which states: '… the Government of the Republic of Indonesia declares that it will apply the Convention on the basis of reciprocity, to the recognition and enforcement of awards made only in the territory of another Contracting States ….' The Court argued that Pakistan, not being a party to the 1958 New York Convention, could not enforce foreign arbitral awards in Indonesia. The Court incorrectly interpreted the term 'another Contracting State', which should mean the country in which the award was made. Thus, the country should have been the UK, as the arbitral award was rendered in London. The requirement of reciprocity stipulated in the Arbitration Act 1999 would also have been satisfied.[69]

An international arbitral award can be recognised and enforced in Indonesia if: (a) the award is rendered in a state that is bound by a bilateral or multilateral convention regarding the recognition and enforcement of international arbitral awards by which Indonesia is also bound; (b) the award is limited to commercial law under Indonesian law; (c) the award is not contrary to public policy in Indonesia; (d) a writ of execution (exequatur) has been

Remedies for International Sellers of Goods, Second Edition, Volume 1 (Juris Publishing, 2014) 817; MN Al-Gozaly, 'The Judicial Expansive Attitude Towards Public Policy in Enforcement of Foreign Arbitral Awards in Indonesia' (2014) 15 *Jurnal Opinio Juris* 127, 167.

[65] Under Art 59, paras (1) and (4) of the Arbitration Act 1999, failure to register domestic arbitral awards within the 30-day period shall render the award unenforceable.

[66] Supreme Court Decision 904K/PDT.SUS/2009 (9 June 2010).

[67] The Arbitration Act 1999, Art 67, para (2).

[68] Supreme Court Decision No 4231/K/Pdt/1986 (4 May 1988).

[69] Soemartono, 'Interpretation and Application' (n 32), 498.

obtained from the Chairman of the Central Jakarta District Court on the basis of the award. If (e) the award involves the Republic of Indonesia as a party to the dispute, it is enforceable only after obtaining an order of exequatur from the Supreme Court of the Republic of Indonesia, and that order has been delegated to the Central Jakarta District Court.[70] In effect, an international arbitral award can only be enforced in Indonesia if the award is made in a contracting state of the 1958 New York Convention, and under the commercial reservation, and not conflicting with Indonesia's public order.[71] In this regard, unlike the national arbitration award, the Arbitration Act imposes no time limit for enforcing an international arbitration award, and many applications for an exequatur remain pending at the District Court.[72] The absence of a time period becomes a tool for parties who are dissatisfied with an arbitration award to delay the execution of the award. If the arbitration award is not registered, the request for the exequatur will not be granted, as happened in the dispute between Pertamina and Karaha Bodas Company.

Regarding legal remedies, the Arbitration Act 1999 also regulates the refusal[73] and annulment (setting aside)[74] of international arbitral awards. The Act defines the grounds upon which recognition and enforcement may be refused at the request of the party against whom the award is invoked, namely on the grounds of public policy and arbitrability.[75] Concerning annulment, the Arbitration Act 1999 does not distinguish between annulment of national and international arbitral awards. The Act stipulates that a party can file an application to the Indonesian courts to set aside an award on the following grounds: (a) false letter or document submitted in the examination; (b) decisive document found that was hidden by the opposing party; (c) the award was a result of fraud committed by one of the parties during the arbitration proceedings.[76] Any alleged grounds for the annulment of an arbitral award must be proven before the court. If the court decides that the reasons for annulment do not exist, the court will reject the application for annulment.[77] In this regard, in 2015 the Constitutional Court issued a decision related to the annulment of arbitral awards as stipulated in Article 70 of the Arbitration Act 1999, through Decision No 15/PUU/XII/2014. The Constitutional Court's ruling annulled the Elucidation of Article 70, but not the Article itself. However, the jurisprudence of the Supreme Court suggests that Indonesian courts may not entertain applications for the annulment of international arbitral awards. The relevant case is *Pertamina v Karaha Bodas Company*, which concerned a Swiss arbitral award that had been annulled by the District Court of Central Jakarta.[78] The Supreme Court, on appeal, overturned the District Court's ruling. The Supreme Court relied on Article V, paragraph (1)(e) of the 1958 New York Convention to determine whether the Indonesian courts had jurisdiction to hear

[70] The Arbitration Act 1999, Art 66. This provision is in accordance with Indonesia's reservation on the 1958 New York Convention and the Supreme Court Regulation No 1 of 1990.

[71] Sukirno, Kadir, and Hirdarisvita, Baker & McKenzie, *The Baker & McKenzie International Arbitration Yearbook* (n 12) 259.

[72] Gerungan, Alizia, and Sitorus, *International Arbitration* (n 7) 168.

[73] The Arbitration Act 1999, Art 68, para (2).

[74] ibid, Art 70.

[75] The Arbitration Act 1999, Art 66.

[76] ibid, Art 70.

[77] Elucidation of the Arbitration Act 1999, Art 70.

[78] District Court of Central Jakarta Decision No 86/PDT.G/2002/PN.JKT.PST (27 August 2002); Supreme Court Decision 01/Banding/Wasit-Int/2002 (8 March 2004); Supreme Court Extraordinary Appeal 444 PK/Pdt/2007 (9 September 2008).

any action to annul a foreign award. The Supreme Court took the view that the phrase '*under the law of which … that award was made*' in the 1958 New York Convention refers to the law of the seat of arbitration. Consequently, the Supreme Court decided that it had no jurisdiction to set aside an award rendered in Geneva under the UNCITRAL rules.[79] This decision is now widely regarded as a 'landmark' standing for the principle that a district court has no jurisdiction to annul an international arbitral award.

These rules and cases have produced confusion regarding who has the authority to annul an international arbitration award. The debate over interpretation arises because Articles 70–71 of the Arbitration Act 1999 do not explicitly state whether the annulment of the award applies to national and international arbitration awards. Therefore, some argue that the annulment of the award in Articles 70–72 of the Arbitration Act 1999 also includes the annulment of an international arbitration award, while others argue that the provisions on annulment apply only to national arbitration awards. Based on the seat of arbitration, the only authority to annul the Genevan arbitration award is held by the court in Switzerland, not the district court in Indonesia. This means that there is no legal basis that can be used by the court to overturn an international arbitration award. For this reason, it is necessary to revise the provisions of Article 70 of the Arbitration Act 1999 to ensure legal certainty and to comply with the principles of international civil law. The Supreme Court has consistently taken this position in subsequent cases. In *PT Bungo Raya Nusantara v PT Jambi Resources*, the Supreme Court confirmed that Indonesian courts have no jurisdiction to set aside SIAC awards made in Singapore. In its decision, the Supreme Court rejected Bungo's application and confirmed that applications for annulment of international arbitral awards can only be filed with the courts in the country in which the award was issued.[80] In *Harvey Nichols and Company Limited v PT Hamparan Nusantara, PT Mitra Adiperkasa Tbk*,[81] the Supreme Court ruled that Indonesian courts lacked jurisdiction to set aside an ad-hoc arbitration award where the seat of arbitration was in London. Similarly, in the case between *PT Daya Mandiri Resource and PT Dayaindo Resources Internasional v SUEK AG*,[82] the Court stated that it had no jurisdiction to annul an award made by the London Court of International Arbitration. In *PT Global Mediacom Tbk v KT Corporation*,[83] the same decision was rendered with respect to setting aside an application against an ICC award made in London. These cases suggest that only a competent authority in the country where the award was issued can annul an international arbitral award. However, note that in the case between *PT Raga Perkasa Ekaguna v Merck Gmbh*, the District Court of Central Jakarta dismissed PT Raga's request for annulment of the LCIA tribunal not because it lacked jurisdiction to decide the issue, but on the basis of PT Raga's failure to prove that the London Court of International Arbitration ('LCIA') award met the substantive requirements stipulated in Article 70 of the Arbitration Act 1999. The case therefore demonstrates that, regardless of the stance promoted by the Supreme Court, Indonesian courts will still apply Article 70 of the Arbitration Act 1999 in examining requests for annulment of international arbitral awards.[84]

[79] Supreme Court Decision 01/Banding/Wasit-Int/2002 (8 March 2004).

[80] Supreme Court Decision 64 K/Pdt.Sus/2010 (26 April 2010).

[81] Supreme Court Decision 631 K/Pdt/Pdt.Sus/2012 (27 December 2012).

[82] District Court of Central Jakarta Decision 117/Pdt.G/Arb/2012/PN.Jkt.Pst (24 October 2012).

[83] Supreme Court Decision 212 K/Pdt.Sus-Arbt/2013 (15 August 2013).

[84] Supreme Court Decision 700 K/PDT/2011 (10 May 2012); See also Sukirno, Kadir, and Hirdarisvita, Baker & McKenzie, *The Baker & McKenzie International Arbitration Yearbook* (n 12).

As stated in the 1958 New York Convention, courts may refuse the recognition and enforcement of an award if the award violates public policy.[85] But how to define public policy (some jurisdictions refer to public order, which has the same meaning) has been the subject of disagreement.[86] Even today, it remains a highly debated, controversial and complex issue. The concrete manifestations of the 'public policy' concept may substantially vary from one state jurisdiction to another, causing differences in interpretation and understanding. Although over time, the laws and practices of arbitration have tried to align the public policy concept across states, so that states may benefit from a universally accepted concept, the different approaches of national courts have made this task hard if not impossible.[87] Turning to domestic Indonesian law, as mentioned above, the Arbitration Act 1999includes incompatibility with public order as one of the reasons for the refusal of a request for the recognition and enforcement of an international arbitral award. In other words, public order may limit the entry into force of an international arbitration award if the award is deemed to be contrary to the fundamental aspects of Indonesia's legal system and society.[88] But the Arbitration Act 1999does not further explain the meaning of public order. This lack of clarity has the potential to make the term public order a flexible reason for use, both by those who are dissatisfied with the arbitral award and the courts, in refusing an application for an arbitral award. In Indonesia, the first case that rejected the enforcement of an international arbitral award (exequatur) on the grounds of public policy after the enactment of the Supreme Court Regulation No 1 of 1990 was *E.D. & F. Man (Sugar) Limited v Yani Haryanto*.[89] The Supreme Court argued that the award made in London violated the public policy of Indonesia, since the sugar purchase agreement made between the parties (ED & F Man (Sugar) Ltd, and Haryanto) was not valid under Indonesian law. The only body with authority to export and import sugar was the government-owned logistic body, BULOG. This type of agreement, according to the Supreme Court, is null and void as a violation of public policy.[90]

Since *E.D. & F. Man (Sugar) Limited v Yani Haryanto*, various laws have been promulgated. However, public policy was not, nor is it now, clearly defined in law or in jurisprudence. The courts therefore have considerable discretion when applying this concept. Acts in Indonesia generally contain the term public policy, and sometimes provide a definition of the term. For example, Act No 9 of 2004 on the Administrative Court (the Administrative Court Act 2004) states that public policy is the interest of the nation and state and/or the interest of the people and/or the interest of the development of law and society in accordance with

[85] The 1958 New Yok Convention, Art V, para 2(b).

[86] S Batubara and O Purba, *Arbitrase Internasional, Penyelesaian Sengketa Investasi Asing Melalui ICSID, UNCITRAL, dan SIAC* (Raih Asa Sukses, 2013) 150.

[87] S Sattar, 'Enforcement of Arbitral Awards and Public Policy: Same Concept, Different Approach?' (2011) 5 *Transnational Dispute Management* 1, 2 www.transnational-dispute-management.com/article.asp?key=1759 (accessed 15 March 2020).

[88] A Jebabun and others, *Initial Assessment Problems of Court Decision Enforcement System in Indonesia (*Asesmen Awal Permasalahan Eksekusi Putusan Perkara Perdata di Indonesia) (*Lembaga Kajian & Advokasi Independensi Peradilan*, 2018) 61 https://leip.or.id/wp-content/uploads/2018/10/LeIP_Asesmen-Awal-Eksekusi-Putusan-Perdata.pdf (accessed 2 November 2019).

[89] Supreme Court Decision 1205K/Pdt/1990 (4 December 1991); High Court of Jakarta Decision High Court of Jakarta Decision 486/Pdt/1989/PT.DKI (14 October 1989); District Court of Central Jakarta Decision 499/Pdt/G/VI/1988/PN.JKT.PST. (29 June 1989).

[90] Batubara and Purba, *Arbitrase Internasional* (n 86) 216–217.

existing regulations.[91] Yet this definition makes the term public policy exceedingly broad. It connects the concept not only with the interest of the state or nation but also with the people and national development. But it provides no explanation of what the interests of the state or nation might be. In this regard, the issue of the protection and use of the state's assets or money may be classified as falling within the scope of public policy.[92] The Judicial Power Act 2009[93] and the Anti-Monopoly Act 1999[94] also contain the term 'public policy'; but these acts also provide a very broad definition of the term's meaning. In addition, the Supreme Court Regulation 1990 defines public policy quite generally as 'the basic principles of the entire Indonesian legal system and social system'.[95] This definition did little to clarify the interpretation of the extent of public policy. Its breadth meant judges continued to take different views on the scope of public policy when examining applications for the enforcement of international arbitration awards. In the past, this often led judges to decline to enforce international arbitral awards.[96] Scholars have also offered their opinion about public policy. A professor of private international law, Sudargo Gautama, defined public policy as a condition that is contrary to the principles and values of the legal system and national interests of a state. Because of the potential breadth of the concept, public policy grounds for refusal to recognise or enforce an award should be used strictly and be applied cautiously. Gautama further noted that public policy should be an escape clause and should be confined to use as a 'shield not a sword'.[97] The Arbitration Act itself does not define public policy or its limits. In the drafting of the Act, there was considerable discussion as to whether such a definition should be included so that the concept could become equitable and workable in the context of arbitration. However, the Act emerged without any such clarification. Article 66(c) only specifies that international arbitration awards may be enforced in Indonesia when not contrary to public order, without further explanation.

Based on the latest survey in 2010, there were about 29 foreign arbitral awards (cases) registered with the District Court of Central Jakarta.[98] Among them, there are just two cases addressing the application of the principle of public policy in Indonesia: *Bankers Trust Company and Bankers Trust International PLC* ('BT') *v PT Mayora Indah Tbk.* ('Mayora') in 1999,[99] and *Astro Nusantara International v PT Ayunda Primamitra* in 2010. The first

[91] The Administrative Court Act 2004, Art 49; 'the Administrative Court shall not have the power to adjudicate and decide the disputes concerning the decisions made by the authorities where the decisions are made in the interest of public policy based on the applicable laws'.

[92] H Adolf, 'Public Policy under Indonesia Arbitration Law' (*Global Arbitration Review*, 30 May 2018) https://globalarbitrationreview.com/print_article/gar/chapter/1170062/public-policy-under-indonesian-arbitration-law?print=true (accessed 11 December 2019).

[93] Elucidation to Article 16 of the Judicial Power Act 2009 provides that the public interest concerns with the interest of the society in general.

[94] For example, Art 1(b) of the Anti-Monopoly Act 1999 explains that the unfair competition may include an unfair competition which harms 'the society in general'.

[95] Supreme Court Regulation No 1 of 1990, Art 4, para (2).

[96] S Gautama, *Perkembangan Arbitrase Dagang Internasional di Indonesia ('International Trade Arbitration Developments in Indonesia')* (PT Eresco, 1989) 62.

[97] Prof Sudargo Gautama's opinion of public policy is discussed in: Tuegeh-Longdong, *Asas Ketertiban* (n 19) 24; Adolf, 'Public Policy' (n 92).

[98] M Hikmah, 'Pelaksanaan Putusan Arbitrase Internasional di Indonesia Berdasarkan Undang-Undang Arbitrase' (PhD thesis, Universitas Pelita Harapan, 2010) 256.

[99] The first case was between *Bankers Trust Company and Bankers Trust International Plc v PT Mayora Indah Tbk*, and the second case was between *Bankers Trust Company and Bankers Trust International Plc v PT Jakarta International Hotels & Development.*

case occurred in a dispute between BT and Mayora submitted to the London Court of International Arbitration. As the losing party, Mayora requested the annulment of the International Swaps and Derivatives Association ('ISDA') agreement in the District Court of South Jakarta, arguing that the transaction was a violation of public policy in Indonesia. The judgment ruled in favour of Mayora.[100] At the same time, BT had also requested an exequatur for the award. The District Court of Central Jakarta refused to issue an exequatur,[101] taking into account the ongoing process of a related dispute in the District Court of South Jakarta. The Chief Justice stated that the execution of an award before the final and binding judgment by the District Court of South Jakarta would be in violation with civil procedural law. This judgment was further strengthened by the Supreme Court.[102] This case shows that enforcing a foreign award will breach public policy if involves an arbitral award still subject to ongoing litigation in Indonesia.[103] The second case, *Astro Nusantara BV v PT Ayunda Prima Mitra*, arose out of an unsuccessful joint venture agreement. The failure of the agreement led to a dispute at the Singapore International Arbitration Centre in accordance with the Subscription and Shareholders Agreement ('SSA'). While the dispute was being heard at the SIAC, the respondent brought the dispute to the District Court of South Jakarta. The arbitrators at SIAC ruled in favour of the claimant and issued an order, among others, for the respondent to stop the court proceedings it had initiated in Indonesia. The arbitrators argued that the SSA forbid the parties to submit their dispute to national courts. The claimant shortly thereafter submitted a copy of the arbitration award to the District Court of Central Jakarta, requesting that the Court execute the award. At the same time, the respondent requested the District Court of Central Jakarta to reject the application for execution, on the basis of, among other arguments, the violation of public policy. In its decision, the Court held in favour of the respondent. The claimant appealed to the Supreme Court, questioning whether the arbitral body's intervention in the court's processes amounted to a violation of public policy.[104] On the substantive matter, the Supreme Court argued in favour of the District Court of Central Jakarta, stating that the order of the arbitration award to stop the process of the proceedings in the Indonesian court was a violation of the principle of sovereignty. No foreign power or body may intervene in the Indonesian legal process.[105] The Supreme Court also argued that the subject matter of the dispute fell within procedural law, and was not a commercial dispute.[106]

It is important to note that the legal system in Indonesian does not acknowledge the principle of binding precedent and therefore, courts are not bound to follow any previous judgments. Despite criticisms of the uncertainty of the concept of public policy, there is some consistency between the decisions of the Supreme Court, insofar as they hold that violation of public policy includes intervention in ongoing proceedings of domestic courts.

[100] District Court of South Jakarta Decision No 46/Pdt.G/1999/PN.Jkt.Sel (9 December 1999).

[101] District Court of Central Jakarta Decision No 001/Pdt/Arb.Int/1999/PN.JKT.PST and No 002/Pdt/Arb.Int/1999/PN.JKT.PST jo 02/Pdt.P/2000/PNJKT.PST (3 February 2000).

[102] Supreme Court Decision 02K/Ex'r/Arb.Int/Pdt/2000 (5 September 2000).

[103] S Butt, 'Arbitration in Indonesia: Largely Dependable Recognition and Enforcement' in A Reyes and W Gu, *The Developing World of Arbitration, A Comparative Study of Arbitration Reform in the Asia Pacific* (Hart Publishing, 2018) 200.

[104] Supreme Court Decision No 01 K/Pdt.Sus/2010 (24 February 2010), 35–36.

[105] ibid, 36.

[106] ibid, 37.

In summary, it is difficult to conclude whether or not Indonesia is a friendly jurisdiction for arbitration awards or not, due to uncertainty in the approaches the courts use. Although the Arbitration Act has been enacted for almost 20 years, the Supreme Court has not provided a uniform interpretation of public policy as a reason to annul or refuse an international arbitral award. Given this uncertainty, arbitration practitioners should not be surprised if the court deviates further from its past decisions.

II. Investment Treaty Arbitration

As an effort to promote foreign direct investment during the administration of President Soeharto, Indonesia ratified the ICSID Convention,[107] through the Investment Disputes Settlement between States and Foreign Nationals Act 1968. Under the Indonesian judicial system, the ICSID is similar to an administrative court, which oversees cases in which an individual or private entity is suing the government for its actions. However, unlike an administrative court, the ICSID can grant compensation to the investors as the plaintiff.

A. Jurisdiction of the Arbitral Tribunal

As stated earlier, the Arbitration Act stipulates that a dispute can be settled by means of arbitration if it is of a commercial nature and involves the rights of the disputed parties.[108] Objects having a commercial nature include, among others, investment.[109] Where an arbitration agreement exists between the parties, district courts must decline to hear any disputes.

In terms of investment treaty arbitration, the jurisdiction of the arbitral tribunal is often regulated in an investment treaty (either bilateral or multilateral). Since 1968, Indonesia has signed 72 bilateral investment treaties ('BITs'),[110] of which 26 are still in force.[111] A 2018 BIT with Singapore is the latest BIT signed by the Government of the Republic of Indonesia, although it has not yet been published. No standard terms or model languages have been adopted in the BITs. Nevertheless, all BITs to which Indonesia is a party choose arbitration as the mechanism dispute settlement among the parties. Almost half of the publicly available BITs contain largely similar provisions regulating disputes between an investor and the host state, allowing the investor, six months after an attempt to settle the dispute amicably via consultation or negotiations, to submit the dispute to domestic judicial procedures in the host state or to international arbitration or conciliation under the

[107] Convention on the Settlement of Investment Disputes between States and Nationals of Other States (the ICSID Convention). The ICSID Convention and the Regulations and Rules adopted pursuant to it are reprinted in ICSID Convention, Regulations and Rules, Doc. ICSID/15 (April 2006) and also available on the ICSID website, www.worldbank.org/icsid.

[108] The Arbitration Act 1999, Art 5, para (1).

[109] Elucidation of The Arbitration Act 1999, Art 66.

[110] UNCTAD, 'Indonesia' (*Investment Policy Hub*, 13 February 2019) https://investmentpolicy.unctad.org/international-investment-agreements/countries/97/indonesia (accessed 18 November 2019).

[111] ibid.

auspices of ICSID.[112] Indonesia has been involved in a total of seven investment disputes at the ICSID, making this institution the most popular investor-state dispute settlement ('ISDS') mechanism for Indonesia.[113] Some of the publicly available BITs provide for the possibility of the investor submitting the dispute, after an attempt at settling the dispute amicably, to international arbitration under either ICSID or to an ad hoc tribunal under UNCITRAL Rules,[114] as in the case between *Indian Metals & Ferro Alloys Ltd v Republic of Indonesia*.[115] The Indonesia-Singapore BIT provides an additional option for the investor to submit the arbitration to any regional centre for arbitration in ASEAN.[116] Other than that, the Indonesia-Cuba BIT does not provide an option of arbitration under ICSID, opting instead for arbitration by the Court of Arbitration of the ICC in Paris under UNCITRAL Rules.[117] Notably, however, some BITs do not contain provisions on investor-state dispute resolution,[118] while others require the investor to pursue local remedies before it may submit the dispute to arbitration.[119] In addition, Indonesia has signed the ASEAN Comprehensive Investment Agreement ('ACIA') in 2009,[120] and the Agreement on Promotion, Protection and Guarantee of Investments among member states of the Organization of Islamic Conferences ('OIC') in 1981.[121] The most significant treaty relating to investment protection within ASEAN is the ASEAN Comprehensive Investment Agreement ('ACIA'). Investors from other ASEAN states that have also ratified the ACIA can therefore look to the ACIA for protection of their investments in Indonesia.

Pursuant to the ICSID Convention, the jurisdiction of the Centre extends to any legal dispute arising directly out of an investment, between a contracting state (or any constituent subdivision or agency of a contracting state designated to the Centre by that state) and a national of another contracting state, which the parties to the dispute consent in writing to submit to the Centre. Arbitral Tribunals have the authority to determine the scope of the investment based on the competence-competence doctrine.[122] From such jurisdiction,

[112] For example, Indonesia-Mongolia BIT (Art 8); Indonesia-Algeria BIT; Indonesia-Bangladesh BIT, Indonesia-Germany BIT (Art 10); Indonesia-Morocco BIT, Indonesia-Pakistan BIT, Indonesia-Sri Lanka BIT; Indonesia-Sudan BIT; Indonesia-Syria BIT, Indonesia-Yemen BIT, Indonesia-Zimbabwe BIT.

[113] The seven cases are *Amco Asia Corporation and others v Republic of Indonesia*, ICSID Case No ARB/81/1; *Cemex Asia Holdings Ltd v Republic of Indonesia*, ICSID Case No ARB/04/3; *Government of the Province of East Kalimantan v PT Kaltim Prima Coal and others*, ICSID Case No ARB/07/3; *Rafat Ali Rizvi v Republic of Indonesia*, ICSID Case No ARB/11/13; *Churchill Mining PLC and Planet Mining Pty Ltd v Republic of Indonesia*, ICSID Case No ARB/12/14 and 12/40; *Nusa Tenggara Partnership B.V. and PT Newmont Nusa Tenggara v Republic of Indonesia*, ICSID Case No ARB/14/15; and *Oleovest Pte. Ltd v Republic of Indonesia*, ICSID Case No ARB/16/26.

[114] Indonesia-Croatia BIT, Indonesia-Czech Republic BIT, Indonesia-Jamaica BIT, Indonesia-India BIT, Indonesia-Singapore BIT.

[115] *Indian Metals & Ferro Alloys Ltd v Republic of Indonesia*, PCA Case No 2015-40, Award (29 March 2019); In this case, Indonesia has won a US$469 million arbitration case against India's Metal Ferro and Alloys Ltd (IMFA) after nearly four years of court battles, at an arbitration court in The Hague, Netherlands.

[116] Indonesia-Singapore BIT, Art VIII, para 2b.

[117] Indonesia-Cuba BIT, Art VIII, para 3.

[118] Indonesia-Switzerland BIT; Indonesia-Denmark BIT.

[119] Indonesia-Sweden BIT; Indonesia-Korea BIT; Indonesia-Spain BIT.

[120] ASEAN Comprehensive Investment Agreement available at http://investasean.asean.org/files/upload/Doc%2005%20-%20ACIA.pdf.

[121] Agreement on Promotion, Protection and Guarantee of Investments among member states of the Organisation of Islamic Conferences available at https://investmentpolicyhubold.unctad.org/IIA/countryGrouping /45/treaty/3092; Hamzah, 'Bilateral Investment Treaties (BITS) in Indonesia: A Paradigm Shift, Issues and Challenges' (2018) 21 *Journal of Legal, Ethical and Regulatory Issues* 1, 1.

[122] ICSID Convention, Art 41, para (1); See also GB Born, *International Arbitration: Law and Practice*, 2nd edn (Kluwer Law International, 2016) 56.

at least three things must be considered in terms in investment in Indonesia. First, the scope of investment, which is regulated in Indonesia's new investment Act No 25 of 2007 concerning investment (the Investment Act 2007), replacing Act No 1 of 1967 concerning Foreign Investment. This Act addresses both domestic and foreign investment. Foreign capital investment is an activity which involves the investing of capital in order to operate businesses within the territory of the Republic of Indonesia, and which is undertaken by foreign investors, either through the use of foreign capital in its entirety or as a part of ventures which are undertaken with domestic investors.[123] Foreign investment must be in the form of a Limited-Liability Company under Indonesian law and domiciled in the territory of the Republic of Indonesia, unless otherwise stipulated by law.[124] In terms of dispute settlement, the Investment Act differentiates between domestic and foreign investment. While both disputes must first be settled through negotiation in order that an amicable solution be reached, disputes that arise between the government and domestic investors should be resolved through domestic arbitration or the courts, whereas disputes between the government and foreign investors can be settled through the international arbitration mechanism.[125] Note that portfolio investment is excluded from the scope of investment as defined under the Investment Act 2007, even though it is not explicitly mentioned under the definition of investment.[126]

Second, investment licences. In Indonesia, the *Badan Koordinasi Penanaman Modal* ('BKPM') (Investment Coordinating Board) is the non-ministerial government agency concerned with approving foreign investment.[127] Unfortunately, BKPM's authority does not cover all types of investments in Indonesia. Investments in the following business sectors are not supervised by the BKPM: (a) the banking and financial services sector (where approval is granted by Indonesia's Financial Service Authority); (b) the upstream oil and gas sector (which is regulated through production sharing contracts with the oil and gas contracting agency, the Indonesian Special Task Force for Upstream Oil and Gas Business Activities (SKK Migas)); and (c) a portfolio investment through the purchase of securities in the capital markets.[128] Although various business sectors are not administered by the BKPM, it is evident that Indonesia only intends to protect investments that are admitted and supervised under the BKPM regime. In the case of *Rafat Ali Rizvi v the Republic of Indonesia*,[129] Indonesia objected to the Tribunal's jurisdiction on the basis that the investment at issue fell outside of the protection of the Indonesia-UK BIT as it had not been granted approval by the BKPM, falling outside BKMP's jurisdiction.[130] Despite stating that the Indonesia-UK BIT also encompasses investments where the relevant sector is open to investment, such as the banking sector in which conditions of admission are administered by Bank Indonesia, the Tribunal found that there was insufficient evidence that the investment had been approved

[123] The Investment Act 2007, Art 1, para (3).
[124] ibid, Art 5, para (2).
[125] ibid, Art 32.
[126] Elucidation of Article 2 of the Investment Act 2007.
[127] The BKPM was established through the issuance of Presidential Regulation No 90 of 2007 concerning investment coordinating board.
[128] Widyawan, 'Legal Guide to Investment in Indonesia' (Widyawan & Partners, July 2014) 7 www.widyawanpartners.com/english/pubs/Investing-in-Indonesia.pdf (accessed 19 November 2019).
[129] *Rafat Ali Rizvi v Republic of Indonesia*, ICSID Case No ARB/11/13, Award (16 July 2013).
[130] ibid, para 80.

by Bank Indonesia,[131] and the investment did not fall within the scope of the BIT. For these reasons, the Tribunal held that it had no jurisdiction over the claim. In *Churchill Mining Plc v Indonesia*,[132] despite Indonesia's argument that the BKPM approvals provided to Churchill did not contain consent to ICSID arbitration,[133] the tribunal held that in any event, the consent to ICSID arbitration in BKPM's approval can be found in Section IX(4) of the 2005 BKPM Approval. Section IX(4) states that in the event of a dispute between the company and the government of Indonesia that cannot be settled by consultation, the government is prepared/ready/willing to follow settlement according to the provision of ICSID. The Tribunal is of the view that the BKPM has the power to grant consent to ICSID arbitration, since it is a government body reporting directly to the President and vested with authority to handle foreign investments.[134] As regards the parties, in the case *the Government of Province of East Kalimantan v PT. Kaltim Prima Coal*,[135] in the award of jurisdiction rendered on 28 December 2009, the Tribunal found that the claimant (the Government of East Kalimantan) had no right claims under the ICSID Convention because it was neither a contracting state nor a designated constituent subdivision of the Indonesian Government.

Third, such disputes brought to international arbitration must be agreed upon by the parties in written form. The word 'agreed' in the article proves that a dispute can only be resolved through arbitration if it has been mutually agreed upon by the parties.[136] In other words, without the consent of the parties, the dispute cannot be resolved through arbitration. This aligns with the requirement that the legal terms of the agreement must be in writing, either in the form of BIT (treaty based) or through international contract (contract based). The *Churchill Mining Plc v Indonesia* case also disputed this matter and, in doing so, attracted both national and international public attention.[137] With regards to the jurisdiction of the ICSID, the Tribunal found that Article 7, paragraph (1) contains a standing offer to arbitrate any dispute that may arise in connection with an investment before ICSID. In particular, contrary to Indonesia's position that the words 'shall assent' in Article 7, paragraph (1) of the BIT meant that subsequent consent from Indonesia was required, the Tribunal concluded that 'shall assent' was functionally equivalent to 'hereby consents' or similar wording and constituted consent in advance of arbitration.[138]

The cases and awards above provide useful insights into the practice of arbitration law in Indonesia. First, they reaffirm that only foreign direct investments are protected in Indonesia (through BIT), with indirect investments (portfolio investments) excluded from protection. Second, they also emphasise that permission or approval from BKPM is an absolute requirement for an investment to be protected. Accordingly, the Indonesian

[131] ibid, para 198, 223.

[132] *Churchill Mining PLC and Planet Mining Pty Ltd v Republic of Indonesia*, ICSID Case No ARB/12/14 and 12/40.

[133] ibid. Decision on Jurisdiction (24 February 2014) para 77.

[134] See Article 1 of Presidential Decree No 33 of 1981 concerning the capital investment coordinating board; Article 1 paragraph (2) of Presidential Decree No. 29 of 2004 concerning implementation of capital investment within the framework of foreign capital investment and domestic capital investment through the one-roof service system.

[135] *Government of the Province of East Kalimantan v PT Kaltim Prima Coal and others*, ICSID Case No. ARB/07/3, Award (28 December 2009).

[136] Elucidation of Art 7, para (3) of the Investment Act 2007.

[137] *Churchill Mining PLC and Planet Mining Pty Ltd v Republic of Indonesia*, ICSID Case No ARB/12/14 and 12/40.

[138] ibid. Decision on Jurisdiction (24 February 2014) para 230.

Government affirms that it may or may not use ICSID as the forum for alternative dispute settlement in the field of foreign capital investment. Based on the ICSID Convention, as modified, any contracting state at the time of ratification, acceptance, or approval of the Convention or at any time thereafter is to notify ICSID of the classes of disputes that it would or would not consider submitting to the jurisdiction of ICSID. This provision formed part of the legal basis of Presidential Decree No 31 of 2012 concerning disputes that are not submitted to the jurisdiction of ICSID, which determined to exclude disputes arising from state administrative decisions issued by Regencies (*Kabupaten*) from the types of disputes that may be settled by the ICSID.[139] However, the exclusion of Regency-level decisions will not apply retroactively. In light of recent events involving cases in the field of foreign capital investment in Indonesia, the issuance of the Presidential Decree may stimulate concerns among investors about how the Indonesian Government provides legal certainty to their investments, particularly as many government decisions affecting foreign investment are issued at the local level (ie, provinces and regencies) under the system of Regional Autonomy.

B. Choice of Law

Being an arbitral process, investment treaty arbitration in no way differs from international commercial arbitration in that the principle of party autonomy is the primary rule governing the arbitration, including with regard to the law applicable to the substance of the dispute. When the applicable law has been chosen by the parties, the arbitrators have a duty to apply the law chosen and nothing but that law.[140] Only in the absence of a choice by the parties are the arbitrators entitled to exercise a degree of discretion in determining the applicable law.[141] ICSID operates under the same approach, whereby parties are explicitly given the power to choose the law that applies to the investment. ICISD directs arbitral tribunals to decide the dispute in accordance with such rules of law as may be agreed by the parties. If the parties agree upon a certain law, the tribunal must apply that law.[142] Parties are not restricted in their choice of law. They can choose the law of the home state, the host state, a third state, or some other set of rules. They can even rely on international law broadly or general principles common to civilised nations. The choice could, in principle, be virtually anything including a modern *lex mercatoria*, *Sharia* law, or even a regime drafted by the parties for just this purpose. In practice, the chosen law is often the law of the host state.[143]

[139] Presidential Decree No 31 of 2012 concerning disputes that are not submitted to the jurisdiction of ICSID; ICSID received the government's notification on 27 September 2012.

[140] ICSID Convention, Art 42, para (1); UNCITRAL Arbitration Rules, Art 33, para (1); Stockholm Chamber of Commerce, Art 22, para (1).

[141] Y Banifatemi, 'The Law Applicable in Investment Treaty Arbitration', in K Yannaca-Small, *Arbitration Under International Investment Agreements: A Guide to the Key Issues* (Oxford University Press, 2010) 192.

[142] ICSID Convention, Art 42, para (1).

[143] JH Dalhuisen and AT Guzman, 'The Applicable Law in Foreign Investment Disputes' (*SSRN*, 30 January 2013) 5 http://ssrn.com/abstract=2209503 (accessed 25 November 2019).

As is common with BITs around the world, most BITs to which Indonesia is a party do not contain an express choice of law. Frequently, the BIT is applicable in conjunction with the principles and applicable rules of international law. In the Agreement between the Government of the Republic of Indonesia and the Government of the Republic of India for the Promotion and Protection of Investments for example, it is stated that all investments shall be governed by the laws in force in the territory of the contracting party in which such investments are made, in other words, the law of the host state. The freedom-based approach is also being proposed in the Bill of Indonesian International Civil Law, which was prepared on the initiative of the National Law Development Agency, and which states that the law that must be used first is the law chosen by the parties. However, it is important to note that the choice of law referred to here is a law that applies to the dispute resolution process through arbitration, not through a court. Of course, in determining the choice of law, general legal principles apply, for example the principle that in the absence of agreement between the parties the law that applies to foreign investment is the law of the host state. So, in the event of a dispute between a foreign investor and Indonesia, if the parties have not chosen a governing law, Indonesian law will be used.

Furthermore, the drafters of the ICSID Convention envisaged, among other possibilities, that in the event of a gap in the applicable domestic law, arbitrators might turn to international law to fill the gap.[144] In *Amco Asia v Indonesia*,[145] an early ICSID Arbitration, the tribunal proceeded by relying primarily on general principles of law and public international law in order to award *Amco* considerable compensation for damage. Despite being annulled by Indonesia in 1986 by the ad hoc committee on the grounds that the tribunal failed to apply Indonesian law to the state contract,[146] the newly establish committee dealing with the resubmitted case also took the view that international law was fully applicable to the state contract under review.[147] It is essential to consider that, as in *Amco v Indonesia*, most of the earlier cases in ICSID arbitration were related to contract claims. By contrast, recent cases often concern treaty claims, especially claims relating to BITs. Therefore, the ICSID tribunal has applied the provisions of BITs to the substance of disputes, as well as general international law rules, besides the law of the state concerned.[148]

Mandatory law also needs to be taken into consideration. For example, in the Coal Mining Concession Work Contract or Work Contract in the mineral and coal mining sector, the applicable law is Indonesian law, as stipulated in Indonesia's legislation.[149] Like natural resources, mineral mining is a branch that plays an important role in economic life

[144] ICSID, *Documents Concerning the Origin and the Formulation of the Convention* (ICSID 1968) 803 in AR Parra, 'Applicable Law in Investor-State Arbitration' in AW Rovine (ed), *Contemporary Issues in International Arbitration and Mediation*, (Martinus Nijhoff Publishers, 2007) 6.

[145] *Amco Asia Corporation and others v Republic of Indonesia*, ICSID Case No ARB/81/1, Award (20 November 1984), 1 ICSID Rep 413, para 147–148.

[146] *Amco Asia Corporation and others v Republic of Indonesia*, ICSID Case No ARB/81/1, decision on Annulment (16 May 1985), ICSID Rep 509, para 38–44.

[147] *Amco Asia Corporation and others v Republic of Indonesia*, ICSID Case No ARB/81/1, Award in Resubmitted Proceeding (31 March 1990), 1 ICSID Rep 569, para 40.

[148] Y Caliskan, 'Dispute Settelement in International Invesment Law' in Y Aksar (ed), *Implementing International Economic Law, Through Dispute Settlement Mechanisms* (Martinus Nijhoff Publishers, 2011) 141.

[149] The 1945 Constitution of the Republic of Indonesia, Art 33, paras (2) and (3), Act No 11 of 1967 concerning Basic Provisions of Mining, Arts 10 and 8, para (1).

in order to achieve the prosperity of the Indonesian people. As this is a mandatory law, such contracts are required to always use Indonesian law in the contract.

C. Recognition and Enforcement of Arbitral Awards

Every contracting state of the ICSID is obliged to recognise arbitral awards as binding and to enforce the pecuniary obligations imposed by those awards within its territories as if they were final judgments of a court in that state. Furthermore, the execution of the international arbitral award will be regulated in accordance with the applicable regulations in the state where the execution will be carried out.[150] Pursuant to Article 54(2) of the ICSID Convention, Indonesia has designated its Supreme Court as the court competent for the purpose of recognising and enforcing awards rendered. Following the registration of the award, under the Arbitration Act 1999, an international arbitration award (eg an investment arbitration award) involving Indonesia may be enforced in Indonesia under a writ of execution from the Chief Justice of the Supreme Court which is then delegated to the Central Jakarta District Court.[151] To our knowledge, to date no investment arbitration awards have been registered with the Central Jakarta District Court. The following reasons explain why: (i) ICISD lacked jurisdiction to issue the award, as in the case of *Government of the Province of East Kalimantan v PT Kaltim Prima Coal and others*,[152] and in the case of *Rafat Ali Rizvi v Republic of Indonesia*;[153] (ii) the case was closed with the agreements of the parties, as in the case of *Cemex Asia Holding Ltd v Republic of Indonesia*;[154] (iii) the lawsuit was withdrawn by one of the parties, as in the case of *Oleovest Pte. Ltd v Republic of Indonesia*,[155] and in the case of *Nusa Tenggara Partnership BV and PT Newmont Nusa Tenggara v Republic of Indonesia*,[156] or where Indonesia was the winning party as in the case of *Churchill Mining Plc and Planet Mining Pty Ltd v Republic of Indonesia*.[157]

BKPM has reported that the Government of the Republic of Indonesia is currently drafting a new model BIT, and is renegotiating current investment treaties. In 2004, Indonesia announced that it intended to terminate its BITs by letting them expire. Since then, 25 of the Indonesian BITs have been terminated.[158] This action was motivated by the desire to

[150] ICSID Convention, Art 54; See also Nugroho, *Penyelesaian Sengketa Arbitrase* (n 18) 446.

[151] The Arbitration Act 1999, Art 66 e.

[152] *Government of the Province of East Kalimantan v PT Kaltim Prima Coal and others*, ICSID Case No ARB/07/3, Award (28 December 2009).

[153] *Rafat Ali Rizvi v Republic of Indonesia*, ICSID Case No ARB/11/13, Award (16 July 2013).

[154] *Cemex Asia Holdings Ltd v Republic of Indonesia*, ICSID Case No ARB/04/3, Award (23 February 2007), concluded by agreement of the parties on 23 February 2007. See also UNTAD, '2004 – Cemex v. Indonesia' (*Investment Policy Hub*, 31 December 2019) https://investmentpolicy.unctad.org/investment-dispute-settlement/cases/171/cemex-v-indonesia.

[155] *Oleovest Pte. Ltd v Republic of Indonesia*, ICSID Case No ARB/16/26, Order taking note of the discontinuance of the proceeding pursuant to ICSID Arbitration Rule 43(1) (12 December 2017). See also UNTAD, '2016 – Oleovest v. Indonesia' (*Investment Policy Hub*, 31 December 2019) https://investmentpolicy.unctad.org/investment-dispute-settlement/cases/730/oleovest-v-indonesia.

[156] *Nusa Tenggara Partnership B.V. and PT Newmont Nusa Tenggara v Republic of Indonesia*, ICSID Case No ARB/14/15, Order of the Secretary-General Taking Note of the Discontinuance of the Proceeding (29 August 2014).

[157] *Churchill Mining PLC and Planet Mining Pty Ltd v Republic of Indonesia*, ICSID Case No ARB/12/14 and 12/40.

[158] See UNCTAD, 'Indonesia' (n 110).

renegotiate with better terms, especially regarding clauses on dispute settlement. It was also argued that the Decision on Jurisdiction issued by the tribunal in the case *Churchill Mining Plc v Indonesia* in 2014[159] influenced this action. Indonesia's intention to issue a new model BIT was reported in conjunction with the announcement of intention to terminate existing BITs. There is little information regarding the draft model BIT. However, according to the BKPM, the draft will limit BIT terms to ten years and will exclude the automatic renewal provision that is usually contained in BITs. According to the BKPM, the draft model BIT was scheduled to be finalised and proposed in 2016. Despite signing a new BIT with Singapore on 11 October 2018,[160] the text of such a new model has not yet been made publicly available. At present, the Indonesian draft Model BIT has been described as containing carve-outs, safeguards and clarifications aimed at striking a balance between the right of the state to regulate and the rights of investors, while maintaining the state's policy space.[161]

[159] *Churchill Mining PLC and Planet Mining Pty Ltd v Republic of Indonesia*, ICSID Case No ARB/12/14 and 12/40, Decision on Jurisdiction (24 February 2014).

[160] Ministry of Trade and Industry of Singapore, 'Singapore and Indonesia Sign Bilateral Investment Treaty to Promote Stronger Economic Ties' (2018) www.mti.gov.sg/-/media/MTI/Newsroom/Press-Releases/2018/10/Singapore-and-Indonesia-sign-Bilateral-Investment-Treaty-to-promote-stronger-economic-ties-11Oct2018/press-release-on-signing-of-indonesia-singapore-bit-on-11-oct-2018.pdf (accessed 30 October 2019).

[161] M Scherer, *International Arbitration in the Energy Sector* (Oxford University Press, 2018) 327.

6

The Harmonisation of Private International Law

I. Indonesia's Role in the Work of the Hague Conference, UNCITRAL, UNIDROIT and Other Organisations

The international harmonisation of contract law encourages trade and other commercial interactions across national borders. Efforts towards harmonisation are principally carried out by international institutions and organisations. Work on harmonisation is conducted both by bodies of a public nature, for example the United Nations and its supporting bodies such as UNCITRAL, and by independent international organisations such as UNIDROIT.[1] Indonesia has not directly engaged with this harmonisation process. It has played no active role in the preparation of international instruments concerning harmonisation, neither those establishing 'hard' obligations nor those setting out 'soft' principles. However, this does not mean that Indonesia is unaffected by, or uninvolved with, the international harmonisation of contract law. For example, Indonesia's participation in various international trade contracts has undoubtedly influenced the development of national law towards alignment with international norms. That said, the impact of this process is limited. At present, Indonesian law continues to draw heavily from Dutch colonial law, which in some cases is not compatible with the development or modernisation of international trade activities. This weakness presents an obstacle to international trade transactions conducted by Indonesian parties with partners from other countries.[2] Remedying this, by ensuring Indonesian law and regulations are effective in governing international commercial contracts, will be an important factor in attracting foreign business people to do business in Indonesia.[3] Without harmonisation, Indonesia's positive law will increasingly be marginalised in the international trade arena.[4] It is therefore essential that legal provisions regarding contracts be revised to respond to the needs of international business.

This chapter discusses the role of Indonesia in various international organisations related to the harmonisation of private international law. Also presented are a number of international agreements that are being considered for Indonesian involvement.

[1] UNIDROIT, *UNIDROIT Principles of International Commercial Contracts 2010* (International Institute for the Unification of Private Law, 2010).

[2] IBR Supancana, 'Perkembangan Hukum Kontrak Dagang Intenasional' (Badan Pembinaan Hukum Nasional, 2012) 51 www.bphn.go.id/data/documents/pk-2012-2.pdf (accessed 14 November 2019).

[3] S Mandala, 'The Unidroit Principles of International Commercial Contracts as a Reference for Modern Indonesian Contracts' [2007] *Indonesian Law Journal*, 13, 22.

[4] Taufiqurrahman, 'Upaya Pembaruan Hukum Nasional di Bidang kontrak Jual Beli Barang Internasional', (2010) 25(3) *Yuridika* 269, 270.

First, the Hague Conference on Private International Law (HCCH), an intergovernmental organisation working in the field of private international law. Indonesia is not a member of HCCH. As such, the conventions, protocols, and soft legal instruments produced by HCCH have not been utilised in Indonesia. The Indonesian Government through the Ministry of Law and Human Rights has indicated it wishes to become a Member State of HCCH, but has not given any timetable for this. Nevertheless, many legal instruments provided by the HCCH can be utilised by non-members. Indonesia could engage with these instruments, an act of international cooperation that would strengthen legal certainty and contribute to the building of a healthy investment climate. Yet Indonesia has not availed itself of these opportunities. Of the 38 international conventions in the civil and commercial sectors owned by the HCCH, none have been followed by Indonesia. This is disappointing, but there is reason to hope for increased engagement in future. First, the Government of Indonesia remains active in several Hague Conference meetings.[5] Second, the Indonesian Government is considering accession to a number of HCCH conventions in order to improve Indonesia's ranking in the World Bank's Ease of Doing Business index and achieve the principle of simple, fast, and low-cost justice, pursuant to Article 2, paragraph (4) of the Judicial Power Act 2009. The conventions being considered for accession are:

i. The 1961 Hague Convention Abolishing the Requirement of Legalization for Foreign Public Documents (the Apostille Convention).
   a. Accession would be in line with the vision of the current government administration, namely: improving the quality of public services by eliminating "bureaucratic red tape", encouraging investment/capital from abroad, and realising Indonesia's commitment to continue to encourage open government. In this regard, it must be noted here that one of the benchmarks of success in the National Strategy for Corruption Prevention and Eradication, contained in Presidential Regulation No 55 of 2012, is to increase the index of 'ease of doing business' which is assessed every year by the World Bank. Indonesia's participation in the Apostille Convention would increase the index of ease of doing business in Indonesia.

ii. The 1965 Convention on the Service Abroad of Judicial and Extrajudicial Documents in Civil or Commercial Matters.

iii The 1968 Convention on Taking of Evidence Abroad in Civil or Commercial Matters.

In addition, from the end of 2014 to 2018 an initiative was organised to encourage Indonesia to participate in the 1980 Hague Convention on the Civil Aspects of International Child Abduction, another HCCH convention.[6] At present, an academic paper concerning the

[5] HCCH, 'Conclusions and Recommendations' (The Fourth Asia Pacific Conference of the Hague Conference on Private International Law: The Work Of The Hague Conference On Private International Law, Manila, 26–28 October 2011) https://assets.hcch.net/upload/ap4concl.pdf (accessed 24 November 2019); HCCH, 'Vingt-deuxième session Acte final La Haye, le 2 juillet 2019 (Twenty-Second Session Final Act The Hague, 2 July 2019)' (Twenty-Second Session Recognition and Enforcement of Foreign Judgments, The Hague, on 8 June–2 July 2019) https://assets.hcch.net/docs/f55fc0a1-1a3c-4368-9199-48e8df11ff3e.pdf (accessed 24 November 2019).

[6] The discussion is conducted under the coordination of the Directorate of Central Authority and International Law of the Directorate General of General Administration of Law, the Ministry of Law and Human Rights. Some academics of the Faculty of Law, *Universitas* Indonesia, namely Prof Dr Zulfa Djoko Basuki, Ms Lita Arijati, and Ms Priskila Pratita Penasthika, have been active in the discussion and preparation to accede to this Hague Convention.

Bill on Indonesia's Accession to the 1980 Hague Convention is being prepared by the Directorate General of General Administration of Law, the Ministry of Law and Human Rights.[7] If the Bill becomes law, Indonesia will be bound by the provisions regarding the return of children in the 1980 Hague Convention for cases of international child abduction.

Second, the International Institute for the Unification of Private Law (UNIDROIT), an intergovernmental organisation for the harmonisation of private international law. On 1 January 2009, Indonesia became the 63rd member of UNIDROIT through accession to the UNIDROIT Statute.[8] Indonesia's membership is based on Presidential Regulation No 59 of 2008 concerning the ratification of the statutes of international institutions for the unification of private law. Indonesia is also a member of the UNIDROIT Finance Committee for the period 2018–2021. Indonesia has acceded to one UNIDROIT convention, namely the Cape Town Convention, through Presidential Regulation No 8 of 2007 concerning Ratification of the Convention on International Interests in Mobile Equipment (Cape Town Convention) and Aircraft Equipment Protocol. The ratification of the Cape Town Convention and the promulgation of the Aviation Act 2009 have provided guarantees and legal certainty for the parties to the convention. As a result, Indonesia now boasts a conducive investment climate for investors in the national air transport industry, with subsequent sustained growth of the national air transport industry both in terms of the number of aircraft and the volumes of passengers and cargo. Indonesia has also benefited from the UNIDROIT Principles on International Commercial Contracts (UPICC). These principles are soft law, so not binding in themselves, but can be used as a reference and adjusted based on the specific needs and conditions of a country. Because of its flexible nature and its capacity to provide a general contract law, the UPICC may represent the best source to assist the development of modern Indonesian contract law.[9]

Third, the International Chamber of Commerce (ICC). The ICC itself is based in Paris, but has branches in almost all countries, including Indonesia. ICC Indonesia is the National Committee of Indonesia to the International Chamber of Commerce.[10] Some important international instruments contributing to the ICC include: Uniform Customs and Practice for Documentary Credit ('UCP'); Incoterms 2010; Dispute Board Rules; and the ICC Arbitration Rules. UCP is often used by banks and Indonesian companies that export and import their products with payment by letters of credit. Incoterms is also used in the practice of import and export contracts. Further, rules made by the ICC, although not themselves part of any convention, become standard trade usage (*lex mercatoria*) and are influential for Indonesian commercial law. Indonesia is also active in ICC Arbitration, some of whose court members come from Indonesia.[11]

[7] PP Penasthika, L Arijati, and AG Anggriana, 'International Child Abduction: Bagaimana Indonesia Meresponnya?' (2018) 48 *Jurnal Hukum & Pembangunan* 536; Information provided by Prof Zulfa Djoko Basuki and Ms Lita Arijati who were actively involved in the discussion on the accession to the 1980 Hague Convention on the Civil Aspects of International Child Abduction with the Directorate General of General Administration of Law, the Ministry of Law and Human Rights, 18–20 April 2018.

[8] UNIDROIT, 'Membership/Etats Membres' (*UNIDROIT*, 3 April 2020), www.unidroit.org/about-unidroit/membership (accessed 26 November 2019).

[9] Mandala, 'The Unidroit Principles' (n 3) 21.

[10] See www.iccindonesia.org/.

[11] ICC, 'Court Members' (*ICC*, 1 July 2018) https://iccwbo.org/dispute-resolution-services/icc-international-court-arbitration/court-members/#1478195489936-1a1acd15-7f6d accessed 2 December 2019.

Fourth, the United Nations Commission on International Trade Law (UNCITRAL). UNCITRAL is the main body of the United Nations established to advance the harmonisation and unification of legal provisions in the field of international trade. Indonesia was re-elected as a member of UNCITRAL for the period 2019–2025,[12] together with six other countries – Singapore, Japan, China, Vietnam, South Korea, and Malaysia – as representatives of the Asia Pacific region. Indonesia succeeded in getting 160 votes from a total of 193 countries. The re-election of Indonesia as a member of UNCITRAL shows the trust of the international community in Indonesia's active role in the field of international trade law. Although elected as a member, Indonesia has so far not ratified any UNCITRAL conventions,[13] except the Convention on the Recognition and Enforcement of Foreign Arbitral Awards (the 1958 New York Convention) that was acceded to on 7 October 1981, through Presidential Decree No 34 of 1981 concerning Ratification of the Convention on the Recognition and Enforcement of Foreign Arbitral Awards. This accession was an important step taken by Indonesia towards the implementation of foreign arbitral awards, despite the many obstacles encountered in its implementation as previously discussed in Chapter 5 on Arbitration.

In addition, steps are being taken towards acceding to other conventions under UNCITRAL. Chief among these is the Convention on the Contracts for the International Sale of Goods (CIGS). Indonesia is one of the eight countries in Southeast Asia that have not ratified the CISG. Its ratification is important because most extra-territorial business in Indonesia is carried out with partners from CISG member countries (Singapore, the EU countries, the US, Canada, Australia, and Korea).[14] One important effort towards its ratification is the existence of an academic paper which was prepared by the National Legal Development Agency under the administration of the Ministry of Law and Human Rights.[15] However, the Indonesian Government has remained silent about its intentions regarding accession to the CISG, leading many scholars to attempt to persuade the government to ratify the CISG.[16] Moving towards uniformity of principles in contract law will make the implementation of international trade transactions more effective.[17] Turning to the field of arbitration, Indonesia also has not ratified the 1976 Arbitration Rules concerning the Arbitration Procedure Law and the 1985 UNCITRAL Model Law on International Commercial Arbitration. As discussed in the previous Chapter 5, the legal basis for arbitration is found in the Arbitration Act 1999, which mostly governs domestic arbitration.

[12] Previously, Indonesia was elected twice as a member of UNCITRAL between 1977–1983 and 2013–2019; See UNCITRAL, 'United Nations General Assembly elects new UNCITRAL Members' (UNCITRAL, 2 July 2019) https://uncitral.un.org/en/news/united-nations-general-assembly-elects-new-uncitral-members-0 (accessed 15 November 2019).

[13] UNCITRAL, 'Overview of the status of UNCITRAL Conventions and Model Laws' (UNCITRAL, 15 November 2016) www.uncitral.org/pdf/english/TAC/Status/Overview-Status-Table.pdf (accessed 5 December 2019).

[14] A Kusumadara, 'Pentingnya Ratikasi UN Convention on Contract for The International Sales of Goods oleh Pemerintah Indonesia' [2006] *Jurnal Forum Penelitian* 1, 5.

[15] S Oktaviandra, 'Indonesia and Its Reluctance to Ratify the United Nations Convention on Contracts for the International Sales of Goods (CISG)' (2018) 8(3) *Indonesia Law Review* 243, 249. See also H Juwana, 'Ratifikasi Konvensi PBB Mengenai Kontrak Jual Beli Barang Internasional' (Badan Pembinaan Hukum Nasional, 2013) <www.bphn.go.id/data/documents/na_bbm.pdf (accessed 17 December 2019).

[16] Oktaviandra, 'Indonesia and Its Reluctance' (n 15) 253; M Minarosa, 'The Principles of International Trade Contract as Reference of Indonesian Contract Law' (2018) 21(2) *European Research Studies Journal* 514, 519.

[17] S Hutabarat, 'Harmonisasi Hukum Kontrak dan Dampaknya pada Hukum Kontrak Indonesia' (2016) 2(1) *Veritas et Justitia* 112, 130.

Alignment of the Arbitration Act 1999 with international arbitration rules would have a positive impact on international trade and would provide guarantees to foreign investors who are willing to invest in Indonesia.

Fifth, the Association of Southeast Asian Nations (ASEAN). Indonesia's role in ASEAN is also important in the context of harmonising international trade law. The establishment of the ASEAN Economic Community in 2015, along with the already-existing ASEAN Free Trade Area, has made contract law a very important tool in supporting trade activities and international business transactions in the ASEAN region. This is not an easy matter, given the differences in legal systems amongst ASEAN member countries.[18] There is therefore a strong argument that reform of Indonesian contract law must align with the development of the harmonisation of ASEAN contract law. Accordingly, the amendment of Indonesian contract law, currently contained in the Book III of BW, must comply with the recommendations given by ASEAN. ASEAN recommends that member countries ratify the CISG or reform their national contract law with reference to the CISG. Alternatively, ASEAN suggests member countries use the UNIDROIT Principles of International Commercial Contracts (UPICC) as a reference for the reform of national contract law.

II. Conclusion and the Future of Private International Law

Indonesian private international law remains grounded in Dutch colonial legislation, jurisprudence, and doctrines. In modern times, the Indonesian Government has made some efforts to codify private international law. Initial attempts were made in 1983 and 1997 but, for unknown reasons, the 1983 and 1997 Bills never reached the Parliament. The most recent effort began in 2014, when the Ministry of Law and Human Rights commissioned an academic paper proposing a new Indonesian Private International Law Bill. Though completed in 2015, this Bill still has not reached the Parliament. But the commercial world has not stood still waiting for legislative action. Indonesian people and companies regularly establish civil and commercial relations with foreigners, while the Indonesian Government enters into international agreements, such as the ASEAN Economic Community, that affect Indonesian companies. As a result, Indonesian judges are having to deal with increasing numbers of civil and commercial cases containing foreign elements. Because of the legislature's failure to codify and modernise Indonesian private international law, judges are left without proper guidance on the law. Often, they will apply BW to private international cases,[19] even though the BW contains no provisions on the conflict of laws or private international law.

Hence, two attempts – the 1983 and 1997 Bills – to enact Bills of Private International Law have failed, and the current attempt – the 2015 Bill – does not look like it will become law any time soon. Given this, it might be better that provisions governing private international matters are accommodated in other Bills. It is also suggested that Indonesia adopt

[18] S Mandala, 'Pembaharuan Hukum Kontrak Indonesia dalam Kerangka Harmonisasi Hukum Kontrak ASEAN' (2012) 1(2) *Jurnal Rechtsvinding* 295, 299.

[19] IBR Supancana, *Naskah Akademik Rancangan Undang-Undang tentang Hukum Perdata Internasional (lanjutan)* (Badan Pembinaan Hukum Nasional Kementerian Hukum dan Hak Asasi Manusia RI, 2015) 4–5 www.bphn.go.id/data/documents/na_ruu_ttg_hukum_perdata_internasional_(lanjutan).pdf (accessed 8 July 2018).

model laws or accede to international conventions on private international law, in order to speed up the development of new Indonesian private international law and promote harmonisation with laws and practices found in other countries.

The following paragraphs discuss twelve issues that need to be addressed when drafting the future Indonesian private international law.

First, current Indonesian private international law lacks rules of characterisation, incidental question, *dépeçage*, and *renvoi*. Insofar as these rules are recognised, they are found in doctrines established during the Dutch colonial era. But doctrines are not binding on judges, so at present implementation of these important rules of private international law is left to the whims of individual judges. If the rules of characterisation, incidental question, *dépeçage*, and *renvoi* were to be expressly governed in an Act, they would become binding on Indonesian judges.

Second, current Indonesian civil procedure codes do not have provisions for taking evidence and serving process abroad for the purpose of Indonesian proceedings, nor do they have provisions for taking evidence and serving process in Indonesia for the purpose of foreign proceedings. There has been a sharp increase in the number of Indonesians who experience civil disputes with parties outside of Indonesia, or have civil cases pending outside of Indonesia.[20] To deal with this issue, the Indonesian Government should consider acceding to the 1965 Hague Service Convention and the 1970 Hague Evidence Convention. These instruments respectively provide mechanisms for the service of judicial documents on and the taking of evidence from parties situated in one contracting state for the purpose of civil proceedings in another contracting state.

Third, the new Indonesian private international law must implement the doctrines of *forum non conveniens* and *lis alibi pendens*, and the rules of anti-suit injunctions, interim measures, and choice of court agreements. These well-established doctrines in private international law are often ignored by Indonesian courts, as demonstrated by several cases written in previous chapters. Similarly, the rules of anti-suit injunctions, interim measures, and choice of court agreements in private international cases are also often disregarded by Indonesian courts. If those doctrines and rules are expressly governed in an Act, they will become binding on Indonesian judges. This will provide legal certainty for all parties, both Indonesian and non-Indonesian.

Fourth, rules on state immunity and state-owned enterprises must be expressly governed in the new Indonesian private international law. Currently, the Indonesian Government advocates for the doctrine of absolute immunity, to protect the interests of the Indonesian state in foreign courts. On the other hand, Indonesian courts apply the doctrine of restrictive immunity to protect the interests of Indonesian nationals who conduct commercial transactions with foreign states in Indonesia. Indonesia may resolve this uncertainty in its application of jurisdictional immunities of states by passing a law that governs immunities of states, or by joining the 2004 UN Convention on Jurisdictional Immunities of States and Their Property.

Fifth, a new Indonesian private international law is also needed to provide choice of law rules to determine the applicable law for contracts with foreign elements. Currently,

[20] Nota Kesepahaman Kementerian Luar Negeri Republik Indonesia dan Mahkamah Agung Republik Indonesia tentang Penanganan Permintaan Bantuan Teknis Hukum dalam Masalah Perdata No PRJ/HI/102/02/2018/01 No 01/NK/MA/2/2018, Art 1(2).

in the absence of rules on this issue, the Indonesian courts have developed a tendency of simply applying Indonesian law to contracts in which the parties have validly chosen different governing laws. The Bills of Indonesian Private International Law have adopted the doctrine of freedom of contract, including the freedom of choosing a governing law for the parties in contracts. The 1983, 1998, and 2015 Bills all provide that the law applicable to a contract with foreign elements is the parties' choice of law, whether the choice is made expressly or impliedly. Where the parties do not make a choice of law for their contract, the Bills suggest that the law applicable should be decided through application of the concept of 'characteristic performance'. Although the choice of law rules proposed by the Bills have long been accepted as prevailing legal doctrines by Indonesian scholars, judicial practice is otherwise. Indonesian judges do not always follow the doctrines, preferring instead to simply apply Indonesian law to contracts in which the parties have expressly or impliedly chosen different governing laws. This judicial practice has been demonstrated in several cases of international contracts brought to Indonesian courts, as explained in the previous chapters. The uncertainty concerning the applicable law for contracts with foreign elements may be solved when the Bill of Indonesian Private International Law is passed to become an Act. The choice of law rules in the Act will be binding on all parties in international contracts and on all Indonesian judges that adjudicate the parties' disputes. It is suggested that the Bill of Indonesian Private International Law adopts the Hague Principles on Choice of Law in International Commercial Contracts to bring the Bill in line with the latest principles practiced in other countries.

Sixth, choice of law rules concerning property with foreign elements should also be governed in the new Indonesian Private International Law Act or in other Acts that govern rights to property. Developing more detailed choice of law rules concerning property is important because the current Indonesian Private International Law only governs the applicable law for Indonesian immovable property (Article 17 AB). It does not provide choice of law rules for movable – tangible and intangible – property with foreign elements.

Seventh, as regards the new Indonesian private international law on family matters, all laws and regulations must be drafted to respect the religious laws governing family matters. That is because the substance of family law in Indonesia covers both the national and religious laws of the parties, whether or not the parties are Indonesian nationals or foreigners. In general, family law in the Indonesian legal system is based on the national laws, the Compilation of Islamic Law, BW, and other religious laws. Failure to comply with the substantive requirements of religious laws concerning family matters will render the parties' actions invalid.

Eighth, for family matters relating to children, the Indonesian private international law should apply the law of the children's habitual residence, and be drafted in the best interests of the children, whether they are Indonesian nationals or foreigners. Several conventions have provisions worth being adopted or referred to in Indonesian private international law. These are: the 1996 Hague Convention on Jurisdiction, Applicable Law, Recognition, Enforcement and Co-operation in Respect of Parental Responsibility and Measures for the Protection of Children; the 1993 Hague Convention on Protection of Children and Co-Operation in Respect of Intercountry Adoption; and the 1980 Hague Convention on the Civil Aspects of International Child Abduction. Alternatively, Indonesia could directly accede to these Conventions, so that they will enter Indonesian law upon the accession and approval from the Parliament. These conventions will help protect the best interests of Indonesian children in private international cases.

Ninth, regarding competition law, the Bill that is being drafted to amend the Anti-Monopoly Act 1999 should contain provisions that expressly govern the application of the Single Economic Entity doctrine and the Effect doctrine. Under current competition law, the two doctrines are regularly applied by the Indonesian Commission Competition to cross-border anti-competitive practices, although the doctrines are not written in the Anti-Monopoly Act 1999. Including the two doctrines in the provisions of the future Anti-monopoly Act will provide legal certainty for all business actors. The new Anti-monopoly Act should also accommodate private enforcement claims on competition matters and should govern litigation between private parties whose claims are brought either in a contractual context, or as a tort claim in anti-monopoly matters. This will enable individual plaintiffs to seek compensation for damages, by contrast with the current mechanism which only allows the Commission to bring claims in competition law.

Tenth, in relation to insolvency and bankruptcy law, it is important to adopt the UNCITRAL Model Law on Cross-Border Insolvency. This can be incorporated into the Bill that is being drafted to amend the Bankruptcy and Suspension of Debt Payment Act 2004. The adoption of the UNCITRAL Model Law and establishment of cooperation with neighbouring countries are necessary to deal with cross-border insolvency cases. The current Act does not provide any mechanism for the recognition and enforcement of cross-border insolvency, despite the increasing number of cases of cross-border insolvency.

Eleventh, in the field of shipping claims, the new Shipping Act must have provisions to determine the court that has jurisdiction over a shipping claim. The current Shipping Act 2008 does not provide such choice of court rules. Based on the current judicial practice, the courts that asserted jurisdiction in shipping claims were usually those in the districts where the defendants or ship owners have their residences. The new Shipping Act should also provide detailed rules on the process of ship arrest, which currently is not the subject of any regulation. As a result of this lack of regulation, Indonesian courts are reluctant to issue orders for ship arrest, meaning that claimants have to bring civil lawsuits to district courts to request ship arrest – although civil lawsuit is not required for ship arrest under Article 223, paragraph (1) of the Shipping Act 2008.

Twelfth, there is a prospect of Indonesia joining treaties or conventions on choice of court agreements and on the recognition and enforcement of foreign judgments. However, recognition and enforcement should be limited to foreign judgments on commercial matters. For foreign judgments on civil matters unrelated to commercial transactions, there is little prospect that they can be recognised and enforced in Indonesia. That is because civil matters strongly relate to the culture and beliefs of Indonesian society that are respected by judges, unlike commercial matters that are considered independent from Indonesia's culture and beliefs. Therefore, in future, it is expected that foreign judgments on commercial matters will be recognised and enforced more easily in Indonesia, insofar as the judgments are not in conflict with Indonesian public policy.

Thirteenth and finally, Indonesia needs to pass a new law that specifically governs international arbitration. The current Arbitration Act 1999 contains very few provisions on international arbitration. A specific international arbitration Act will provide foreign parties with legal certainty in the settlement of their disputes with Indonesian parties in Indonesia. It is recommended that the UNCITRAL Model Law on International Commercial Arbitration Law be adopted into this proposed international arbitration Act, to bring the Act in line with the international practices.

GLOSSARY OF TERMS AND ABBREVIATIONS

AB	*Algemene Bepalingen van Wetgeving voor Nederlandsch Indie.* General Provisions of Legislation for the Dutch East Indies. Promulgated by State Gazette No 23 of 1847.
adat	Set of norms, usually unwritten, applicable to the indigenous population of a territory.
BHP	*Balai Harta Peninggalan.* Office for the Administration of Estates.
BKPM	*Badan Koordinasi Penanaman Modal.* Investment Coordinating Board. Non-ministerial government agency for approving domestic and foreign direct investment in Indonesia.
BPSK	*Badan Penyelesaian Sengketa Konsumen.* Consumer Dispute Resolution Body. Quasi-judicial body in all districts in Indonesia.
BW	*Burgerlijk Wetboek voor Nederlandsch-Indie.* Civil Code for the Dutch East Indies. Enacted in 1847 by the Dutch colonial government.
conservatoir beslag	Conservatory seizure. Governed by Articles 226–227 HIR and 261 Rbg.
hifz al-nasl	Preservation of family lineage. An Islamic doctrine.
HIR	*Het Herziene Indonesisch Reglement,* also referred to as *Herziene Indlandsch Reglement.* Literally the Revised Indonesian (Domestic) Regulation. Enacted in 1941 as a revision of the earlier procedure law *Reglement op de uitoefening van de politie, de burgerlijke rechtspleging en de strafvordering onder de Inlanders en de Vreemde Oosterlingen op Java en Madura* 1849 (often abbreviated *Inlandsch Reglement* (IR)).
Hoge Raad	Supreme Court of the Netherlands.
Hooggerechtshof	Supreme Court of the Dutch East Indies and Court of Cassation.
IS	*Indische Staatsregeling.* The Dutch Colonial Constitution applicable to the Dutch East Indies. Promulgated by State Gazette No 415 of 1925 to replace the previous *Reglement op het beleid der regering van Nederlandsch Indie* (1855–1926).
KHI	*Kompilasi Hukum Islam.* Compilation of Islamic Law. Pursuant to Presidential Instruction No 1 of 1991, guidance for judges of the religious courts in matters of Islamic marriage, succession, and trust (*waqaf*).

KPPU (also *ICC)*	*Komisi Pengawas Persaingan Usaha*. Indonesian Competition Commission. Quasi-judicial body with jurisdiction to implement the Anti-Monopoly Act 1999.
Mahkamah Agung	Supreme Court of Indonesia
Mahkamah Pelayaran	Literally, Maritime Court. A panel of experts in maritime matters under the Ministry of Transportation and based in Jakarta. It is not a judicial body.
MK	*Mahkamah Konstitusi*. Constitutional Court of the Republic of Indonesia.
nasab	Family lineage or filiation based on a valid marriage under Islamic law.
Nieuw Burgerlijk Wetboek	New Netherlands Civil Code. Passed in 1992. Only applicable in the Netherlands.
onrechtmatige daad	Unlawful act. Used in BW to designate a tort.
PA	*Pengadilan Agama*. Religious Court. Located in all districts in Indonesia.
Pengadilan Tinggi	High Court. The appellate court situated in the capital city of each province in Indonesia.
PERMA	*Peraturan Mahkamah Agung*. Supreme Court Regulations. Issued from time to time by the Chief Justice of the Supreme Court to regulate court administrative and procedural matters. Unlike SEMA which are only binding on courts, PERMA are binding on all persons.
PK	*Peninjauan Kembali*. Extraordinary appeal. PK is brought before the Supreme Court of Indonesia.
PN	*Pengadilan Negeri*. Court of First Instance in all districts in Indonesia.
PT	*Perseroan Terbatas*. Limited liability company.
PT Tbk	*Perseroan Terbatas Terbuka*. Limited liability company offering shares to the public.
qadi	Islamic jurist. In the context of marriage, the person who solemnises an Islamic marriage.
Raad van Justitie	Court for European inhabitants and foreigners in the Dutch East Indies. The appellate court for judgments of the courts for indigenous inhabitants (*Landraad*).
Rbg	*Rechtsreglement Buitengewesten*. More fully known as *Reglement tot Regeling van het Rechtswezen in de Gewesten Buiten Java en Madura* (Procedure Code for Indigenous Outside of Java and Madura). Enacted in 1855. Code for courts outside of Java and Madura.

Rv	*Reglement op de Burgerlijke Rechtsvordering.* Civil procedure law for the *Raad van Justitie* and the *Hooggerechtshof* of the Dutch East Indies. Enacted in 1847.
SEMA	*Surat Edaran Mahkamah Agung.* Supreme Court Circular Letters. Issued from time to time by the Chief Justice of the Supreme Court to all lower courts in Indonesia, providing guidance on legal issues.
SKK Migas	*Satuan Kerja Khusus Pelaksana Kegiatan Usaha Hulu Minyak Dan Gas Bumi.* Special Task Force for Upstream Oil and Gas Business Activities. Government body that manages upstream oil and gas business activities under a cooperation contract with third parties.
Staatsblad	State Gazette in which the laws of Dutch East Indies were promulgated
talaq	Divorce in Islamic law whereby the husband dissolves a marriage.
Uitvoerbaar bij voorraad judgment	Lower court judgment which is immediately executable. Governed by Art 180 HIR and Art 191 para (1) Rbg.
wali amanat	Bond trustee in the Indonesian security market
wali nikah	Marriage guardian. In an Islamic marriage, the father or one of the male relatives of a bride who must consent to her marriage.
wali	Literally, a guardian.
waqaf	A charitable trust or foundation under Islamic law.
Wetboek van strafrecht voor Nederlandsch-Indie	Penal Code for the Dutch East Indies. Enacted in 1918.
Yayasan	Charitable foundation governed by the Foundation Act 2001 as amended in 2004.

BIBLIOGRAPHY

Books

Abdurrasyid P, *Suatu Pengantar Arbitrase dan Alternatif Penyelesaian Sengketa* (Fikahati Aneska, 2002)

Adolf H, *Dasar-dasar Hukum Kontrak Internasional* rev edn (Refika Aditama, 2007)

Agusman DD, *Treaties Under Indonesian Law: A Comparative Study* (PT Remaja Rosdakarya, 2014)

Bakker T, Siahaan S, and Naibaho U, 'Indonesia' in James H Carter (ed), *The International Arbitration Review* 9th edn (Law Business Research, 2018)

Banifatemi Y, 'The Law Applicable in Investment Treaty Arbitration', in K Yannaca-Small, *Arbitration Under International Investment Agreements: A Guide to the Key Issues* (Oxford University Press, 2010)

Bankas EK, *The State Immunity Controversy in International Law Private Suits Against Sovereign States in Domestic Courts* (Springer, 2005)

Basuki ZD and others, *Materi Pokok Hukum Perdata Internasional. Modul 2* (Universitas Terbuka, 2014)

——, *Materi Pokok Hukum Perdata Internasional. Modul 3* (Universitas Terbuka, 2014)

——, *Materi Pokok Hukum Perdata Internasional. Modul 5* (Universitas Terbuka, 2014)

—— *Materi pokok hukum perdata internasional. Modul 6* (Universitas Terbuka, 2014)

Batubara S and Purba O, *Arbitrase Internasional, Penyelesaian Sengketa Investasi Asing Melalui ICSID, UNCITRAL, dan SIAC* (Raih Asa Sukses, 2013)

Bermann GA, 'Interpretation and Application of the New York Convention by National Courts' in M Schauer and B Verschraegen (ed), *General Reports of the XIXth Congress of the International Academy of Comparative Law, Rapports Généraux du XIXème Congrès de l'Académie Internationale de Droit Comparé, Ius Comparatum- Global Studies in Comparative Law* 1st edn (Springer, 2017)

Born GB, *International Arbitration: Law and Practice* 2nd edn (Kluwer Law International, 2016)

Budidjaja T, *Public Policy as Grounds for Refusal of Recognition and Enforcement of Foreign Arbitral Awards in Indonesia* (PT Tatanusa, 2002)

Butt S, 'Arbitration in Indonesia: Largely Dependable Recognition and Enforcement' in A Reyes and W Gu (eds), *The Developing World of Arbitration, A Comparative Study of Arbitration Reform in the Asia Pacific* (Hart Publishing, 2018)

Caliskan Y, 'Dispute Settelement in International Invesment Law' in Y Aksar (ed), *Implementing International Economic Law, Through Dispute Settlement Mechanisms* (Martinus Nijhoff Publishers, 2011)

Chong A, 'Principle 1 General Principle' in A Chong (ed), *Asian Principles for the Recognition and Enforcement of Foreign Judgments* (Asian Business Law Institute, 2020)

Gautama S, *Hukum Perdata Internasional Indonesia Jilid Dua Bagian Dua Buku Ketiga* (Penerbit Alumni, 1973)

—— *Hukum Perdata Internasional Indonesia Jilid Dua (Bagian Tiga) Buku Keempat* (Penerbit Alumn,i 1973)

—— *Hukum Perdata Internasional Indonesia Buku Ketujuh Jilid Ke-Tiga (Bagian Pertama)* (Penerbit Alumni, 1981)

—— *Pengantar Hukum Perdata Internasional Indonesia* (Binacipta, 1985)

—— *Hukum Perdata Internasional Indonesia Jilid Kedua (Bagian Pertama) Cetakan Ke-3* (Eresco Bandung, 1986)

—— *Hukum Perdata Internasional Indonesia Jilid III Bagian 2 Buku Ke Delapan* (Penerbit Alumni, 1987)

—— *Hukum Perdata Internasional Indonesia Jilid II Bagian 5 Buku Ke enam* (Penerbit Alumni, 1988)

—— *Hukum Perdata Internasional Indonesia Jilid II Bagian 4 Buku Ke 5* (Penerbit Alumni 1992)

—— *Essays in Indonesian Law* (Citra Aditya Bakti, 1991)

—— *Perkembangan Arbitrase Dagang Internasional di Indonesia ('International Trade Arbitration Developments in Indonesia')* (PT Eresco, 1989)

—— *Hukum Perdata Internasional Indonesia, Jilid III Bagian 2 Buku Ke-8* (Alumni 2002)

Gerungan AFM, Alizia L and Sitorus R, 'Indonesia' in J Tirado (ed), *International Arbitration* 1st edn (Global Legal Group, 2015)

Hague Conference on Private International Law, *Principles on Choice of Law in International Commercial Contracts* (The Hague Conference on Private International Law Permanent Bureau, 2015)
Harahap MY, *Hukum Acara Perdata Tentang Gugatan, Persidangan, Penyitaan, Pembuktian, dan Putusan Pengadilan* 16th edn (Sinar Grafika, 2016)
Hartono S, *Pokok-Pokok Hukum Perdata Internasional Indonesia* (Binacipta, 1976)
ICSID, *Documents Concerning the Origin and the Formulation of the Convention* (ICSID, 1968)
Is MS, *Pengantar Ilmu Hukum* (Kencana, 2017)
Kartakusuma GR, 'Indonesia' in Dennis Campbell, *Remedies for International Sellers of Goods, Second Edition*, Vol 1 (Juris Publishing, 2014)
Kusumadara A, *Kontrak Bisnis Internasional Elemen-Elemen Penting dalam Penyusunannya* (Sinar Grafika, 2013)
Lukito L, *Legal Pluralism in Indonesia: Bridging the Unbridgeable* (Routledge, 2013)
Marilang, *Hukum Perikatan, Perikatan yang Lahir dari Perjanjian* (Indonesia Prime, 2017)
Marzuki PM, *An Introduction to Indonesian Law* (Setara Press, 2011)
Mayss AJ, *Principles of Conflict of Laws* 3rd edn (Cavendish Publishing Limited, 1999)
Nugroho SA, *Penyelesaian Sengketa Arbitrase dan Penerapan Hukumnya* (Prenada Media, 2016)
Oppusunggu YU, 'Indonesia' in A Chong (ed), *Recognition and Enforcement of Foreign Judgments in Asia* (Asian Business Law Institute, 2017)
Oppusunggu YU and Bell GF, 'Indonesia' in J Basedow and others (eds) *Encyclopedia of Private International Law*, vol 3 (Edward Elgar, 2017)
Parra AR, 'Applicable Law in Investor-State Arbitration' in AW Rovine (ed), *Contemporary Issues in International Arbitration and Mediation*, (Martinus Nijhoff Publishers, 2007)
Purwosutjipto HMN, *Pengertian Pokok Hukum Dagang Indonesia 1: Pengetahuan Dasar Hukum Dagang* 14 edn (Djambatan, 2007)
Rajagukguk E, *Arbitrase dalam Putusan Pengadilan* (Chandra Pratama, 2000)
Scherer M, *International Arbitration in the Energy Sector* (Oxford University Press, 2018)
Siahaan S and others, 'Indonesia' in J Gosling and T Huzarski (eds), *The Shipping Law Review* 3rd edn (Law Business Research Ltd, 2016)
Soekardono R, *Hukum Dagang Indonesia*, vol 1, 1st edn (Dian Rakyat, 1983)
Soemartono G, *Arbitrase dan Mediasi di Indonesia* (Gramedia Pustaka Utama, 2006)
—— 'Interpretation and Application of the New York Convention in Indonesia', in GA Bermann (ed), *Recognition and Enforcement of Foreign Arbitral Awards, The Interpretation and Application of the New York Convention by National Courts* (Springer, 2017)
—— and Lumbantobing J, 'Indonesia: Indonesian Arbitration Law and Practice in Light of the UNCITRAL Model Law' in GF Bell (ed), *The UNCITRAL Model Law and Asian Arbitration Laws, Implementation and Comparison* (Cambridge University Press, 2018)
Suadi A, *Penyelesaian Sengketa Ekonomi Syariah: Penemuan dan Kaidah Hukum* (Prenada Media, 2018)
Subekti R, *Arbitrase Perdagangan* (Binacipta, 1981)
Sukirno T and Hirdarisvita R, 'Indonesia' in Baker & McKenzie and N Thevenin (eds), *The Baker & McKenzie International Arbitration Yearbook: 2010–2011* (JurisNet, LLC, 2011)
Sukirno T, Kadir AY, and Hirdarisvita R, 'Indonesia' in Baker & McKenzie and N Thevenin (eds), *The Baker & McKenzie International Arbitration Yearbook 2011–2012* (JurisNet, LLC, 2012)
Sutiyoso B, *Penyelesaian Sengketa Bisnis* (Citra Media, 2006)
Tuegeh-Longdong TL, *Asas Ketertiban Umum dan Konvensi New York 1958* (PT Citra Aditya Bakti, 1998)
Tutik TT, *Hukum Perdata Dalam Sistem Hukum Nasional* (Kencana, 2018)
van Caster G, *European Private International Law* 2nd edn (Hart Publishing, 2016)

Official Sources

Agreement on Promotion, Protection and Guarantee of Investments among member states of the Organisation of Islamic Conferences available at https://investmentpolicyhubold.unctad.org/IIA/countryGrouping/45/treaty/3092
Almanach De Gotha, 'Mediatized House of Waldburg' (*the Almanach de Saxe Gotha*) www.almanachdegotha.org/id108.html (accessed 28 March 2020)

ASEAN Comprehensive Investment Agreement available at http://investasean.asean.org/files/upload/Doc%20 05%20-%20ACIA.pdf

Australian Embassy Indonesia, 'Marriage in Indonesia' (*Australian Embassy Indonesia*) https://indonesia.embassy.gov.au/jakt/MarriageInd.html (accessed 10 April 2020)

Co-Rapporteurs of the draft Convention (Professors Francisco J Garcimartín Alférez, Universidad Autónoma de Madrid, Spain and Geneviève Saumier, McGill University, Canada) and the Permanent Bureau, 'Treatment of Intellectual Property-Related Judgments under the November 2017 draft Convention' (*Hague Conference on Private International Law*, May 2018) https://assets.hcch.net/docs/0c2a7a4d-17ed-43b1-9b98-6bdb452f28a7.pdf (accessed 26 March 2019)

Dit. Hukum & Perjanjian Sosial Budaya, 'Alur Masuk' (*Rogatory Online Monitoring*) http://rogatori.kemlu.go.id/flow2 (accessed 17 December 2018)

—— 'Alur Keluar' (*Rogatory Online Monitoring*) 'Rogatory Online Monitoring' http://rogatori.kemlu.go.id/flow1 (accessed 18 December 2018)

—— 'Ketentuan Nasional' (*Rogatory Online Monitoring*) 'Rogatory Online Monitoring' http://rogatori.kemlu.go.id/nasional (accessed 17 December 2018)

—— 'PKS Standardisasi Dokumen 2018' (*Rogatory Online Monitoring*) http://rogatori.kemlu.go.id/assets/pdf/PKS%20Standardisasi%20Dokumen%202018.pdf (accessed 18 December 2018)

Embassy of The Republic of Indonesia In Manila, The Republic of The Philippines, Accredited to The Republic of Marshall Islands and The Republic of Palau, 'Certificate Of Legal Capacity To Marry' (*Kementerian Luar Negeri Repulik Indonesia*) https://kemlu.go.id/manila/en/pages/certificate_of_legal_capacity_to_marry/486/etc-menu (accessed 10 April 2020)

Embassy of Republic of Indonesia Ottawa and Permanent Representative to ICAO Canada, 'Marriage & Divorce' (*Kementerian Luar Negeri Repulik Indonesia*) https://kemlu.go.id/ottawa/en/pages/perkawinan___perceraian/680/about-service (accessed 10 April 2020)

HCCH, 'Conclusions and Recommendations' (The Fourth Asia Pacific Conference of the Hague Conference on Private International Law: The Work Of The Hague Conference On Private International Law, Manila, 26–28 October 2011) https://assets.hcch.net/upload/ap4concl.pdf (accessed 24 November 2019)

—— 'Vingt-deuxième session Acte final La Haye, le 2 juillet 2019 (Twenty-Second Session Final Act The Hague, 2 July 2019)' (Twenty-Second Session Recognition and Enforcement of Foreign Judgments, The Hague, on 8 June–2 July 2019) https://assets.hcch.net/docs/f55fc0a1-1a3c-4368-9199-48e8df11ff3e.pdf (accessed 24 November 2019)

ICC, 'Court Members' (*ICC*, 1 July 2018) https://iccwbo.org/dispute-resolution-services/icc-international-court-arbitration/court-members/#1478195489936-1a1acd15-7f6d (accessed 2 December 2019)

Investment Policy Hub UNCTAD, 'Indonesia' (*International Investment Agreements Navigator*) https://investmentpolicy.unctad.org/international-investment-agreements/countries/97/indonesia (accessed 12 May 2020)

Juwana H, 'Ratifikasi Konvensi PBB Mengenai Kontrak Jual Beli Barang Internasional' (*Badan Pembinaan Hukum Nasional*, 2013) www.bphn.go.id/data/documents/na_bbm.pdf (accessed 17 December 2019).

MAECI, 'Stato Civile' (*Ambasciata d'Italia*, 1 August 2019) https://ambjakarta.esteri.it/ambasciata_jakarta/it/informazioni_e_servizi/servizi_consolari/stato_civile (accessed 10 April 2020).

Margono S, 'Kompendium Hukum Yayasan' (*Badan Pembinaan Hukum Nasional Kementerian Hukum dan Hak Asasi Manusia RI*, 2012) www.bphn.go.id/data/documents/komp_2012_yayasan.pdf (accessed 15 March 2020)

Ministry of Trade and Industry of Singapore, 'Singapore and Indonesia Sign Bilateral Investment Treaty To Promote Stronger Economic Ties' (2018) www.mti.gov.sg/-/media/MTI/Newsroom/Press-Releases/2018/10/Singapore-and-Indonesia-sign-Bilateral-Investment-Treaty-to-promote-stronger-economic-ties-11Oct2018/press-release-on-signing-of-indonesia-singapore-bit-on-11-oct-2018.pdf (accessed 30 October 2019)

Sucharitkul S (Special Rapporteur), 'Fourth Report on Jurisdictional Immunities of States and Their Property' UN Doc A/CN.4/357 and Corr.1 (1982)

Supancana IBR, 'Naskah Akademik Rancangan Undang-Undang tentang Hukum Perdata Internasional (lanjutan)' (*Badan Pembinaan Hukum Nasional Kementerian Hukum dan Hak Asasi Manusia RI*, 2015) www.bphn.go.id/data/documents/na_ruu_ttg_hukum_perdata_internasional_ (lanjutan).pdf (accessed 8 July 2018)

——, 'Perkembangan Hukum Kontrak Dagang Intenasional' (*Badan Pembinaan Hukum Nasional*, 2012) 51 www.bphn.go.id/data/documents/pk-2012-2.pdf (accessed 14 November 2019)

Tawil GS, 'Dispute Settlement International centre for settlement of Investment Disputes (2.6 Applicable Law)' (*United Nations Conference on Trade and Development*, 2003) http://unctad.org/en/Docs/edmmisc232add5_en.pdf (accessed 22 June 2018)

Tim Pokja Laporan Tahunan Mari, *Laporan Tahunan 2017 Mahkamah Agung Republik Indonesia* (Mahkamah Agung RI 2018)

UNCITRAL, 'Overview of the status of UNCITRAL Conventions and Model Laws' (*UNCITRAL*, 15 November 2016) www.uncitral.org/pdf/english/TAC/Status/Overview-Status-Table.pdf (accessed 5 December 2019)

——, 'United Nations General Assembly elects new UNCITRAL Members' (*UNCITRAL*, 2 July 2019) https://uncitral.un.org/en/news/united-nations-general-assembly-elects-new-uncitral-members-0 (accessed 15 November 2019)

UNCTAD, Expropriation – UNCTAD Series on Issues in International Investment Agreements II (UNCTAD/DIAE/IA/2011/7), (New York and Geneva, 2012) available from https://unctad.org/en/Docs/unctaddiaeia2011d7_en.pdf

—— 'Indonesia' (*Investment Policy Hub*, 13 February 2019) https://investmentpolicy.unctad.org/international-investment-agreements/countries/97/indonesia (accessed 18 November 2019)

—— '2004–Cemex v Indonesia' (*Investment Policy Hub*, 31 December 2019) https://investmentpolicy.unctad.org/investment-dispute-settlement/cases/171/cemex-v-indonesia

—— '2016–Oleovest v Indonesia' (*Investment Policy Hub*, 31 December 2019) https://investmentpolicy.unctad.org/investment-dispute-settlement/cases/730/oleovest-v-indonesia

UNIDROIT, 'Membership/Etats Membres' (*UNIDROIT*, 3 April 2020), www.unidroit.org/about-unidroit/membership (accessed 26 November 2019)

Articles

Adolf H, 'Urgensi Pembentukan Undang-Undang tentang Arbitrase Internasional' (2016) 10(2) *Fiat Justicia* 317

Agusman DD, 'Status Hukum Perjanjian Internasional Dalam Hukum Nasional RI Tinjauan Dari Perspektif Praktek Indonesia' (2008) 5 Indonesian Journal of International Law 488 http://ijil.ui.ac.id/index.php/home/article/view/178/pdf_92 (accessed 29 May 2018)

Al-Gozaly MN, 'The Judicial Expansive Attitude Towards Public Policy in Enforcement of Foreign Arbitral Awards in Indonesia' (2014) 15 *Jurnal Opinio Juris* 127

Allagan TMP, 'Intercountry Adoption in Indonesia' (2019) 15 *Indonesian Journal of International Law* 214 http://ijil.ui.ac.id/index.php/home/article/view/725/pdf_603 (accessed 27 June 2020)

Anindita SL, 'Hukum yang Dipergunakan dalam Kontrak Dagang Internasional' (2008) 5 *Indonesian Journal of International Law* 537

Butt S, 'The Position of International Law Within the Indonesian Legal System' (2014) 28(1) *Emory International Law Review* 1 http://law.emory.edu/eilr/content/volume-28/issue-1/recent-developments/international-law-indonesianlegal-system.html (accessed 29 May 2018)

Cairns DJA, 'The Spanish Application of the UNCITRAL Model Law on International Commercial Arbitration' (2006) 22 *Arbitration International* 573

Gautama S, 'International Civil Procedure in Indonesia' (1996) 6 *Asian Yearbook of International Law* 87

——, 'Recognition and Enforcement of Foreign Judgments and Arbitral Awards in The Asean Region' (1990) 32(1) *Malaya Law Review* 173

—— and Wiknjosastro H, 'Some Aspects of Indonesian Private International Law' (1990) 32 *Malaya Law Review* 417 www.jstor.org/stable/24865645 (accessed 26 May 2018)

Hamzah, 'Bilateral Investment Treaties (BITS) in Indonesia: A Paradigm Shift, Issues and Challenges' (2018) 21 *Journal of Legal, Ethical and Regulatory Issues* 1

Hutabarat S, 'Harmonisasi Hukum Kontrak dan Dampaknya pada Hukum Kontrak Indonesia' (2016) 2(1) *Veritas et Justitia* 112

Jebabun A and others, *Initial Assessment Problems of Court Decision Enforcement System in Indonesia* (Asesmen Awal Permasalahan Eksekusi Putusan Perkara Perdata di Indonesia) (*Lembaga Kajian & Advokasi Independensi Peradilan*, 2018) 61 https://leip.or.id/wp-content/uploads/2018/10/LeIP_Asesmen-Awal-Eksekusi-Putusan-Perdata.pdf (accessed 2 November 2019)

Kusumadara A, 'Pentingnya Ratikasi UN Convention on Contract for The International Sales of Goods oleh Pemerintah Indonesia' [2006] *Jurnal Forum Penelitian* 1

Mandala S, 'The Unidroit Principles of International Commercial Contracts as a Reference for Modern Indonesian Contracts' [2007] *Indonesian Law Journal* 13
—— 'Pembaharuan Hukum Kontrak Indonesia dalam Kerangka Harmonisasi Hukum Kontrak ASEAN' (2012) 1(2) *Jurnal Rechtsvinding* 295
Members of The Shiparrested.com Network, 'Ship Arrests in Practice' 11th edn (2018) http://shiparrested.com/wp-content/uploads/2016/07/Final-Ship-Arrests-in-Practice-11th-edition.pdf (accessed 20 April 2020)
Mills K, 'Indonesia' [2018] International Bar Association
Minarosa M, 'The Principles of International Trade Contract as Reference of Indonesian Contract Law' (2018) 21(2) *European Research Studies Journal* 514
Oktaviandra S, 'Indonesia and Its Relunctance to Ratify the United Nations Convention on Contracts for the International Sales of Goods (CISG)' (2018) 8(3) *Indonesia Law Review* 243
Peari S, 'Substance and Procedure in Private International Law by Richard Garnett – Book Review' (2013) 14(1) *Melbourne Journal of International Law* 1 https://law.unimelb.edu.au/__data/assets/pdf_file/0011/1687448/11Peari1.pdf (accessed 11 August 2018)
Penasthika PP, Arijati L, and Anggriana AG, 'International Child Abduction: Bagaimana Indonesia Meresponnya?' (2018) 48 *Jurnal Hukum & Pembangunan* 521
Santy M, 'Gangguan Ketenangan Hidup (Hinder dan Nuisance): Analisis Perbandingan Perbuatan Melawan Hukum Indonesia dan Inggris' (*Universitas Indonesia Library*, 2017) www.lib.ui.ac.id/naskahringkas/2019-11/S66236-Meyliana%20Santy (accessed 6 June 2020)
Sattar S, 'Enforcement of Arbitral Awards and Public Policy: Same Concept, Different Approach?' (2011) 5 TDM 1 www.transnational-dispute-management.com/article.asp?key=1759 (accessed 15 March 2020)
Situmorang M, 'Pelaksanaan Putusan Arbitrase Nasional di Indonesia' (2017) 17(4) *Jurnal Penelitian Hukum De Jure* 309
Soemartono RMGP, 'Finalitas Putusan Arbitrase Internasional: Analisis Pasal 52 Konvensi "ICSID"' (1997) 4(3) *Era Hukum. Jurnal Ilmiah Hukum* 60
Sujayadi and Yuniarti, 'Pelaksanaan Sita Jaminan Dalam Hukum Acara Arbitrase' (2010) 25 Yuridika 227 https://e-journal.unair.ac.id/YDK/article/view/255 (accessed 3 January 2020)
Sutiyoso B, 'Akibat Pemilihan Forum dalam Kontrak yang Memuat Klausula Arbitrase' (2012) 24 *Mimbar Hukum* 159
Taufiqurrahman, 'Upaya Pembaruan Hukum Nasional di Bidang kontrak Jual Beli Barang Internasional' (2010) 25(3) *Yuridika* 269.
Tektona RI, 'Arbitrase sebagai Alternatif Solusi Penyelesaian Sengketa Bisnis di Luar Pengadilan' (2011) 6(1) *Pandecta* 86
Toha K and Retnaningsih S, 'Legal Policy Granting Status of Fresh Start to the Individual Bankrupt Debtor in Developing the Bankruptcy Law in Indonesia' (2020) 9(2) *Academic Journal of Interdisciplinary Studies* 157.

Theses

Alfianti R, 'Pembatalan Perkawinan Poligami Beda Kewarganegaraan Tanpa Izin Isteri Disertai Dengan Pemalsuan Identitas (Studi Kasus Putusan Pengadilan Agama Depok Nomor 324/Pdt.G/2006/PA.Dpk)' (Master thesis, Universitas Indonesia, 2011)
Allagan TMP, 'International mixed marriage in Indonesia and ASEAN: international mixed marriage and its recognition in Indonesia towards one ASEAN community' (PhD thesis, University of Groningen, 2019)
Hak N, 'Kedudukan dan Hak Anak Luar Nikah Pasca Putusan Mahkamah Konstitusi Nomor 46/Puu-VIII/2010 Tentang Status Anak Luar Nikah (Studi Persepsi Hakim Pengadilan Agama Se-Wilayah Pengadilan Tinggi Agama Bengkulu)' (Doctoral thesis, Universitas Islam Negeri (UIN) Raden Intan Lampung, 2018)
Hikmah M, 'Pelaksanaan Putusan Arbitrase Internasional di Indonesia Berdasarkan Undang-Undang Arbitrase' (PhD thesis, Universitas Pelita Harapan 2010)
Oestreicher Y, 'Recognition and Enforcement Of Foreign Intellectual Property Judgments: Analysis And Guidelines For A New International Convention' (S.J.D. thesis, Duke University School of Law, 2004)
Pratiwi A, 'Aspek-aspek Hukum Acara Perdata Internasional dalam Perceraian di Indonesia' (Undergraduate thesis, Universitas Indonesia, 2011)

Rani OM, 'Pengesampingan Pasal 1266 dan Pasal 1267 Kitab Undang-undang Hukum Perdata Dalam Putusan Pengadilan' (Master thesis, Universitas Islam Indonesia, 2015)
Sahabati M, 'Perjanjian Nominee Dalam Kaitannya Dengan Kepasian Hukum bagi Pihak Pemberi Kuasa Ditinjau Dari Undang-Undang Pokok Agraria, Undang-Undang Tentang Penanaman Modal, Dan Undang-Undang Kewarganegaraan' (Master thesis, Universitas Indonesia, 2011)
Subijakto C, 'Tinjauan tentang Talak Setelah Berlakunya Undang-undang Nomor 1 Tahun 1974' (Undergraduate thesis, Universitas Airlangga, 1989)
Yasmin M, 'Akibat Perkawinan Campuran Terhadap Anak dan Harta Benda yang Diperoleh Sebelum dan Sesudah Perkagataguwinan (Studi Banding Indonesia-Malaysia)' (Undergraduate thesis, Universitas Indonesia, 2011)

Websites and Blogs

Adolf H, 'Public Policy under Indonesia Arbitration Law' (*Global Arbitration Review*, 30 May 2018) https://globalarbitrationreview.com/print_article/gar/chapter/1170062/public-policy-under-indonesian-arbitration-law?print=true (accessed 11 December 2019)
Ali, 'Pengadilan Boleh Sita Harta BUMN' (*hukumonline.com*, 18 October 2010) www.hukumonline.com/berita/baca/lt4cbc1bcd43fa9/pengadilan-boleh-sita-harta-bumn?page=all (accessed 18 July 2020)
Anthony, 'Ketika Profesor Digugat Sang Putri Salah Satu Rumah Sudargo di Jakarta' (*Gatra*, 7 April 2008) http://arsip.gatra.com/2008-04-07/majalah/artikel.php?pil=23&id=113936 (accessed 12 February 2019)
Aurora L, 'New York Court Rules in Favor of Asia Pulp and Paper' (*Jawawa Indonesian Business & Finance News*, 16 February 2004) https://jawawa.id/newsitem/new-york-court-rules-in-favor-of-asia-pulp-andpaper-1447893297 (accessed 18 October 2019)
Coles D, 'Special Report Overview of Indonesia's Insolvency and Restructuring Regime' (*Conventus Law*, May 2016) www.conventuslaw.com/special-report/overview-of-indonesias-insolvency-and/ (accessed 2 May 2020)
detikNews, 'MA Perintahkan Hakim Laksanakan Putusan MK Soal Hak Anak Hasil Zina' (*detiknews*, 4 February 2013) https://news.detik.com/berita/d-2160080/ma-perintahkan-hakim-laksanakan-putusan-mk-soal-hak-anak-hasil-zina (accessed 27 June 2020)
—— 'Pria Hidung Belang Tak Beri Nafkah Anak Hasil Zina Bisa Dipenjara!' (*detiknews*, 4 February 2013) https://news.detik.com/berita/d-2160115/pria-hidung-belang-tak-beri-nafkah-anak-hasil-zina-bisa-dipenjara (accessed 27 June 2020)
Dalhuisen JH and Guzman AT, 'The Applicable Law in Foreign Investment Disputes' (*SSRN*, 30 January 2013) 5 http://ssrn.com/abstract=2209503 (accessed 25 November 2019)
Devita I, 'Pembuatan Wasiat Oleh Orang Asing' (*Irmadevita.com*, 5 December 2018) https://irmadevita.com/2012/pembuatan-wasiat-oleh-orang-asing/ (accessed 17 May 2020)
Drobnig UM, Hay P, and Rheinstein M, 'Conflict of Laws – Choice of Law' (*Encyclopædia Britannica, inc.*, 12 April 2018) www.britannica.com/topic/conflict-of-laws (accessed 21 June 2018)
Dutch Civil Law, 'Obligatory claims and obligations' (*Dutch Civil Law*) www.dutchcivillaw.com/content/dutchcivillaw033.htm (accessed 11 June 2020)
Firman I, 'Ship Arrest Process in Indonesia' (*Indra Firman & Associates*, 14 September 2016) http://indrafirman.com/en/2016/09/14/ship-arrest-process-in-indonesia/ (accessed 3 May 2019)
Hasanah S, 'Ulasan lengkap: Akibat Hukum Jika Merusak Barang Orang Lain Tanpa Sengaja' (*hukumonline*, 15 September 2016) www.hukumonline.com/klinik/detail/ulasan/lt539a466693874/akibat-hukum-jika-merusak-barang-orang-lain-tanpa-sengaja/ (accessed 6 June 2020)
Hukumonline, 'MA Batalkan Penetapan Pengampuan Prof. Sudargo' (*hukumonline*, 29 March 2008) www.hukumonline.com/berita/baca/hol18857/ma-batalkan-penetapan-pengampuan-prof-sudargo (accessed 11 February 2019)
—— 'Gugatan Konsumen Rokok Salah Alamat' (*hukumonline*, 15 May 2008) www.hukumonline.com/berita/baca/hol19246/gugatan-konsumen-rokok-salah-alamat/ (accessed 9 February 2020)
—— 'Gugatan Konsumen, Haruskah Sesuai Domisili?' (*hukumonline*, 29 May 2008) www.hukumonline.com/berita/baca/hol19346/gugatan-konsumen-haruskah-sesuai-domisili (accessed 9 February 2020)
—— 'Gugatan PT Ayunda Terhadap Astro Tidak Dapat Diterima' (*hukumonline*, 19 September 2009) www.hukumonline.com/berita/baca/hol23180/gugatan-pt-ayunda-terhadap-astro-tidak-dapatditerima/ (accessed 25 October 2019)

—— 'Pernyataan Menkumham Bertolak Belakang dengan Suratnya' (*hukumonline*, 5 February 2010) www.hukumonline.com/berita/baca/lt4b6b97f03c20a/pernyataan-menkumham-bertolak-belakang-dengansuratnya (accessed 17 January 2019)

—— 'UU Bahasa Batalkan Kontrak Bisnis Internasional' (*hukumonline*, 12 October 2013) www.hukumonline.com/berita/baca/lt5258d22c06dfe/uu-bahasa-batalkan-kontrak-bisnis-internasional (accessed 17 January 2019)

Islami AI, 'Dialektika Status Dan Hak Keperdataan Anak Luar Kawin' (*Mahkamah Agung Republik Indonesia Pengadilan Agama* Sidoarjo, 14 January 2020) <https://pa-sidoarjo.go.id/informasi-pengadilan/241-dialektika-status-dan-hak-keperdataan-anak-luar-kawin> accessed 27 June 2020

Laiman AD and others, 'The Indonesian Legal System and Legal Research' (*Globalex*, September 2009) www.nyulawglobal.org/globalex/Indonesia.html#sourcesoflaw (accessed 29 May 2018)

Lim D, 'SICC Releases Its First Decision' (*Financier Worldwide*, August 2016) www.financierworldwide.com/sicc-releases-its-first-decision#.Xbs2ROgzaUk (accessed 17 November 2019)

Mapes T, 'New York Judge Orders APP To End Efforts to Nullify Bonds' (*Wall Street Journal*, 28 November 2003) www.wsj.com/articles/SB106995908981230100 (accessed 18 October 2019)

Nursobah A, 'MA Dan Kemlu Sepakati Kerjasama Penanganan Permintaan Bantuan Teknis Hukum Dalam Masalah Perdata Lintas Yurisdiksi Negara' (*Kepaniteraan Mahkamah Agung RI*, 21 February 2018) https://kepaniteraan.mahkamahagung.go.id/index.php/kegiatan/1578-ma-dan-kemlu-sepakati-kerjasamapenanganan-permintaan-bantuan-teknis%E2%80%A6 (accessed 27 September 2018)

Qodir A, 'Banyak Pesawat Batavia Ditarik Pemilik Sebelum Dinyatakan Pailit' (*Tribunnews.com*, 31 Januari 2013) www.tribunnews.com/nasional/2013/01/31/banyak-pesawat-batavia-ditarik-pemilik-sebelum-dinyatakan-pailit (accessed 16 March 2019)

Santy M, 'Gangguan Ketenangan Hidup (Hinder dan Nuisance): Analisis Perbandingan Perbuatan Melawan Hukum Indonesia dan Inggris' (Universitas Indonesia Library, 2017) www.lib.ui.ac.id/naskahringkas/2019-11/S66236-Meyliana%20Santy (accessed 6 June 2020)

Saputra A, '3 Kedubes Asing Belum Laksanakan Putusan MA, Ini Kata Menlu RI' (*detikNews*, 28 Desember 2015) https://news.detik.com/berita/d-3105829/3-kedubes-asing-belum-laksanakan-putusan-ma-ini-kata-menluri (accessed 3 August 2019)

Shietra H, 'Aspek Hukum Uang Paksa (Dwangsom) dalam Praktik Litigasi Perdata' (Shietra and Partners, May 2016) www.hukum-hukum.com/2016/05/aspek-hukum-uang-paksa-dwangsom-dalam.html (accessed 4 January 2019)

Suastha RD, 'Kasus Perdata WNI Di Luar Negeri Meningkat 91 Persen' (*CNN Indonesia*, 20 February 2018) www.cnnindonesia.com/internasional/20180220174425-106-277523/kasus-perdatawni-di-luar-negeri-meningkat-91-persen (accessed 3 October 2018)

Thereoff P, 'Waldburg' (09 December 2019) www.angelfire.com/realm/gotha/gotha/waldburg.html (accessed 28 March 2020)

Widyawan, 'Legal Guide to Investment in Indonesia' (Widyawan & Partners, July 2014) 7 www.widyawanpartners.com/english/pubs/Investing-in-Indonesia.pdf (accessed 19 November 2019)

Yasin M, 'Bahasa Hukum: Sumber Hukum Formal Bernama "Yurisprudensi"' (*hukumonline*, 7 February 2018) www.hukumonline.com/berita/baca/lt5a7ad95871d1a/bahasa-hukum--sumber-hukumformal-bernama-yurisprudensi (accessed 28 May 2018)

INDEX

Lightning Source UK Ltd.
Milton Keynes UK
UKHW052353301022
411371UK00003B/174

9 781509 924332